Lecture Notes in Artificial Intelligence   3264

Edited by J. G. Carbonell and J. Siekmann

Subseries of Lecture Notes in Computer Science

Georgios Paliouras   Yasubumi Sakakibara (Eds.)

Grammatical Inference: Algorithms and Applications

7th International Colloquium, ICGI 2004
Athens, Greece, October 11-13, 2004
Proceedings

 Springer

Series Editors

Jaime G. Carbonell, Carnegie Mellon University, Pittsburgh, PA, USA
Jörg Siekmann, University of Saarland, Saarbrücken, Germany

Volume Editors

Georgios Paliouras
National Center of Scientific Research (NCSR), "Demokritos"
Institute of Informatics and Telecommunications
P.O.Box 60228, Ag. Paraskevi, Attiki, 15310, Greece
E-mail: paliourg@iit.demokritos.gr

Yasubumi Sakakibara
Keio University
Dept. of Biosciences and Informatics
3-14-1 Hiyoshi, Kohoku-ku, Yokohama, 223-8522, Japan
E-mail: yasu@bio.keio.ac.jp

Library of Congress Control Number: 2004112896

CR Subject Classification (1998): I.2, F.4, F.3

ISSN 0302-9743
ISBN 3-540-23410-1 Springer Berlin Heidelberg New York

Springer is a part of Springer Science+Business Media

springeronline.com

© Springer-Verlag Berlin Heidelberg 2004
Printed in Germany

Typesetting: Camera-ready by author, data conversion by Olgun Computergrafik
Printed on acid-free paper   SPIN: 11332824   06/3142   5 4 3 2 1 0

Preface

The 7th International Colloquium on Grammatical Inference (ICGI 2004) was held in the National Centre for Scientific Research "Demokritos", Athens, Greece on October 11–13, 2004. ICGI 2004 was the seventh in a series of successful biennial international conferences in the area of grammatical inference. Previous meetings were held in Essex, UK; Alicante, Spain; Montpellier, France; Ames, Iowa, USA; Lisbon, Portugal; and Amsterdam, The Netherlands. This series of conferences seeks to provide a forum for the presentation and discussion of original research papers on all aspects of grammatical inference.

Grammatical inference, the study of learning grammars from data, is an established research field in artificial intelligence, dating back to the 1960s, and has been extensively addressed by researchers in automata theory, language acquisition, computational linguistics, machine learning, pattern recognition, computational learning theory and neural networks. ICGI 2004 emphasized the multidisciplinary nature of the research field and the diverse domains in which grammatical inference is being applied, such as natural language acquisition, computational biology, structural pattern recognition, information retrieval, Web mining, text processing, data compression and adaptive intelligent agents.

We received 45 high-quality papers from 19 countries. The papers were reviewed by at least two – in most cases three – reviewers. In addition to the 20 full papers, 8 short papers that received positive comments from the reviewers were accepted, and they appear in a separate section of this volume. The topics of the accepted papers vary from theoretical results of learning algorithms to innovative applications of grammatical inference, and from learning several interesting classes of formal grammars to estimations of probabilistic grammars.

In conjunction with ICGI 2004, a context-free grammar learning competition, named Omphalos, took place. In an invited paper in this volume, the organizers of the competition report on the peculiarities of such an endeavor and some interesting theoretical findings. Last but not least, we are honored by the contributions of our invited speakers Prof. Dana Angluin, from Yale University, USA, and Prof. Enrique Vidal, from Universidade Politecnica de Valencia, Spain.

The editors would like to acknowledge the contribution of the Program Committee and the Additional Reviewers in reviewing the submitted papers, and thank the Organizing Committee for their invaluable help in organizing the conference. Particularly, we would like to thank Colin de la Higuera, Menno van Zaannen, Georgios Petasis, Georgios Sigletos and Evangelia Alexopoulou for their additional voluntary service to the grammatical inference community, through this conference. We would also like to acknowledge the use of the Cyberchair software, from Borbala Online Conference Services, in the submission and reviewing process. Finally, we are grateful for the generous support and sponsorship of the conference by NCSR "Demokritos", the PASCAL and KDnet European Networks of Excellence, and Biovista: Corporate Intelligence in Biotechnology.

October 2004   Georgios Paliouras and Yasubumi Sakakibara

Technical Program Committee

Pieter Adriaans — Perot Systems Corporation, and University of Amsterdam, The Netherlands

Dana Angluin — Yale University, USA

Walter Daelemans — University of Antwerp, The Netherlands

Pierre Dupont — Université Catholique de Louvain, Belgium

Dominique Estival — Defence Science and Technology Organisation (DSTO), Australia

Colin de la Higuera — EURISE, Univ. de St. Etienne, France

Vasant Honavar — Iowa State University, USA

Makoto Kanazawa — University of Tokyo, Japan

Laurent Miclet — ENSSAT, Lannion, France

Gopalakrishnaswamy Nagaraja — Indian Institute of Technology, Bombay, India

Jacques Nicolas — IRISA, France

Tim Oates — University of Maryland Baltimore County, USA

Arlindo Oliveira — Lisbon Technical University, Portugal

Jose Oncina Carratala — Universidade de Alicante, Spain

Rajesh Parekh — Blue Martini, USA

Lenny Pitt — University of Illinois at Urbana-Champaign, USA

Arun Sharma — University of New South Wales, Australia

Giora Slutzki — Iowa State University, USA

Etsuji Tomita — University of Electro-Communications, Japan

Esko Ukkonen — University of Helsinki, Finland

Menno van Zaanen — Tilburg University, The Netherlands

Enrique Vidal — Universidade Politécnica de Valencia, Spain

Takashi Yokomori — Waseda University, Japan

Thomas Zeugmann — University at Lübeck, Germany

Additional Reviewers

Cláudia Antunes
O. Boeffard
Miguel Bugalho
Rafael Carrasco
François Coste
Daniel Fredouille
Akio Fujiyoshi
Rebecca Hwa
François Jacquenet

Christine Largeron
J.A. Laxminarayana
Thierry Murgue
Katsuhiko Nakamura
Takeshi Shinohara
Yasuhiro Tajima
Franck Thollard
Mitsuo Wakatsuki
Satoshi Kobayashi

Organizing Committee

Georgios Paliouras, NCSR "Demokritos", Greece
Colin de la Higuera, Univ. de St. Etienne, France
Georgios Petasis, NCSR "Demokritos", Greece
Georgios Sigletos, NCSR "Demokritos", Greece

Sponsoring Organizations

 National Center for Scientific Research
(NCSR) "Demokritos"

 PASCAL Network of Excellence

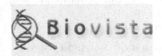 KDnet Network of Excellence

Biovista: Corporate Intelligence
in Biotechnology

Table of Contents

Invited Papers

Regular Papers

Poster Papers

Learning and Mathematics

Dana Angluin

Yale University
P.O. Box 208285, New Haven, CT 06520-8285, USA
angluin@cs.yale.edu
http://www.cs.yale.edu/people/faculty/angluin.html

Our formal models of learning seem to overestimate how hard it is to learn some kinds of things, including grammars. One possible reason for this is that our models generally do not represent learning a concept as an incremental addition to a rich collection of related concepts. This raises the question of how to make a good model of a "rich collection of related concepts." Rather than start by trying to make a general model, or adapting existing formalisms (e.g., logical theories) for the purpose, I have undertaken an extended look at a particular domain, namely mathematics. Mathematics certainly qualifies as a rich collection of related concepts, and has the advantage of thousands of years of effort devoted to improving its representations and clarifying its interconnections. This talk will present some of the issues I have encountered, and will probably consist of more questions than answers.

An anecdote will begin to raise some questions. At a workshop some years ago, a colleague asked me if I was familiar with the following problem. Given a nonempty finite set U of cardinality n, and two positive integers $s \leq t \leq n$, find the minimum cardinality of a collection C of subsets of U of size t such that every subset of U of size s is a subset of some element of C. Since I was not familiar with the problem, she continued to ask others at the workshop, until finally someone gave her the name of the problem and a pointer to work on it.

The meaning of the problem is clear (to someone with some mathematical training) from a very short description. What kind of representation would it take for us to be able to give something like this description to a search engine and be referred to papers that dealt with it? We already are expected to make our papers available in machine readable form on the web, or risk their irrelevance. Perhaps some enhancement of that representation could make such searches possible?

As another example, students in an elementary discrete mathematics course are often introduced to the concepts of permutations and combinations by means of concrete examples. Liu [1] asks the reader to imagine placing three balls, colored red, blue, and white, into ten boxes, numbered 1 through 10, in such a way that each box holds at most one ball. The problem is to determine the number of ways that this may be done. Lovász, Pelikán and Vesztergombi [2] describe a party with seven participants, each of whom shakes hands once with each of the others, and ask how many handshakes there have been in total. An introductory textbook will typically contain many examples and exercises of this kind.

G. Paliouras and Y. Sakakibara (Eds.): ICGI 2004, LNAI 3264, pp. 1–2, 2004.
© Springer-Verlag Berlin Heidelberg 2004

The situations used involve familiar elements, are easily imagined, and are intended to engage the student's intuitions in helpful ways. However, some students find it quite difficult to get the hang of the implicit rules for these problems. What will *not* help such students is the customary explicit and detailed formalization of the domain as a logical theory. What *might* help would be a somewhat more concrete model in terms of actions and state spaces. This is reminiscent of Piaget's emphasis upon an individual's actions as a basis for more abstract understanding.

These issues provide a window on other questions about mathematical reasoning and representation. It is likely that we will make more and more use of computers to help us create and use mathematics. Questions of how best to do that are far from settled, and will require a deep understanding of the multitude of ways that people actually do mathematics. Ironically, those for whom mathematics is difficult may provide some of the clearest evidence of what is involved.

References

1. C. L. Liu. *Elements of Discrete Mathematics*. McGraw-Hill, 1977.
2. L. Lovász, J. Pelikán, and K. Vesztergombi. *Discrete Mathematics: Elementary and Beyond*. Springer, 2003.

Learning Finite-State Models
for Machine Translation[*]

Enrique Vidal and Francisco Casacuberta

Departamento de Sistemas Informáticos y Computación
Instituto Tecnológico de Informática, Universidad Politécnica de Valencia
46071 Valencia, Spain
{evidal,fcn}@iti.upv.es

Abstract. In formal language theory finite-state transducers are well-know models for "input-output" rational mappings between two languages. Even if more powerful, recursive models can be used to account for more complex mappings, it has been argued that the input-output relations underlying most usual natural language pairs are essentially rational. Moreover, the relative simplicity of these mappings has recently lead to the development of techniques for learning finite-state transducers from a training set of input-output sentence pairs of the languages considered. Following these arguments, in the last few years a number of machine translation systems have been developed based on stochastic finite-state transducers. Here we review the statistical statement of Machine Translation and how the corresponding modelling, learning and search problems can be solved by using stochastic finite-state transducers. We also review the results achieved by the systems developed under this paradigm. After presenting the traditional approach, where transducer learning is mainly solved under the grammatical inference framework, we propose a new approach where learning is explicitly considered as a statistical estimation problem and the whole stochastic finite-state transducer learning problem is solved by expectation maximisation.

1 Introduction

Machine translation (MT) is one of the most appealing (and challenging) applications of human language processing technology. Because of its great social and economical interest, in the last 20 years MT has been considered under almost every imaginable point of view: from strictly linguistics-based methods to pure statistical approaches including, of course, formal language theory and the corresponding learning paradigm, *grammatical inference* (GI). Different degrees of success have been achieved so far using these approaches.

Basic MT consists in transforming text from a source language into a target language, but several extensions to this framework have been considered. Among the most interesting of these extensions are *speech-to-speech* MT (STSMT) and

---

[*] This work was partially supported by the European Union project TT2 (IST-2001-32091) and by the Spanish project TEFATE (TIC 2003-08681-C02-02).

G. Paliouras and Y. Sakakibara (Eds.): ICGI 2004, LNAI 3264, pp. 3–15, 2004.

computer assisted (human) *translation* (CAT). In STSMT, which is generally considered significantly harder than pure text MT, the system has to accept a source-language utterance and produce corresponding human-understandable target-language speech. In CAT, on the other hand, the input is source-language text and both the system and the human translator have to collaborate with each other in an attempt to produce high quality target text.

Here we consider MT, STSMT and CAT models that can be be automatically learned through suitable combinations of GI and statistical methods. In particular we are interested in *stochastic finite-state transducers*. Techniques for learning these models have been studied by several authors, in many cases with special motivation for their use in MT applications. [1–12].

2   General Statement of MT Problems

The (*text-to-text*) MT problem can be statistically stated as follows. Given a sentence $\mathbf{s}$ from a source language, search for a target-language sentence $\hat{\mathbf{t}}$ which maximises the posterior probability[1]:

$$\hat{\mathbf{t}} = \operatorname*{argmax}_{\mathbf{t}} \Pr(\mathbf{t}\,|\,\mathbf{s}) \ . \tag{1}$$

It is commonly accepted that a convenient way to deal with this equation is to transform it by using the Bayes' theorem:

$$\hat{\mathbf{t}} = \operatorname*{argmax}_{\mathbf{t}} \Pr(\mathbf{t}) \cdot \Pr(\mathbf{s}\,|\,\mathbf{t}) \ , \tag{2}$$

where $\Pr(\mathbf{t})$ is a target *language model* – which gives high probability to well formed target sentences – and $\Pr(\mathbf{s}\,|\,\mathbf{t})$ accounts for source-target word(-position) relations and is based on *stochastic dictionaries* and *alignment models* [13, 14].

Alternatively the conditional distribution in Eq. 1 can be transformed into a joint distribution:

$$\hat{\mathbf{t}} = \operatorname*{argmax}_{\mathbf{t}} \Pr(\mathbf{s}, \mathbf{t}) \ , \tag{3}$$

which can be adequately modelled by means of *stochastic finite-state transducers* (SFST) [15]. This is the kind of models considered in the present work.

Let us now consider the STSMT problem. Here an acoustic representation of a source-language utterance $\mathbf{x}$ is available and the problem is to search for a target-language sentence $\hat{\mathbf{t}}$ that maximises the posterior probability[2]:

$$\hat{\mathbf{t}} = \operatorname*{argmax}_{\mathbf{t}} \Pr(\mathbf{t}\,|\,\mathbf{x}) \ . \tag{4}$$

Every possible decoding of a source utterance $\mathbf{x}$ in the source language can be considered as the value of a hidden variable $\mathbf{s}$ [15] and, assuming $\Pr(\mathbf{x}|\mathbf{s}, \mathbf{t})$ does not depend on $\mathbf{t}$, Eq. 4 can be rewritten as:

---

[1] For simplicity, $\Pr(X = x)$ and $\Pr(X = x \mid Y = y)$ are denoted as $\Pr(x)$ and $\Pr(x \mid y)$.

[2] From $\hat{\mathbf{t}}$, a target utterance can be produced by using a *text-to-speech* synthesiser.

$$\hat{\mathbf{t}} = \underset{\mathbf{t}}{\operatorname{argmax}} \sum_{\mathbf{s}} \Pr(\mathbf{s}, \mathbf{t}) \cdot \Pr(\mathbf{x}|\mathbf{s}) \ . \tag{5}$$

As in plain MT, $\Pr(\mathbf{s}, \mathbf{t})$ can be modelled by a SFST. The term $\Pr(\mathbf{x}|\mathbf{s})$, on the other hand, can be modelled through *hidden Markov models* (HMM) [16], which are the standard acoustic models in automatic speech recognition. Thanks to the homogeneous finite-state nature of both SFST and HMMs, and approximating the sum with a maximisation, Eq. 5 can be easily and efficiently solved by the well-known *Viterbi algorithm* [15].

Finally, let us consider a simple statement of CAT [17]. Given a source text $\mathbf{s}$ and a fixed *prefix* of the target sentence $\mathbf{t}_p$ –previously validated by the human translator–, the problem is to search for a *suffix* of the target sentence $\hat{\mathbf{t}}_s$ that maximises the posterior probability:

$$\hat{\mathbf{t}}_s = \underset{\mathbf{t}_s}{\operatorname{argmax}} \Pr(\mathbf{t}_s | \mathbf{s}, \mathbf{t}_p) \ . \tag{6}$$

Taking into account that $\Pr(\mathbf{t}_p | \mathbf{s})$ does not depend on $\mathbf{t}_s$, we can write:

$$\hat{\mathbf{t}}_s = \underset{\mathbf{t}_s}{\operatorname{argmax}} \Pr(\mathbf{s}, \mathbf{t}_p \mathbf{t}_s) \ , \tag{7}$$

where $\mathbf{t}_p \mathbf{t}_s$ is the concatenation of the given prefix $\mathbf{t}_p$ and a suffix $\mathbf{t}_s$ suggested by the system. Eq. 7 is similar to Eq. 3, but here the maximisation is constrained to a set of suffixes, rather than full sentences. As in Eq. 3, this joint distribution can be adequately modelled by means of SFSTs [18].

All the above problem statements share the common *learning problem* of estimating $\Pr(\mathbf{s}, \mathbf{t})$, which can be approached by training a SFST from a parallel text corpus.

3   Stochastic Finite-State Transducers

Different types of SFSTs have been applied with success in some areas of machine translation and other areas of natural language processing [3, 19, 4, 8, 11, 9, 20]. Here only conventional and *subsequential* SFSTs are considered. A SFST $\mathcal{T}_P$ is a tuple $\langle \Sigma, \Delta, Q, q_0, p_T, f_T \rangle$, where Σ is a finite set of *source words*, Δ is a finite set of *target words*, Q is a finite set of *states*, q_0 is the initial state and p_T and f_T are two functions $p_T : Q \times \Sigma \times \Delta^\star \times Q \rightarrow [0, 1]$ (*transition probabilities*) and $f_T : Q \rightarrow [0, 1]$ (*final-state probability*), that verify:

$$\forall q \in Q, \quad f_T(q) \quad + \sum_{(a, \omega, q') \in \Sigma \times \Delta^\star \times Q} p_T(q, a, \omega, q') = 1.$$

Given $\mathcal{T}_P$, the joint probability of a pair $(\mathbf{s}, \mathbf{t}) \in \Sigma^\star \times \Delta^\star$ –denoted as $\Pr_{\mathcal{T}_P}(\mathbf{s}, \mathbf{t})$– is the sum of the probabilities of all sequences of states that deal with $(\mathbf{s}, \mathbf{t})$; that is, the concatenation of the source (target) words of the transitions between each pair of adjacent states in the sequence of states is the source sentence $\mathbf{s}$ (target sentence $\mathbf{t}$) [21]. The probability of a particular state sequence is the product of the corresponding transition probabilities, times the final-state probability of the last state in the sequence [21].

If $\mathcal{T}_P$ has not useless states, $\mathrm{Pr}_{\mathcal{T}_P}(\mathbf{s}, \mathbf{t})$ describes a probability distribution on $\Sigma^\star \times \Delta^\star$ which is called *stochastic regular translation*. This distribution is used to model the joint probabilities introduced in Eq. 3 in the previous section.

Given a SFST $\mathcal{T}_P$, a non-probabilistic counterpart $\mathcal{T}$, called *characteristic finite-state transducer of $\mathcal{T}_P$* (FST), can be defined. The *transitions* are those tuples in $Q \times \Sigma \times \Delta^\star \times Q$ with probability greater than zero and the *set of final states* are those states in Q with final-state probability greater than zero.

A particularly interesting transducer model is the *subsequential transducer (SST)* which is a finite-state transducer with the basic restriction of being deterministic. This implies that if two transitions have the same starting state and the same source word, then both ending states are the same state and both the target strings are also the same target string. In addition, SSTs can produce a target substring when the end of the input string has been detected.

Any SFST has two embedded stochastic regular languages, one for the source alphabet and another for the target alphabet. These languages correspond to the two marginals of the joint distribution modelled by the SFST [21].

SFSTs exhibit properties and problems similar to those exhibited by stochastic regular languages. One of these properties is the formal basis of the GIATI technique for transducer inference presented in Section 6. It can be stated as the following theorem [21]: *Each stochastic regular translation can be obtained from a stochastic local language and two alphabetic morphisms*. The morphisms allow for building the components of a pair in the regular translation from a string in the local language [21].

On the other hand, one of the problems of SFSTs is the *stochastic translation problem* [22]: given a SFST $\mathcal{T}_P$ and $\mathbf{s} \in \Sigma^\star$, search for a target string $\hat{\mathbf{t}}$ that maximise $\mathrm{Pr}_{\mathcal{T}_P}(\mathbf{s}, \mathbf{t})$. While this is proved to be a **NP**-Hard problem [22], a generally good approximation can be obtained in polynomial time through a simple extension to the Viterbi algorithm [10].

4   Learning Stochastic Finite-State Transducers

Following the statistical framework adopted in the previous sections, three main families of techniques can be used to learn a SFST from a parallel corpus of source-target sentences:

- *Traditional syntactic pattern recognition paradigm*: a) Learn the SFST "topology" (the *characteristic transducer*) and b) Estimate its probabilities from the same data.
- *Hybrid methods*: Under the *traditional* paradigm, use statistical methods to guide the structure learning.
- *Pure statistical approach*: a) Adequately parametrise the SFST structure and consider it as a hidden variable and b) estimate everything by expectation maximisation (EM).

To estimate the probabilities in the *traditional* approach, *maximum likelihood* or other possible criteria can be used [10]. As in every estimation problem, an important issue is the modelling of unseen events. In our case, a general approach to this *smoothing* problem consists of using *stochastic error-correcting parsing* [23, 24]. Alternatively, it can be tackled as in language modelling; either in the estimation of the probabilities of the SFST themselves [25] or within of the process of learning both the structural and probabilistic SFST components [20].

5   Traditional Syntactic Pattern Recognition Paradigm: OSTIA

The formal model of translation used in this section is the SST. A transducer of this kind can delay the production of target words until enough source words have been seen to determine the correct target words. Therefore, the sates of a SST hold the "memory" of the part of the sentence seen so far. This allows the whole context of a word to be taken into account, if necessary, for the translation of the next word. A very efficient technique for automatically learning these models from a training set of sentence pairs is the so called *onward subsequential transducer inference algorithm* (OSTIA) [3].

OSTIA starts building up an initial representation of the original paired data in the form of a tree (the *onward prefix tree transducer*). Then appropriate states of this transducer are merged to build a FST in which those transitions sharing some structural properties are merged together in oder to generalise the seen samples. To this end, the tree is traversed level by level and the states in each level are considered to be merged with those previously visited. Only those pairs of states which are compatible according to the output strings of their subtrees are effectively merged. If the training pairs were produced by an unknown SST, $\mathcal{T}$, –which can be considered true, at least for many common pairs of natural languages– and the amount of training data is sufficiently large and/or representative, then OSTIA is guaranteed to converge to a canonical (*onward*) SST which generates the same translation pairs as $\mathcal{T}$ [3].

The state merging process followed by OSTIA tries to generalise the training pairs as much as possible. This often leads to very compact transducers which adequately translate correct source text of the learned task into the target language. However, this compactness often entails an excessive generalisation of the source and the target languages, allowing meaningless source sentences to be accepted, and even worse target sentences to be produced. This is not a problem for perfectly correct source text, but becomes important when not exactly correct text or speech is to be used as input.

A possible way to overcome this problem consists in further restricting state merging so that the resulting SST only accepts source sentences and produces target sentences that are consistent with given source and target (regular) language models. These models are known as *domain* and *range* language models, respectively. A version of OSTIA called OSTIA-DR [26, 4] enforces these restrictions in the learning process. N-grams [16], generally trained from the source and target sentences in the given corpus, are usually adopted as domain and range language models for OSTIA-DR.

OSTIA and OSTIA-DR have been applied to many relatively simple MT tasks, including speech-input MT. The first works, reported in [27], were carried out on the so called MLA and EuTRANS-0 tasks.

MLA (*miniature language acquisition*) was a small task, with vocabularies of about 30 words, involving the Spanish-English translation of sentences used to describe and manipulate simple visual scenes. OSTIA-DR achieved almost perfect *text-input* results on this simple task by training with with a large number of pairs (50,000). *Speech-input* experiments were also carried out, leading to very good performance: less than 3% *translation word error rate* (TWER)[3].

EuTRANS-0, called *traveller task* in [27], was a much larger and practically motivated task established in the framework of the European Union speech-to-speech MT project EuTRANS [28]. The task involved human-to-human communication situations in the front-desk of a hotel. A large parallel corpus for this task was produced in a semi-automatic way [8]. The resulting Spanish-English[4] corpus contained $500,000$ ($171,481$ different) sentence pairs, with Spanish/English vocabulary sizes of 689/514 words and test-set bigram perplexities of 6.8/5.6, respectively. Since the total size of this corpus was considered unrealistically large, a much reduced corpus, called EuTRANS-I, was built by randomly selecting $10k$ ($6,813$ different) sentence pairs for training and $3k$ (all different) for testing.

Very good results, in both text- and speech-input experiments with EuTRANS-0 were reported in [27] and additional results, both for EuTRANS-0 and EuTRANS-I, can be seen in [8]. Using a categorised[5] version of the huge EuTRANS-0 training corpus, OSTIA-DR produced almost perfect models, with text- and (microphone) speech-input TWER lower than 1% and 2%, respectively. However, results degraded significantly when the more realistically sized EuTRANS-I training corpus was used. Since the learned models were clearly under-trained, error-correcting smoothing was needed in this case, leading to a text-input TWER close to 10% [28]. Without using categories, no useful results were obtained.

6   Hybrid Methods: OMEGA and GIATI

OSTIA has proved able to learn adequate transducers for real (albeit limited) tasks if a sufficiently large amount of training pairs is available. However, as the amount of training data shrinks, its performance drops dramatically. Clearly, in order to convey enough information to learn structurally rich transducers, prohibitively large amounts of examples are required. Therefore, in order to

---

[3] TWER is (a rather pessimistic measure) computed as the minimum number of word insertions, substitutions and deletions needed to match the system output with a single target sentence reference.

[4] Similar Spanish-German and Spanish-Italian corpora were also produced. For the sake of brevity, only Spanish-English data and results will be discussed here.

[5] Seven categories: proper names, numbers, dates and times of day, etc. Each instance of these categories was substituted by a corresponding non-terminal symbol.

render training data demands realistic, additional, explicit information about the relation of source-target words involved in the translation seems to be needed. The two techniques discussed in this section are explicitly based on this idea.

OMEGA

This algorithm, called "OSTIA modified for employing guarantees and alignments" (OMEGA) [6], is an improvement over OSTIA-DR to learn SSTs.

As with OSTIA, there are two main training phases: building an initial tree from the training pairs and state-merging. Apart from the OSTIA-DR state-merging restrictions, including those derived from (n-gram) source and target language models, two additional knowledge sources are employed to avoid over-generalisation: a *bilingual dictionary* and *word alignments*. They are used to ensure that target words are only produced after having seeing the source words they are translation of. These dictionaries and alignments can be obtained from the training pairs by means of pure statistical methods such as those described in [13, 29].

To enforce the new constraints, each state is labelled with two sets: the *"guarantees"* and the *"needs"*. The first set indicates which words can appear in the output because the corresponding input has already been seen. The second set contains those words that should appear since they will be output somewhere along the target subsequences departing from the state [6].

OMEGA was tested on the EUTRANS-0 and EUTRANS-I corpora described above. While results on EUTRANS-0 were similar to or slightly worse than those of OSTIA, on the much smaller EUTRANS-I corpus OMEGA was clearly better. Without using categories, OMEGA achieved error-correcting text-input TWER better than 7% [28] whereas, under the same conditions, OSTIA completely failed to produce useful results. OMEGA transducers learned with EUTRANS-I were also tested with speech-input, achieving moderately good results of less than 13% and 18% TWER for microphone and telephone speech, respectively [15]. These results correspond to 336 Spanish test utterances from several speakers.

Apart from the Spanish-English corpora considered so far, an additional Italian-English MT corpus was produced in the EUTRANS project [28]. This corpus, referred to as EUTRANS-II, corresponds to a task significantly more complex and closer real life than those previously considered. In this case, a speech corpus was acquired by recording real phone calls to the (simulated) front desk of a hotel. An associated text corpus was obtained by manually transcribing the acquired Italian utterances and translating them into English. The resulting corpus is much smaller than the previous ones, while having 4 times larger vocabularies ($2,459/1,701$ words). From this corpus, approximately $3,000$ pairs of sentences were used for training the translation model and about 300 sentences (and the corresponding utterances, from 24 speakers) were used for testing.

OSTIA could not be used at all in this task and OMEGA produced only moderately acceptable results: less than 38% and 42% TWER for text and speech input, respectively [6, 15]. This prompted the need for even less data-hungry transducer learning techniques, leading to the approach discussed below.

GIATI

This approach, called *grammatical inference and alignments for transducer inference* (GIATI), also makes use of information obtained by means of pure statistical methods. However, in this case, the alignments are used to define an adequate *bilingual segmentation* of the training pairs of sentences.

Given a finite sample of string pairs, GIATI relies on the two-morphisms theorem mentioned in Section 3 [21], to propose the following steps for the inference of a transducer [22]:

1. Using a bilingual segmentation of each training pair of sentences, the pair is transformed into a single string from an *extended alphabet.*
2. A stochastic regular grammar, typically an n-gram, is inferred from the set of strings obtained in first step.
3. The terminal symbols of the grammar rules from the second step are transformed back into source/target symbols by applying adequate morphisms. This converts the stochastic grammars into the learned transducer.

The main problem with this approach is the first (and correspondingly the third) step(s), i.e. to adequately transform a parallel corpus into a string corpus. The transformation of the training pairs must capture the correspondences between words of the input and the output sentences and must allow the implementation of the inverse transformation of the third step. As previously mentioned, this is achieved with the help of bilingual segmentation [20].

The probabilities associated with the transitions of a SFST learned in this way are just those of the corresponding stochastic regular grammar inferred in *step 2*. Therefore, an interesting feature of GIATI is that it can readily make use of all the smoothing techniques known for n-grams [30] and stochastic regular grammars [25]. Other interesting properties of GIATI can be found in [21].

This technique was tested with all the corpora of the EuTRANS project. TWER smaller than 7% and 25% were obtained for text input with EuTRANS-I and EuTRANS-II, respectively [20]. For telephone speech-input, on the other hand, less 13% and 30% TWER were obtained on the same corpora, and less than 8% for microphone speech with EuTRANS-I [20, 15]. These results, particularly those of EuTRANS-II, are clearly better than those achieved by OMEGA under the same conditions. Overall, GIATI was among the best techniques tested in the framework of the EuTRANS project [28].

Recently, GIATI has also been used in the context of the computer assisted translation (CAT) project *Trans-Type 2* (TT2) [18]. One of the corpora considered in this project, referred to as "XEROX", contains a collection of technical Xerox manuals written in English, Spanish, French and German. The sizes of the training subsets are around $600,000$ words for each language. In this case performance is assessed in terms of the Key-Stroke Ratio (KSR). It measures the percentage of keys-strokes that a human translator has to type with respect to the those needed to type the entire text without the help of the CAT system.

Results are promising. For English to Spanish translation, KSR smaller 26% have been achieved, while KSR about 30%, 54%, 54%, 60% and 54% have been obtained for Spanish to English, English to French, French to English, English to German and German to English, respectively [18]. Apart from these results GIATI has been used as the basis of one of the prototypes which have shown better practical behaviour according to real human tests on the XEROX task [18].

7   Pure Statistical Approach: GIATI Revisited

The original GIATI technique was developed from some properties of the formal language theory [21], however, this technique can also be derived from a pure statistical point of view. Such derivation has the advantage that it no longer has to relay on "external" statistical techniques to obtain a bilingual segmentation or make use of heuristics to transform pairs of sentences into conventional strings.

Let J and I be the *given* lengths of the source and the target sentences, respectively. Both of these sentences are assumed to be segmented into the same number of segments, K, for all possible K. Segmentations can be described as two functions, γ and μ, for the source and the target sentence, respectively:

$$\gamma : \{1, ..., K\} \to \{1, ..., J\} \text{ with } \gamma_{k+1} \geq \gamma_k \text{ for } 1 \leq k < K \text{ and } \gamma_K = J ,$$

$$\mu : \{1, ..., K\} \to \{1, ..., I\} \text{ with } \mu_{k+1} \geq \mu_k \text{ for } 1 \leq k < K \text{ and } \mu_K = I .$$

Under these assumptions, Eq. 3 can be rewritten as[6]:

$$\Pr(\mathbf{s}, \mathbf{t}) = \Pr(J, I) \cdot \sum_K \Pr(K|J, I) \cdot \sum_{\gamma_1^K, \mu_1^K} \Pr(\mathbf{s}_1^J, \mathbf{t}_1^I, \gamma_1^K, \mu_1^K | J, I, K) , \quad (8)$$

Assuming that $\Pr(\gamma_1^K, \mu_1^K | J, I, K)$ is uniform and that the correspondence among source and target segments is one-to-one and monotone, the last term in the right side of Eq. 8 can be rewritten as:

$$\Pr(\mathbf{s}_1^J, \mathbf{t}_1^I, \gamma_1^K, \mu_1^K | J, I, K)$$
$$\propto \prod_{k=1}^{K} \Pr(\mathbf{s}_{\gamma_{k-1}+1}^{\gamma_k}, \mathbf{t}_{\mu_{k-1}+1}^{\mu_k} | J, I, K, \mathbf{s}_1^{\gamma_{k-1}}, \mathbf{t}_1^{\mu_{k-1}}, \gamma_1^K, \mu_1^K) . \quad (9)$$

A convenient type of segmentation is when $\gamma_j = j$ for $1 \leq j \leq J$; that is, source word-by-word. Then $K = J$ and it is not necessary to use γ_1^K explicitly:

$$\Pr(\mathbf{s}_1^J, \mathbf{t}_1^I, \mu_1^K | J, I, K) \propto \prod_{k=1}^{J} \Pr(\mathbf{s}_k, \mathbf{t}_{\mu_{k-1}+1}^{\mu_k} | J, I, K, \mathbf{s}_1^{k-1}, \mathbf{t}_1^{\mu_{k-1}}, \mu_1^K) . \quad (10)$$

The right part of Eq.10 can be approximated by using n-grams of the sequences of monotonically paired segments. This amounts to representing the right side of the conditional probabilities, $(J, I, K, \mathbf{s}_1^{k-1}, \mathbf{t}_1^{\mu_{k-1}}, \mu_1^K)$, by means of the concept of (equivalence class of) "history" $(H(J, I, K, \mathbf{s}_1^{k-1}, \mathbf{t}_1^{\mu_{k-1}}, \mu_1^K))$ [16].

---

[6] Following a notation used in [13], a sequence of the form $z_i, \ldots, z_j$ is denoted as z_i^j. For some positive integers N and M, the image of a function $f : \{1, ..., N\} \to \{1, ..., M\}$ for n is denoted as f_n, and all the possible values of the function as f_1^N.

With n-grams in particular and with stochastic finite-state automata in general, the equivalence classes of histories correspond to the states of the model. Finally, if it is assumed that $\Pr(J, I)$ and $\Pr(K|J, I)$ in Eq. 8 are single parameters that are independent of J, I and K, Eq. 8 can be written as:

$$\Pr(\mathbf{s}, \mathbf{t}) \propto \sum_K \sum_{\mu_1^K} \prod_{k=1}^J \Pr(\mathbf{s}_k, \mathbf{t}_{\mu_{k-1}+1}^{\mu_k} | H(J, I, K, \mathbf{s}_1^{k-1}, \mathbf{t}_1^{\mu_{k-1}}, \mu_1^K)) \ . \tag{11}$$

Given a set of training pairs, all the probabilities of the Eq. 11 can be estimated using the EM algorithm [31]. Note that the existence of hidden variables related to the assumed bilingual segmentation makes EM estimation the method of choice, instead of using simple relative frequency.

On the other hand, as an estimation of a joint distribution, Eq.11 suggests an approximate implementation as a SFST. The states of the SFST are the equivalence classes of histories $H(J, I, K, \mathbf{s}_1^{k-1}, \mathbf{t}_1^{\mu_{k-1}}, \mu_1^K)$, and the probabilities in Eq. 11 correspond to the transition probabilities between states with $\mathbf{s}_k$ as source word and $\mathbf{t}_{\mu_{k-1}+1}^{\mu_k}$ as target string.

The extension of this procedure to the most general setting of Eq. 9, which deals with source strings rather than single source words, is straightforward.

In practice, when SFSTs are used, the finite-length characteristic of source and target strings is modelled through the explicit introduction of a special "end" symbol $\$$, which is not in the source or the target language: $\mathbf{s}\$$ and $\mathbf{t}\$$, instead of explicit length modelling (I, J). This is the usual way to represent finite-length strings when n-gram models are used. In this case, and using n-grams, Eq. 11 becomes:

$$\Pr(\mathbf{s}, \mathbf{t}) \propto \sum_K \sum_{\mu_1^K} \prod_{k=1}^J \Pr(\mathbf{s}_k, \mathbf{t}_{\mu_{k-1}+1}^{\mu_k} | \mathbf{s}_{k-n+1}^{k-1}, \mathbf{t}_{\mu_{k-n+1}}^{\mu_{k-1}}) \cdot \Pr(\$, \$ | \mathbf{s}_{J-n+2}^J, \mathbf{t}_{\mu_{J-n+2}}^{\mu_J}) \ .$$

$$\tag{12}$$

The states of the SFST are all possible $(\mathbf{s}_{k-n+1}^{k-1}, \mathbf{t}_{\mu_{k-n+1}}^{\mu_{k-1}})$ in the training set[7]. The probabilities in Eq. 12 correspond to transition probability between two states with $\mathbf{s}_k$ as source symbol and $\mathbf{t}_{\mu_{k-n+1}}^{\mu_{k-1}}$ as the target string associated to the transition are similar to those in Eq. 11 and the probability that a state $(\mathbf{s}_{k-n+1}^{k-1}, \mathbf{t}_{\mu_{k-n+1}}^{\mu_{k-1}})$ is a final state is $\Pr(\$, \$ | \mathbf{s}_{k-n+1}^{k-1}, \mathbf{t}_{\mu_{k-n+1}}^{\mu_{k-1}})$.

An important difference of this proposal, with respect to the version of GIATI previously described in section 6, is the number of segmentations that are represented in the model: In the present case, all possible segmentations of the training set are considered, while in the previous one, only one segmentation was used: the one derived from the best word alignments between source and target strings obtained by an external statistical alignment algorithm.

---

[7] Note that varying K and μ_1^K, all the target segments from training set are generated.

8   Conclusions

A number of techniques to learn stochastic finite-state transducers for machine translation have been reviewed. The review has started with techniques mainly falling under the traditional grammatical Inference paradigm. While these techniques have proven able to learn very adequate MT models for non-trivial tasks, the amount of training sentence pairs needed often becomes prohibitive in real-world situations. Other techniques are also reviewed that circumvent this problem by increasingly relying on statistically-derived information.

As task complexity increases, we think that statistically-based learning is the most promising framework, particularly when data becomes scarce, which is the typical condition encountered in practical situations. Consequently, in the final part of this article, one of the reviewed techniques has been revisited so as to derive it using only statistical arguments.

All the reviewed techniques have been tested on practical MT tasks considered in many Spanish and European projects and company contracts, involving a large variety of languages such as Spanish, English, Italian, German, French, Portuguese, Catalan and Basque. As a result of these projects a number of prototypes have been implemented and successfully tested under real (or at least realistic) conditions. On-line demonstrations of some of these prototypes are available at http://prhlt.iti.es/demos/demos.htm.

References

1. Vidal, E., García, P., Segarra, E.: Inductive learning of finite-state transducers for the interpretation of unidimensional objects. In Mohr, R., Pavlidis, T., Sanfeliu, A., eds.: Structural Pattern Analysis. World Scientific pub (1989) 17–35
2. Knight, K., Al-Onaizan, Y.: Translation with finite-state devices. In: Proceedings of the 4th. ANSTA Conference. (1998)
3. Oncina, J., García, P., Vidal, E.: Learning subsequential transducers for pattern recognition interpretation tasks. IEEE Transactions on Pattern Analysis and Machine Intelligence **15** (1993) 448–458
4. Castellanos, A., Vidal, E., Varó, A., Oncina, J.: Language Understanding and Subsequential Transducer Learning. Computer Speech and Language **12** (1998) 193–228
5. Mäkinen, E.: Inferring finite transducers. Technical Report A-1999-3, University of Tampere (1999)
6. Vilar, J.M.: Improve the learning of subsequential transducers by using alignments and dictionaries. In: Grammatical Inference: Algorithms and Applications. Volume 1891 of Lecture Notes in Artificial Intelligence. Springer-Verlag (2000) 298–312
7. Casacuberta, F.: Inference of finite-state transducers by using regular grammars and morphisms. In: Grammatical Inference: Algorithms and Applications. Volume 1891 of Lecture Notes in Computer Science. Springer-Verlag (2000) 1–14
8. Amengual, J., Benedí, J., Casacuberta, F., Castaño, A., Castellanos, A., Jiménez, V., Llorens, D., Marzal, A., Pastor, M., Prat, F., Vidal, E., Vilar, J.: The EuTrans-I speech translation system. Machine Translation **15** (2000) 75–103
9. Alshawi, H., Bangalore, S., Douglas, S.: Learning dependency translation models as collections of finite state head transducers. Computational Linguistics **26** (2000)

10. Picó, D., Casacuberta, F.: Some statistical-estimation methods for stochastic finite-state transducers. Machine Learning **44** (2001) 121–141
11. Bangalore, S., Riccardi, G.: A finite-state approach to machine translation. In: Proceedings of the North American ACL2001, Pittsburgh, USA (2001)
12. Casacuberta, F., Vidal, E.: Machine translation with inferred stochastic finite-state transducers. Computational Linguistics **30** (2004) 205–225
13. Brown, P.F., Pietra, S.A.D., Pietra, V.J.D., Mercer, R.L.: The mathematics of statistical machine translation: Parameter estimation. Computational Linguistics **19** (1993) 263–311
14. Ney, H., Nießen, S., Och, F.J., Sawaf, H., Tillmann, C., Vogel, S.: Algorithms for statistical translation of spoken language. IEEE Transactions on Speech and Audio Processing **8** (2000) 24–36
15. Casacuberta, F., Ney, H., Och, F.J., Vidal, E., Vilar, J.M., Barrachina, S., García-Varea, I., Llorens, D., Martínez, C., Molau, S., Nevado, F., Pastor, M., Picó, D., Sanchis, A., Tillmann, C.: Some approaches to statistical and finite-state speech-to-speech translation. Computer Speech and Language **18** (2004) 25–47
16. Jelinek, F.: Statistical Methods for Speech Recognition. The MIT Press, Cambridge, Massachusetts (1998)
17. Langlais, P., Foster, G., Lapalme, G.: TransType: a computer-aided translation typing system. In: Proceedings of the Workshop on Embedded Machine Translation Systems (NAACL/ANLP2000), Seattle, Washington (2000) 46–52
18. Civera, J., Vilar, J., Cubel, E., Lagarda, A., Casacuberta, F., Vidal, E., Picó, D., González, J.: A syntactic pattern recognition approach to computer assisted translation. In Fred, A., Caelli, T., Campilho, A., Duin, R.P., de Ridder, D., eds.: Advances in Statistical, Structural and Syntactical Pattern Recognition. Lecture Notes in Computer Science. Springer-Verlag, Lisbon (2004)
19. Mohri, M.: Finite-state transducers in language and speech processing. Computational Linguistics **23** (1997) 269–311
20. Casacuberta, F., Vidal, E.: Machine translation with inferred stochastic finite-state transducers. Computational Linguistics **30** (2004) 205–225
21. Casacuberta, F., Vidal, E., Picó, D.: Inference of finite-state transducers from regular languages. Pattern Recognition (2004) In press
22. Casacuberta, F., de la Higuera, C.: Computational complexity of problems on probabilistic grammars and transducers. In: Grammatical Inference: Algorithms and Applications. Volume 1891 of Lecture Notes in Computer Science., Springer-Verlag (2000) 15–24
23. Amengual, J., Vidal, E.: Efficient Error-Corecting Viterbi Parsing. IEEE Transactions on Pattern Analysis and Machine Intelligence **20** (1998) 1109–1116
24. Amengual, J., Sanchis, A., Vidal, E., Benedí, J.: Language simplification through error-correcting and grammatical inference techniques. Machine Learning **44** (2001) 143–159
25. Llorens, D., Vilar, J.M., Casacuberta, F.: Finite state language models smoothed using n-grams. International Journal of Pattern Recognition and Artificial Intelligence **16** (2002) 275–289
26. Oncina, J., .Varó, M.: Using domain information during the learning of a subsequential transducer. In: Grammatical Inference: Learning Syntax from Sentences. Volume 1147 of Lecture Notes on Computer Science. (1996) 313–325
27. Vidal, E.: Finite-State Speech-to-Speech Translation. In: Proceedings of the International Conference on Acoustics Speech and Signal Processing (ICASSP-97), proc., Vol.1, Munich (1997) 111–114

28. EuTrans: Example-based language translation systems. Final report. Technical report, Instituto Tecnológico de Informática, Fondazione Ugo Bordoni, Rheinisch Westfälische Technische Hochschule Aachen Lehrstuhl für Informatik VI, Zeres GmbH Bochum: Long Term Research Domain, Project Number 30268 (2000)
29. Och, F., Ney, H.: A systematic comparison of various statistical alignment models. Computational Linguistics **29** (2003) 19–51
30. Ney, H., Martin, S., Wessel, F.: Statistical language modeling using leaving-one-out. In Young, S., Bloothooft, G., eds.: Corpus-Based Statiscal Methods in Speech and Language Processing. Kluwer Academic Publishers (1997) 174–207
31. Moon, T.K.: The expectation-maximization algorithm. IEEE Signal Processing Mahazine (1996) 47–59

The Omphalos Context-Free Grammar Learning Competition

Bradford Starkie[1], François Coste[2], and Menno van Zaanen[3]

[1] Telstra Research Laboratories
770 Blackburn Rd Clayton, Melbourne, Victoria, Australia 3127
Brad.Starkie@telstra.com.au
http://www.cs.newcastle.edu.au/~bstarkie
[2] IRISA, Campus de Beaulieu, 35042 Rennes, France
francois.coste@irisa.fr
http://www.irisa.fr/symbiose/people/coste
[3] Tilburg University, Postbus 90153, 5000LE, Tilburg, The Netherlands
mvzaanen@uvt.nl
http://ilk.uvt.nl/~mvzaanen

Abstract. This paper describes the Omphalos Context-Free Grammar Learning Competition held as part of the International Colloquium on Grammatical Inference 2004. The competition was created in an effort to promote the development of new and better grammatical inference algorithms for context-free languages, to provide a forum for the comparison of different grammatical inference algorithms and to gain insight into the current state-of-the-art of context-free grammatical inference algorithms. This paper discusses design issues and decisions made when creating the competition. It also includes a new measure of the complexity of inferring context-free grammars, used to rank the competition problems.

1 Introduction

Omphalos is a context-free language learning competition held in conjunction with the International Colloquium on Grammatical Inference 2004[1]. The aims of the competition are:

- to promote the development of new and better grammatical inference (GI) algorithms,
- to provide a forum in which the performance of different grammatical inference algorithms can be compared on a given task, and
- to provide an indicative measure of the complexity of grammatical inference problems that can be solved with the current state-of-the-art techniques.

2 The Competition Task

The competition task was to infer a model of a context-free language from unstructured examples. During the development of the competition, two main design issues needed to be resolved as follows:

---

[1] The competition data will continue to be available after the completion of the competition and can be accessed via http://www.irisa.fr/Omphalos/.

G. Paliouras and Y. Sakakibara (Eds.): ICGI 2004, LNAI 3264, pp. 16–27, 2004.

Method of evaluation. A method of determining the winner of the competition needed to be decided upon. For instance entries could be judged by measuring the difference between the inferred language and the target language, or, alternatively, entries could be judged by measuring the difference between the derivation trees assigned to sentences by the inferred grammar and the derivation trees assigned to sentences by the target grammar.

Complexity of tasks. As one of the goals of the competition was to determine the state-of-the-art in grammatical inference, the competition tasks should be selected so as to be neither too simple, nor too difficult to solve. That is the complexity of the learning task should be quantifiable.

Both of these issues will be discussed in the following subsections below.

2.1 Method of Evaluation

The evaluation approach selected to be used by the competition should be automatic, objective and easy. Van Zaanen et al. [1] describe several approaches to the evaluation of grammatical inference systems. These include the following:

Rebuilding known grammars. Using a pre-defined grammar, unstructured data is generated. Based on this data, the GI system tries to induce the original grammar. The problem here is that for most languages, there is more than one grammar that can be used to describe that language. Although all regular grammars can be transformed into a canonical form, no such canonical form exists for context-free grammars. Therefore there is no automated way to determine that the language described by a grammar submitted by a competitor and the target grammar are the same.

Comparison of labelled test data with treebank. Plain data is extracted from a set of structured sentences. A GI system must now find the original structure using the unstructured data. A distance measure is then used to rank the similarity between the derivation trees assigned to test sentences by the inferred grammar and derivation trees assigned to test sentences by the target grammar. Once again because for most languages there is more than one grammar describing that language a grammar submitted by a competitor may describe the target language exactly, but would rank poorly according to the distance measure. In addition the approach is problematic when ambiguity occurs in either the target or inferred grammar as multiple solutions are then possible.

Classification of unseen examples. The GI systems receive unstructured (positive or positive and negative) training data. This training data is generated according to an underlying grammar. Next, test data is provided and the system designed by competitors should assign language membership information to this test data. In other words, the system must say for each sentence if it is contained in the language described by the underlying grammar. The main disadvantage of this evaluation approach is that since this task is a classification task, no real grammatical information has to be learned as such.

Precision and recall. Each GI system receives unstructured training data generated according to a target grammar. From this training data a grammar is inferred. Next, previously unseen sentences that are in the target language are provided to the system. The percentage of these sentences that are in the inferred grammar is measured. This measure is known as the recall. Next sentences are generated according to the inferred grammar. The number of these sentences that exist in the target language is then measured. This measure is known as the precision. Recall and precision can then be merged into a single measure known as the F-score. The F-Score is a measure of the similarity between the target and inferred languages. A problem with this technique is that once a test sentence has been used to measure recall it cannot be used to measure recall a second time. This because that test sentence can also be used as an additional training example. In addition this technique requires that all grammatical inference systems be capable of generating example sentences.

All these evaluation methods have problems when applied to a generic GI competition. It was decided however that for the Omphalos competition, the technique of "classification of unseen examples" would be used to identify the winner of the competition. This was the same evaluation method that was used for the Abbadingo [2] DFA (regular language) learning competition. For Omphalos however competitors needed to tag the test sentences with 100% accuracy compared with 99% accuracy for the Abbadingo competition. This stricter requirement was used in an effort to encourage the development of new truly context-free learning algorithms. The main benefit of this technique is that it places few restrictions upon the techniques used to classify the data. In addition if the inferred grammar describes the target language exactly it will classify the test examples exactly. The main disadvantage of this technique is that it is possible for a classifier to classify all of the test examples exactly without the classifier having an accurate model of the target language. One way to overcome this problem is to only consider the problem to be solved when the precision of the inferred grammar is greater than a threshold value. We have decided not to implement this additional constraint, since it is believed that if the test sets contain negative examples that are sufficiently close to positive examples, then classification accuracy is a suitable measure of how close the inferred grammar is to the target grammar.

2.2   Complexity of the Competition Tasks

The target grammars, training and testing sentences were created with the following objectives in mind:

Requirement 1. The learning task should be sufficiently difficult. Specifically the task should be just outside of the current state-of-the-art, but not so difficult that it is unlikely that a winner will be found.

Requirement 2. It should be provable that the training sentences are sufficient to identify the target language.

From [3] it is known that it is impossible to learn a context-free grammar from positive examples only without reference to a statistical distribution, however:

- It is possible to learn a context-free grammar if both positive and negative examples are available and,
- If sufficient additional prior knowledge is known, such as a statistical distribution, it is possible to learn a context-free grammar with positive data only.

Therefore it was decided to include problems that included learning grammars from positive examples only as well as learning grammars from positive as well as negative examples.

To determine whether or not Requirement 1 was met, a measure of the complexity of the learning task was derived. This measure was derived by creating a model of the learning task based upon a brute force search. To do this a hypothetical grammatical inference algorithm called the *BruteForceLearner* algorithm was created. This model was also used to determine if the training data was sufficient to identify the target grammar. The details of the algorithm, the proof that it can identify any context-free grammar in the limit from positive and negative data, as well as the definition of the complexity measure itself can be found in [4].

The summary of these proofs is as follows:

- For each context-free grammar G there exists a set of positive examples $O(G)$ such that when $O(G)$ is presented to the *BruteForceLearner* algorithm, the *BruteForceLearner* algorithm constructs a set of grammars X such that there exists a grammar G_2 in X with the property that $L(G) = L(G_2)$. We call this set the characteristic set, and use the notation $O(G)$ to define the characteristic set of G.
- Given G there exists a simple technique to construct $O(G)$. This technique involves generating a sentence s for each rule P in G, such that all derivations of s are derived using P. This technique was used in the Omphalos competition to construct some of the training examples.
- When presented with the training examples $O(G)$ the *BruteForceLearner* need only construct a finite number of candidate grammars. Equation 1 described below defines the number of candidate grammars that could be constructed that would be sufficient to include the target language.

$$\#\text{candidate grammars} = 2^{(((\sum_j (2|O_j|-2))+1)^3 + ((\sum_j (2|O_j|-2)+1)T(O)))} \qquad (1)$$

Where G is any context-free grammar, O is a set of positive examples in a characteristic set of G, and $T(O)$ is the number of terminals in O.

- Given G and $O(G)$, there exists an additional set of positive and negative examples $O_2(G)$ such that when $O_2(G)$ is presented to the *BruteForceLearner* algorithm after $O(G)$, the *BruteForceLearner* algorithm identifies the target language exactly.

The following technique can be used to construct $O_2(G)$;

- Given O(G) construct the set of hypothesis grammars H that is sufficiently large to ensure that it contains the target grammar.
- For each H_i ∈H such that $L(O(H_i)) \subset L(G)$ add one sentence, marked as a positive example, to $O_2(G)$ that is an element of G but not an element of H_i.
- For all other H_i ∈H where $L(O(H_i)) \neq L(G)$ add one sentence, marked as a negative example, to $O_2(G)$ that is an element of H_i but not an element of G.

Note that this is the only known technique for constructing the set $O_2(G)$. The number of possible grammars given $O(G)$ is described by Equation 1 which is not polynomial. Therefore the construction of the negative data using this technique is not computable in polynomial time using this technique.

3   Creation of the Example Problems

As a result of the proofs contained in [4] and summarized in the previous section, Equation 1 was considered to be a suitable measure of the complexity of the learning tasks of the Omphalos competition. This is because it defines a hypothesis space used by at least one algorithm that is guaranteed to identify any context-free language in the limit using positive and negative data. Equation 1 was also used to benchmark the target problems against other grammatical inference problems that were known to be solved using other algorithms. In addition the proofs contained in [4] showed that for all grammars, other than those that could generate all strings of a given alphabet, the *BruteForceLearner* algorithm required negative data to ensure that it uniquely identified any context-free language. As described in the previous section, the only known way that could be used to construct sufficient negative data to ensure that at least one known algorithm could identify the language exactly from positive data was not computable in polynomial time. Therefore if a target grammar was chosen that was small enough to enable sufficient negative training examples to be calculated, then the learning task would become too simple. Therefore no such set of negative data was calculated, and it is not known if for any of the competition problems the training examples are sufficient to uniquely identify the target language.

The following technique was used to construct the training sets for the Omphalos competition:

- For each target grammar a set of positive sentences were constructed, such that for every rule in the target grammar, a positive sentence was added to the training set that is derived using that rule.
- A set of positive examples were then randomly created from the target grammar of length up to five symbols longer than the longest sentence in the characteristic.
- A set of negative sentences was then created for each target grammar. For problems 1 to 6 these were constructed by randomly creating strings up to the maximum length using the symbols of the grammar. For problems 6.1 to 10 the negative examples were created from "surrogate" grammars such as regular approximations to the target languages.

The number of training examples was selected to be between 10 and 20 times as large as the characteristic set.

3.1 Creation of the Target Grammars

Firstly the literature was reviewed to identify pre-existing benchmark grammatical inference problems. The work in [5] and [6] identified some benchmark problems, i.e. grammars that can be used as some sort of standard to test the effectiveness of a GI system by trying to learn these grammars. The grammars were taken from [7] and [8]. Using Equation 1 the complexities of these grammars were calculated. A description of these grammars and their complexity measures are listed in Table 1.

Table 1. Complexity of Benchmark Inference Problems from [5] and [6].

	Description	Example phrase	$\log_2$ compl.	Properties
1	(aa)∗	aa, aaaa, aaaaaa	1.34×10^3	Regular
2	(ab)∗	ab, abab, ababab	2.22×10^3	Regular
3	Operator precedence (small)	(a+(b+a))	9.37×10^3	Not regular
4	Parentheses	(), (()), ()(), ()(())	2.22×10^3	Not regular
5	English verb agreement (small)	that is a woman, i am there	5.33×10^5	Finite
6	English lzero grammar	a circle touches a square, a square is below a triangle	4.17×10^6	Finite
7	English with clauses (small)	a cat saw a mouse that saw a cat	6.59×10^5	Not regular
8	English conjugations (small)	the big old cat heard the mouse	9.13×10^5	Regular
9	Regular expressions	ab∗(a)∗	9.39×10^3	Not regular
10	$\{\omega = \omega^\mathbb{R}, \omega \in \{a,b\}\{a,b\}+\}$	aaa, ba	6.90×10^4	Not regular
11	Number of a's=number of b's	aabbaa	4.29×10^4	Not regular
12	Number of a's=2×number of b's	aab, babaaa	3.01×10^5	Not regular
13	$\{\omega\omega|\omega \in \{a,b\}+\}$	aba, aa	9.12×10^4	Regular
14	Palindrome with end delimiter	aabb\$, ab\$, baab\$	1.18×10^5	Not regular
15	Palindrome with center mark	aca, abcba	4.96×10^3	Not regular
16	Even length palindrome	aa, abba	9.30×10^3	Not regular
17	Shape grammar	da, bada	2.45×10^4	Not regular

Using the results of Table 1 the complexities of the target grammars of the competition problems were selected. The grammars were then created as follows:

1. The number of non-terminals, terminals and rules were selected to be greater than in grammars shown in Table 1.
2. A set of terminals and non-terminals were created. Rules were then created by randomly selecting terminals and non-terminals. A fixed number of rules were created to contain only terminal strings.

3. Useless rules were then identified. If a non-terminal could not generate a terminal string, a terminal rule was added to it. If a non-terminal was not reachable from the start symbol, rules were added to ensure the rule was reachable from the start symbol. For instance if the non-terminal N was unreachable from the start symbol, a rule was created with the start symbol on the left hand side of the rule, and N on the right hand side of the rule.
4. Additional rules were added to ensure that the grammar did not represent a regular language. Specifically rules containing center recursion were added.
5. A characteristic set of sentences was generated for the grammar. If the complexity of the grammar was not in the desired range, then the grammar was deleted.

Using this technique six grammars were created as listed in Table 2. Tests were undertaken to ensure that grammars 1–4 represented deterministic languages. Specifically $LR(1)$ parse tables were constructed from the grammars using bison. To ensure that grammars 4 and 5 represented non-deterministic languages, rules were added to the target grammars. It should be noted that these grammars are complex enough that they cannot be learned using a brute force technique in time to be entered into the Omphalos competition. Having said that, even the smallest of grammars could not be inferred using the *Brute-ForceLearner*. After problem 6 was solved, problems 7 to 10 were added to the competition. Problems 6.1 to 6.6 were added some time later.

The grammars listed in Table 2 represent three axes of difficulty in grammatical inference. Specifically:

1. The complexity of the underlying grammar,
2. whether or not negative data is available and,

Table 2. Complexities of Benchmark Inference Problems in Omphalos Competition.

	Training data	Properties	$\log_2$ compl.
1	Positive and negative	Not regular, deterministic	1.10×10^9
2	Positive only	Not regular, deterministic	7.12×10^8
3	Positive and negative	Not regular, deterministic	1.65×10^{10}
4	Positive only	Not regular, deterministic	1.13×10^{10}
5	Positive and negative	Not regular, non-deterministic	5.46×10^{10}
6	Positive only	Not regular, non-deterministic	6.55×10^{10}
6.1	Positive and negative	Not regular, deterministic	1.10×10^9
6.2	Positive only	Not regular, deterministic	7.12×10^8
6.3	Positive and negative	Not regular, deterministic	1.65×10^{10}
6.4	Positive only	Not regular, deterministic	1.13×10^{10}
6.5	Positive and negative	Not regular, non-deterministic	5.46×10^{10}
6.6	Positive only	Not regular, non-deterministic	6.55×10^{10}
7	Positive and negative	Not regular, deterministic	5.88×10^{11}
8	Positive only	Not regular, deterministic	1.63×10^{11}
9	Positive and negative	Not regular, non-deterministic	1.08×10^{12}
10	Positive only	Not regular, non-deterministic	9.92×10^{11}

3. how similar the negative examples in the test set are to positive examples of the language. For instance whether or not the test set includes sentences that can be generated by regular approximations to the target language but not the target language itself.

The competition adopted a linear ordering for the benchmark problems based upon these axes. Correctly labelling a test set in which the negative sentences closely resembled the positive sentences was ranked higher than correctly labelling a test set where the negative examples differed greatly from the positive examples. For instance, problem 6.1 is ranked higher than problem 1 and even problem 6. Similarly, solving a problem with a higher complexity measure was ranked higher than solving one with a lower complexity measure. For instance, problem 3 is ranked higher than problem 1. Solving a problem without using negative data was considered to be a more difficult problem than when negative data was used. For instance, problem 2 is ranked higher than problem 1. In addition it has been noted by [6] that the inference of non-deterministic languages is a more difficult task than the inference of deterministic languages. Therefore solving those problems that involved non-deterministic languages was ranked higher than solving those problems that involved deterministic languages.

3.2   Construction of Training and Testing Sets

Once the target grammars were constructed, characteristic sets were constructed for each grammar. Sets of positive examples were then created using the GenR-GenS software [9].

For the first six problems additional examples were then created by randomly generating sentences of length up to five symbols more than the length of the longest sentence in the characteristic set. These sentences were then parsed using the target grammar and were labeled as being either in or out of the target language. This set of sentences was then randomized and split into testing and training sets, but in such a way as to ensure that the training set contained a characteristic set. For those problems that were to be learned from positive data only the training sets had all negative examples removed.

For problems 6.1 to 10 a more rigorous method of constructing negative data was used as follows:

- For each context-free grammar an equivalent regular grammar was constructed using the superset approximation method based on Recursive Tree Network (RTN) described in [10]. Sentences that could be generated from this regular approximation to the target language were included as negative data. These sentences were included to distinguish between competitors who had created regular approximations to the underlying context-free languages, and competitors who had identified a non-regular language.
- A context-free grammar that was larger than the target language was constructed by treating the target grammar as a string rewriting system, and normalizing the right hand sides of rules using the normalization algorithm

described in [11]. That is, a context-free grammar was constructed that described a language that was a superset of the target language, but in which the right hand side of each rule could not be parsed by the right hand side of any other rule. Negative examples were then created from this approximation to the target language.

- Each target grammar in the competition included some deliberate constructs designed to trick grammatical inference algorithms. For instance most included sequences that where identical to center recursion expanded to a finite depth. An example is $A^n B^n$ where $n < m$, m is an integer > 1. To ensure that the training and testing examples tested the ability of the inferred grammars to capture these nuances, the target grammars were copied and hand modified changing the $A^n B^n$ where $n < m$ to become $A^n B^n$ where $n > 1$. In addition, where center recursion existed of the form $A^n B^n$ in the target grammar the regular approximations $A^* B^*$ were included in the "tricky" approximation to the target grammar. Negative examples where then created from these approximations to the target grammar and added to the test set.
- There were an equal number of positive and negative examples in the test sets.

In addition for problems 6.1 to 10:

- The longest training example was shorter than the longest test example.
- The grammar rules for problems 7 to 10 were shorter than for problems 1 to 6.6 and had more recursion. Some non-$LL(1)$ constructs were also added to the target grammars for problems 7 to 10.

4   Preliminary Results

The timetable of the competition was constructed such that the competition ended two weeks prior to the ICGI 2004 conference in which this paper appears. Due to the deadlines involved in publishing the proceedings the results of the competition cannot be contained within this paper. The following table includes some important dates on the time line of the competition.

4.1   Problem 1

Problem 1 was solved by Joan Andreu Sánchez from the Departament de Sistemes Informàtics i Computació, Universitat Politècnica de València. Although Sánchez originally tried to solve the problem using the Inside-Outside algorithm, he actually solved it manually. After discovering the regularities in the positive examples he used a regular expression constructed by hand to classify the test examples as being either positive or negative. Although the target grammar was not a regular language the test sets did not include a single non-regular example. This in addition to the speed in which the problem was solved suggests that the first task was overly simple, and the negative examples were too different from the positive examples to be an accurate test of whether or not the language had been successfully learned.

Table 3. Competition time line.

Date	Event
February 15th 2004	Competition begins
February 20th 2004	Problem 1 solved by Joan Andreu Sánchez
March 22nd 2004	Problems 3, 4, 5 and 6 were solved by Erik Tjong Kim Sang
April 14th 2004	Problems 7, 8, 9 and 10 were added
June 7th 2004	New larger testing sets were added for problems 1 to 6
October 1st 2004	Competition closed
October 11th 2004	Competition winner announced
October 11th–13th 2004	Omphalos session at ICGI-2004

4.2   Problems 3, 4, 5, and 6

Problems 3, 4, 5, and 6 were solved by Erik Tjong Kim Sang from the CNTS – Language Technology Group at the University of Antwerp in Belgium. Tjong Kim Sang used a pattern matching system that classifies strings based on n-grams of characters that appear either only in the positive examples or only in the negative examples. With the exception of problem 1 this technique was not sufficient to solve the problem, so Tjong Kim Sang generated his own negative data, using the principle that the majority of randomly generated strings would not be contained within the language. His software behaved as follows;

1. Firstly it loaded in positive examples from the training file.
2. It then generated an equal number of unseen random strings, and added these to the training data as negative examples.
3. A n-gram classifier was then created as follows: A count was made of n-grams of length 2 to 10 that appeared uniquely in the positive examples or uniquely in the negative examples. A weighted (frequency) count of such n-grams in the test strings was then made. For each sentence in the test set. If the positive count was larger than the negative count then the string was classified as positive, otherwise it was classified as negative. If a string contained two zero counts then that sentence was classified as unknown.
4. Steps 2 and 3 were repeated thirty times.
5. Strings that were always classified as positive in all thirty tests were then assumed to be positive examples. Strings that were classified as negative one or more time were classified as negative. Other strings were classified as unknown.

The techniques used by Sánchez and Tjong Kim Sang suggested that more effort was required to generate negative data, to ensure that the testing sets were accurate indications of whether or not the competitor had successfully constructed a context-free grammar that was close to the exact solution. In particular the testing sets needed to include negative sentences that were in regular approximations of the target language, but not in the target language itself. As result, additional problems were added to the competition on April

14th. In addition, on June 7th additional test sets for problems 1 to 6 were added to the competition. Because the correct classification of these test sets was a more difficult task than the correct classification of the earlier test sets, these test sets became problems 6.1 to 6.6.

5   Conclusions

In conclusion, at the time of the writing of this paper the competition is yet to achieve the goal of encouraging the development of new grammatical inference algorithms that can infer truly context-free languages. We believe there are two reasons for this; Firstly, generic machine learning classifiers have been used to solve the "easy" problems, so GI researchers do not attempt to re-solve these. Secondly, the Omphalos problems were designed to be just out of reach of the current state-of-the-art. Since the data-sets will stay available for some time, we expect these problems to be solved in the near future. The goal of providing an indicative measure of the complexity of grammatical inference problems that can be solved using current state of the art techniques has however been partially achieved. An equation (Equation 1) has been developed that defines the size of a set of context-free grammars that can be constructed from a set of training sentences, such that the target language is guaranteed to be contained in this set of context-free grammars.

References

1. Menno van Zaanen, Andrew Roberts, and Eric Atwell. A multilingual parallel parsed corpus as gold standard for grammatical inference evaluation. In Lambros Kranias, Nicoletta Calzolari, Gregor Thurmair, Yorick Wilks, Eduard Hovy, Gudrun Magnusdottir, Anna Samiotou, and Khalid Choukri, editors, *Proceedings of the Workshop: The Amazing Utility of Parallel and Comparable Corpora; Lisbon, Portugal*, pages 58–61, May 2004.
2. Kevin J. Lang, Barak A. Pearlmutter, and Rodney A. Price. Results of the Abbadingo One DFA learning competition and a new evidence-driven state merging algorithm. In V. Honavar and G. Slutzki, editors, *Proceedings of the Fourth International Conference on Grammar Inference*, volume 1433 of *Lecture Notes in AI*, pages 1–12, Berlin Heidelberg, Germany, 1994. Springer-Verlag.
3. E. Mark Gold. Language identification in the limit. *Information and Control*, 10:447–474, 1967.
4. B. Starkie. A complexity measure for the grammatical inference of context-free languages. Technical Report RLR8561, Telstra Research Laboratories, Clayton, Australia, 2004.
5. A. Stolcke. Boogie. `ftp://ftp.icsi.berkeley.edu/pub/ai/stolcke/software/boogie.shar.Z`, 2003.
6. K. Nakamura and M. Matsumoto. Incremental learning of context-free grammars. In Pieter Adriaans, Henning Fernau, and Menno van Zaanen, editors, *Grammatical Inference: Algorithms and Applications (ICGI); Amsterdam, the Netherlands*, volume 2482 of *Lecture Notes in AI*, pages 174–184, Berlin Heidelberg, Germany, September 23–25 2002. Springer-Verlag.

7. Craig M. Cook, Azriel Rosenfeld, and Alan R. Aronson. Grammatical inference by hill climbing. *Informational Sciences*, 10:59–80, 1976.

8. J.E. Hopcroft, R. Motwani, and J.D. Ullman. *Introduction to automata theory, languages, and computation*. Addison-Wesley Publishing Company, Reading:MA, USA, 2001.

9. Alain Denise, Frédéric Sarron, and Yann Ponty. GenRGenS. URL: `http://www.lri.fr/~denise/GenRGenS/`, 2001.

10. Mark-Jan Nederhof. Practical experiments with regular approximation of context-free languages. *Computational Linguistics*, 26(1):17–44, 2000.

11. F. Otto. On deciding the confluence of a finite string-rewriting system on a given congruence class. *Journal of Computer and System Sciences*, 35:285–310, 1987.

Mutually Compatible and Incompatible Merges for the Search of the Smallest Consistent DFA

John Abela[1], François Coste[2], and Sandro Spina[1]

[1] Department of Computer Science & AI, University of Malta
{jabel,sandro}@cs.um.edu.mt
[2] INRIA/IRISA, Campus de Beaulieu, 35042 Rennes Cedex, France
francois.coste@irisa.fr

Abstract. State Merging algorithms, such as Rodney Price's EDSM (Evidence-Driven State Merging) algorithm, have been reasonably successful at solving DFA-learning problems. EDSM, however, often does not converge to the target DFA and, in the case of sparse training data, does not converge at all. In this paper we argue that is partially due to the particular heuristic used in EDSM and also to the greedy search strategy employed in EDSM. We then propose a new heuristic that is based on minimising the risk involved in making merges. In other words, the heuristic gives preference to merges, whose evidence is supported by high compatibility with other merges. Incompatible merges can be trivially detected during the computation of the heuristic. We also propose a new heuristic limitation of the set of candidates after a backtrack to these incompatible merges, allowing to introduce diversity in the search.

1 Introduction

Most real world phenomena can be represented as syntactically structured sequences. Examples of such sequences include DNA, natural language sentences, electrocardiograms, speech signals, chain codes, etc. Grammatical inference addresses the problem of extracting/learning finite descriptions/representations, from examples of these syntactically structured sequences. Deterministic finite state automata (DFA) are an example of a finite representation, used to learn these sequences. Section 2 presents to the reader some preliminary definitions. Section 3 describes the current leading DFA-learning algorithm EDSM, whereas sections 4 and 5 introduce a novel heuristic for EDSM, namely S-EDSM, and the backtracking heuristic. Finally, sections 6 and 7 document the initial results of this new heuristic.

2 Preliminary Definitions

This section introduces the reader with the terms and definitions used throughout this paper. It is being assumed that the reader is already familiar with the definitions and results in set theory and formal languages, as well as the area of DFA learning in particular state merging DFA learning algorithms.

G. Paliouras and Y. Sakakibara (Eds.): ICGI 2004, LNAI 3264, pp. 28–39, 2004.

2.1   Transition Trees

Transition trees represent the set of string suffixes of a language L from a particular state. Transition trees are *mapped* onto each other by taking the state partitions of the two transition trees and joining them into new blocks to form a new state set partition. The mapping operation is recursively defined as follows:

Definition 1 (Map) *A transition tree t_1 is **mapped** onto transition tree t_2 by recursively joining together blocks of the set partitions of t_1 and t_2, for each common string prefix present in t_1 and t_2. The result of this mapping operation is a set partition π, consisting of a number of blocks b. Each block in π, is a set of states which have been merged together.*

2.2   State Compatibility and Merges

States in a hypothesis DFA are either unlabeled or labeled as accepting or rejecting. Two state labels A,B are **compatible** in all cases except when, A is accepting and B is rejecting, or, A is rejecting and B is accepting. Two states are **state compatible** if they have compatible labels. The set of all possible merges is divided between the set of **valid** merges, $\mathcal{M_V}$, and that of **invalid** merges, $\mathcal{M_I}$. A valid merge is defined in terms of the transition trees mapping operation as follows:

Definition 2 (Valid Merge) *A **valid merge** M_V in a hypothesis DFA H is defined as (q, q'), where q and q' are the states being merged, such that, the mapping of q' onto q results in a state partition π of H, with a number of blocks b, such that for each block $b \in \pi$, all states in b are **state compatible** with each other.*

3   State Merging Algorithms

The first state merging algorithm is due to Trakhtenbrot and Barzdin [1]. In their algorithm all the states of the APTA are labeled, hence the algorithm does not make any labeling decisions. We then see Gold's algorithm, in which the algorithm determines the label of unlabeled states in the APTA. Clearly, the order in which merges occur, determines the effectiveness of the learning process. In this algorithm only compatibility is considered, and evidence is not taken into account. EDSM improves on this algorithm by ordering merges on the amount of evidence of each *individual* merge. [2] describes the search space of the regular inference.

3.1   EDSM

The Evidence Driven State Merging (EDSM) algorithm developed by Price [3] emerged from the Abbadingo One DFA learning competition organised by Lang and Pearlmutter [3] in 1998. EDSM searches for a target DFA within a lattice of hypotheses (automata) enclosed between the augmented prefix tree acceptor (APTA) and the Universal Acceptor Automaton (UA) [2]. EDSM only considers DFAs that are consistent with the training examples. It is assumed that the target DFA lies in the search space of EDSM. It therefore follows, that at least one sequence of merges exists that will lead to the target DFA. The algorithm starts by constructing an augmented prefix tree acceptor (APTA) and then progressively performing merges. The search is guided by an evidence heuristic which determines which pair of states are to be merged [3]. The heuristic is based upon a score, that computes the number of compatible states found in the transition trees of the two states under consideration. At each iteration, all possible pairs of states in the current hypothesis are evaluated[1]. The pair with the highest evidence score is chosen for the next merge. This procedure is repeated until no more states can be merged.

3.2   Problems with EDSM

Although EDSM was one of the winners of Abbadingo One, it still could not solve the hardest four problems. These problems were characterised by very sparse training sets. If EDSM is to find the target DFA (or some other DFA that is close to it) it must, at each iteration of the algorithm, make a 'correct' merge. The scoring function is therefore critical in determining the direction to be taken within the set of possible merges. Since EDSM is a greedy depth-first search it is very sensitive to mistakes made in early merges. The algorithm does not backtrack to undo a 'bad' merge. In general, it is not possible to determine when a 'bad' merge had been made. Very often, EDSM converges to a DFA that is of much larger size than the target DFA. This is evidently because, EDSM makes some 'bad' merges in the beginning.

4   Shared Evidence

In order to improve on what EDSM does, we need to somehow gather more evidence from what is available. We propose that evidence can be augmented by gathering and combining together, the information derived from the interactions between all these valid merges. This combination of individual merge evidence, referred to as *shared evidence*, results in an improvement on the heuristic score. These sets of compatible merges, empirically prove to be valuable in two aspects. Initially they minimise the risk of making mistakes with the initial merges, thus decreasing the size of the hypothesis DFA from that generated by EDSM. Secondly, they prune the search tree (when a search strategy is applied) in such a way that equivalent merges are grouped together and need not be traversed individually. The strategy can also be seen as a kind of lookahead, computing an expectation of the score that you can expect in the next choices.

Shared evidence driven state merging (S-EDSM), is an attempt at a heuristic that tries to minimise the risk of a merge. Undoubtedly there exist no risk

---

[1] W-EDSM, also presented in [3], takes only a subset of all the possible merges.

free merges, however as opposed to EDSM, S-EDSM tries to share this risk across multiple merges. In this paper we are proposing a subset of a *preliminary* calculus, which specifically deals with how merges interact. A heuristic is then developed based on some of the properties derived from this analysis.

4.1   Pairwise and Mutual Compatible Merges

The most basic interaction between two merges is compatibility. Merge M is said to be *pairwise compatible* to merge M' if after performing merge M, M' remains a valid merge in the hypothesis automaton as changed by M. From this point onwards we will refer to merges which are elements of $\mathcal{M}_\mathcal{V}$. More formally two merges are pairwise compatible, if the following property holds:

Definition 3 (Pairwise Compatible) *Let π_1 and π_2 be the state partitions resulting from the application of the map operator to the two merges M_1 and M_2 on hypothesis H. Let H_1 and H_2 be the hypotheses resulting from π_1, π_2 respectively. M_1 and M_2 are **pairwise compatible** if for each state $s \in H$, $s \in H_1$ is state compatible with $s \in H_2$.*

Table 1. Score Calculation for Pairwise Compatible States

Current Merge	EDSM Score	S-EDSM Score	Pairwise Compatible Merges
$M1$	7	7+2	$\{M8\}$
$M2$	6	6+5+2+1	$\{M3, M8, M10\}$
$M3$	5	5+6+5+4+2	$\{M2, M4, M6, M8\}$
$M4$	5	5+5+4+2	$\{M3, M5, M8\}$
$M5$	4	4+5+3+2+1	$\{M4, M7, M8, M10\}$
$M6$	4	4+5+2	$\{M3, M8\}$
$M7$	3	3+4+2	$\{M5, M8\}$
$M8$	2	2+7+6+5+5	$\{M1, M2, M3, M4, M5,$
		4+4+3+1+1	$M6, M7, M9, M10\}$
$M9$	1	1+2+1	$\{M8, M10\}$
$M10$	1	1+6+4+2+1	$\{M2, M5, M8, M9\}$

Consider the set $V \subseteq \mathcal{M}_\mathcal{V}$, consisting of the 10 merges $\{M1 \, .. \, M10\}$. Table 1 lists merges $M1$ to $M10$, together with the set of merges which are pairwise compatible to each merge. For instance, merges $M3$ and $M8$ are both pairwise compatible with $M2$. However, note that this does not necessarily imply that $M3$ is pairwise compatible with $M8$. Moreover from the definition of pairwise compatibility it follows that, if $M3$ is pairwise compatible with $M4$ then $M4$ is pairwise compatible with $M3$. This means that the order in which the two merges are executed does not change the resulting state partition.

Let pairwise compatibility between two states be denoted by the symbol $\uparrow$. Pairwise compatibility induces the binary relation $\uparrow \subseteq \mathcal{M}_\mathcal{V} \times \mathcal{M}_\mathcal{V}$. Thus, $M1 \uparrow M2$ denotes that $M1$ is pairwise compatible with $M2$. Moreover, $M1 \uparrow \{M2, M3, M4\}$ denotes that, $M1$ is pairwise compatible with $M2$, $M3$, and $M4$. Note that $\uparrow$ is a symmetric relation.

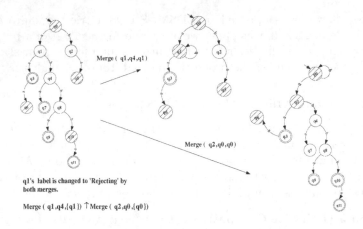

Fig. 1. Simple example of two pairwise compatible merges

$$M1 \uparrow M2 \rightarrow M2 \uparrow M1$$

Let us now consider the possibility that more that just two merges are compatible with each other. This means that for a particular hypothesis H, there *might exist* n valid merges with $n >$ two such that the execution of merges M_1 to M_{n-1} does not effect the validity of merge M_n. In this case we need to extend the definition of pairwise compatibility to include more than two merges. *Mutual compatibility* is defined as follows:

Definition 4 (Mutual Compatibility) *Let n be equal to an arbitrary number of valid merges. Let $\pi_1, \pi_2, ..., \pi_n$ be the state partitions created when applying the map operator to the n merges $M_1, M_2, ..., M_n$ on hypothesis H. Let $H_1, H_2, ..., H_n$ be the hypotheses resulting from $\pi_1, \pi_2, ..., \pi_n$ respectively. $M_1, ..., M_n$ are **mutually compatible** if, for each state $s \in H$, s is state compatible with $s \in H_1 \wedge ... \wedge s \in H_{n-1} \wedge s \in H_n$.*

5   Merge Heuristic

Shared Evidence Driven State Merging (S-EDSM) is the algorithm based on the definitions presented in the previous section. Only pairwise compatibility is used in the heuristic. There are plans, however, to extend the heuristic to also incorporate other ideas such as merge mutual compatibility, merge dominance, merge coverage and merge intersection. The term **shared** was used to underline the basic notion that, the heuristic works by gathering and combining, thus sharing, the information of individual merges.

5.1   Increasing Evidence

Consider a scenario, where a number of valid merges can be performed. Table 1 shows ten potential merge candidates, with $M1$'s heuristic score being the highest and $M10$'s heuristic score the lowest. While EDSM just executes the merge with the highest heuristic score (in this case $M1$), S-EDSM first checks for pairwise compatibility between all the merges and creates a list of *pairwise compatible merges* for each merge. Table 1 also shows an example of how these merges can be grouped through pairwise compatibility. The second column in this table indicates the EDSM score for the merge listed in the first column. Hence, the first row in the column is read as $M1 \uparrow \{M8\}$ and the second row as $M2 \uparrow \{M3, M8, M10\}$. Note that the sets are not checked for mutual compatibility. When EDSM merges $M1$ (the merge with the highest evidence score), merges $M2$, $M3$, $M4$, $M5$, $M6$, $M7$, $M9$ and $M10$ become invalid. This means that for the next merge selection procedure only merge $M8$ is possible, since this is the only merge which is pairwise compatible with $M1$. On the other hand, S-EDSM proceeds by first re-ordering the merges according to the pairwise compatibility of the merges. Column 3 of table 1 shows how the scores are re-calculated for all the merges. For the time being scores are simply added together. For instance, in the case of $M2$, the new score is added to $M3$'s score (5), $M8$'s score (2), and $M10$'s score (1). Thus, the score of the pairwise compatible set of $M2$ is set to 13. Simply adding the scores might however not be the best way of re-calculating evidence.

$M8$ is executed first by S-EDSM, since $M8$ is supported by evidence from all the other valid merges. $M4$ is the second merge to be executed, followed by $M3$. Once $M3$ is done, no more merges are possible. The merge sequence created by EDSM consists of two merges, $M1$ and $M8$. S-EDSM creates a merge sequence of three merges, $M8$, $M4$, then $M3$. The overall EDSM heuristic score for this sequence is 9, whereas for S-EDSM it is 12. Thus, it seems that overall S-EDSM has performed a sequence of merges which is better than the one chosen by EDSM. However, one should note that for the time being only pairwise compatibility is being considered. Pairwise compatibility alone *does not* give sufficient knowledge of how many states are actually giving **distinct evidence**. By distinct evidence we mean, the evidence that is given uniquely by a state through a state compatibility check. With pairwise compatibility sets, the same state compatibility check may account (and in practice it usually does) for increasing the evidence score of the pairwise compatible set when summing the individual EDSM scores. Consider for example figure 2. In this simple example, we have two possible merges $(q3, q2, \{q2\})$ and $(q2, q1, \{q1\})$ with EDSM evidence scores of one and two respectively. Clearly these two merges are pairwise compatible. Note however that when re-calculating the scores for S-EDSM, the evidence given by $q2$ is counted twice when calculating the S-EDSM score for the pairwise compatible set of $q1$.

5.2   Pairwise Compatibility – A Lookahead Strategy

Recall that EDSM's main problem is that when only a few states are labeled in the APTA, it is very difficult for the heuristic to determine which merge to perform. S-EDSM, by using pairwise compatibility for single merges, tries to

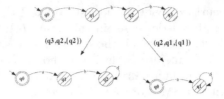

Fig. 2. Two simple merges

alleviate this problem by making use of a *lookahead strategy*. Lookahead occurs because of the following two factors:

- By gathering evidence for a single merge M from multiple merges pairwise compatible with M, and
- By increasing the number of labeled states (labeled by M) before recalculating the EDSM scores of the pairwise compatible states of M.

The execution of each valid merge M, before calculating the pairwise compatibility set of M, actually accounts for more evidence in terms of state labels which can now be used. S-EDSM works by always calculating these sets for each step in the search. Consider the DFA illustrated in figure 1. We know that for merge M1 $= (q0, q2, \{q0\})$ and merge M2 $= (q1, q4, \{q1\})$, $M1 \uparrow M2$. M1's EDSM score is equal to zero simply because there are no states which are state compatible, which are both accepting or rejecting in the respective transition trees of $q0$ and $q2$. However, when calculating the pairwise compatible set for merge $M2$, EDSM's score for merge $M1$ becomes one, since now $q1$ has been labeled as rejecting by $M2$. This new evidence supports the execution of $M2$.

5.3   Calculating the Evidence Score

Computing the set of pairwise compatible merges for such a large number of merges is not feasible. The strategy adopted by S-EDSM is to include a parameter which determines the set $\mathcal{M_S}$, of valid merges which are taken in consideration. Two possibilities have been implemented, with the first option used for the experiments.

- Identify the merge M_H with the highest evidence score. Include in $\mathcal{M_S}$, all those merges whose EDSM score falls into a percentage from this score (typically 70% of the best score in the experiments).
- Include in $\mathcal{M_S}$, a percentage of all the valid merges ordered by EDSM score in descending order.

5.4   Using Incompatible Merges in Backtrack

How to backtrack efficiently in the state merging framework is still an open question when the search space is too big for complete algorithms. Since the

---

Algorithm 1 Merge Score Calculation for S-EDSM

Require: A hypothesis H
Require: A set $\mathcal{V} \subseteq \mathcal{M}_\mathcal{V}$ on H
  for $j = 1$ to size($\mathcal{V}$) **do**
    enableTrackingOfMergeChangesOnStack
    $H \leftarrow executeMerge(V_j)$
    for $k = 1$ to size($\mathcal{V}$) **do**
      if V_k is still a valid merge **then**
        V_k is pairwise compatible to V_j
        include V_k in set of pairwise compatible merges of V_j
        $score\ V_j = score\ V_j + score\ V_k$
      else
        V_k is not pairwise compatible to V_j
        $score\ V_j = score\ V_j\ \text{-}\ score\ V_k$
      end if
    end for
    restoreMergeChangesFromStack
  end for
  $H \leftarrow executeMerge(highestScore(\mathcal{V}))$

Abbadingo competition, it is admitted that the first choices of EDSM are less informed when learning data become sparse and thus that the earlier merges are the most critical ones. After the winning but cpu demanding approach of Juillé [4], only few proposals have been made, focusing essentially on this first choices by a wrapper technique [5] or even by choosing randomly the first merge [6]. We believe that these methods have been moderately fruitful because they fail escaping from the neighbourhood of the first solution, visiting always the same area of the search space.

We propose here to introduce diversity in the exploration of the search space by limiting the choice of candidate merges after a backtrack to the set of incompatible merges with the undone merge. The set of incompatible merges with the merge with the highest score can be easily memorised with a small modification of algorithm 1: when V_k is not pairwise compatible to V_j, V_k can be added to a set of incompatible merges of V_j (Let us remark that only two sets of incompatible merges are needed: the current one and the one of the best candidate, denoted hereafter $\mathcal{I}$).

A simple implementation of the backtrack scheme may then consist in replacing the last line of algorithm 1 by:

  enableTrackingOfMergeChangesOnStack
  $H \leftarrow executeMerge(highestScore(\mathcal{V}))$
  restoreMergeChangesFromStack
  $H \leftarrow executeMerge(highestScore(\mathcal{V} \cap \mathcal{I}))$

More subtle implementations around this scheme can be developed by choosing to propagate the limitation of the candidates to the next choices, but these have to be chosen carefully according to the search strategy and the heuristic.

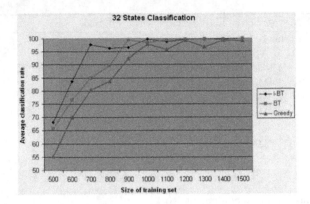

Fig. 3. Ten 32 state Gowachin Problems – Average Classification Rate

We show only here some preliminary results without propagation on small target automata. In these experiments, the backtrack has been limited to the three first merges. Figure 3 shows that using the incompatible merges backtrack scheme (I-BT) allows to outperform the reference algorithm with the same S-EDSM score calculation (BT) on sparser training samples.

6   S-EDSM Classification Rate

Classification of testing data is the best indicator of how well a learning algorithm performs. A comparison on classification rate between EDSM and S-EDSM is not a straightforward task. This is because there are numerous examples, when sparse training sets are used, were both algorithms perform poorly. Suppose EDSM achieves a classification rate of 0.51 and S-EDSM achieves a classification rate of 0.55. In these situations, there is really no difference between the two hypotheses. For this reason, classification rate experiments were carried out as follows. For a given problem, the target DFA was inferred by using a large training set. Portions of this training set are then systematically removed and the two learning algorithms are then applied on the new test sets. With this method we can check which algorithm requires the least amount of training strings in order to infer a good DFA. Since the target DFA is not known, training sets with 30,000 strings are initially used to exactly infer the target DFAs. The graphs of figure 4 show the average classification rates for ten DFAs with target sizes of 256, 192 and 128 states respectively. The three sets of ten problems each, have been sequentially downloaded from Gowachin.

With 128 states, the main difference between S-EDSM and EDSM occurs when the training set is reduced below 6,000 strings. The average classification rate for EDSM degenerates to 1,581 correctly classified strings (i.e. 87%). S-EDSM maintains (although still decreasing) an average classification rate of 1,737 (i.e. 96%). This indicates that, S-EDSM is somewhat less sensitive to sparse training sets. For the 256 states problems, S-EDSM starts to better classify

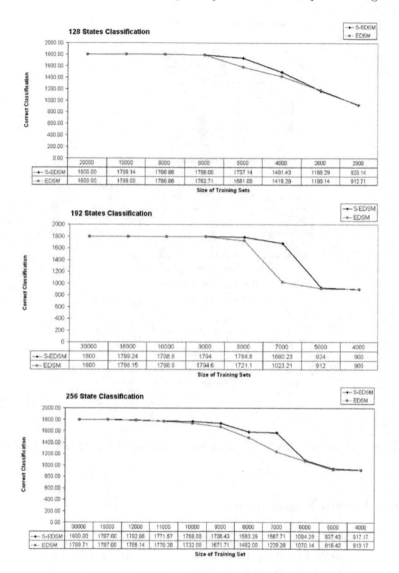

Fig. 4. Ten 128, 192 and 256 state Gowachin Problems - Average Classification Rate

the testing set with 10,000 strings. With 9,000 strings in the training set, the distance in classification rate between EDSM and S-EDSM increases. S-EDSM on average classifies correctly 1,736 strings (96%), while EDSM classifies 1,671 (92%). The biggest difference in classification rate occurs when the training set contains 7,000 strings. The average classification rate for S-EDSM remains high, while EDSM's classification rate drops considerably. Finally, for the set of ten 192 state problems, a similar behaviour is observed.

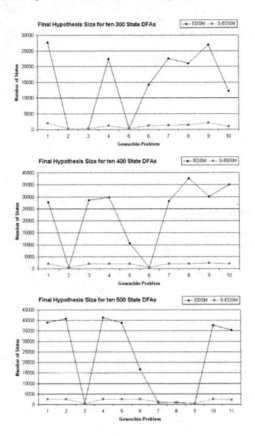

Fig. 5. Ten 300, 400 and 500 state Gowachin Problems - Final Hypothesis Size Comparison

7   Final Hypothesis Size

The final hypothesis size, gives an indication of how well a learning algorithm is searching the lattice of automata compatible with the training set. However, if using Occam's razor, when both algorithms give a classification rate of 0.5, we can argue that the size of the final hypothesis constitutes a measure which can be used to discriminate between the two algorithms. Essentially, the smaller the number of states used, to generalise a finite set of examples, the better. Figure 5 shows thirty consecutively downloaded Gowachin problems with a target size of 500 (24000 strings), 400 (20000) and 300 (12000) states. Although thirty problems certainly do not constitute an exhaustive sample of problems, the sample is enough to demonstrate a trend in the target sizes of the final hypothesis.

It is clear from these thirty problems that, when the percentage of the labeled nodes goes under 20%, S-EDSM outperforms EDSM heavily in target size convergence. S-EDSM's heuristic seems to be paying back in terms of target size convergence.

8   Conclusion and Perspectives

Initial results on S-EDSM's heuristic show that there is an improvement in both classification rate and final hypothesis size. The reason for this can be attributed to the fact that, S-EDSM augments its evidence score by combining the information of multiple valid merges. By doing so, S-EDSM avoids very 'bad' merges in the beginning, when the information is sparse. Considering both compatible merges and incompatible merges seems also promising and we think that S-EDSM coupled with a backtrack heuristic based on incompatible merges is worth being studied more systematically on artificial and also real data.

References

1. B. Trakhtenbrot and Ya. Barzdin. *Finite Automata: Behavior and Synthesis*. North Holland Pub. Comp., Amsterdam, 1973.
2. P. Dupont, L. Miclet, and E. Vidal. What is the search space of the regular inference ? In *Grammatical Inference and Applications, ICGI'94*, number 862 in Lecture Notes in Artificial Intelligence, pages 25–37. Springer Verlag, 1994.
3. K. Lang, B. Pearlmutter, and R. Price. Results of the abbadingo one dfa learning competition and a new evidence-driven state merging algorithm. *Grammatical Inference. ICGI 1998.*, LNAI 1433:1–12, 1998.
4. H. Juillé and J.B. Pollack. A stochastic search approach to grammar induction. In *Grammatical Inference*, number 1433 in Lecture Notes in Artificial Intelligence, pages 126–137. Springer-Verlag, 1998.
5. K. Lang. Evidence driven state merging with search. Technical report, NEC Research Institute, October 1998.
6. Orlando Cicchello and Stefan C. Kremer. Beyond edsm. *Grammatical Inference:Algorithms and Applications. ICGI 2002.*, 2002.

Faster Gradient Descent Training of Hidden Markov Models, Using Individual Learning Rate Adaptation

Pantelis G. Bagos, Theodore D. Liakopoulos, and Stavros J. Hamodrakas

Department of Cell Biology and Biophysics, Faculty of Biology, University of Athens
Panepistimiopolis, Athens 15701, Greece
{pbagos,liakop}@biol.uoa.gr, shamodr@cc.uoa.gr

Abstract. Hidden Markov Models (HMMs) are probabilistic models, suitable for a wide range of pattern recognition tasks. In this work, we propose a new gradient descent method for Conditional Maximum Likelihood (CML) training of HMMs, which significantly outperforms traditional gradient descent. Instead of using fixed learning rate for every adjustable parameter of the HMM, we propose the use of independent learning rate/step-size adaptation, which has been proved valuable as a strategy in Artificial Neural Networks training. We show here that our approach compared to standard gradient descent performs significantly better. The convergence speed is increased up to five times, while at the same time the training procedure becomes more robust, as tested on applications from molecular biology. This is accomplished without additional computational complexity or the need for parameter tuning.

1 Introduction

Hidden Markov Models (HMMs) are probabilistic models suitable for a wide range of pattern recognition applications. Initially developed for speech recognition [1], during the last few years they became very popular in molecular biology for protein modeling [2,3] and gene finding [4,5].

Traditionally, the parameters of an HMM (emission and transition probabilities) are optimized according to the Maximum Likelihood (ML) criterion. A widely used algorithm for this task is the efficient Baum-Welch algorithm [6], which is in fact an Expectation-Maximization (EM) algorithm [7], guaranteed to converge to at least a local maximum of the likelihood. Baldi and Chauvin later proposed a gradient descent method capable of the same task, which offers a number of advantages over the Baum-Welch algorithm, including smoothness and on-line training abilities [8].

When training an HMM using labeled sequences [9], we can either choose to train the model according to the ML criterion, or to perform Conditional Maximum Likelihood (CML) training which is shown to perform better in several applications [10]. ML training could be performed (after some trivial modifications) with the use of standard techniques such as the Baum-Welch algorithm or gradient descent, whereas for CML training one should rely solely on gradient descent methods.

The main advantage of the Baum-Welch algorithm (and hence the ML training) is due to its simplicity and the fact that requires no parameter tuning. Furthermore com-

G. Paliouras and Y. Sakakibara (Eds.): ICGI 2004, LNAI 3264, pp. 40–52, 2004.

pared to standard gradient descent, even for ML training, the Baum-Welch algorithm achieves significantly faster convergence rates [11]. On the other hand gradient descent (especially in the case of large models) requires careful search in the parameter space for an appropriate learning rate in order to achieve the best possible performance.

In the present work, we extend the gradient descent approach for CML training of HMMs. We then, adopting ideas from the literature regarding training techniques applied on feed-forward back-propagated multilayer perceptrons, introduce a new scheme for gradient descent optimization for HMMs. We propose the use of independent learning rate/step-size adaptation for every trainable parameter of the HMM (emission and transition probabilities), and we show that not only outperforms significantly the convergence rate of the standard gradient descent, but also leads to a much more robust training procedure whereas at the same time it is equally simple enough, since it requires almost no parameter tuning.

In the following sections we will first establish the appropriate notation for describing a Hidden Markov Model with labeled sequences, following mainly the notation used in [2] and [12]. We will then briefly describe the algorithms for parameter estimation with ML and CML training and afterwards we will introduce our proposal, of individual learning rate adaptation as a faster and simpler alternative to standard gradient descent. Eventually, we will show the superiority of our approach on a real life application from computational molecular biology, training a model for the prediction of the transmembrane segments of β-barrel outer membrane proteins.

2 Hidden Markov Models

A Hidden Markov Model is composed of a set of (hidden) states, a set of observable symbols and a set of transition and emission probabilities. Two states k, l are connected by means of the transition probabilities α_{kl}, forming a 1st order Markovian process. Assuming a protein sequence $\mathbf{x}$ of length L denoted as:

$$= \tag{1}$$

where the x_i's are the 20 amino acids, we usually denote the "path" (i.e. the sequence of states) ending up to a particular position of the amino acid sequence (the sequence of symbols), by π. Each state k is associated with an emission probability $e_k(x_i)$, which is the probability of a particular symbol x_i to be emitted by that state. When using labeled sequences, each amino acid sequence $\mathbf{x}$ is accompanied by a sequence of labels $\mathbf{y}$ for each position i in the sequence:

$$= \tag{2}$$

Consequently, one has to declare a new probability distribution, in addition to the transition and emission probabilities, the probability $\Delta_k(c)$ of a state k having a label c. In almost all biological applications this probability is just a delta-function, since a particular state is not allowed to match more than one label. The total probability of a sequence **x** given a model is calculated by summing over all possible paths:

$$(\quad \theta) = \quad (\pi \quad \theta) = \quad _\pi \prod_\pi \quad _{\pi\pi_.} \quad (3)$$

This quantity is calculated using a dynamic programming algorithm known as the forward algorithm, or alternatively by the similar backward algorithm [1]. In [9] Krogh proposed a simple modified version of the forward and backward algorithms, incorporating the concept of labeled data. Thus we can also use, the joint probability of the sequence **x** and the labeling **y** given the model:

$$(\quad \theta) = \quad (\pi \quad \theta) = \quad (\pi \quad \theta) = \quad _\pi \prod_\pi \quad _{\pi\pi_.} \quad (4)$$

The idea behind this approach is that summation has to be done only over those paths Π_y that are in agreement with the labels **y**. If multiple sequences are available for training (which is usually the case), they are assumed independent, and the total likelihood of the model is just a product of probabilities of the form (3) and (4) for each of the sequences. The generalization of Equations (3) and (4) from one to many sequences is therefore trivial, and we will consider only one training sequence **x** in the following.

2.1 Maximum Likelihood and Conditional Maximum Likelihood

The Maximum Likelihood (ML) estimate for any arbitrary model parameter, is denoted by:

$$\theta \quad = \quad _\theta \quad (\quad \theta) \quad (5)$$

The dominant algorithm for ML training is the elegant Baum-Welch algorithm [6]. It is a special case of the Expectation-Maximization (EM) algorithm [7], proposed for Maximum Likelihood (ML) estimation for incomplete data. The algorithm, updates iteratively the model parameters (emission and transition probabilities), using their expectations, computed with the use of forward and backward algorithms. Convergence to at least a local maximum of the likelihood is guaranteed, and since it requires no initial parameters, the algorithm needs no parameter tuning. It has been shown, that maximizing the likelihood with the Baum-Welch algorithm can be done equivalently with a gradient descent method [8]. It should be mentioned here, as it is apparent from the above equations where the summation is performed over the entire training set, that we consider only batch (off-line) mode of training. Gradient descent could also be performed on on-line mode, but we will not consider this option in this work since the collection of heuristics we present are especially developed for batch mode of training.

In the CML approach (which is usually referred to as discriminative training) the goal is to maximize the probability of correct labeling, instead of the probability of the sequences [9, 10, 12]. This is formulated as:

$$\theta = \quad (\quad \theta) = \frac{(\quad \theta)}{(\quad \theta)} \tag{6}$$

When turning to negative log-likelihoods this is equivalent to minimizing the difference between the logarithms of the quantities in Equations (4) and (3). Thus the log-likelihood can be expressed as the difference between the log-likelihood in the *clamped* phase and that of the *free-running* phase [9]

$$\ell = - \quad (\quad \theta) = \ell - \ell \tag{7}$$

where

$$\ell = - \quad (\quad \theta) \tag{8}$$

$$\ell = - \quad (\quad \theta) \tag{9}$$

The maximization procedure cannot be performed with the Baum-Welch algorithm [9, 10] and a gradient descent method is more appropriate. The gradients of the log-likelihood, w.r.t. the transition and emission probabilities according to [12] are:

$$\frac{\partial \ell}{\partial} = \frac{\partial \ell}{\partial} - \frac{\partial \ell}{\partial} = - \frac{-}{} \tag{10}$$

$$\frac{\partial \ell}{\partial\,(\,)} = \frac{\partial \ell}{\partial\,(\,)} - \frac{\partial \ell}{\partial\,(\,)} = - \frac{-}{} \tag{11}$$

The superscripts c and f in the above expectations correspond to the *clamped* and *free-running* phase discussed earlier. The expectations A, E, are computed as described in [12], using the forward and backward algorithms [1, 2].

2.2 Gradient Descent Optimization

By calculating the derivatives of the log-likelihood with respect to a generic parameter θ of the model, we proceed with gradient-descent and iteratively update these parameters according to:

$$\theta^{(+)} = \theta^{()} - \eta \frac{\partial \ell^{()}}{\partial \theta} \tag{12}$$

where η is the learning rate. Since the model parameters are probabilities, performing gradient descent optimization would most probably lead to negative estimates [8]. To avoid the risk of obtaining negative estimates, we have to use a proper parameter transformation, namely the normalization of the estimates in the range [0,1] and perform gradient-descent optimization on the new variables [8,12]. For example, for the transition probabilities, we obtain:

$$\alpha = \frac{(\quad)}{(\quad\cdot\,)} \tag{13}$$

Now, doing gradient descent on z's,

$$(+) = (\,) - \frac{\partial \ell^{(\,)}}{\partial} \tag{14}$$

yields the following update formula for the transitions:

$$\alpha^{(+)} = \frac{\alpha^{(\,)} \quad -\eta \dfrac{\partial \ell^{(\,)}}{\partial}}{\alpha^{(\,)} \quad -\eta \dfrac{\partial \ell^{(\,)}}{\partial \cdot}} \tag{15}$$

The gradients with respect to the new variables z_{kl} can be expressed entirely in terms of the expected counts and the transition probabilities at the previous iteration. Similar results could be obtained for the emission probabilities. Thus, when we train the model according to the CML criterion the derivatives of the log-likelihood w.r.t. a transition probability is:

$$\frac{\partial \ell}{\partial} = - \quad - \quad - \quad ,\left(\quad - \quad\right) \tag{16}$$

Substituting now Equation (16) into Equation (15), we get an expression entirely in terms of the model parameters and their expectations.

$$\alpha^{(+)} = \frac{\alpha^{(\,)} \quad -\eta \quad - \quad - \quad \left(\quad - \quad\right)}{\alpha^{(\,)} \quad -\eta \quad - \quad - \quad \left(\quad - \quad\right)} \tag{17}$$

The last equation describes the update formula for the transitions probabilities according to CML training with standard gradient descent [12]. The main disadvantage of gradient descent optimization is that it can be very slow [11]. In the following section we introduce our proposal for a faster version of gradient descent optimization, using information included only in the first derivative of the likelihood function.

These kinds of techniques have been proved very successful in speeding up the convergence rate of back-propagation in multi-layer perceptrons, and at the same time they are also improving the stability during training. However, even though they are a natural extension to the gradient descent optimization of HMMs, to our knowledge no such effort has been done in the past.

3 Individual Learning Rate Adaptation

One of the greatest problems in training large models (HMMs or ANNs) with gradient descent is to find an optimal learning rate [13]. A small learning rate will slow down the convergence speed. On the other hand, a large learning rate will probably cause oscillations during training, finally leading to divergence and no useful model would be trained. A few ways of escaping this problem have been proposed in the literature of the machine learning community [14]. One option is to use some kind of adaptation rule, for adapting the learning rate during training. This could be done for instance starting with a large learning rate and decrease it by a small amount at each iteration, forcing it though to be the same for every model parameter, or alternatively to adapt it individually for every parameter of the model, relying on information included in the first derivative of the likelihood function [14]. Another approach is to turn on second order methods, using information of the second derivative. Here we consider only methods relying on the first derivative, and we developed two algorithms that use individual learning rate adaptation that are presented below.

The first, denoted as Algorithm 1, alters the learning rate according to the sign of the two last partial derivatives of the likelihood w.r.t. a specific model parameter. Since we are working with transformed variables, the partial derivative, which we consider, is that of the new variable. For example, speaking for transition probabilities we will use the partial derivative of the likelihood w.r.t. the z_{kl} and not w.r.t. the original α_{kl}. If the partial derivative possesses the same sign for two consecutive steps, the learning rate is increased (multiplied by a factor of $a^+ > 1$), whereas if the derivative changes sign, the learning rate is decreased (multiplied by a factor of $a^- < 1$). In the second case, we set the partial derivative equal to zero and thus prevent an update of the model parameter. This ensures that in the next iteration the parameter is modified according to the reduced learning rate, using though the actual gradient. We chose to have the learning rates bound by some minimum and maximum values denoted by the parameters η_{min} and η_{max}. In the following section Algorithm 1 is presented, for updating the transition probabilities. It is completely straightforward to derive the appropriate expressions for the emission probabilities as well. In the following, the *sign* operator of an argument returns 1 if the argument is positive, -1 if it is negative and 0 otherwise, whereas *min* and *max* operators are the usual minimum and maximum of two arguments.

The second algorithm denoted Algorithm 2, constitutes a more radical approach and is based on a modified version of the RPROP algorithm [15]. The RPROP algorithm is perhaps the fastest first-order learning algorithm for multi-layer perceptrons, and it is designed specifically to eliminate the harmful influence of the size of the partial derivative, on the weight step-size [14, 15]. Algorithm 2 is almost identical to the one discussed above, with the only difference being the fact that the step-size (the amount of change of a model parameter) at each iteration is independent of the magnitude of the partial derivative. Thus, instead of modifying the learning rate and multiplying it by the partial derivative, we chose to modify directly an initial step-size for every model parameter denoted by Δ, and then use only the sign of the partial derivative to determine the direction of the change. Algorithm 2 is presented below. Once again we need the increasing and decreasing factors a^+ and a^- and the minimum and maximum values for the step-size, now denoted by Δ_{min} and Δ_{max} respectively.

Algorithm 1

> **for each** k
> {
>> **for each** l
>> {

$$\frac{\partial \ell}{\partial}^{()} \quad \frac{\partial \ell}{\partial}^{(-)} >$$

$$\eta^{()} = \left(\eta^{(-)} \, {}^+ \, \eta \right)$$

$$\frac{\partial \ell}{\partial}^{()} \quad \frac{\partial \ell}{\partial}^{(-)} <$$

$$\eta^{()} = \left(\eta^{(-)} \, {}^- \, \eta \right)$$

$$\frac{\partial \ell}{\partial}^{()} =$$

$$\alpha^{(+)} = \frac{\alpha^{()} \quad -\eta^{()} \dfrac{\partial \ell}{\partial}^{()}}{\alpha^{()} \quad -\eta^{()} \dfrac{\partial \ell}{\partial}^{()}}$$

It should be mentioned that the computational complexity and memory requirements of the two proposed algorithms is similar to standard gradient descent for CML training. The algorithms need to store only two additional matrices with dimensions equal to the total number of the model parameters, the matrix with the partial derivatives at the previous iteration and the matrix containing the individual learning rates (or step-sizes) for every model parameter. In addition, a few additional operations are required per iteration compared to standard gradient descent. In HMMs the main computational bottleneck is the computation of the expected counts, requiring running the forward and backward algorithms. Thus, the few additional operations and memory requirements introduced here are practically negligible.

Algorithm 2

> **for each** k
> $\{$
> > **for each** l
> > $\{$

$$\frac{\partial \ell^{()}}{\partial} \frac{\partial \ell^{(-)}}{\partial} >$$

$$\Delta^{()} = \left(\Delta^{(-)} + \Delta \right)$$

$$\frac{\partial \ell^{()}}{\partial} \frac{\partial \ell^{(-)}}{\partial} <$$

$$\Delta^{()} = \left(\Delta^{(-)} - \Delta \right)$$

$$\frac{\partial \ell^{()}}{\partial} =$$

$$\alpha^{(+)} = \frac{\alpha^{()} - \frac{\partial \ell^{()}}{\partial} \Delta^{()}}{\alpha^{()} - \frac{\partial \ell^{()}}{\partial} \Delta^{()}}$$

4 Results and Discussion

In this section we present results comparing the convergence speed of our algorithms against the standard gradient descent. We apply our proposed algorithms in a real problem from molecular biology, training a model to predict the transmembrane regions of β-barrel membrane proteins [16]. These proteins are localized on the outer membrane of the gram-negative bacteria, and their transmembrane regions are formed by antiparallel, amphipathic β-strands, as opposed to the α-helical membrane proteins, found in the bacterial inner membrane, and in the cell membrane of eukaryotes, that have their membrane spanning regions formed by hydrophobic α-helices [17].

The topology prediction of β-barrel membrane proteins, i.e. predicting precisely the amino-acid segments that span the lipid bilayer, is one of the hard problems in current bioinformatics research [16]. The model that we used is cyclic with 61 states with some of them sharing the same emission probabilities (hence named tied states). The full details of the model are presented in [18]. We have to note, that similar HMMs, are found to be the best available predictors for α-helical membrane protein topology [19], and this particular method, currently performs better for β-barrel membrane protein topology prediction, outperforming significantly, two other Neural Network-based methods [20]. For training, we used 16 non-homologous outer membrane proteins with structures known at atomic resolution, deposited at the Protein Data Bank (PDB) [21]. The sequences **x**, are the amino-acid sequences found in PDB, whereas the labels **y** required for the training phase, were deduced by the three dimensional structures. We use one label for the amino-acids occurring in the membrane-spanning regions (TM), a second for those in the periplasmic space (IN) and a third for those in the extracellular space (OUT). In the prediction phase, the input is only the sequence **x**, and the model predicts the most probable path of states with the corresponding labeling **y**, using the Viterbi algorithm [1, 2].

For standard gradient descent we use learning rates (η), ranging from 0.001 to 0.1 for both emission and transition probabilities, whereas the same values were used for the initial parameters η^0 (in algorithm 1) and Δ^0 (in algorithm 2), for every parameter of the model. For the two algorithms that we proposed, we additionally used $a^+=1.2$ and $a^-=0.5$, for increasing and decreasing factors, as originally proposed for the RPROP algorithm, even though the algorithms are not sensitive to these parameters. Finally, for setting the minimum and maximum allowed learning rates we used η_{min} (algorithm 1) and Δ_{min} (algorithm 2) equal to 10^{-20} and η_{max} (algorithm 1) and Δ_{max} (algorithm 2) equal to 10.

The results are summarized in Table 1. It is obvious that both of our algorithms perform significantly better than standard gradient descent. The training procedure with the 2 newly proposed algorithms is more robust, since even choosing a very small or a very large initial value for the learning rate, the algorithm eventually converges to the same value of negative log-likelihood. This is not the case for standard gradient descent, since a small learning rate ($\eta = 0.001$) will cause the algorithm to converge extremely slowly (negative log-likelihood equal to 391.5 at 250 iterations) or even get trapped in local maxima of the likelihood, while at the same time a large value will cause the algorithm to diverge (for $\eta > 0.03$). In real life applications, one has to conduct an extensive search in the parameter space in order to find the optimal problem-specific learning rate. It is interesting to note, that no matter the initial values of the learning rates we used, after 50 iterations, our 2 algorithms, converge to approximately the same negative log-likelihood, which is in any case better compared to that obtained by standard gradient descent. Furthermore, we should mention that Algorithm 1 diverged only for $\eta_{kl} = 0.1$, whereas Algorithm 2 did not diverge in the range of the initial parameters we used.

Table 1. Evolution of negative log-likelihoods for algorithm 1, algorithm 2 and standard gradient descent, using different initial values for the learning rate, #: negative log-likelihood greater than 10000, meaning that the algorithm diverged

		Iterations				
		50	**100**	**150**	**200**	**250**
Standard Gradient Descent	0.001	459.7871	424.3475	408.3465	398.4966	391.5139
	0.005	391.7835	372.7111	363.2065	357.1393	352.8225
	0.010	372.8962	357.1751	349.5669	344.9322	341.8101
	0.020	357.1228	344.7693	342.7547	337.6631	335.6162
	0.030	353.7927	342.4032	338.8682	337.3911	336.5716
	0.040	#	#	#	#	#
	0.050	#	#	#	#	#
	0.100	#	#	#	#	#
Algorithm 1	kl					
	0.001	331.0293	328.6714	327.4731	326.1206	325.3529
	0.005	330.0261	328.4753	327.2319	326.0366	325.3092
	0.010	329.9236	328.4093	327.4881	326.5018	325.7104
	0.020	329.6344	328.3149	327.1772	326.0632	325.1964
	0.030	329.5086	328.1867	326.8927	325.7983	325.1218
	0.040	330.2231	328.7799	327.7404	326.7106	325.6933
	0.050	475.0815	332.7297	328.3895	327.6025	327.0391
	0.100	#	#	#	#	#
Algorithm 2	Δ_{kl}					
	0.001	330.1204	328.2821	327.3199	326.6095	325.9399
	0.005	329.4728	327.8869	327.0973	326.3861	325.8135
	0.010	329.5845	327.9141	326.8738	325.9267	325.4198
	0.020	329.2549	327.8328	327.0722	326.4339	325.8361
	0.030	329.0184	327.6231	326.8671	326.1906	325.5751
	0.040	329.1602	327.7389	327.0219	326.2906	325.7256
	0.050	329.0520	327.7299	326.9171	326.1581	325.5698
	0.100	328.7986	327.4951	326.6774	325.9476	325.5050

On the other hand, the 2 newly proposed algorithms are much faster than standard gradient descent. From Table 1 and Figure 1, we observe that standard gradient descent, even when an optimal learning rate has been chosen ($\eta = 0.02$), requires as much as five times the number of iterations in order to reach the appropriate log-likelihood. We should mention here, that in real life applications, we would have chosen a threshold for the difference in the log-likelihood, between two consecutive iterations (for example 0.01). In such cases the training procedure would have been stopped much earlier, using the two proposed algorithms, than with the standard gradient descent.

We should note here, that the observed differences in the values of negative log-likelihood correspond also to better predictive performance of the model. By the use of our two proposed algorithms the correlation coefficient for the correctly predicted residues, in a two state mode (transmembrane vs. non-transmembrane), ranges between 0.848-0.851, whereas for standard gradient descent ranges between 0.819-0.846. Similarly, the fraction of the correctly predicted residues in a two state mode ranges between 0.899-0.901, while at the same time the standard gradient descent

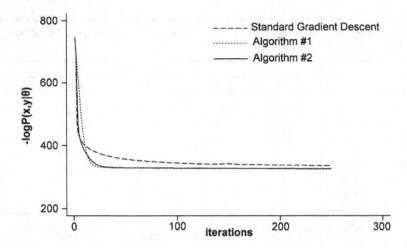

Fig. 1. Evolution of the negative log-likelihoods obtained using the three algorithms, with the same initial values for the learning rate (0.02). This learning rate was found to be the optimal for standard gradient descent. Note that after 50 iterations the lines for the two proposed algorithms are practically indistinguishable, and also that convergence is achieved much faster, compared to standard gradient descent

yields a prediction in the range of 0.871–0.885. In all cases these measures were computed without counting the cases of divergence, where no useful model could be trained. Obviously, the two algorithms perform consistently better, irrespective of the initial values of the parameters.

If we used different learning rates for the emission and transition probabilities, we would probably perform a more reliable training for standard gradient descent. Unfortunately, this would result in having to optimize simultaneously two parameters, which it would turn out to require more trials for finding optimal values for each one. Our two proposed algorithms on the other hand, do not depend that much on the initial values, and thus this problem is not present.

5 Conclusions

We have presented two simple, yet powerful modifications of the standard gradient descent method for training Hidden Markov Models, with the CML criterion. The approach was based on individually learning rate adaptation, which have been proved useful for speeding up the convergence of multi-layer perceptrons, but up to date no such kind of study have been performed on HMMs. The results obtained from this study are encouraging; our proposed algorithms not only outperform, as one would expect, the standard gradient descent in terms of training speed, but also provide a much more robust training procedure. Furthermore, in all cases the predictive performance is better, as judged from the measures of the per-residue accuracy mentioned earlier. In conclusion, the two algorithms presented here, converge much faster to the same value of the negative log-likelihood, and produce better results. Thus, it is clear that they are superior compared to standard gradient descent. Since the required parameter tuning is minimal, without increasing the computational complexity or the memory requirements, our algorithms constitute a potential replacement for the standard gradient descent for CML training.

References

1. Rabiner, L.: A tutorial on hidden Markov models and selected applications in speech recognition. Proc IEEE. 77(2) (1989) 257-286
2. Durbin, R., Eddy, S., Krogh, A., Mithison, G.: Biological sequence analysis, probabilistic models of proteins and nucleic acids. Cambridge University Press (1998)
3. Krogh, A., Larsson, B., von Heijne, G., Sonnhammer, E.L.: Predicting transmembrane protein topology with a hidden Markov model, application to complete genomes. J. Mol. Biol. 305(3) (2001) 567-80
4. Henderson, J., Salzberg, S., Fasman, K.H.: Finding genes in DNA with a hidden Markov model. J. Comput. Biol. 4(2) (1997) 127-142
5. Krogh, A., Mian, I.S., Haussler, D.: A hidden Markov model that finds genes in E. coli DNA. Nucleic Acids Res. 22(22) (1994) 4768-78
6. Baum, L.: An inequality and associated maximization technique in statistical estimation for probalistic functions of Markov processes. Inequalities. 3 (1972) 1-8
7. Dempster, A.P., Laird, N.M., Rubin, D.B.: Maximum likelihood from incomplete data via the EM algorithm. J. Royal Stat. Soc. B. 39 (1977) 1-38
8. Baldi, P., Chauvin, Y.: Smooth On-Line Learning Algorithms for Hidden Markov Models. Neural Comput. 6(2) (1994) 305-316
9. Krogh, A.: Hidden Markov models for labeled sequences, Proceedings of the 12th IAPR International Conference on Pattern Recognition (1994) 140-144
10. Krogh, A.: Two methods for improving performance of an HMM and their application for gene finding. Proc Int Conf Intell Syst Mol Biol. 5 (1997) 179-86
11. Bagos, P.G., Liakopoulos, T.D., Hamodrakas, S.J.: Maximum Likelihood and Conditional Maximum Likelihood learning algorithms for Hidden Markov Models with labeled data-Application to transmembrane protein topology prediction. In Simos, T.E. (ed): Computational Methods in Sciences and Engineering, Proceedings of the International Conference 2003 (ICCMSE 2003), World Scientific Publishing Co. Pte. Ltd. Singapore (2003) 47-55
12. Krogh, A., Riis, S.K.: Hidden neural networks. Neural Comput. 11(2) (1999) 541-63
13. Bishop, C.M.: Neural Networks for Pattern Recognition. Oxford University Press (1998)
14. Schiffmann, W., Joost, M., Werner, R.: Optimization of the Backpropagation Algorithm for Training Multi-Layer Perceptrons. Technical report (1994) University of Koblenz, Institute of Physics.
15. Riedmiller, M., Braun, H.: RPROP-A Fast Adaptive Learning Algorithm, Proceedings of the 1992 International Symposium on Computer and Information Sciences, Antalya, Turkey, (1992) 279-285
16. Schulz, G.E.: The structure of bacterial outer membrane proteins, Biochim. Biophys. Acta., 1565(2) (2002) 308-17
17. Von Heijne, G.: Recent advances in the understanding of membrane protein assembly and function. Quart. Rev. Biophys., 32(4) (1999) 285-307

18. Bagos, P.G., Liakopoulos, T.D., Spyropoulos, I.C., Hamodrakas, S.J.: A Hidden Markov Model capable of predicting and discriminating β-barrel outer membrane proteins. BMC Bioinformatics 5:29 (2004)
19. Moller S., Croning M.D., Apweiler R.: Evaluation of methods for the prediction of membrane spanning regions. Bioinformatics, 17(7) (2001) 646-53
20. Bagos, P.G., Liakopoulos, T.D., Spyropoulos, I.C., Hamodrakas, S.J.: PRED-TMBB: a web server for predicting the topology of beta-barrel outer membrane proteins. Nucleic Acids Res. 32(Web Server Issue) (2004) W400-W404
21. Berman, H.M., Battistuz, T., Bhat, T.N., Bluhm, W.F., Bourne, P.E., Burkhardt, K., Feng, Z., Gilliland, G.L., Iype, L., Jain, S., et al: The Protein Data Bank. Acta Crystallogr. D Biol. Crystallogr., 58(Pt 6 No 1) (2002) 899-907

Learning Mild Context-Sensitiveness: Toward Understanding Children's Language Learning*

Leonor Becerra-Bonache[1] and Takashi Yokomori[2]

[1] Research Group on Mathematical Linguistics (GRLMC)
Rovira i Virgili University
Pl. Imperial Tárraco 1, 43005, Tarragona, Spain
leonor.becerra@estudiants.urv.es

[2] Department of Mathematics, School of Education
Waseda University
1-6-1 Nishiwaseda, Shinjuku-ku, 169-8050, Tokyo, Japan
yokomori@waseda.jp

Abstract. The aim of this paper is to try to understand the process of children's language acquisition by using the theory of inference of formal grammars. Toward this goal, we introduce an extension of Marcus External Contextual grammars which constitutes a Mildly Context-Sensitive language family, and study their learnability in the limit from positive data. Finally, we briefly indicate our future research direction.

1 Introduction

Grammatical Inference is known as one of the most attractive paradigms of scientific learning that is nowadays a classical, but still active, discipline. It refers to the process of learning grammars and languages from data. Gold originated this study trying to construct a formal model of human language acquisition. A remarkable amount of research has been done since his seminal work to establish a theory of Grammatical Inference, to find effective and efficient methods for inferring grammars, and to apply those methods to practical problems (i.e., Natural Language Processing, Computational Biology). Grammatical Inference has been investigated within many research fields, including machine learning, computational learning theory, pattern recognition, computational linguistics, neural networks, formal language theory, and many others (see [1]).

Grammatical inference and linguistic studies are close in proximity, especially with linguistic studies of Chomsky's inspiration. These studies conceive grammar as a machine (in the sense of the Theory of Formal Languages) that children develop and reconstruct very fast during the first years of their lives. Children infer and select the grammar of their language from the data (from the examples of the language) that the surrounding world offers them, but the facility with

---

* This research was supported by a FPU Fellowship from the Spanish Ministry of Education and Science.

G. Paliouras and Y. Sakakibara (Eds.): ICGI 2004, LNAI 3264, pp. 53–64, 2004.

which children acquire language belies the complexity of the task. This idea accords with the belief of the biologically determined character of the human linguistic capacity.

Hence, the study of grammatical inference is highly interdisciplinary, drawing from computer science, linguistic and cognitive science. We will try to bring together the *Theory of the Grammatical Inference* and *Studies of Language Acquisition* (which are connected areas, but they belong to different scientific traditions).

2   Which Formal Grammars Are Adequate to Describe Natural Languages?

The question of determining the location of natural languages in the *Chomsky hierarchy* has been subject of debate for a long time. Several authors have proven the non-context-freeness of natural languages presenting examples of natural language structures that cannot be described using a context-free grammar. Next, we will present several such non-context-free structures [2]:

– **Dutch:** The following example shows a duplication-like structure $\{w\bar{w} \mid w \in \{a,b\}^*\}$, where $\bar{w}$ is the word obtained from w by replacing each letter with its barred copy.

   ...dat Jan Piet Marie de Kinderen zag helpen laten zwemmen
   (That Jan saw Piet help Marie make the children swim)

This is only *weakly* non-context-free, i.e., only in the deep structure.

– **Bambara:** A duplication structure is found in the vocabulary of the African language Bambara, demonstrating a *strong* non-context-freeness, i.e., on the surface and in the deep structure:

   malonyininafilèla o malonyininafilèla o

   (one who searches for rice watchers + one who searches for rice watchers = whoever searches for rice watchers)

This has the structure $\{wcw \mid w \in \{a,b\}^*\}$. But also the *crossed agreement* structure $\{a^n b^m c^n d^m \mid m, n>0 \}$ can be inferred.

– **Swiss German:** The following example is a strong non-context-free structure, again showing crossed agreement:

   Jan säit das mer (d'chind)^m (em Hans)^n es huus haend wele (laa)^m (hälfe)^n aastriiche

   (Jan said that we wanted to let the children help Hans paint the house)

This has the structure $xwa^m b^n yc^m d^n z$, where *a, b* stand for accusative, dative noun phrases, respectively, and *c, d* for the corresponding accusative, dative verb phrases, respectively.

The Chomsky hierarchy does not provide a specific demarcation of language families having the desired properties [2]. The family of context-free languages has good computational properties, but it does not contain some important formal languages that appear in human languages. On the other hand, the family of context-sensitive languages contains all important constructions that occur in natural languages, but it is believed that the membership problem for languages in this family cannot be solved in deterministic polynomial time.

The difficulty of working with context-sensitive grammars has obliged researchers to look for ways to generate non-context-free structures using context-free rules. This idea has led to *Regulated Rewriting* in Formal Language Theory [3] and to the so-called *Mildly Context-Sensitive Devices* in Linguistics [4].

Hence, the Mildly Context-Sensitive languages are the most appropriate to describe natural language because they: (a) include non-context-free constructions that were found in the syntax of natural languages; (b) are computationally feasible, i.e., the membership problem for them is solvable in deterministic polynomial time.

In this paper, by a *Mildly Context-Sensitive family of languages* we mean a family $\mathcal{L}$ of languages that satisfies the following conditions [2]:

(i) each language in $\mathcal{L}$ is semilinear
(ii) for each language in $\mathcal{L}$ the membership problem is solvable in deterministic polynomial time
(iii) $\mathcal{L}$ contains the following three non-context-free languages:
   - *multiple agreements*: $L_1 = \{a^n b^n c^n \mid n \geq 0\}$
   - *crossed agreements*: $L_2 = \{a^n b^m c^n d^m \mid n, m \geq 0\}$
   - *duplication*: $L_3 = \{ww \mid w \in \{a, b\}^*\}$

There exist different mechanisms to fabricate mildly context-sensitive families: *tree adjoining grammars* ([4]), *head grammars* [5], *combinatory categorial grammars* [6], *linear indexed grammars* [7], *simple matrix grammars* [8], etc. We will study another mechanism, which is a natural extension of Marcus External Contextual grammars [2]. This mechanism is (technically) much simpler than any other models found in the literature on Mildly Context-Sensitive families of languages. It does not involve nonterminals, and it does not have rules of derivation except one general rule: to adjoin contexts. Although this mechanism generates a proper subclass of simple matrix languages, it is still Mildly Context-Sensitive.

3   Learnability Model to Study Children's Language Acquisition

Within Computational Learning Theory, there are three major established formal models for learning from examples or for grammatical inference[1]:

– **Gold:** *identification in the limit model* [9]. In the second half of the 1960's, Gold first formulated the process of learning formal languages. Motivated by observing children's language learning process, he proposed an idea that learning is the process of making guesses of grammars and it does not terminate in a finite number of steps. It is only able to converge at a correct grammar in the limit. *Identification in the limit* provides a learning model where an infinite sequence of examples of the unknown grammar G is presented to the inference algorithm M, and the eventual or limiting behavior of the algorithm is used as the criterion of its success.

– **Angluin:** *query learning model* [10]. Angluin considered a learning paradigm in which the learner has access to an expert teacher. The teacher is a fixed set of oracles that can answer specific kinds of queries made by the learner (inference algorithm) on the unknown grammar G. Typical types of queries include the following:

(i) *Membership.* The input is a string $w \in \Sigma^*$ and the output is "yes" if w is generated by G and "no" otherwise.
(ii) *Equivalence.* The input is a grammar G' and the output is "yes" if G' generates the same language as G (G' is equivalent to G) and "no" otherwise. If the answer is "no" a string w in the symmetric difference of the language $L(G)$ generated by G and the language $L(G')$ generated by G' is returned. This returned string w is called a *counterexample.*

– **Valiant:** *PAC learning model* [11]. Valiant introduced *probably approximately correct learning* (PAC learning, in short), which is a distribution-independent probabilistic model of learning from random examples. In this model, the inference algorithm takes a sample as input and produces a grammar as output. A successful inference algorithm is one that *with high probability* (at least 1 - δ) finds a grammar *whose error is small* (less than ε).

What model is the most adequate to study children's language acquisition? We will distinguish two stages in the process of language acquisition:

– **1st stage: learning from positive data.** It is widely believed that children do not receive negative examples (examples of sentences that are not in the language). They get only positive data from the surroundings, namely linguistic constructions that are grammatically correct.

– **2nd stage: learning from correction queries.** Children need to communicate more complex ideas, and therefore must increase the complexity of their constructions beyond the level acquired in the first stage. Hence, in this stage, receiving only positive data is not enough: they need to ask questions about the grammar of their language.

Therefore, we propose here a novel learning model inspired by Gold's model and Angluin's model: *learnability in the limit from positive data and correction queries.*

Correction queries are an extension of *membership queries.* The output in a membership query is "yes" if the string is generated by a unknown grammar G and "no" otherwise. In the case of correction queries, if the answer is "no", then a *corrected* string is returned. However, in this paper, we will study the learnability in the limit from only positive data. See the conclusion for a discussion of corrected strings.

4   Basic Definitions

The following basic notations and definitions 1–4 are taken directly from [2].

For an alphabet Σ, let Σ^* be the free monoid generated by Σ with the identity λ. The free semigroup generated by Σ is $\Sigma^+ = \Sigma^* - \{\lambda\}$. Elements in $\Sigma^*(\Sigma^+)$ are referred to as *words* (*nonempty words*); λ is the *empty word*. Assume that $a \in \Sigma$ and $w \in \Sigma^*$; the length of w is denoted by $|w|$, while the number of occurrences of a in w is denoted by $|w|_a$. A *context* is a pair of words, i.e., (u, v), where $u, v \in \Sigma^*$. N denotes the set of natural numbers.

A minimal linear language is a language generated by a minimal linear grammar, that is, a linear grammar with just one nonterminal.

The families of regular, minimal linear, linear, context-free, and context-sensitive languages are denoted by $REG, MinLIN, LIN, CF$, and CS, respectively.

Assume that $\Sigma = \{a_1, a_2, ..., a_k\}$. The *Parikh mapping*, denoted by ψ, is:

$$\psi \colon \Sigma^* \longrightarrow N^k, \ \psi(w) = (|w|_{a_1}, |w|_{a_2}, ..., |w|_{a_k}).$$

If L is a language, then the *Parikh set* of L is defined by:

$$\psi(L) = \{\psi(w) \mid w \in L\}.$$

A *linear set* is a set $M \subseteq N^k$ such that $M = \{v_0 + \sum_{i=1}^{m} v_i x_i \mid x_i \in N\ \}$, for some $v_0, v_1, ..., v_m$ in N^k. A *semilinear set* is a finite union of linear sets, and a *semilinear language* is a language L such that $\psi(L)$ is a semilinear set.

The reader can find supplementary information regarding the basic notions on formal languages we use in this paper in [12].

4.1   Marcus External Contextual Grammars

Contextual grammars were firstly considered in Marcus [13] to model some natural aspects from descriptive linguistics, for instance, the acceptance of a word (construction) only in certain contexts. There are many variants of Marcus Contextual grammars, but all of them are based on context adjoining. The differences are in the way of adjoining contexts, the sites where contexts are adjoined, the use of selectors, etc. For a detailed introduction to the topic, the reader is referred to the monograph [14].

Definition 1 *A Marcus External Contextual grammar is $G = (\Sigma, B, C)$, where Σ is the alphabet of G, B is a finite subset of Σ^* called the base of G, and C is a finite set of contexts, i.e. a finite set of pairs of words over Σ. C is called the set of contexts of G.*

The direct derivation relation with respect to G is a binary relation between words over Σ, denoted $\Rightarrow_G$, or $\Rightarrow$ if G is understood from the context. By definition, $x \Rightarrow_G y$, where $x, y \in \Sigma^*$, iff $y = uxv$ for some $(u, v) \in C$. The derivation relation with respect to G, denoted $\Rightarrow_G^*$, or $\Rightarrow^*$ if G is understood from the context, is the reflexive and transitive closure of $\Rightarrow_G$.

Definition 2 *Let* $G = (\Sigma, B, C)$ *be a Marcus External Contextual grammar.*
The language generated by G, *denoted by* $L(G)$, *is defined as:*

$$L(G) = \{\ y \in \Sigma^* \mid \text{there exists } x \in B \text{ such that } x \Rightarrow_G^* y\ \}.$$

One can verify that the language generated by $G = (\Sigma, B, C)$ is the smallest
language L over Σ such that:

(i) $B \subseteq L$
(ii) if $x \in L$ and $(u, v) \in C$, then $uxv \in L$

The family of all Marcus External Contextual languages is denoted by $\mathcal{EC}$.

Remark 1. $\mathcal{EC} = MinLIN$, which is a strict subfamily of LIN, incomparable
with REG (see [14]).

4.2   Marcus Many-Dimensional External Contextual Grammars

Marcus many-dimensional External Contextual grammars are an extension of
Marcus External Contextual grammars, but they work with vectors of words
and vectors of contexts [2] .

Let $p \geq 1$ be a fixed integer, and let Σ be an alphabet. A *p-word* x over
Σ is a p-dimensional vector whose components are words over Σ, i.e., $x = (x_1, x_2, ..., x_p)$, where $x_i \in \Sigma^*, 1 \leq i \leq p$. A *p-context* c over Σ is a p-dimensional
vector whose components are contexts over Σ, i.e., $c = [c_1, c_2, ..., c_p]$ where $c_i = (u_i, v_i), u_i, v_i \in \Sigma^*, 1 \leq i \leq p$. We denote vectors of words with round brackets,
and vectors of contexts with square brackets.

Definition 3 *Let* $p \geq 1$ *be an integer. A Marcus p-dimensional External Con-*
textual grammar is $G = (\Sigma, B, C)$, *where* Σ *is the alphabet of* G, B *is a finite*
set of p-words over Σ *called the base of* G, *and* C *is a finite set of p-contexts*
over Σ. C *is called the set of contexts of* G.

The direct derivation relation with respect to G is a binary relation be-
tween p-words over Σ, *denoted by* $\Rightarrow_G$, *or* $\Rightarrow$ *if* G *is understood from the con-*
text. Let $x = (x_1, x_2, ..., x_p)$ *and* $y = (y_1, y_2, ..., y_p)$ *be two p-words over* Σ.
By definition, $x \Rightarrow_G y$ *iff* $y = (u_1 x_1 v_1, u_2 x_2 v_2, ..., u_p x_p v_p)$ *for some p-context*
$c = [(u_1, v_1), (u_2, v_2), ..., (u_p, v_p)] \in C$. *The derivation relation with respect to* G,
denoted by $\Rightarrow_G^*$, *or* $\Rightarrow^*$ *if no confusion is possible, is the reflexive and transitive*
closure of $\Rightarrow_G$.

Definition 4 *Let* $G = (\Sigma, B, C)$ *be a Marcus p-dimensional External Contex-*
tual grammar. The language generated by G, *denoted* $L(G)$, *is defined as:*

$$L(G) = \{y \in \Sigma^* \mid \text{there exists } (x_1, x_2, ..., x_p) \in B \text{ such that } (x_1, x_2, ..., x_p) \Rightarrow_G^*$$
$(y_1, y_2, ..., y_p)$ *and* $y = y_1 y_2 ... y_p\}$.

The family of all Marcus p-dimensional External Contextual languages is
denoted by $\mathcal{EC}_p$.

The trivial (empty) context $[(\lambda, \lambda), (\lambda, \lambda), ..., (\lambda, \lambda)]$ is not necessary, therefore
we will not consider in the remainder of this paper.

Remark 2. Note that $\mathcal{EC} = \mathcal{EC}_1$ and $\mathcal{EC}_p \subseteq \mathcal{EC}_q$, for all $1 \leq p \leq q$ (see [2]).

Remark 3. Any family $\mathcal{EC}_p$ for $p \geq 2$ is a subfamily of linear simple matrix languages (see [2]).

5 The Simple p-Dimensional External Contextual Case

It is clear that not all regular languages over the alphabet of, say, English are subsets of it. Certainly, some authors pointed out this in the past in a more or less informal way (see [15]). Hence, natural languages could occupy an eccentric position in the Chomsky hierarchy. Therefore, we need a new hierarchy, which should certainly hold strong relationships with the Chomsky hierarchy, but which should not coincide with it. In a certain sense, the new hierarchy should be incomparable with the Chomsky hierarchy and pass across it [2].

Since the families of languages generated by many-dimensional External Contextual grammars have the property of transversality, they appear to be appropriate candidates to model natural language syntax and, therefore, the most adequate towards our goal of understanding the process of children's language acquisition.

In this paper, we will study the learnability of this family of languages from only positive data. Therefore, we will understand the process of language acquisition in the first stage.

It is desirable that learning can be achieved using only positive data, but it is generally impossible to learn a certain family of languages in the limit from positive data. Gold proves in [9] that, as soon as a class of languages contains all of the finite languages and at least one infinite language (called a *superfinite class*), it is not identifiable in the limit from positive data. Hence, regular, context-free and context-sensitive languages are not learnable from positive data in Gold's model. They only can be identified in the limit when the learner has access to both positive and negative evidence.

How do children overcome Gold's theoretical hurdle? The answer could rely on the supposition that children do not need superfinite language, therefore learning from only positive data is possible.

According to the general definition, the $\mathcal{EC}_p$ grammar family is superfinite, since the base of G can be any finite set of p-words. Hence, we need to put some restrictions to make it possible to learn this class in the limit from only positive data.

Definition 5 *A Simple Marcus p-dimensional External Contextual grammar is* $G = (\Sigma, B, C)$, *where Σ is the alphabet of G, B is a singleton of p-words over Σ called the base of G, and C is a finite set of p-contexts over Σ. C is called the set of contexts of G.*

The family of all Simple Marcus p-dimensional External Contextual languages is denoted by $\mathcal{SEC}_p$.

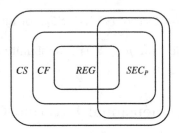

Fig. 1. The $\mathcal{SEC}_p$ family occupies an eccentric position in the Chomsky hierarchy.

Note 1. In what follows, we use the notation $\mathcal{SEC}_p$ for referring to families of both languages and grammars, as far as no confusion arises from the context.

Since the base of G is a singleton, this class is not superfinite (as seen later). Moreover, even if B is a singleton, it is enough to describe the three non-context-free languages described in the third condition on page 3 (a necessary condition for a family $\mathcal{L}$ of languages to be a *Mildly Context-Sensitive family of languages*). It is easy to construct $\mathcal{SEC}_p$ grammars for each of these languages, but we omit the proof due to lack of space.

The properties of this class with which we propose to study language acquisition shows its adequacy to develop our goal. Like an $\mathcal{EC}_p$ grammar, a $\mathcal{SEC}_p$ grammar has the following properties:

(a) Any family $\mathcal{SEC}_p$ for $p \geq 2$ is a subfamily of linear simple matrix languages.
(b) For every integer $p \geq 2$, the family $\mathcal{SEC}_p$ is a mildly context-sensitive family of languages.
(c) If $1 \leq p < q$, then $\mathcal{SEC}_p \subset \mathcal{SEC}_q$ (i.e., the inclusion is proper).
(d) The families $(\mathcal{SEC}_p)$ $p \geq 2$ define an infinite hierarchy of mildly context-sensitive languages.
(e) $\mathcal{SEC}_p$ is strictly contained in the family CS and is incomparable with the families CF and REG.

All these properties are immediately true due to [2].

Moreover, the $\mathcal{SEC}_p$ grammar has another property with regard to $\mathcal{EC}_p$ grammars. We can find some languages showing the proper inclusion:

$$\mathcal{SEC}_p \subset \mathcal{EC}_p$$

For example, $L = \{a, b, c\}$. It is generated by an $\mathcal{EC}_p$ grammar, but never could be generated by a $\mathcal{SEC}_p$ grammar because of the restricted features of $\mathcal{SEC}_p$ grammars. This demonstrates that $\mathcal{SEC}_p$ is not superfinite.

Figure 1 shows the location of the $\mathcal{SEC}_p$ family in the Chomsky hierarchy.

5.1 Learnability of $\mathcal{SEC}_p$ Languages from Only Positive Data

Now, we direct our attention to see if the class of languages generated by $\mathcal{SEC}_p$ grammars is learnable from positive data.

From a result by Shinohara [16], the class of languages generated by CS grammars with a fixed number of rules is learnable from only positive data. Hence, if we can transform a given $\mathcal{SEC}$ grammar with dimension p and degree q into an equivalent $LSMG$ (linear simple matrix grammar [3]) with dimension p' and degree q' and this into an equivalent CS grammar with a fixed number of rules, we will achieve our goal.

First, we need to define p, q, p' and q'.

(i) $\mathcal{SEC}_{p,q}$:
   - p: dimension (in the same sense as $\mathcal{SEC}_p$),
   - q: degree (the number of contexts).
(ii) $\mathcal{LSMG}_{p',q'}$:
   - p': number of nonterminals in the right hand of the unique rule of the $LSMG$ started by S.
   - q': number of matrices.

We will give the following constructive demonstration to prove that $\mathcal{SEC}_{p,q}$ $\subset \mathcal{LSMG}_{p',q'} \subset CS$ grammars with a fixed number of rules.

Let $G = (\Sigma, B, C)$ be a $\mathcal{SEC}_{p,q}$ grammar, where

- B $= \{(\gamma_1, ..., \gamma_p)\}$
- C $= \{\ c_1 = [(\alpha_1^1, \beta_1^1), ..., (\alpha_p^1, \beta_p^1)], ..., c_q = [(\alpha_1^q, \beta_1^q), ..., (\alpha_p^q, \beta_p^q)]\ \}$

We can transform this $\mathcal{SEC}$ grammar with dimension p and degree q into an equivalent LSMG with dimension p' and degree q'.

G' $= (N_1, ..., N_p, \Sigma, P, S)$, where

- P $= \{$ S $\longrightarrow A_1...A_p$,
$(A_1 \longrightarrow \gamma_1, ..., A_p \longrightarrow \gamma_p)$,
$(A_1 \longrightarrow \alpha_1^1 A_1 \beta_1^1, ..., A_p \longrightarrow \alpha_p^1 A_p \beta_p^1)$,
$(...)$,
$(A_1 \longrightarrow \alpha_1^q A_1 \beta_1^q, ..., A_p \longrightarrow \alpha_p^q A_p \beta_p^q)\}$

for $A_i \in N_i, \gamma_i, \alpha_i^j, \beta_i^j \in \Sigma^*, 1 \leq i \leq p, 1 \leq j \leq q$

The number of rules of an equivalent CSG will be proportional to p' · q'. Generally, there exists a CSG with the number of rules $\leq k \cdot p' \cdot q'$ (k is a constant).

We now illustrate this method using a grammar as follows. As a simple example, consider a $\mathcal{SEC}_{p,q}$ with $p = 2$ and $q = 2$.

Let $G = (\{a, b, c, d\}, B, C)$ be a $\mathcal{SEC}_{p,q}$ grammar, where

- B $= \{(ab, cd)\}$
- C $= \{\ c_1 = [(a, \lambda), (c, \lambda)],\ c_2 = [(\lambda, b), (\lambda, d)]\ \}$

Note that $L(G) = \{a^m b^n c^m d^n | m, n > 0\}$.

We can transform this $\mathcal{SEC}$ grammar with dimension p and degree q into an equivalent LSMG with dimension p' and degree q'.

$G' = (\{S, A, A'\}, \{a, b, c, d\}, P, S)$, where

$-\text{P} = \{\ m_0\colon \text{S} \longrightarrow \text{AA'},$
$m_1\colon (\text{A} \longrightarrow \text{ab}, \text{A'} \longrightarrow \text{cd}),$
$m_2\colon (\text{A} \longrightarrow \text{aA}, \text{A'} \longrightarrow \text{cA'}),$
$m_3\colon (\text{A} \longrightarrow \text{Ab}, \text{A'} \longrightarrow \text{A'd})\ \}.$

Now, we can construct a CSG: G" = $(\ V_N, \text{T}, \text{P'}, \text{S})$, where

$V_N = \{S, A, A', M, R_1, R_2, R_3\}$

$\text{P'} = \{S \longrightarrow AMA'$

$AM \longrightarrow abR_1$	$R_1b \longrightarrow bR_1$	$R_1c \longrightarrow cR_1$	$bM \longrightarrow Mb$
$AM \longrightarrow aAR_2$	$R_2b \longrightarrow bR_2$	$R_2c \longrightarrow cR_2$	$cM \longrightarrow Mc$
$AM \longrightarrow AbR_3$	$R_3b \longrightarrow bR_3$	$R_3c \longrightarrow cR_3$	

$R_1A' \longrightarrow Mcd \qquad R_1A' \longrightarrow cd$
$R_2A' \longrightarrow McA' \qquad R_2A' \longrightarrow cA'$
$R_3A' \longrightarrow MA'd \qquad R_3A' \longrightarrow A'd\}$

Note that the set of rules presented here may contain some redundancy. However, we gave a priority to the consistency of the manner of constructing corresponding CSGs for general cases.

It is easy to prove that $L(G) = L(G') = L(G'')$, but we omit the proof due to lack of space.

Hence, there are clear relationships between $\mathcal{SEC}_{p,q}$, $\mathcal{LSMG}_{p',q'}$ and CSG.

(i) $p' = p$ (in our example, p is equal to 2; therefore, the number of nonterminals in the right hand of the unique rule of the $LSMG$ started by S is 2).
(ii) $q' = q+1$ (in our example, q is equal to 2; therefore, the number of matrices of $LSMG$ has to be 3).
(iii) *The fixed number of rules of CSG is proportional to $p'\cdot q'$.* Generally, one can have G'' with $O(p' \cdot q')$ number of rules. Since p' and q' are given, G'' has a bounded number of rules.

From a result by Shinohara [16], we can obtain the following theorem:

Theorem 1. *Given $p' > 0$ and $q' > 0$, the class of languages generated by linear simple matrix grammars with dimension p' and degree q' is learnable from positive data.*

Corollary 1. *Given $p > 0$ and $q > 0$, the class of languages generated by simple external contextual grammars with dimension p and degree q is learnable from positive data.*

6   Conclusions

The grammar introduced in this paper, $\mathcal{SEC}_p$ grammar, is an appropriate candidate to attain our goal: to understand the process of children's language acquisition.

We have briefly reported on research attempting to apply formal grammars to the study of natural language. We have seen that the most appropriate formal grammars to describe natural language are the Mildly Context-Sensitive grammars. One of the simpler mechanism to fabricate Mildly Context-Sensitive families is a natural extension of Marcus External Contextual grammars: the many-dimensional Marcus External Contextual grammars.

We have also referred to the most adequate model to study children's language acquisition. We have distinguished two stages in the acquisition of the language: (1) learning from only positive data; (2) learning from correction queries. So, we have proposed here a novel learning model inspired by the Gold's model and Angluin's model: *learnability in the limit from positive data and correction queries*.

In this paper, we have studied the learnability from only positive data. To begin with, by making a certain restriction on the grammar, we have considered a subfamily of the Marcus p-dimensional External Contextual grammars, called Simple Marcus p-dimensional External Contextual grammars.

Finally, we have shown that the class of languages generated by simple external contextual grammars with fixed dimension and degree is learnable from positive data, from Shinohara's results [16]. The learning algorithm straightforwardly derived from our main result is enumerative in nature and therefore not time-efficient, but we have obtained positive learnability result as the first step toward our final goal.

Of special interest in the future will be:

- To improve this algorithm and to obtain a time-efficient algorithm in practical cases.
- To study the learnability from correction queries and to explain the acquisition of language in the second stage. In our future research schema, by *correction queries* we intend to define as an oracle that takes a string w as input and produces as output a *corrected string* w_c (if w is close to an element w_c of the target L) and "No" (otherwise), where w being close to w_c is defined by a certain measure (such as "one-letter" difference or Hamming distance).
- To connect the concept of approximately learning with linguistics motivations (extending our results). This kind of learning could be appropriate for our purpose.

In this way, we will see that the $\mathcal{SEC}_p$ grammar is truly adequate to understand children's language acquisition.

References

1. Sakakibara, Y.: Recent advances of grammatical inference. Theoretical Computer Science **185** (1997) 15–45
2. Kudlek, M., Martín-Vide, C., Mateescu, A., Mitrana, V.: Contexts and the concept of mild context-sensitivity. Linguistics and Philosophy **26** (2002) 703–725
3. Dassow, J., Păun, G.: Regulated Rewriting in Formal Language Theory. Springer-Verlag, New York (1990)
4. Joshi, A.K., Schabes, Y.: Tree-adjoining grammars. In Rozenberg, G., Salomaa, A., eds.: Handbook of Formal Languages. Volume 3. Springer-Verlag, Berlin (1997) 69–123
5. Roach, K.: Formal properties of head grammars. In Manaster Ramer, A., ed.: Mathematics of Language. John Benjamins, Amsterdam (1987) 293–348
6. Steedman, M.: Dependency and coordination in the grammar of Dutch and English. Language **61** (1985) 523–568
7. Gazdar, G., Pullum, G.K.: Computationally relevant properties of natural languages and their grammars. New Generation Computing **3** (1985) 273–306
8. Ibarra, O.: Simple matrix languages. Information and Control **17** (1970) 359–394
9. Gold, E.: Language identification in the limit. Information and Control **10** (1978) 447–474.
10. Angluin, D.: Queries and concept learning. Machine Learning **2** (1988) 319–342
11. Valiant, L.: A theory of the learnable. Communications of the ACM **27** (1984) 1134–1142.
12. Rozenberg, G., Salomaa, A.: Handbook of Formal Languages. Volume 1–3. Springer-Verlag, Berlin (1997)
13. Marcus, S.: Contextual grammars. Revue Roumaine des Mathématiques Pures et Appliquées **14** (1969) 1525–1534
14. Păun, G.: Marcus Contextual Grammars. Kluwer, Dordrecht (1997)
15. Manaster Ramer, A.: Some uses and abuses of mathematics in linguistics. In Martín-Vide, C., ed.: Issues in Mathematical Linguistics. John Benjamins, Amsterdam (1999) 73–130
16. Shinohara, T.: Rich classes inferable from positive data: Length-bounded elementary formal systems. Information and Computation **108** (1994) 175–186

Learnability of Pregroup Grammars

Denis Béchet[1], Annie Foret[2], and Isabelle Tellier[3]

[1] LIPN - UMR CNRS 7030, Villetaneuse
Denis.Bechet@lipn.univ-paris13.fr
[2] IRISA - IFSIC, Campus de Beaulieu, Rennes
Annie.Foret@irisa.fr
[3] MOSTRARE project RU Futurs INRIA*
GRAppA & Inria Futurs, Lille
tellier@univ-lille3.fr

Abstract. This paper investigates the learnability of Pregroup Grammars, a context-free grammar formalism recently defined in the field of computational linguistics. In a first theoretical approach, we provide learnability and non-learnability results in the sense of Gold for sub-classes of Pregroup Grammars. In a second more practical approach, we propose an acquisition algorithm from a special kind of input called Feature-tagged Examples, that is based on sets of constraints.

Keywords: Learning from positive examples, Pregroup grammars, Computational linguistics, Categorial Grammars, Context-Free grammars.

1 Introduction

Pregroup Grammars [1] (PGs in short) is a context-free grammar formalism used in the field of computational linguistics. This recently-defined formalism for syntax allies expressivity (in this respect it is close to Lambek Grammars) and computational efficiency. Subtle linguistic phenomena have already been treated in this framework [2, 3]. PGs share many features with Categorial Grammars of which they are inheritors, especially their lexicalized nature.

Since the seminal works of Kanazawa[4], a lot of learnability results in Gold's model [5] have been obtained for various classes of Categorial Grammars and various input data. But the learnability of PGs has yet received very little attention except a negative result in [6]. In the first part of this paper, we prove several results of learnability or of non-learnability for classes of PGs. But these results are mainly theoretical and are not associated with learning algorithms.

In the second part of the paper, we define an acquisition algorithm to specify a set of PGs compatible with input data. The input data considered, called Feature-tagged Examples, are richer than strings but chosen to be language-independent (inspired by [7–9]). The originality of the process is that it allows to reconsider the learning problem as a constraints resolution problem.

* This research was partially supported by: "CPER 2000-2006, Contrat de Plan état - région Nord/Pas-de-Calais: axe TACT, projet TIC"; fonds européens FEDER "TIC - Fouille Intelligente de données - Traitement Intelligent des Connaissances" OBJ 2-phasing out - 2001/3 - 4.1 - n 3. And by "ACI masse de données ACIMDD".

G. Paliouras and Y. Sakakibara (Eds.): ICGI 2004, LNAI 3264, pp. 65–76, 2004.
© Springer-Verlag Berlin Heidelberg 2004

2   Pregroup Grammars

2.1   Background

Definition 1 (Pregroup). *A* pregroup *is a structure* $(P, \leq, \cdot, l, r, 1)$ *such that* $(P, \leq, \cdot, 1)$ *is a partially ordered monoid*[1] *and* l, r *are two unary operations on* P *that satisfy:* $\forall a \in P \colon a^l a \leq 1 \leq aa^l$ *and* $aa^r \leq 1 \leq a^r a$. *The following equations follow from this definition:* $\forall a, b \in P$, *we have* $a^{rl} = a = a^{lr}$, $1^r = 1 = 1^l$, $(a \cdot b)^r = b^r \cdot a^r$, $(a \cdot b)^l = b^l \cdot a^l$. *Iterated adjoints*[2] *are defined for* $i \in \mathbb{Z}$: $a^{(0)} = a$, *for* $i \leq 0 \colon a^{(i-1)} = \left(a^{(i)}\right)^l$, *for* $i \geq 0 \colon a^{(i+1)} = \left(a^{(i)}\right)^r$

Definition 2 (Free Pregroup). *Let* $(P, \leq)$ *be a partially ordered set of primitive categories,* $P^{(\mathbb{Z})} = \{p^{(i)} \mid p \in P, i \in \mathbb{Z}\}$ *is the set of atomic categories and* $Cat_{(P, \leq)} = \left(P^{(\mathbb{Z})}\right)^* = \{p_1^{(i_1)} \cdots p_n^{(i_n)} \mid 1 \leq k \leq n, p_k \in P, i_k \in \mathbb{Z}\}$ *is the set of categories. For* $X, Y \in Cat_{(P, \leq)}$, $X \leq Y$ *iff this relation is deducible in the system in Fig. 1 where* $p, q \in P$, $n, k \in \mathbb{Z}$ *and* $X, Y, Z \in Cat_{(P, \leq)}$. *This construction, proposed by Buskowski, defines a pregroup that extends* $\leq$ *on* P *to* $Cat_{(P, \leq)}$.

$$X \leq X \;\; (Id) \qquad \frac{XY \leq Z}{Xp^{(n)}p^{(n+1)}Y \leq Z} \, (A_L) \qquad \frac{Xp^{(k)}Y \leq Z}{Xq^{(k)}Y \leq Z} \, (IND_L)$$

$$\frac{X \leq Y \;\; Y \leq Z}{X \leq Z} \, (Cut) \qquad \frac{X \leq YZ}{X \leq Yp^{(n+1)}p^{(n)}Z} \, (A_R) \qquad \frac{X \leq Yp^{(k)}Z}{X \leq Yq^{(k)}Z} \, (IND_R)$$

$$q \leq p \text{ if } k \text{ is even or } p \leq q \text{ if } k \text{ is odd}$$

Fig. 1. System for Pregroup Grammars

Cut Elimination. *Every derivable inequality has a cut-free derivation.*

Simple Free Pregroup. *A* simple free pregroup *is a free pregroup where the order on primitive categories is equality.*

Definition 3 (Pregroup Grammars). $(P, \leq)$ *is a finite partially ordered set. A free pregroup grammar based on* $(P, \leq)$ *is a lexicalized*[3] *grammar* $G = (\Sigma, I, s)$ *such that* $s \in P$; G *assigns a category* X *to a string* $v_1 \cdots v_n$ *of* Σ^* *iff for* $1 \leq i \leq n, \exists X_i \in I(v_i)$ *such that* $X_1 \cdots X_n \leq X$ *in the free pregroup based on* $(P, \leq)$. *The language* $\mathcal{L}(G)$ *is the set of strings in* Σ^* *that are assigned* s *by* G.

Rigid and k-Valued Grammars. Grammars that assign at most k categories to each symbol in the alphabet are called *k-valued grammars*; 1-valued grammars are also called *rigid* grammars.

Width. We define the width of a category $C = p_1^{u_1} \ldots p_n^{u_n}$ as $wd(C) = n$ (the number of atomic categories).

---

[1] A *monoid* is a structure $< M, \cdot, 1 >$, such that $\cdot$ is associative and has a neutral element 1 ($\forall x \in M : 1 \cdot x = x \cdot 1 = x$). A partially ordered monoid is a monoid $(M, \cdot, 1)$ with a partial order $\leq$ that satisfies $\forall a, b, c \colon a \leq b \Rightarrow c \cdot a \leq c \cdot b$ and $a \cdot c \leq b \cdot c$.

[2] We use this notation in technical parts

[3] A lexicalized grammar is a triple (Σ, I, s): Σ is a finite alphabet, I assigns a finite set of categories to each $c \in \Sigma$, s is a category associated to correct sentences.

Example 1. Our first example is taken from [10] with the basic categories: π_2 = second person, s_1 = statement in present tense, p_1 = present participle, p_2 = past participle, o = object. The sentence "You have been seeing her" gets category s_1 ($s_1 \leq s$), with successive reductions on $\pi_2 \pi_2^r \leq 1$, $p_2^l p_2 \leq 1$, $p_1^l p_1 \leq 1$, $o^l o \leq 1$:

$$\begin{array}{ccccc} \text{You} & \text{have} & \text{been} & \text{seeing} & \text{her} \\ \pi_2 & (\pi_2^r \ \underline{s_1} \ p_2^l) & (p_2 \ p_1^l) & (p_1 \ o^l) & o \end{array}$$

2.2   Parsing

Pregroup languages are context-free languages and their parsing is polynomial. We present in this section a parsing algorithm working directly on lists of words. For that, we first extend the notion of inference to lists of categories, so as to reflect the separations between the words of the initial string. The relations noted $\Gamma \vdash_{\mathcal{R}} \Delta$ where $\mathcal{R}$ consists in one or several rules are defined on lists of categories (p, q are atomic, X, Y range over categories and Γ, Δ over lists of categories):

M (merge): $\Gamma, X, Y, \Delta \vdash_M \Gamma, XY, \Delta$.

I (internal): $\Gamma, Xp^{(n)}q^{(n+1)}Y, \Delta \vdash_I \Gamma, XY, \Delta$, if $q \leq p$ and n is even or if $p \leq q$ and n is odd.

E (external): $\Gamma, Xp^{(n)}, q^{(n+1)}Y, \Delta \vdash_E \Gamma, X, Y, \Delta$, if $q \leq p$ and n is even or if $p \leq q$ and n is odd.

$\vdash_{\mathcal{R}}^*$ is the reflexive-transitive closure of $\vdash_{\mathcal{R}}$. This system is equivalent with the deduction system when the final right element is a primitive category. As a consequence, parsing can be done using $\vdash_{MIE}^*$.

Lemma 1. *For $X \in Cat_{(P,\leq)}$ and $p \in P$, $X \leq p$ iff $\exists q \in P$ such that $X \vdash_{MIE}^* q$ and $q \leq p$.*

Corollary 1. *$G = (\Sigma, I, s)$ generates a string $v_1 \cdots v_n$ iff for $1 \leq i \leq N$, $\exists X_i \in I(v_i)$ and $\exists p \in P$ such that $X_1, \cdots, X_n \vdash_{MIE}^* p$ and $p \leq s$.*

All $\vdash_I^*$ can be performed before $\vdash_M^*$ and $\vdash_E^*$ as the next lemma shows.

Lemma 2. *(easy) $\Gamma_1 \vdash_{MIE}^* \Gamma_2$ iff $\exists \Delta$ such that $\Gamma_1 \vdash_I^* \Delta$ and $\Delta \vdash_{ME}^* \Gamma_2$*

The external reductions corresponding to the same couple and a merge reduction can be joined together such that, at each step, the number of categories decreases.

E$^+$ (external+merge): For $k \in \mathbb{N}$,
$\Gamma, Xp_1^{(n_1)} \cdots p_k^{(n_k)}, q_k^{(n_k+1)} \cdots q_1^{(n_1+1)}Y, \Delta \vdash_{E^+} \Gamma, XY, \Delta$, if $q_i \leq p_i$ and n_i is even or if $p_i \leq q_i$ and n_i is odd, for $1 \leq i \leq k$.

Lemma 3. *For a list of categories Γ and $p \in P$, $\Gamma \vdash_{ME}^* p$ iff $\Gamma \vdash_{E^+}^* p$.*

To define a polynomial algorithm, we finally constraint the application of $\vdash_{E^+}^*$ such that the width of the resulting category is never greater than the maximal width of the two initial categories: one category plays the role of an argument and the other plays the role of a functor even if the application is partial. The rule is thus called Functional. In fact, there is a small difference between left and right functional reductions (see the two different conditions $wd(X) \leq k$ or $wd(Y) < k$) to avoid some redundancies. The last condition $wd(Y) = 0$ is necessary when Δ is empty and $k = 0$ to mimic a (degenerated) merge reduction.

F (functional): For $k \in \mathbb{N}$,
$$\Gamma, X p_1^{(n_1)} \cdots p_k^{(n_k)}, q_k^{(n_k+1)} \cdots q_1^{(n_1+1)} Y, \Delta \vdash_F \Gamma, XY, \Delta, \text{ if } q_i \leq p_i \text{ and } n_i \text{ is}$$
even or if $p_i \leq q_i$ and n_i is odd, for $1 \leq i \leq k$ and if $wd(X) \leq k$ or $wd(Y) < k$ or $wd(Y) = 0$.

Lemma 4. *For a list of categories Γ and $p \in P$, $\Gamma \vdash_{E+}^* p$ iff $\Gamma \vdash_F^* p$.*

Proof. The proof is based on the fact that for any planar graph where the vertice are put on a line and where the edges are only on one side of this line, there always exists at least one vertex that is connected only to one of its neighbours or to both of them but not to any other vertex. This vertex is then associated to its neighbour if it is connected to only one neighbour. If it is connected to its two neighbours, we choose the one that interacts the most with the vertex.

The parsing of a string with n words consists in the following steps:
1. Search for the categories associated to the n words through the lexicon.
2. Add the categories deduced with $\vdash_I^*$.
3. Compute recursively the possible categories associated to a contiguous segment of words of the string with $\vdash_F$.

The third step uses a function that takes the positions of the first and last words in the segment as parameters. The result is a set of categories with a bounded width (i.e. by the maximum width of the categories in the lexicon).

Property 1 *For a given grammar, this algorithm is polynomial (wrt. the number of words of input strings).*

Example 2. Parsing of "whom have you seen ?". The categories are as follows in the lexicon ($q' \leq s$):

$$\begin{array}{cccc} \text{whom} & \text{have} & \text{you} & \text{seen} \\ q'o^{ll}q^l & qp_2^l\pi_2^l & \pi_2 & p_2o^l \end{array}$$

	...whom	...have	...you	...seen
seen...				$\{p_2o^l\}$
you...			$\{\pi_2\}$	$\emptyset$
have...		$\{qp_2^l\pi_2^l\}$	$\{qp_2^l\}$	$\{qo^l\}$
whom...	$\{q'o^{ll}q^l\}$	$\emptyset$	$\emptyset$	$\{q'\}$

The cell of line i (numbered from the bottom) and column j contains the category computed for the fragment starting at the ith word and ending at the jth word.

3   Learning

3.1   Background

We now recall some useful definitions and known properties on learning in the limit [5]. Let $\mathcal{G}$ be a class of grammars, that we wish to learn from positive examples. Formally, let $\mathcal{L}(G)$ denote the language associated with a grammar G, and let V be a given alphabet, a learning algorithm is a function ϕ from finite sets of words in V^* to $\mathcal{G}$, such that $\forall G \in \mathcal{G}$, $\forall(e_i)_{i \in N}$ such that $\mathcal{L}(G) = (e_i)_{i \in N}$ $\exists G' \in \mathcal{G}$ and $\exists n_0 \in \mathbb{N}$ such that $\forall n > n_0$ $\phi(\{e_1, \ldots, e_n\}) = G' \in \mathcal{G}$ and $\mathcal{L}(G') = \mathcal{L}(G)$.

Limit Points. A class $\mathcal{CL}$ of languages has *a limit point* iff there exists an infinite sequence $< L_n >_{n \in N}$ of languages in $\mathcal{CL}$ and a language $L \in \mathcal{CL}$ such that: $L_0 \subsetneq L_1 \ldots \subsetneq L_n \subsetneq \ldots$ and $L = \bigcup_{n \in N} L_n$ (L is *a limit point* of $\mathcal{CL}$). If the languages of the grammars in a class $\mathcal{G}$ have a limit point then the class $\mathcal{G}$ is *unlearnable* in Gold's model.

Elasticity. A class $\mathcal{CL}$ of languages has *infinite elasticity* iff there exists $(e_i)_{i \in N}$ a sequence of sentences and $(L_i)_{i \in N}$ a sequence of languages in $\mathcal{CL}$ such that: $\forall i \in N$: $e_i \notin L_i$ and $\{e_1, \ldots, e_i\} \subseteq L_{i+1}$. It has *finite elasticity* in the opposite case. If $\mathcal{CL}$ has *finite elasticity* then the corresponding class of grammars is learnable in Gold's model.

3.2 Non-learnability from Strings – A Review

The class of rigid (also k-valued for any k) PGs has been shown not learnable from strings in [11] using [12]. So, no learning algorithm is possible. This has also been shown for subclasses of rigid PGs as summarized below (from [6]).

Pregroups of Order n and of Order $n+1/2$. A PG on $(P, \leq)$ is of order $n \in \mathbb{N}$ when its primitive categories are in $\{a^{(i)} | a \in P, -n \leq i \leq n\}$; it is of order $n+1/2, n \in \mathbb{N}$ when its primitive categories are in $\{a^{(i)} | a \in P, -n-1 \leq i \leq n\}$.

Construction of Rigid Limit Points. We have proved [6] that the smallest such class (except order 0) has a limit point. Let $P = \{p, q, r, s\}$ and $\Sigma = \{a, b, c, d, e\}$. We consider grammars on $(P, =)$:

$G_n = (\Sigma, I_n, s)$	$G_* = (\Sigma, I_*, s)$
$a \mapsto (p^l)^n q^l$	$a \mapsto q^l$
$b \mapsto qpq^l$	$b \mapsto qp^l q^l$
$c \mapsto qr^l$	$c \mapsto qr^l$
$d \mapsto rp^l r^l$	$d \mapsto rpr^l$
$e \mapsto rp^n s$	$e \mapsto rs$

Theorem 1 *The language of G_* is a limit point for the languages of grammars G_n on $(P, =)$ in the class of languages of rigid simple free PGs of order $1/2$: for $n \geq 0$, $\mathcal{L}(G_n) = \{ab^k cd^k e \mid 0 \leq k \leq n\}$ and $\mathcal{L}(G_*) = \{ab^k cd^k e \mid k \geq 0\}$.*

Corollary 2. *The classes $\mathcal{CG}_{n/2}^k$ of k-valued simple free pregroups of order $n/2, n \geq 0$ are not learnable from strings.*

3.3 Learnability for Restricted Categories

We consider three cases of restricted categories. Case (ii) is used in next section.

(i) *Width and Order* Bounds. Here, by the *order* of a category $C = p_1^{u_1} \ldots p_n^{u_n}$ we mean its integer order : $max\{ |u_i| / 1 \leq i \leq n\}$.

It is first to be noted that when we bind the width and the order of categories, as well as the number of categories per word (k-valued), the class is learnable from strings (since we have a finite number of grammars -up to renaming-).

(ii) *Width* Bounded Categories. By normalizing with translations, we get:

Theorem 2 *The class of rigid (also k-valued for each k) PGs with categories of width less than N is learnable from strings for each N.*

Proof. Let G denote a rigid PG on Σ and n be the maximum width of G, we can show that G is equivalent (same language) to a similar PG of order $\leq 2n|\Sigma|$. This PG is a normalized version of G obtained by repeating translations as follows: consider possible iterations of r; if two consecutive exponents never appear in any iterated adjoints (a hole), decrease all above exponents; proceed similarly for iterations of l. Therefore, a bounded width induces a bounded order for rigid PGs; we then apply the learnability result for a class with a width bound and an order bound. In the k-valued case, we proceed similarly with an order $\leq 2n|\Sigma|k$.

(iii) *Pattern* of Category. We infer from known relationships between categorial formalisms, a case of learnability from strings for PGs. We refer to [13, 14] for definitions and details on formalisms.

From Lambek Calculus to Pregroup. We have a transformation $A \to [A]$ on formulas and sequents from $L_\emptyset$ (Lambek calculus allowing empty sequents) to the simple free pregroup, that translates a valid sequent into a valid inequality[4]:

$$[A] = A \quad \text{when } A \text{ is primitive}$$
$$[A \setminus B] = [A]^r[B] \quad ; \quad [B / A] = [B][A]^l$$
$$[A_1, \ldots, A_n \vdash B] = [A_1] \cdots [A_n] \leq [B]$$

The *order of a category* $o(A)$ for Categorial Grammars is:

$$o(A)=0 \quad \text{when } A \text{ is primitive; } o(A \setminus B)=o(B / A)=max(o(A)+1, o(B))$$

Lemma 5. [15] *If B is primitive and $o(A_i) \leq 1$ for $1 \leq i \leq n$ then:*
$$A_1, \ldots, A_n \vdash_{AB} B \quad \textit{(Classical or AB Categorial Grammars)}$$
iff $A_1, \ldots, A_n \vdash_{L_\emptyset} B$ *(Lambek)*
iff $[A_1] \cdots [A_n] \leq B$ *(simple free pregroup)*

We infer the following result:

Theorem 3 *The class $\mathcal{C}_L^k$ of k-valued (simple free) PGs with categories of the following pattern (P_1) : $g_n^r \ldots g_1^r p d_1^l \ldots d_m^l$, where $n \geq 0$ and $m \geq 0$ is learnable from strings in Gold's model.*

Proof. The class of k-valued AB grammars is learnable from strings [4]. Lemma 5 shows that the class of PGs that are images of k-valued Lambek Grammars of order 1 (also k-valued AB-grammars with the same language) is also learnable. And when $o(A) \leq 1$, then $[A]$ must be written as: $g_n^r \ldots g_1^r p d_1^l \ldots d_m^l$.

Relevance of Pattern P_1. We have observed that many linguistic examples follow the pattern P_1 or are images of these by some *increasing function,*

---

[4] The converse is not true :
$$[(a \cdot b) / c] = abc^l = [a \cdot (b / c)] \qquad \text{but} \quad (a \cdot b) / c \not\vdash a \cdot (b / c)$$
$$[(p / ((p / p) / p)) / p] = pp^{ll}p^{ll}p^l p^l \leq [p] \text{ but } (p / ((p / p) / p)) / p \not\vdash p$$

i.e. a function h such that $X \leq h(X)$ (for example type-raised introduction $h_{raise}(X) = ss^l X$); moreover if G assigns $h_i(t_i)$ to c_i, where all h_i are increasing and all t_i have the pattern P_1, we consider G_{P_1} assigning t_i to c_i and get : $L(G) \subseteq L(G_{P_1})$ and the class of G_{P_1} is learnable from strings.

3.4   Learning Pregroup Grammars from Feature-Tagged Examples

Previous learnability results lead to non tractable algorithms. But an idea from Categorial Grammars learning is worth being applied to PGs: the learnability from Typed Examples. Types are to be understood here in the sense Montague's logic gave them. Under some conditions specifying the link between categories and types, interesting subclasses of AB-Categorial Grammars and of Lambek Grammars have been proved learnable from Typed Examples, i.e. from sentences where each word is associated with its semantic type [8, 9].

To adapt this idea to PGs, the first problem is that the link between PGs and semantics is not clearly stated. So, the notion of semantic types has no obvious relevance in this context and our first task is to identify what can play the role of language-independent features in PGs. We call Feature-tagged Examples the resulting input data. We then define a subclass of PGs learnable from Feature-tagged Examples in the sense of Gold. Finally, we present an algorithm whose purpose is to identify every possible PG of this class compatible with a set of Feature-tagged Examples. An original point is that this set will be specified by a set of constraints. We provide examples showing that this set can be exponentially smaller than the set of grammars it specifies.

Specification of Input Data. Let us consider how the various possible word orders for a basic sentence expressing a statement at the present tense, with a third person subject S, a transitive verb V and a direct object O would be treated by various PGs (Figure 2): The common points between every possible analysis

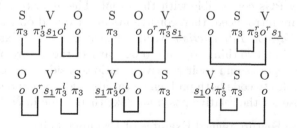

Fig. 2. Pregroup Grammars and possible word orders

are the primitive categories associated with S and O. The category of V is always a concatenation (in various orders) of the elements of the set $\{s_1, \pi_3^u, o^v\}$ where u and v are either r or l: this set simply expresses that V expects a subject and an object. But the nature of the exponent (r or l or a combination of them) and their relative positions in the category associated with V are language-specific.

This comparison suggests that multisets of primitive categories play the role of language-independent features in PGs. For any set $(P, \leq)$, we call $\mathcal{M}(P)$ the set of multisets of elements of P and f_P the mapping from $Cat_{(P,\leq)}$ to $\mathcal{M}(P)$ that transforms any category into the multiset of its primitive categories.

Definition 4. *For any PG $G = (\Sigma, I, s)$, the Feature-tagged Language of G, noted $FT(G)$, is defined by: $FT(G) = \{\langle v_1, T_1 \rangle ... \langle v_n, T_n \rangle | \forall i \in \{1, ..., n\} \exists X_i \in I(v_i)$ such that $X_1 ... X_n \leq s$ and $T_i = f_P(X_i)\}$*

Example 3. Let $P = \{\pi_3, o, s, s_1\}$ with $s_1 \leq s$, $\Sigma = \{he, loves, her\}$ and let $G = (\Sigma, I, s)$ with $I(he) = \{\pi_3\}$, $I(loves) = \{\pi_3^r s_1 o^l\}$, $I(her) = \{o\}$. We have: $\langle he, \{\pi_3\} \rangle \langle loves, \{s_1, \pi_3, o\} \rangle \langle her, \{o\} \rangle \in FT(G)$. An element of $FT(G)$ is a Feature-tagged Example. We study how PGs can be learned from such examples.

Definition 5. *For any sets Σ and P, we call $\mathcal{G}_f$ the set of PGs $G = (\Sigma, I, s)$ satisfying: $\forall v \in \Sigma, \forall X_1, X_2 \in I(v): f_P(X_1) = f_P(X_2) \Longrightarrow X_1 = X_2$*

Theorem 4. *The class $\mathcal{G}_f$ is learnable in Gold's model from Feature-tagged Examples (i.e. where, in Gold's model, FT plays the role of $\mathcal{L}$ and $V = \Sigma \times \mathcal{M}(\mathcal{P})$).*
Proof. The theorem is a corollary of Theorem 2, where k and N can be computed from any sequence of Feature-tagged Examples that enumerates $FT(G)$:
- the condition satisfied by a PG for being an element of $\mathcal{G}_f$ implies that the number of distinct multisets associated with the same word in Feature-tagged Examples is the same as the number of distinct categories associated to it by function I. So k can be easily obtained.
- the width of a category is exactly the number of elements in the corresponding multiset, so N can also be easily obtained.

Acquisition Algorithm. Our algorithm takes as input a set of Feature-tagged Examples for some $G \in \mathcal{G}_f$ and provides a set of PGs. We conjecture (although we haven't proved yet) that the output is exactly, up to basic transformations, the set of every PGs compatible with the input. The algorithm has two steps: first variables are introduced, then constraints are deduced on their values.

First Step: Variable Introduction. Although Feature-tagged Examples provide a lot of information, two things remain to be learned: the nature of the potential exponents of categories and their relative positions inside a concatenation. We introduce variables to code both problems. Variables for the exponents take their value in $\mathbb{Z}$, those for the relative positions take their value in $\mathbb{N} \setminus \{0\}$.

Example 4. The Feature-tagged Example of Example 3 gives:
he: $T_1 = \{(\pi_3^u, x_{11})\}$
loves: $T_2 = \{(s_1^v, x_{21}), (\pi_3^{v'}, x_{22}), (o^{v''}, x_{23})\}$
her: $T_3 = \{(o^w, x_{31})\}$
with $u, v, v', v'', w \in \mathbb{Z}$. $\forall i, j, x_{ij} \in \mathbb{N} \setminus \{0\}$ is the position of the jth primitive category of the ith word. The following constraints and consequences are available:
$\{x_{11}\} = \{1\} \Longrightarrow x_{11} = 1$; $\{x_{21}, x_{22}, x_{23}\} = \{1, 2, 3\}$; $\{x_{31}\} = \{1\} \Longrightarrow x_{31} = 1$

This coding allows to reformulate the learning problem into a variable assignment problem. Furthermore, as the Feature-tagged Examples belong to the same $FT(G)$ for some G in $\mathcal{G}_f$, the *same variables* are used for every occurrence of the same couple $\langle word, multiset \rangle$ in the set of Feature-tagged Examples.

Second Step: Constraints Deduction. This step consists in deducing constraints applying on the variables. Each Example is treated one after the other. For a given Example, we call T_i the multiset associated with the ith word. Each initial sentence of n words is then replaced by a sequence of n multisets. Constraint deduction takes the form of rules that mimic the rules I and F used for the parsing of PGs in section 2.2. Constraints coming from the same syntactic analysis are linked by a conjunction, constraints from distinct alternative syntactic analyses are linked by a disjunction. For each sentence, we thus obtain a disjunction of conjunctions of basic constraints (that we call *data constraint*) where each basic constraint consists in an exponent part and a position part.

Let $T_m = \{(p_{mi}^u, x_{mi})_{1 \leq i \leq k}\}$ and $T_{m'} = \{(p_{m'j}^{u'}, x_{m'j})_{1 \leq j \leq k'}\}$ be two consecutive sets (at the beginning: $m' = m+1$). If $\exists (p_{mi_0}^u, x_{mi_0}) \in T_m$ and $\exists (p_{m'j_0}^{u'}, x_{m'j_0}) \in T_{m'}$ such that $p_{mi_0} \leq p_{m'j_0}$ or $p_{m'j_0} \leq p_{mi_0}$ then:

- Position constraints:
  - $\forall i \neq i_0, \forall x_{mi} \in T_m$: $x_{mi_0} > x_{mi}$
  - $\forall j \neq j_0, \forall x_{m'j} \in T_{m'}$: $x_{m'j_0} < x_{m'j}$
- Exponent constraints:
  - (all cases) $u' = u + 1$
  - IF $p_{m'j_0} < p_{mi_0}$ THEN: u is odd
  - IF $p_{mi_0} < p_{m'j_0}$ THEN: u is even
- Next sets:
  - $T_m \longleftarrow T_m - (p_{mi_0}^u, x_{mi_0})$
  - $T_{m'} \longleftarrow T_{m'} - (p_{m'j_0}^{u'}, x_{m'j_0})$

For internal reductions, where $m = m'$, the Position constraint is replaced by: $\forall i \neq i_0, i \neq j_0$: $x_{mi} < x_{mi_0}$ or $x_{mj_0} < x_{mi}$

Whenever a set T_i becomes empty, drop it. The process ends when the list gets reduced to some $\{(p^u, x)\}$ where $p \leq s$ (the constraint $u = 0$ is deduced).

If a primitive category satisfying the precondition of the rules has several occurrences in a multiset, any of them can be chosen (they are interchangeable). By convention, take the one associated with the position variable of smallest index. Example 6 (further) illustrates this case. To efficiently implement these rules, an interesting strategy consists in following the parsing steps of section 2.2.

Example 5. Let us see what this algorithm gives on our basic Example 4 where the initial sequence of multisets is: $T_1 T_2 T_3$:

- $(\pi_3^u, x_{11}) \in T_1$ and $(\pi_3^{v'}, x_{22}) \in T_2$ satisfy the precondition. The position constraints obtained are: $x_{22} < x_{21}$ and $x_{22} < x_{23}$. The exponent constraint is: $v' = u + 1$, and the remaining sets are the following: $T_1 = \emptyset$, $T_2 = \{(s_1^v, x_{21}), (o^{v''}, x_{23})\}$, $T_3 = \{(o^w, x_{31})\}$

– then $(o^{v''}, x_{23}) \in T_2$ and $(o^w, x_{31}) \in T_3$ satisfy the precondition. We deduce: $x_{23} > x_{21}$, $w = v'' + 1$ and $T_2 = \{(s_1^v, x_{21})\}$, $T_3 = \emptyset$. As $s_1 \leq s$, we obtain $v = 0$ and the algorithm stops.

From the constraints: $\{x_{21}, x_{22}, x_{23}\} = \{1, 2, 3\}$, $x_{22} < x_{21}$, $x_{22} < x_{23}$ and $x_{23} > x_{21}$ we deduce: $x_{21} = 2$, $x_{22} = 1$ and $x_{23} = 3$. The PGs specified by these constraints are defined up to a translation on the exponents. If we set $u = 0 = w$, then $v' = 1$ (or $v' = r$) and $v'' = -1$ (or $v'' = l$): the only remaining PG associates $\pi_3^r s_1 o^l$ with "loves". But, in general, solution PGs are only specified by a set of constraints. We will see that this set can be exponentially smaller than the set of classes (up to translations) of PGs it specifies.

In an acquisition process, each example gives rise to a new data constraints that is conjoined to the previous ones. We get a convergence property as follows:

Property 2 *Let $G \in \mathcal{G}_f$, and $FT(G) = \{e_i\}_{i \in \mathbb{N}}$, the data constraints $\mathcal{DC}_i$ obtained from the successive e_i converges[5]: $\exists n_0 \in \mathbb{N} \; \forall n \geq n_0 : \mathcal{DC}_{n+1} = \mathcal{DC}_n$*

Proof. At some stage N of the acquisition process, the set of primitive categories and the widths of the categories assigned to each word become known; after this N, we have only a finite number of possibilities for data constraints, that must therefore converge.

Even if our acquisition algorithm finds every possible PG compatible with a set of Feature-tagged Example, it is not enough to make it a learning algorithm in the sense of Gold. A remaining problem is to identify a unique PG in the limit. Inclusion tests between Feature-tagged languages may be necessary for this purpose, and we do not even know if these tests are computable. They can nevertheless be performed for Feature-tagged Example of bounded length (this is Kanazawa's strategy for learning k-valued AB-Categorial Grammars from strings) but, of course, make the algorithm intractable in practice.

Why Pregroup Grammars and Constraints Are Efficient. The main weakness of known learning algorithms for Categorial Grammars is their algorithmic complexity. The only favourable case is when rigid AB-Grammars are to be learned from Structural Example but this situation is of limited interest. Our algorithm can still sometimes lead to combinatorial explosion but seems more tractable than previous approaches, as shown by the following two examples.

Example 6 (First exponential gain). The first gain comes from the associativity of categories in PGs. Let a word "b" be associated with a category expecting $2n$ arguments of a category associated with a word "a", n of which are on its right and the other n on its left. The corresponding Feature-tagged Example is:

$$\underbrace{\underset{e \ldots e}{\text{a} \ldots \text{a}}}_{n \; times} \quad \underbrace{\{s, \underset{e, \ldots, e}{\text{b}}\}}_{2n \; times} \quad \underbrace{\underset{e \ldots e}{\text{a} \ldots \text{a}}}_{n \; times}$$

---

[5] we consider constraints written in a format without repetition

This case is equivalent with the problem of learning AB or Lambek Categorial Grammars from the following Typed Example [7, 9]:

$$\underbrace{a \ldots a}_{} \qquad b \qquad \underbrace{a \ldots a}_{}$$
$$\underbrace{e \ldots e}_{n \; times} \underbrace{\langle e, \langle e, \ldots \langle e, t \rangle \rangle \ldots \rangle}_{2n \; times} \underbrace{e \ldots e}_{n \; times}$$

There are $\binom{2n}{n}$ different Categorial Grammars compatible with this input. This situation occurs with transitive verbs, whose category is $T\backslash(S/T)$ or $(T\backslash S)/T$ (both corresponding to the same type $\langle e, \langle e, t \rangle \rangle$, i.e. the example with $n = 1$). The distinct categories assigned to "b" by each solution are deductible from one another in the Lambek calculus. Lambek Grammars are associative, but at the *rule level*, whereas PGs are associative at the *category level*. The only compatible PG (up to translations) is the one assigning $\underbrace{e^r \ldots e^r}_{n \; times} s \underbrace{e^l \ldots e^l}_{n \; times}$ to b.

Example 7 (Second exponential gain). Another exponential gain can be earned from the reduction of the learning problem to a constraints resolution problem. In the following example, position variables are shown under for readability:

$$a \qquad\qquad b \qquad\qquad c \qquad\qquad d$$
$$\{s, m, n\} \qquad \{m, n, o, p\} \qquad \{o, p, q, r\} \qquad \{q, r\}$$
$$\{x_{11}, x_{12}, x_{13}\} \; \{x_{21}, x_{22}, x_{23}, x_{24}\} \; \{x_{31}, x_{32}, x_{33}, x_{34}\} \; \{x_{41}, x_{42}\}$$

There are several PGs compatible with this input, all of which sharing the same values for exponent variables, but differing in the way they embed the two reductions to be applied on each distinct category (one solution -up to translations- is shown above, the other one is shown under). As each choice is independent, there are $2^3 = 8$ different PGs compatible with this example but defined by a conjunction of 3 constraints (the first one is displayed on the right).

$$sm^l n \; n^r mo^l p \; p^r oq^l r \; r^r q$$
$$a \qquad b \qquad c \qquad d \quad ((x_{12} < x_{13}) \wedge (x_{22} < x_{21})) \vee ((x_{13} < x_{12}) \wedge (x_{21} < x_{22}))$$
$$snm^l \; mn^r po^l \; op^r rq^l \; qr^r$$

4   Conclusion

Pregroup Grammars appear to be an interesting compromise between simplicity and expressivity. Their link with semantics is still an open question. As far as learnability is concerned, very few was known till now. This paper provides theoretical as well as practical approaches to the problem. Theoretical results prove that learning PGs is difficult unless limitations are known. The practical approach shows that the limitations can be weakened when rich input data is provided. These data take the form of Feature-tagged sentences which, although very informative, are arguably language-independent. The interest of working with constraints is that the solution grammars are only implicitly defined by the output. The combinatorial explosion of solution grammars is then sometimes delayed to the constraint resolution mechanism, as displayed in the examples. As many current learning algorithms are unification-based [4, 16], the use of constraints may also be seen as a natural generalization of such techniques. What remains to be done is to study further the properties of our algorithm, both from the point of view of tractability, and from the point of view of formal properties and to exploit further the good properties of bounded width grammars.

References

1. Lambek, J.: Type grammars revisited. In Lecomte, A., Lamarche, F., Perrier, G., eds.: Logical aspects of computational linguistics: Second International Conference, LACL '97, Nancy, France, September 22–24, 1997; selected papers. Volume 1582., Springer-Verlag (1999)
2. Bargelli, D., Lambek, J.: An algebraic approach to french sentence structure. [17]
3. Casadio, C., Lambek, J.: An algebraic analysis of clitic pronouns in italian. [17]
4. Kanazawa, M.: Learnable classes of categorial grammars. Studies in Logic, Language and Information. FoLLI & CSLI (1998) distributed by Cambridge University Press.
5. Gold, E.: Language identification in the limit. Information and control **10** (1967) 447–474
6. Béchet, D., Foret, A.: Remarques et perspectives sur les langages de prégroupe d'ordre 1/2. In ATALA, ed.: Actes de la conférence internationale Traitement Automatique des Langues Naturelles (TALN'2003). (2003) (Poster in French).
7. Dudau-Sofronie, D., Tellier, I., Tommasi, M.: Learning categorial grammars from semantic types. In: Proccedings of the 13rd Amsterdam Colloquium. (2001) 79–84
8. Dudau-Sofronie, D., Tellier, I., Tommasi, M.: A learnable class of ccg from typed examples. In: Proccedings of the 8th conference on Formal Grammar (FGVienna). (2003) 77–88
9. Dudau-Sofronie, D., Tellier, I.: A study of learnability of lambek grammars from typed examples. In: Categorial Grammars 04. (2004) 133–147
10. Lambek, J.: Mathematics and the mind. In Abrusci, V., Casadio, C., eds.: New Perspectives in Logic and Formal Linguisitics, Proceedings Vth ROMA Workshop, Bulzoni Editore (2001)
11. Foret, A.: Some unlearnability results for lambek categorial and pregroup grammars (oral communication). In: ESSLII, Trento, Italy (2002)
12. Foret, A., Le Nir, Y.: Lambek rigid grammars are not learnable from strings. In: COLING'2002, 19th International Conference on Computational Linguistics, Taipei, Taiwan (2002)
13. Buszkowski, W.: Mathematical linguistics and proof theory. [18] chapter 12 683–736
14. Moortgat, M.: Categorial type logic. [18] chapter 2 93–177
15. Buszkowski, W.: Lambek grammars based on pregroups. [17]
16. Nicolas, J.: Grammatical inference as unification. Technical Report 3632, IRISA, Unité de Recherche INRIA Rennes (1999)
17. de Groote, P., Morrill, G., Retoré, C., eds.: Logical aspects of computational linguistics: 4th International Conference, LACL 2001, Le Croisic, France, June 2001. Volume 2099., Springer-Verlag (2001)
18. van Benthem, J., ter Meulen, A., eds.: Handbook of Logic and Language. North-Holland Elsevier, Amsterdam (1997)

A Markovian Approach to the Induction of Regular String Distributions

Jérôme Callut and Pierre Dupont

Department of Computing Science and Engineering, INGI
Université catholique de Louvain
Place Sainte-Barbe 2
B-1348 Louvain-la-Neuve, Belgium
{jcal,pdupont}@info.ucl.ac.be

Abstract. We propose in this paper a novel approach to the induction of the structure of Hidden Markov Models (HMMs). The notion of partially observable Markov models (POMMs) is introduced. POMMs form a particular case of HMMs where any state emits a single letter with probability one, but several states can emit the same letter. It is shown that any HMM can be represented by an equivalent POMM. The proposed induction algorithm aims at finding a POMM fitting a sample drawn from an unknown target POMM. The induced model is built to fit the dynamics of the target machine observed in the sample. A POMM is seen as a lumped process of a Markov chain and the induced POMM is constructed to best approximate the stationary distribution and the mean first passage times (MFPT) observed in the sample. The induction relies on iterative state splitting from an initial maximum likelihood model. The transition probabilities of the updated model are found by solving an optimization problem to minimize the difference between the observed MFPT and their values computed in the induced model.

Keywords: HMM topology induction, Partially observable Markov model, Mean first passage time, Lumped Markov process, State splitting algorithm.

1 Introduction

Hidden Markov Models (HMMs) are widely used in many pattern recognition areas, including applications to speech recognition [15], biological sequence modeling [6], information extraction [7, 8] and optical character recognition [11], to name a few. In most cases, the model structure, also referred to as topology, is defined according to some prior knowledge of the application domain. Automatic techniques for inducing the HMM topology are interesting as the structures are sometimes hard to define *a priori* or need to be tuned after some task adaptation. The work described here presents a new approach towards this objective.

Probabilistic automata (PA) form an alternative representation class to model distributions over strings, for which several induction algorithms have been proposed. PA and HMMs actually form two families of equivalent models, according to whether or not final probabilities are included. In the former case,

G. Paliouras and Y. Sakakibara (Eds.): ICGI 2004, LNAI 3264, pp. 77–90, 2004.

the models generate distributions over words of finite length, while, in the later case, distributions are defined over complete finite prefix-free sets [5].

The equivalences between PA and HMMs can be used to apply induction algorithms in either formalism to model the same classes of string distributions. Nevertheless, previous works with HMMs mainly concentrated either on hand-built models (*e.g.* [7]) or heuristics to refine predefined structures [8]. More principled approaches are the Bayesian merging technique due to Stolcke [18] and the maximum likelihood state-splitting method of Ostendorf and Singer [14]. The former approach however has been applied only to small problems while the later is specific to the subclass of left-to-right HMMs modeling speech signals.

In contrast, PA induction techniques are often formulated in theoretical learning frameworks. These frameworks typically include adapted versions of the *PAC* model [16], *Identification with probability one* [1, 2] or *Bayesian learning* [19]. Other approaches use error-correcting techniques [17] or statistical tests as a model fit induction bias [10]. All these approaches, while being interesting, are still somehow limited. From the theoretical viewpoint, PAC learnability is only feasible for restricted subclasses of PAs (see [5], for a review). The general PA class is identifiable with probability one [2] but this learning framework is weaker than the PAC model. In particular, it guarantees asymptotic convergence to a target model but does not bound the overall computational complexity of the learning process. From a practical viewpoint, several induction algorithms have been applied, typically to language modeling tasks [4, 3, 19, 12]. The experiments reported in these works show that automatically induced PA hardly outperform well smoothed *discrete Markov chains* (MC), also known as *N-grams* in this context. Hence even though HMMs and PA are more powerful than simple Markov chains, it is still unclear whether these models should be considered when no strong prior knowledge can help to define their structure.

The present contribution describes a novel approach to the structural induction of HMMs. The general objective is to induce the structure and to estimate the parameters of a HMM from a sample assumed to have been drawn from an unknown target HMM. The goal however is not the identification of the target model but the induction of a model sharing with the target the main features of the distribution it generates. We restrict here our attention to features that can be deduced from the sample. These features are closely related to fundamental quantities of a Markov process, namely the *stationary distribution* and *mean first passage times*. In other words, the induced model is built to fit the dynamics of the target machine observed in the sample, not necessarily to match its structure.

We show in section 2 that any HMM can be converted into an equivalent *Partially Observable Markov Model* (POMM). Any state of a POMM emits with probability 1 a single letter, but several states can emit the same letter. Several properties of standard Markov chains are reviewed in section 3. The relation between a POMM and a lumped process in a Markov chain is detailed in section 4. This relation forms the basis of the induction algorithm presented in section 5.

2   Hidden Markov Models and Partially Observable Markov Models

We recall in this section the classical definition of a HMM and we show that any HMM can be represented by an equivalent partially observable model.

Definition 1 (HMM). *A* discrete *Hidden Markov Model (HMM)* (with state emission) *is a 5-tuple* $M = \langle \Sigma, Q, A, B, \iota \rangle$ *where* Σ *is an alphabet,* Q *is a set of states,* $A : Q \times Q \to [0,1]$ *is a mapping defining the probability of each transition,* $B : Q \times \Sigma \to [0,1]$ *is a mapping defining the emission probability of each letter on each state, and* $\iota : Q \to [0,1]$ *is a mapping defining the initial probability of each state. The following stochasticity* (or properness) *constraints must be satisfied:* $\forall q \in Q, \sum_{q' \in Q} A(q, q') = 1; \; \forall q \in Q, \sum_{a \in \Sigma} B(q, a) = 1; \; \sum_{q \in Q} \iota(q) = 1.$

Figure 1 presents a HMM defined as follows:
$\Sigma = \{a, b\}$, $Q = \{1, 2\}$, $\iota(1) = 0.4$; $\iota(2) = 0.6$;
$A(1,1) = 0.1; A(1,2) = 0.9; A(2,1) = 0.7; A(2,2) = 0.3$;
$B(1,a) = 0.2; B(1,b) = 0.8; B(2,a) = 0.9; B(2,b) = 0.1$

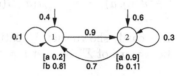

Fig. 1. HMM example.

Definition 2 (HMM path). *Let* $M = \langle \Sigma, Q, A, B, \iota \rangle$ *be a HMM. A* path *in* M *is a word defined on* Q^*. *For any path* ν, ν_i *denotes the i-th state of* ν, *and* $|\nu|$ *denotes the path length. For any word* $u \in \Sigma^*$ *and any path* $\nu \in Q^*$, *the probabilities* $P_M(u, \nu)$ *and* $P_M(u)$ *are defined as follows:*

$$P_M(u, \nu) = \begin{cases} \iota(\nu_1) \prod_{i=1}^{l-1} [B(\nu_i, u_i) A(\nu_i, \nu_{i+1})] B(\nu_l, u_l) \text{ if } l = |u| = |\nu| > 0, \\ 1 \text{ if } |u| = |\nu| = 0 \text{ and} \\ 0 \text{ otherwise.} \end{cases}$$

$$P_M(u) = \sum_{\nu \in Q^*} P(u, \nu).$$

$P_M(u, \nu)$ is the probability to emit word u while following path ν. $P_M(u)$ can be interpreted as the probability of observing a finite word u as part of a random walk through the model. For instance, the probability of the word ab in the HMM of Fig. 1 is given by: $P_M(ab) = P_M(ab, 11) + P_M(ab, 12) + P_M(ab, 21) + P_M(ab, 22) = 0.0064 + 0.0072 + 0.3024 + 0.0162 = 0.3322$.

Definition 3 (POMM). *A Partially Observable Markov Model (POMM)* is a *HMM* $M = \langle \Sigma, Q, A, B, \iota \rangle$ *with emission probabilities satisfying:* $\forall q \in Q, \exists a \in \Sigma$ *such that* $B(q, a) = 1$.

In other words, any state in a POMM emits a specific letter with probability 1. Hence we can consider that POMM states only emit a single letter. This model is called *partially* observable since, in general, several distinct states can emit the same letter. As for a HMM, the observation of a word emitted during a random walk does not allow to identify the states from which each letter was emitted.

However, the observations define *state subsets* from which each letter may have been emitted. Theorem 1 shows that the class of POMMs is equivalent to the class of HMMs, as any distribution generated by a HMM can be represented by a POMM.

Theorem 1 (Equivalence between HMMs and POMMs). *Let $M = \langle \Sigma, Q, A, B, \iota \rangle$ be a HMM, there exists an equivalent POMM $M' = \langle \Sigma, Q', A', B', \iota' \rangle$.*

Proof. Let M' be defined as follows.

- $Q' = Q \times \Sigma$,
- $B'((q, a), x) = 1$ if $x = a$, and 0 otherwise,
- $A'((q, a), (q', b)) = B(q, b)A(q, q')$,
- $\iota'((q, a)) = \sum_{q' \in Q} \iota(q')B(q', a)A(q', q)$.

It is easily shown that M' satisfies the stochasticity constraints. Let $u = u_1 \ldots u_l$ be a word of Σ^* and let $\nu = ((q_1, u_1) \ldots (q_l, u_l))$ be a path in M'. We have:

$$P_{M'}(u, \nu) = \iota'((q_1, u_1)) \prod_{i=1}^{l-1} [B'((q_i, u_i), u_i)A'((q_i, u_i), (q_{i+1}, u_{i+1}))]B'((q_l, u_l), u_l)$$

$$= \sum_{q' \in Q} \iota(q')B(q', u_1)A(q', q_1) \prod_{i=1}^{l-1} [B(q_i, u_{i+1})A(q_i, q_{i+1})]$$

$$= \sum_{q' \in Q} P_M(u, q'q_1 \ldots q_{l-1})A(q_{l-1}, q_l)$$

Summing up over all possible paths of length $l = |u|$ in M', we obtain:

$$P_{M'}(u) = \sum_{\nu \in Q'^l} P_{M'}(u, \nu) = \sum_{\nu_1 \in Q^{l-1}} \sum_{q' \in Q} P_M(u, q'\nu_1) \sum_{q \in Q} A(q_{|\nu_1|}, q)$$
$$= \sum_{\nu_2 \in Q^l} P_M(u, \nu_2) = P_M(u)$$

Hence, M and M' generate the same distribution.   □

The proof of theorem 1 is adapted from a similar result showing the equivalence between PA without final probabilities and HMMs [5]. An immediate corollary of this theorem is the equivalence between PA and POMMs. Hence we call *regular string distribution*, any distribution generated by these models[1]. Figure 2 shows an HMM and its equivalent POMM.

---

[1] More precisely, these models generate distributions over complete finite prefix-free sets. A typical case is a distribution defined over Σ^n, for some positive integer n. See [5] for further details.

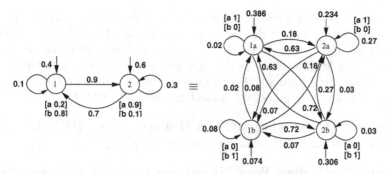

Fig. 2. Transformation of a HMM into an equivalent POMM.

It should be stressed that all transition probabilities of the form $A'((q, \_), (q', b))$ are necessarily equal as the value of $A'((q, a), (q', b))$ does not depend on a in a POMM constructed in this way. A state (q, a) in this model represents the state q reached during a random walk in the original HMM after having emitted the letter a on any state.

3   Markov Chains, Stationary Distribution and Mean First Passage Times

The notion of POMM introduced in section 2 is closely related to a standard Markov Chain (MC). Indeed, in the particular case where all states emit a different letter, the process of a POMM is fully observable. Moreover the Markov property is satisfied as, by definition, the probability of any transition only depends on the current state. Some fundamental properties of a Markov chain are recalled in this section. The links between a POMM and a MC are further detailed in section 4.

Definition 4 (Discrete Time Markov Chain). *A discrete time Markov Chain (MC) is a stochastic process $\{X_t\}$ where the random variable X takes its value at any discrete time t in a countable set Q and such that: $P[X_{t+1} = q \,|\, X_t, X_{t-1}, \ldots, X_0] = P[X_{t+1} = q \,|\, X_t]$. This condition states that the probability of the next outcome only depends on the last value of the process. This is known as the (first-order) Markov property. When the set Q is finite the process forms a finite state MC.*

Definition 5 (Finite State MC Representation). *A finite state representation of a MC is a 3-tuple $T = \langle Q, A, \iota \rangle$ where Q is a finite set of states, $A = Q \times Q \to [0, 1]$ is a mapping defining the transition probability function and $\iota : Q \to [0, 1]$ is the initial probability of each state. The following stochasticity constraints must be satisfied: $\sum_{q \in Q} \iota(q) = 1$; $\forall q \in Q, \sum_{q' \in Q} A(q, q') = 1$*

In this context, the Markov property simply states that the probability of reaching the next state only depends on the current state. For a finite MC, the transition probability function can be represented as a $|Q| \times |Q|$ transition matrix.

In the sequel, A both denotes this function and its matrix representation, with $A_{qq'} = A(q, q')$. Similarly, the function ι is associated with a $|Q|$−dimensional initial probability vector, with $\iota_q = \iota(q)$. We will use interchangeably MC to denote a finite Markov chain or its finite state representation. A finite MC can also be constructed from a HMM by ignoring the emission probabilities and the alphabet. We call this model the *underlying MC* of a HMM.

Definition 6 (Underlying MC of a HMM). *Given a HMM $M = \langle \Sigma, Q, A, B, \iota \rangle$, the* underlying Markov chain T *is the 3-tuple* $\langle Q, A, \iota \rangle$.

Definition 7 (Random Walk String). *Given a MC, $T = \langle Q, A, \iota \rangle$, a* random walk string s *can be defined on Q^* as follows. A random walker is positioned on a state q according to the initial distribution ι. The random walker next moves to some state q' according to the probability $A(q, q')$. Repeating this operation n times results in a n-steps random walk. The string s is the sequence of states visited during this walk.*

In the present work, we focus on *regular* Markov chains. For such chains, there is a strictly positive probability to be in any state after n steps, no matter the starting state.

Definition 8 (Regular MC). *A MC with transition matrix A is* regular *if and only if for some $n \in \mathbb{N}$, the power matrix $A^{(n)}$ has no zero entries.*

In other words, the transition graph of a regular MC is *strongly connected*[2] and all states are *aperiodic*[3]. The *stationary distribution* and *mean first passage times* are fundamental quantities characterizing the dynamics of random walks in a regular MC. These quantities form the basis of the induction algorithm presented in section 5.2.

Definition 9 (Stationary Distribution). *Given a regular MC, $T = \langle Q, A, \iota \rangle$, the* stationary distribution *is a $|Q|$−dimensional stochastic vector π such that $\pi A = \pi$.*

This vector is also known as the *equilibrium vector* or *steady-state vector*. A regular MC is started at equilibrium when the initial distribution ι is set to the stationary distribution π. The q-th entry of the vector π can be interpreted as an expected proportion of the time the steady-state process reaches state q.

Definition 10 (Mean First Passage Time). *Given a regular MC, $T = \langle Q, A, \iota \rangle$, the* first passage time *is a function $f = Q \times Q \to \mathbb{N}$ such that $f(q, q')$ is the number of steps before reaching state q' for the first time, leaving initially from state q.*

$$f(q, q') = \inf\{t \geq 1 \mid X_t = q' \text{ and } X_0 = q\}$$

The Mean First Passage Time *(MFPT) denotes the expectation of this function. It can be represented by the MFPT matrix M, with $M_{qq'} = E[f(q, q')]$.*

---

[2] The chain is said to be *irreducible*.

[3] A state i is *aperiodic* if $A_{ii}^{(n)} > 0$ for all sufficiently large n.

For a regular MC, the MFPT values can be obtained by solving the following linear system [9]:

$$\forall q, q' \in Q, M_{qq'} = \begin{cases} 1 + \displaystyle\sum_{q'' \neq q'} A_{qq''} M_{q''q'} & \text{, if } q \neq q' \\ \dfrac{1}{\pi_q} & \text{, otherwise.} \end{cases}$$

The values M_{qq} are usually called *recurrence times*[4].

4   Relation Between Partially Observable Markov Models and Markov Chains

Given a MC, a partition can be defined on its state set and the resulting process is said to be *lumped*.

Definition 11 (Lumped Process). *Given a regular MC, $T = \langle Q, A, \iota \rangle$, let $q^{(t)}$ be the state reached at time t during a random walk in T. $\kappa = \{\kappa_1, \kappa_2, \ldots, \kappa_r\}$ denotes a partition of the set of states Q. $K_\kappa = Q \to 2^Q$ denotes a function that, given a state q, returns the block of κ, or state subset, containing q. The* lumped *process $T/\!/\kappa$ outcomes $K_\kappa(q^{(t)})$ at time t.*

Consider for example the regular MC T_1 illustrated[5] in Fig. 3. A partition κ is defined on its states set, with $\kappa_1 = \{1, 3\}, \kappa_2 = \{2\}$ and $\kappa_3 = \{4\}$. The random walk 312443 in T_1 corresponds to the following observations in the lumped process $T_1/\!/\kappa$: $\kappa_1 \kappa_1 \kappa_2 \kappa_3 \kappa_3 \kappa_1$.

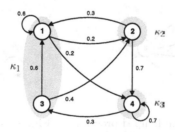

Fig. 3. A regular Markov chain T_1 and the partition $\kappa = \{\{1, 3\}, \{2\}, \{4\}\}$.

While the states are fully observable during a random walk in a MC, a lumped process is associated to random walks where only state *subsets* are observed. In this sense, the lumped process makes the MC only partially observable as it is

---

[4] An alternative definition, $M_{qq} = 0$, is possible when it is not required to leave the initial state before reaching the destination state for the first time [13].

[5] For the sake of clarity, the initial probability of each state is not depicted. Moreover, as we are mostly interested in MC being in steady-state mode, the initial distribution is assumed to be equal to the stationary distribution deriving from the transition matrix (see Def. 9).

the case for a POMM. Conversely, a random walk in a POMM can be considered as a lumped process of its underlying MC with respect to an *observable partition* of its state set. Each block of the observable partition corresponds to the state(s) emitting a specific letter.

Definition 12 (Observable Partition). *Given a POMM* $M = \langle \Sigma, Q, A, B, \iota \rangle$, *the* observable partition κ *is defined as follows:* $\forall q, q' \in Q, K_\kappa(q) = K_\kappa(q') \Leftrightarrow \exists a \in \Sigma, B(q, a) = B(q', a) = 1$

The underlying MC T of a POMM M has the same state set as M. Thus the observable partition κ of M is also defined for the state set of T. If each block of this partition is labeled by the associated letter, M and $T /\!/ \kappa$ define the same string distribution.

It is important to notice that the Markov property is not necessarily satisfied for a lumped process. For example, the lumped MC in Fig. 3 satisfies $P[X_{t+2} = \kappa_2 \mid X_{t+1} = \kappa_1, X_t = \kappa_2] = 0.2$ and $P[X_{t+2} = \kappa_2 \mid X_{t+1} = \kappa_1, X_t = \kappa_3] = 0.4$, which clearly violates the *first-order* Markov property. In general, the Markov property is not satisfied when, for a fixed length history, it is impossible to decide unequivocally which state the process has reached in a given block while the next step probability differs for several states in this block. This can be the case no matter the length of the history considered. This is illustrated by the MC depicted in Fig. 4 and the partition $\kappa = \{\{1, 2\}, \{3\}\}$. Even if the complete history of the lumped process is given, there is no way to know the state reached in κ_1. Thus, the probability $P[X_t = \kappa_2 \mid X_{t-1} = \kappa_1, X_{t-2}, \ldots, X_0]$ cannot be unequivocally determined and the lumped process is not markovian for any order. Hence the definition of *lumpability*.

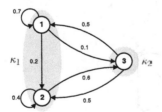

Fig. 4. A non markovian lumped process.

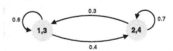

Fig. 5. The MC T_1 lumped with respect to the partition $\kappa' = \{\{1, 2\}, \{3, 4\}\}$.

Definition 13 (Lumpability). *A MC* T *is lumpable with respect to a partition* κ *if the lumped process* $T /\!/ \kappa$ *satisfies the first-order Markov property for any initial distribution.*

When a MC T is lumpable with respect to a partition κ, the lumped process $T /\!/ \kappa$ defines itself a Markov chain.

Theorem 2 (Necessary and sufficient conditions for lumpability [9]).
A MC is lumpable with respect to a partition κ *if and only if for every pair of blocks* κ_i *and* κ_j *the probability* $A_{ij} /\!/ \kappa$ *to reach some state of* κ_j *is equal from every state in* κ_i:

$$\forall \kappa_i, \kappa_j \in \kappa, \forall q, q' \in \kappa_i, \ A_{ij}/\!/\kappa \triangleq \sum_{q'' \in \kappa_j} A_{qq''} = \sum_{q'' \in \kappa_j} A_{q'q''}$$

The values $A_{ij}/\!/\kappa$ form the transition matrix of the lumped chain. For example, the MC T_1 given in Fig. 3 is not lumpable with respect to the partition $\kappa = \{\{1,3\}, \{2\}, \{4\}\}$ while it is lumpable with respect to the partition $\kappa' = \{\{1,3\}, \{2,4\}\}$. The lumped chain $T_1/\!/\kappa'$ is illustrated in Fig. 5.

Even though a lumped process is not necessarily markovian, it is useful for the induction algorithm presented in section 5.2 to define the mean first passage times between the blocks of a lumped process. To do so, it is convenient to introduce some notions from absorbing Markov chains. In a MC, a state q is said to be *absorbing* if there is a probability 1 to go from q to itself. In other words, once an absorbing state has been reached in a random walk, the process will stay on this state forever. A MC for which there is a probability 1 to end up in an absorbing state is called an *absorbing MC*. In such a model, the state set can be divided into the absorbing state set Q_A and its complementary set, the transient state set Q_T. The transition submatrix between transient states is denoted A_T. A related notion is the *mean time to absorption*.

Definition 14 (Mean Time to Absorption).
Given an absorbing MC, $T = \langle\{Q_A, Q_T\}, A, \iota\rangle$, the time to absorption is a function $g = Q_T \to \mathbb{N}$ such that $g(q)$ is the number of steps before absorption, leaving initially from a transient state q.

$$g(q) = \inf\{t \geq 1 \mid X_t \in Q_A, X_0 = q\}$$

The Mean Time to Absorption (MTA) *denotes the expectation of this function. It can be represented by the vector $\mathbf{z}$ computed as $\mathbf{z} = (I - A_T)^{-1}.\mathbf{1}$, where $\mathbf{1}$ denotes a $|Q_T|-$dimensional vector with each component being equal to 1.*

The q-th entry of $\mathbf{z}$ represents the mean time to absorption, leaving initially from the transient state q.

Definition 15 (MFPT for a Lumped Process). *Given a regular MC $T = \langle Q, A, \iota\rangle$, κ a partition of Q and κ_i, κ_j two blocks of κ, an absorbing MC T^j is created from T by transforming every state of κ_j to be absorbing. Furthermore, let $\mathbf{z}^j$ be the MTA vector of T^j. The mean first passage time $M_{ij}/\!/\kappa$ from κ_i to κ_j in the lumped process $T/\!/\kappa$ is defined as follows:*

$$M_{ij}/\!/\kappa = \begin{cases} \dfrac{1}{\pi_{\kappa_i}} & \text{if } \kappa_i = \kappa_j \\[2ex] \displaystyle\sum_{q \in \kappa_i} \dfrac{\pi_q}{\pi_{\kappa_i}} z_q^j & \text{otherwise} \end{cases}$$

where π_q is the stationary distribution of state q in T and $\pi_{\kappa_i} = \sum_{q \in \kappa_i} \pi_q$ is the stationary distribution of the block κ_i in the lumped process $T/\!/\kappa$.

In a lumped process, states subsets are observed instead of the original states of the Markov chain. A related, but possibly different, process is obtained when the states of the original MC are *merged* to form a *quotient Markov chain*.

Definition 16 (Quotient MC). *Given a MC $T = \langle Q, A, \iota \rangle$ and a partition $\kappa = \{\kappa_1, \kappa_2, \dots, \kappa_r\}$ on Q, the quotient T/κ is a r-states MC with transition matrix A/κ and initial vector I/κ defined as follows:*

$$A_{ij}/\kappa = \sum_{q \in \kappa_i} \sum_{q' \in \kappa_j} \frac{\pi_q}{\pi_{\kappa_i}} A_{qq'}, \; I_i/\kappa = \sum_{q \in \kappa_i} \iota(q)$$

where π is the stationary distribution of T and $\pi_{\kappa_i} = \sum_{q \in \kappa_i} \pi_q$.

Note that for any regular MC T, the quotient T/κ has always the Markov property while, as mentioned before, this is not necessarily the case for the lumped process $T/\!\!/\kappa$. The following theorem specifies under which condition the distributions generated by T/κ and $T/\!\!/\kappa$ are identical.

Theorem 3. *If a MC T is lumpable with respect to a partition κ then T/κ and $T/\!\!/\kappa$ generate the same distribution in steady-state.*

Proof. When T is lumpable with respect to κ, the transition probabilities between any pair of blocks κ_i, κ_j are the same in both models:
$A_{i,j}/\kappa = \sum_{q \in \kappa_i} \frac{\pi_q}{\pi_{\kappa_i}} \sum_{q' \in \kappa_j} A_{qq'} = A_{ij}/\!\!/\kappa \sum_{q \in \kappa_i} \frac{\pi_q}{\pi_{\kappa_i}} = A_{ij}/\!\!/\kappa$

$\square$

5   A Markovian Approach to the Induction of Regular Distributions

As explained in section 4, a random walk in a POMM can be seen as a lumped process of its underlying MC lumped with respect to the observable partition. We present now an induction algorithm making use of this relation. Given a data sample, assumed to have been drawn from a target POMM TP, our induction algorithm estimates a model EP fitting the dynamics of the MC related to TP. The estimation relies on the stationary distribution and the mean first passage times which can be derived from the sample. In the present work, we focus on distributions that can be represented by POMMs without final probabilities and with regular underlying MC. Since the target process TP never stops, the sample is assumed to have been observed in steady-state. Furthermore, as the transition graph of TP is strongly connected, it is not restrictive to assume that the data is a unique finite string s resulting from a random walk through TP observed during a finite time[6]. Under these assumptions, all transitions of the target POMM and all letters of its alphabet will tend to be observed in the sample. Such a sample can be called *structurally complete*. The sample estimates are detailed in section 5.1 and an algorithm for POMMs induction is proposed in section 5.2.

---

[6] The statistics described in section 5.1 could equivalently be computed from repeated finite samples observed in steady-state.

5.1   Sample Estimates

As the target process TP can be considered as a lumped process, each letter of the sample s is associated to a unique state subset of the observable partition κ. All estimates introduced here are related to the state subsets of the target lumped process. First, we introduce the *stationary maximum likelihood model*. This model is the starting point of the induction algorithm presented in section 5.2.

Definition 17 (Stationary Maximum Likelihood MC). *Given a string s on an alphabet Σ, the stationary maximum likelihood MC $ML = \langle Q, \hat{A}, \hat{\imath} \rangle$ is defined as follows: $Q = \Sigma$; $\forall a, b \in Q, \hat{A}_{ab} = \frac{count(a,b)}{count(a)}$; $\forall a \in Q, \hat{\imath}_a = \hat{\pi}_a$; where $count(a, b)$ is the number of times the letter a is immediately followed by the letter b in s, $count(a) = \sum_{b \in \Sigma} count(a, b)$ and $\hat{\pi}$ is the stationary vector computed from $\hat{A}$ (see Def. 9).*

The ML model is a maximum likelihood estimate of the quotient MC TP/κ, where κ is the observable partition. Furthermore the stationary distribution of TP/κ fits the letter distribution observed in the sample. The letter distribution is however not sufficient to reproduce the dynamics of the target machine. For instance, if the letters of s were alphabetical sorted, the stationary distribution of the ML model would be unchanged. In order to better fit the target dynamics, the induced model is further required to comply with the MFPT between the blocks of $TP/\!/\kappa$, that is between the letters observed in the sample.

Definition 18 (MFPT Matrix Estimate). *Given a string s defined on an alphabet Σ, $\hat{M}$ is a $|\Sigma| \times |\Sigma|$ matrix where $\hat{M}_{ab}$ is the average number of symbols after an occurrence of a in s to observe the first occurrence of b.*

5.2   Induction Algorithm

Given a target POMM TP and a random walk string s built from TP, the objective of our induction algorithm is to construct a model fitting the stationary distribution and the MFPT estimated from the sample. This algorithm starts from the stationary maximum likelihood model ML, which complies with the stationary distribution. Iterative state splitting in the current model allows to increase the fit to the MFPT, while preserving the stationary distribution. The induction algorithm is sketched hereafter.

At each iteration, a state q is selected by the function `selectStateToSplit` in an arbitrary order. During the call to `splitState`, the state q is split into two new states q_1 and q_2 as depicted in Fig. 6. The *input states* $i_1, \ldots, i_k$ and *output states* $o_1, \ldots, o_l$ are those directly connected to q in the current model in which all transitions probabilities A are known. Input and output states are not necessarily disjoint.

The topology after splitting provides additional degrees of freedom in the transition probabilities. The new transitions probabilities x, y, z form the variables of an optimization problem, which can be represented by the matrices X $(k \times 2), Y$ $(2 \times l)$ and Z (2×2). The objective function to be *minimized* is $W(X, Y, Z) = \sum_{i,j=1}^{|\Sigma|} (\hat{M}_{ij} - M_{ij}/\!/\kappa)^2$. In other words, the goal is to find values

Algorithm MARKOVIANSTATESPLIT
Input: A string s resulting from a target POMM TP
    A precision parameter ϵ
Output: A POMM EP

$EP \;\leftarrow$ estimateML(s);   // *Build the ML model (see Def. 17)*
$\hat{M} \;\leftarrow$ sampleMFPT(s);   // *MFPT between the blocks of $TP /\!\!/ \kappa$ (Def. 18)*
$M /\!\!/ \kappa \leftarrow$ blockMFPT(EP);   // *MFPT between the blocks of EP (Def. 15)*

// *Iterate till the MFPT of the current model are close enough to those estimated from s*
while $\sum_{i,j=1}^{|\Sigma|} (\hat{M}_{ij} - M_{ij} /\!\!/ \kappa)^2 \geq \epsilon$ **do**

$\quad q \qquad\;\; \leftarrow$ selectStateToSplit$(EP, \hat{M}, M /\!\!/ \kappa)$;
$\quad EP \;\;\leftarrow$ splitState$(EP, q, \hat{M}, M /\!\!/ \kappa)$; // *Update the current model*
$\quad M /\!\!/ \kappa \leftarrow$ blockMFPT(EP);   // *Recompute MFPT between the blocks of EP*

return EP

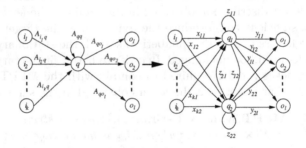

Fig. 6. Splitting of state q.

for X, Y and Z such that the MFPT of the new model are as close as possible to those estimated from s. After the splitting of state q, the blockMFPT function recomputes the MFPT between the blocks of EP. The algorithm is iterated until the squared difference of the MFPT between $TP /\!\!/ \kappa$ and EP fall below the precision threshold ϵ.

Stochastic constraints have to be satisfied in order to keep a proper POMM. Moreover we require the stationary distribution to be preserved for any state $q' \neq q$ and $\pi_{q_1} = \pi_{q_2} = \frac{\pi_q}{2}$. All these constraints can easily be formulated on the problem variables:

$$\forall j = 1, \ldots, k : x_{j1} \geq 0, x_{j2} \geq 0, \; x_{j1} + x_{j2} = A_{i_j q};$$
$$\forall j = 1, \ldots, l : y_{1j} \geq 0, y_{2j} \geq 0, \; y_{1j} + y_{2j} = 2A_{qo_j};$$
$$z_{11}, z_{12}, z_{21}, z_{22} \geq 0, \; z_{11} + z_{12} + z_{21} + z_{22} = 2A_{qq};$$
$$z_{11} + z_{12} + \textstyle\sum_{j=1}^{l} y_{1j} = 1, \; z_{21} + z_{22} + \textstyle\sum_{j=1}^{l} y_{2j} = 1.$$

6   Conclusion and Future Work

We propose in this paper a novel approach to the induction of HMMs. Firstly, the notion of partially observable Markov models (POMMs) is introduced. They form a particular case of HMMs where any state emits a single letter with probability one, but several states can emit the same letter. It is shown that any HMM can be represented by an equivalent POMM. Our induction algorithm aims at finding a POMM fitting a sample drawn from an unknown target POMM. The induced model is built to fit the dynamics of the target machine observed in the sample, not necessarily to match its structure. To do so, a POMM is seen as a lumped process of a Markov chain and the induced POMM is built to fit the stationary distribution and the mean first passage times (MFPT) observed in the sample.

Our ongoing work includes several issues. The `selectStateToSplit` function defines the order in which states are selected for splitting in our induction algorithm. Among all candidate states for splitting, the one providing the largest decrease of the objective function after the split could be considered in the first place. A simple implementation would compute the values of the objective function for all candidate states and would then select the best candidate. More efficient ways for computing this optimal state are under study.

A general solver could be used to solve the optimization problem at each iteration of the MARKOVIANSTATESPLIT algorithm. An efficient implementation of this optimization procedure is under development.

A systematic experimental study of the proposed approach is our very next task. We will focus in particular on practical comparisons with standard probabilistic automata induction algorithms and EM estimation of HMMs using greedy approaches to refine predefined structures. Other perspectives include a formal study of the convergence of this approach as a function of the precision parameter ϵ and extensions to models for which the underlying Markov chain is no longer assumed to be regular.

References

1. R. Carrasco and J. Oncina. Learning deterministic regular gramars from stochastic samples in polynomial time. *Theoretical Informatics and Applications*, 33(1):1–19, 1999.
2. F. Denis and Y. Esposito. Learning classes of probabilistic automata. In *Proc. of 17th Annual Conference on Learning Theory (COLT)*, number 3120 in Lecture Notes in Computer Science, pages 124–139, Banff, Canada, 2004. Springer Verlag.
3. P. Dupont and J.C. Amengual. Smoothing probabilistic automata: an error-correcting approach. In A. Oliveira, editor, *Grammatical Inference: Algorithms and Applications*, number 1891 in Lecture Notes in Artificial Intelligence, pages 51–64, Lisbon, Portugal, 2000. Springer Verlag.
4. P. Dupont and L. Chase. Using symbol clustering to improve probabilistic automaton inference. In *Grammatical Inference, ICGI'98*, number 1433 in Lecture Notes in Artificial Intelligence, pages 232–243, Ames, Iowa, 1998. Springer Verlag.

5. P. Dupont, F. Denis, and Y. Esposito. Links between Probabilistic Automata and Hidden Markov Models: probability distributions, learning models and induction algorithms. *Pattern Recognition*, 2004. to appear in Special Issue on Grammatical Inference Techniques & Applications.
6. R. Durbin, S. Eddy, A. Krogh, and G. Mitchison. *Biological sequence analysis*. Cambridge University Press, 1998.
7. D. Freitag and A. McCallum. Information extraction with hmms and shrinkage. In *Proc. of the AAAI-99 Workshop on Machine Learning for Information Extraction*, 1999.
8. D. Freitag and A. McCallum. Information extraction with HMM structures learned by stochastic optimization. In *Proc. of the Seventeenth National Conference on Artificial Intelligence, AAAI*, pages 584–589, 2000.
9. J.G. Kemeny and J.L. Snell. *Finite Markov Chains*. Springer-Verlag, 1983.
10. C. Kermorvant and P. Dupont. Stochastic grammatical inference with multinomial tests. In P. Adriaans, H. Fernau, and M. van Zaanen, editors, *Proceedings of the 6th International Colloquium on Grammatical Inference: Algorithms and Applications*, number 2484 in Lecture Notes in Artificial Intelligence, pages 149–160, Amsterdam, the Netherlands, September 2002. Springer Verlag.
11. E. Levin and R. Pieraccini. Planar hidden markov modeling: from speech to optical character recognition. In C.L. Giles, S.J. Hanton, and J.D. Cowan, editors, *Advances in Neural Information Processing Systems*, volume 5, pages 731–738. Morgan Kauffman, 1993.
12. D. Llorens, J.-M. Vilar, and F. Casacuberta. Finite state language models smoothed using n-grams. *International Journal of Pattern Recognition and Artificial Intelligence*, 16(3):275–289, 2002.
13. J. R. Norris. *Markov Chains*. Cambridge University Press, United Kingdom, 1997.
14. M. Ostendorf and H. Singer. Hmm topology design using maximum likelihood successive state splitting. *Computer Speech and Language*, 11:17–41, 1997.
15. L. Rabiner and B.-H. Juang. *Fundamentals of Speech Recognition*. Prentice-Hall, 1993.
16. D. Ron, Y. Singer, and N. Tishby. Learning probabilistic automata with variable memory length. In *Proceedings of the Seventh Annual Conference on Computational Learning Theory*, New Brunswick, NJ, 1994. ACM Press.
17. H. Rulot and E. Vidal. An efficient algorithm for the inference of circuit-free automata. In G. Ferraté, T. Pavlidis, A. Sanfeliu, and H. Bunke, editors, *Advances in Structural and Syntactic Pattern Recognition*, pages 173–184. NATO ASI, Springer-Verlag, 1988.
18. A. Stolcke. *Bayesian Learning of Probabilistic Language Models*. Ph. D. dissertation, University of California, 1994.
19. F. Thollard, P. Dupont, and C. de la Higuera. Probabilistic DFA Inference using Kullback-Leibler Divergence and Minimality. In *Seventeenth International Conference on Machine Learning*, pages 975–982. Morgan Kauffman, 2000.

Learning Node Selecting Tree Transducer from Completely Annotated Examples*

Julien Carme, Aurélien Lemay, and Joachim Niehren

Mostrare project, INRIA Futurs, Lille, France

Abstract. A base problem in Web information extraction is to find appropriate queries for informative nodes in trees. We propose to learn queries for nodes in trees automatically from examples. We introduce *node selecting tree transducer* (NSTT) and show how to induce deterministic NSTTs in polynomial time from completely annotated examples. We have implemented learning algorithms for NSTTs, started applying them to Web information extraction, and present first experimental results.

Keywords: Web information extraction, tree automata and logics, grammatical inference.

1 Introduction

Web documents in HTML or XML form trees with nodes containing text. The tree structure is relevant for Web information extraction (IE) from well structured documents as created by databases. Many recent approaches to Web IE therefore focus on tree structure [5, 10, 14] rather than pure text [15, 22].

A base problem in Web information extraction (IE) is to find appropriate queries for informative nodes in trees. In Fig. 1, for instance, one might want to extract all Email addresses (single-slot IE). This can be done by querying for all links in the last line of each table, i.e., for all A-nodes whose TR-node ancestor is the last child of some TABLE-node. Alternatively, one might want to ask for all pairs of names and email addresses (multi-slots IE). This problem can be reduced to iterated single-slot IE: first search for all tables that encompass the pairs and then extract the components from the tables.

Gottlob et. al. [10] advocate for monadic Datalog as representation language for node queries in trees. This logic programming language is highly expressive (all regular node queries in trees can be expressed) while enjoying efficient algorithms for answering queries. The Lixto system for multi-slot IE [1] supplies a graphical user interface by which to interactively specify and test node queries in monadic Datalog.

Tree automata yield an alternative representation formalism [18, 21, 8, 3] that is particularly relevant for grammatical inference. Run-based node queries by

---

* This research was partially supported by: "CPER 2000-2006, Contrat de Plan état – région Nord/Pas-de-Calais: axe TACT, projet TIC"; fonds européens FEDER "TIC – Fouille Intelligente de données – Traitement Intelligent des Connaissance" OBJ 2-phasing out – 2001/3 – 4.1 – n 3. And by "ACI masse de données ACIMDD"

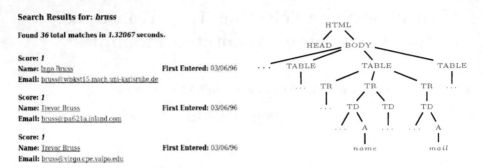

Fig. 1. A simple Web page, its corresponding tree.

tree automata can be translated in linear time into monadic Datalog, and in non-elementary time back due to Thatcher and Wright's famous theorem [23]. A more recent problem here is to deal with the *unrankedness* of trees [3] as in HTML and XML, by encoding into binary trees.

The objective of the present paper is to learn tree automata that represent node queries in trees from completely annotated examples. Query induction might be useful in order to circumvent manual query specification as in Lixto. Completely annotated examples consist of trees where all nodes are annotated by Booleans, stating whether a node is selected or not. We introduce *node selecting tree transducers* (NSTT) for representing node queries in trees, and show how to infer *deterministic* NSTTs from examples by variants of the RPNI algorithm [19]. We have implemented several versions of our learning algorithm and started to apply them to Web IE, so that we can present first experimental results.

Related Work. Kosala et. al. [14] learn tree automata representing node queries in trees from less informative examples, which specify selected nodes but not unselected ones. This has the advantage that complete annotations for all nodes are not needed, but restricts the class of learnable queries to those representable by local or k-testable tree automata. Deterministic NSTTs, in contrast, can represent all regular node queries in trees (see subsequent work [2]).

Node queries of bounded length in monadic-second order (MSO) logic over trees are shown PAC learnable in [11]. Variants of RPNI for inducing sub-sequential text transducers were proposed in [12]; these transducers may alter the structure of words in contrast to NSTTs which only relabel nodes in trees. Chidlovskii [4] proposes induction of word transducers for Web IE.

2   Node Queries in Binary Trees

Before considering the particularities of HTML and XML trees, we will deal with node queries for binary trees. We start from an finite alphabet Σ consisting of binary function symbols f and constants a. A *binary tree* t over Σ is a term that satisfies the grammar:

$$t ::= f(t_1, t_2) \mid a$$

For every tree t let $\mathsf{nodes}(t) \subseteq \{1,2\}^*$ be the set of *nodes* of tree t. This set determines the shape t, i.e., two trees have the same shape if and only if they have the same node sets. The empty word ϵ always addresses the root of a tree; the first child of node v is node $v1$ and its second child is $v2$. We write $t(v)$ for the label of nodes $v \in \mathsf{nodes}(t)$. The size $|t|$ is the cardinality of $\mathsf{nodes}(t)$. The tree $t = f_1(a_1, f_2(a_1, a_2))$, for instance, has the node set $\{\varepsilon, 1, 2, 21, 22\}$. Its root is labeled by $t(\varepsilon) = f_1$ while its third leaf is labeled by $t(22) = a_2$.

Definition 1. *A (monadic) node query in binary trees is a function q that associates to each binary tree t a set of nodes $q(t) \subseteq \mathsf{nodes}(t)$.*

The query **leaf** associates the set of leaves to a given tree, i.e., those nodes that don't have children. If $t = f(a_1, f(a_1, a_2))$ then $\mathbf{leaf}(t) = \{11, 21, 22\}$.

3   Tree Automata

We are interested in regular node queries in trees that can be defined equivalently by tree automata, in monadic Datalog, or MSO over trees. (See [3] for the case of unranked trees.) Here, we recall a representation formalisms for node queries based on successful runs of tree automata [21, 8, 3].

A *tree automaton* A over signature Σ consists of a finite set $\mathsf{states}(A)$ of states, a set $\mathsf{final}(A) \subseteq \mathsf{states}(A)$ of final states, and a finite set $\mathsf{rules}(A)$ of rules of the form $f(p_1, p_2) \to p$ or $a \to p$ where $p, p_1, p_2 \in \mathsf{states}(A)$, f a binary function symbol and a a constant in Σ. The *size* $|A|$ of a tree automaton A is the number of its states plus the number of symbols occurring in its rules.

A *run* r of a tree automaton A on a tree t is a binary tree over $\mathsf{states}(A)$ of the same shape, i.e. $\mathsf{nodes}(r) = \mathsf{nodes}(t)$, such that for all $v \in \mathsf{nodes}(t)$ and $f, a \in \Sigma$: if $t(v) = f$ then $f(r(v1), r(v2)) \to r(v) \in \mathsf{rules}(A)$, and if $t(v) = a$ then $a \to r(v) \in \mathsf{rules}(A)$. A run r of A on t is *successful* if $r(\varepsilon) \in \mathsf{final}(A)$.

Let A_0 be an automaton with 3 states $0, 1, 2$, a single final state 2, and the rules: $a \to 0$, $a \to 1$, $f(0, 1) \to 2$. The tree $f(a, a)$ has a unique successful run by A_0, the tree $2(0, 1)$; no other tree permits a successful run with A_0.

Definition 2. *A tree automaton is (bottom-up) deterministic if no two rules have the same left-hand side and unambiguous if no tree permits two successful runs.*

Every deterministic tree automaton is clearly unambiguous, but not conversely. The automaton A_0 above yields a counter example. It is nondeterministic given that tree a permits two distinct runs with A_0, but nevertheless unambiguous given that none of these two runs is successful.

We write $\mathsf{runs}_A(t)$ for the set of all runs of automaton A on tree t and $\mathsf{succ\_runs}_A(t)$ for the subset of all successful runs. A tree automaton *recognizes* all trees t that permit a successful run of A on t. The *language* $L(A)$ of an automaton A contains all trees that A recognizes.

A pair of a tree automaton A over Σ and a set of selection states $P \subseteq$ states(A) defines a node query in trees $t \in \text{tree}_\Sigma$:

$$\text{query}_{A,P}(t) = \{v \mid r \in \text{succ\_runs}_A(t), r(v) \in P\}$$

We call a monadic query q *regular* if it is equal to some $\text{query}_{A,P}$. Thatcher and Wright's famous theorem [23] proves that a query is regular if and only if it can be defined by a MSO-formula over binary trees with a single free node variable.

4   Node Selection Tree Transducer

We will introduce NSTTs, a new representation formalism for regular node queries in trees suitable for grammatical inference.

Every subset $q(t) \subseteq \text{nodes}(t)$ can be identified with a tree over Bool with the same shape, such that the Boolean values $q(t)(v)$ satisfy for all $v \in \text{nodes}(t)$:

$$q(t)(v) \leftrightarrow v \in q(t)$$

The query application $\mathbf{leaf}(f(a, g(a, b)))$, for instance, yields the Boolean tree false(true, false(true, true)).

Given two trees t over Σ and β over Bool with the same shape, we define a tree $t \times \beta$ over $\Sigma \times$ Bool by requiring for all $v \in \text{nodes}(t) = \text{nodes}(\beta) = \text{nodes}(t \times \beta)$:

$$(t \times \beta)(v) = (t(v), \beta(v))$$

A tree language L over $\Sigma \times$ Bool is *functional* (resp. *total*) if for all $t \in \text{tree}_\Sigma$ there exists at most (resp. at least) one tree $\beta \in \text{tree}_{\text{Bool}}$ such that $t \times \beta \in L$.

We associate tree languages lan_q over $\Sigma \times$ Bool to queries q in trees over Σ:

$$\text{lan}_q = \{t \times q(t) \mid t \in \text{tree}_\Sigma\}$$

Tree languages lan_q are always functional and total. Conversely, we will associate queries to functional tree languages. Let $\text{total}(L)$ be the functional total language containing L and contained in $L \cup \text{tree}_{\Sigma \times \{\text{false}\}}$. Functional languages L define node queries in trees that satisfies for all trees $t \in \text{tree}_\Sigma$ and $\beta \in \text{tree}_{\text{Bool}}$:

$$\text{query}_L(t) = \beta \text{ iff } t \times \beta \in \text{total}(L)$$

We have $\text{query}_{\text{lan}_q} = q$ for all node queries q in trees and $\text{lan}_{\text{query}_L} = \text{total}(L)$ for all functional tree languages L. For every functional tree language L there exists exactly one query q with $\text{lan}_q = L$, but for some queries q there exist many functional tree languages L with $\text{total}(L) = \text{lan}_q$. This ambiguity has to be treated carefully.

Definition 3. *An* NSTT *is a tree automaton A whose language $L(A)$ is functional. A* NSTT*-query has the form* $\text{query}_{L(A)}$ *where A is an* NSTT.

Proposition 1. NSTT*-queries are regular.*

Proof. Given a NSTT A we define a projection tree automaton $\pi(A)$ over Σ. We set $\mathsf{states}(\pi(A)) = \mathsf{states}(A) \times \mathsf{Bool}$, $\mathsf{final}(\pi(A)) = \mathsf{final}(A) \times \mathsf{Bool}$, and fix the following automata rules by:

$$\frac{(f,b)(p_1,p_2) \rightarrow p \in \mathsf{rules}(A)}{f((p_1,b_1),(p_2,b_2)) \rightarrow (p,b) \in \mathsf{rules}(\pi(A))} \qquad \frac{(a,b)(p_1,p_2) \rightarrow p \in \mathsf{rules}(A)}{a \rightarrow (p,b) \in \mathsf{rules}(\pi(A))}$$

The subsequent Lemma 1 yields $\mathsf{query}_{L(A)} = \mathsf{query}_{\pi(A),\mathsf{states}(A) \times \{\mathsf{true}\}}$.

Lemma 1. $r \in \mathsf{runs}_A(t \times \beta)$ *iff* $r \times \beta \in \mathsf{runs}_{\pi(A)}(t)$.

The converse of Prop. 1 holds as proved by the authors a follow up paper [2]. The construction in the proof shows NSTT-queries can be answered efficiently, in that $\mathsf{query}_{L(A)}(t)$ can be computed in time $O(|A| * |t|)$ from NSTTs A and trees t. It is sufficient to transform NSTT-queries into automata queries (in linear time) which can be answered in linear time. We finally present a new polynomial time algorithm for testing whether a deterministic automaton A is an NSTT.

Proposition 2. *The language of a deterministic tree automaton A over $\Sigma \times \mathsf{Bool}$ is functional if and only if the projection $\pi(A)$ to Σ is unambiguous.*

Proof. For the one direction, let A be deterministic (and thus unambiguous) and $L(A)$ functional. Suppose $r_1 \times \beta_1, r_2 \times \beta_2 \in \mathsf{succ\_runs}_{\pi(A)}(t)$ for some $t \in \mathsf{tree}_\Sigma$. Lemma 1 yields $r_1 \in \mathsf{succ\_runs}_A(t \times \beta_1)$ and $r_2 \in \mathsf{succ\_runs}_A(t \times \beta_2)$. The functionality of A implies that $t \times \beta_1 = t \times \beta_2$ and thus $\beta_1 = \beta_2$. The unambiguity of A yields $r_1 = r_2$ so that $r_1 \times \beta_1 = r_2 \times \beta_2$. This proves that $\pi(A)$ is unambiguous.

For the converse, assume that $\pi(A)$ is unambiguous and suppose $t \times \beta_1, t \times \beta_2 \in L(A)$. Let $r_1 \in \mathsf{succ\_runs}_A(t \times \beta_1)$ and $r_2 \in \mathsf{succ\_runs}_A(t \times \beta_2)$. Lemma 1 yields $r_1 \times \beta_1, r_2 \times \beta_2 \in \mathsf{succ\_runs}_{\pi(A)}(t)$. The unambiguity of $\pi(A)$ implies $\beta_1 = \beta_2$, i.e., $L(A)$ is functional.

Proposition 3. *Unambiguity of tree automata can be tested in polynomial time.*

Proof. An algorithm for word automata can be found in [6]. Here, we test unambiguity for tree automata A. The algorithm is based on the binary relation $\mathsf{drst}_A \subseteq \mathsf{states}(A) \times \mathsf{states}(A)$, where $\mathsf{drst}_A(p,p')$ means that two distinct runs of A label the root of the same tree with respectively p and p'.

$$\mathsf{drst}_A(p,p') \text{ iff } \exists t \in \mathsf{tree}_\Sigma \exists r,r' \in \mathsf{runs}_A(t).\ r \neq r' \wedge r(\epsilon) = p \wedge r'(\epsilon) = p'$$

The automaton A is ambiguous if and only if there exists $p \in \mathsf{final}(A)$ such that $\mathsf{drst}_A(p,p)$. It remains to compute the relation drst_A. We assume that A does not contain useless states, which are not used in any runs. We compute the relation by applying the rules of Fig. 2 exhaustively.

The first rule permits to derive runs for constant a-trees leading into distinct states. If we can apply the second rule, there are trees t_1, t_2 with runs into states p_1, p_2 respectively, since there are no useless states. The tree $f(t_1, t_2)$ then

$$\mathsf{drst}_A(p, p') \Leftrightarrow$$

$(a \to p \in \mathsf{rules}(A) \wedge a \to p' \in \mathsf{rules}(A) \wedge p \neq p')$
$\vee\ (f(p_1, p_2) \to p \in \mathsf{rules}(A) \wedge f(p_1, p_2) \to p' \in \mathsf{rules}(A) \wedge p \neq p')$
$\vee\ (f(p_1, p_2) \to p \in \mathsf{rules}(A) \wedge f(p'_1, p_2) \to p' \in \mathsf{rules}(A) \wedge \mathsf{drst}_A(p_1, p'_1))$
$\vee\ (f(p_1, p_2) \to p \in \mathsf{rules}(A) \wedge f(p_1, p'_2) \to p' \in \mathsf{rules}(A) \wedge \mathsf{drst}_A(p_2, p'_2))$
$\vee\ (f(p_1, p_2) \to p \in \mathsf{rules}(A) \wedge f(p'_1, p'_2) \to p' \in \mathsf{rules}(A) \wedge \mathsf{drst}_A(p_1, p'_1) \wedge \mathsf{drst}_A(p_2, p'_2))$

Fig. 2. Testing non-ambiguity.

permits two distinct runs in p'_1 and p'_2. The third rule is recursive. Suppose, there are distinct runs on t_1 leading to p_1 and p'_1 and a run on t_2 into p_2, then there exists distinct runs on $f(t_1, t_2)$ leading into p and p' respectively (even if $p = p'$). The forth and fifth rule are similar.

The whole algorithm is polynomial in the size of A. We can apply at most $\mathsf{states}(A)^2$ rules, when avoid to infer the same pair $\mathsf{drst}_A(p, p')$ twice. Every rule application can be done in polynomial time in the size of the automaton.

Corollary 1. *Testing whether a deterministic tree automaton over $\Sigma \times \mathsf{Bool}$ is an NSTT can be done in polynomial time.*

Proof. For a deterministic NSTT A, we check the non-ambiguity of its projection $\pi(A)$ (Prop. 2). This can be done in polynomial time (Prop. 3).

5   Inducing NSTT-Queries

We show how to induce NSTT-queries for nodes in trees from completely annotated examples, i.e., pair trees of the form $t \times \beta$. Let $\mathsf{samples}^a$ be the set of all completely annotated examples. Every tree $t \times q(t)$ is a completely annotated example for q. Complete annotations thus specify for all nodes of a tree, whether they are selected or not. Given that completely annotated examples express positive and negative information, it should not come as a surprise that we will learn by the RPNI algorithm for regular positive and negative inference [16, 19, 20].

5.1   Identification in the Limit

We recall the learning model of identification in the limit [9] and apply it to identification of node queries in trees.

Definition 4. *Let* class *and* examples *be sets related by a binary relation called consistency, and $\equiv$ an equivalence relation on* class. *Let* samples *be the set of all finite subset of* examples. *A sample in* samples *is consistent with a class member if all its examples are.*

Members of class *are identifiable in the limit from* examples *if there are computable functions* learner : samples $\to$ class *mapping samples to class members and* char : class $\to$ samples *computing consistent samples for all class members – called characteristic samples – such that* learner$(S) \equiv M$ *for every member $M \in$* class *and sample $S \supseteq$* char(M) *consistent with M.*

Identification of NSTT-queries from completely annotated examples is an instance of Def. 4 where class $= \{\text{query}_{L(A)} \mid A \text{ is an NSTT}\}$, examples contains all completely annotated examples, and equivalence $\equiv$ of NSTT-queries is equality. An annotated example $t \times \beta$ is consistent with a query q if $q(t) = \beta$.

Identifying deterministic NSTTs from completely annotated samples is another case. Here class $= \{A \mid A \text{ is an NSTT}\}$, and an NSTT A is consistent with a completely annotated example if $\text{query}_{L(A)}$ is. The equivalence $A \equiv A'$ is total language equality $\text{total}(L(A)) = \text{total}(L(A'))$.

Identification of regular tree languages from positive and negative examples is the third case. Given some set $T = T_\Sigma$ of trees, let class $\subseteq 2^{2^T}$ be a class of regular tree languages. A *positive example* is an element of $T \times \{\text{true}\}$, a *negative example* an element of $T \times \{\text{false}\}$. Let $\text{samples}(T)$ be the set all samples with positive or a negative example. An example (t, b) is consistent with a language $L \in$ class if $t \in L \Leftrightarrow b$. Equivalence $\equiv$ of tree languages is language equality.

Identification of deterministic tree automata from positive and negative examples is similar. Again, two automata are equivalent if they have the same language; an automaton is consistent with an examples if its language is.

Proposition 4. *Identification of NSTT-queries from completely annotated examples can be reduced to identification of regular tree languages from positive and negative examples.*

Proof. Completely annotated examples $t \times \beta$ for a query q correspond positive examples $(t \times \beta, \text{true})$ for lan_q and furthermore imply negative example $(t \times \beta', \text{false})$ for all $\beta' \neq \beta$. Let $T = \text{tree}_{\Sigma \times \text{Bool}}$. We define a function pn : $\text{samples}^a \to \text{samples}(T)$ by samples with completely annotated examples to samples of positive and negative examples:

$$\text{pn}(S) = \{(t \times \beta', b) \mid t \times \beta \in S, b \Leftrightarrow (\beta = \beta')\}$$

Let class the class of regular tree languages over T. We assume that languages in class can be identified from positive and negative examples by functions learner : $\text{samples}(T) \to$ class and char : class $\to \text{samples}(T)$.

Let class$'$ be the set of NSTT-queries. We show that queries in class$'$ can be identified from completely annotated example by the following functions:

learner$'$: samples$^a \to$ class$'$, learner$'(S) = \text{query}_{\text{learner}(\text{pn}(S))}$
char$'$: class$' \to$ samples^a,   char$'(q) = \{t \times \beta \in \text{lan}_q \mid (t \times \beta', b) \in \text{char}(\text{lan}_q)\}$

First note that char$'(q)$ is always consistent with q. If $t \times \beta \in$ char$'(q)$ then by definition $t \times \beta \in \text{lan}_q$ and thus $q(t) = \beta$.

Second, notice that $\text{pn}(\text{char}'(q)) \supseteq \text{char}(\text{lan}_q)$. For positive examples $t \times \beta' \in$ char(lan_q), clearly $t \times \beta' \in$ char$'(q)$. For negative examples $(t \times \beta', \text{false}) \in$ char(lan_q) there is some $t \times \beta \in \text{lan}_q$ since lan_q is total, with $\beta \neq \beta'$ since lan_q is functional and char(lan_q) consistent with lan_q. Hence $t \times \beta \in$ char$'(q)$ so that $(t \times \beta', \text{false}) \in \text{pn}(\text{char}'(q))$.

Let $q \in$ class and $S \supseteq$ char$'(q)$ consistent with L. Then $\text{pn}(S) \supseteq \text{char}(q)$ and $\text{pn}(S)$ consistent with lan_q. Identifying regular languages yields $\text{learner}(\text{pn}(S)) = \text{lan}_q$, i.e. learner$'(S) = \text{query}_{\text{lan}_q} = q$ as required for identifying NSTT-queries.

Theorem 1. *NSTT-queries for nodes in trees can be identified in the limit from completely annotated examples.*

Proof. The problem is equivalent to identifying regular tree languages from positive and negative examples (Prop. 4) which can be done by RPNI [16, 19, 20]. □

5.2   Identification in Polynomial Time and Data

We now show how to identify deterministic NSTTs in polynomial time from completely annotated examples.

Identification in polynomial time and data is identification in the limit with functions learner in polynomial time and char in polynomial space [7].

The classical RPNI-algorithm identifies deterministic automata from positive and negative examples in polynomial time and data [19, 16]. It applies to tree languages similarly as to word languages [20]. For a given signature, it computes a polynomial time function learner$_{\text{RPNI}}$ mapping samples of positive and negative examples to deterministic tree automata, and polynomial space function char$_{\text{RPNI}}$ of the inverse type.

Theorem 2. *Let a completely annotated example $t \times \beta$ be consistent with a NSTT A if query$_{L(A)}(t) = \beta$, and two NSTTs be equivalent if they define the same queries. Given this consistency and equivalence relations, we can identify deterministic NSTTs in polynomial time and data from completely annotated examples.*

Proof. For identifying deterministic NSTTs from completely annotated examples, we want to compute the function learner$_{\text{RPNI}} \circ$ pn which inputs completely annotated examples over $\Sigma \times$ Bool, transforms them into positive and negative examples and then outputs the result of the RPNI learner for the signature $\Sigma \times$ Bool. This output is a NSTT whose associated language is total, which is the representant of its equivalence class.

Unfortunately, the function pn is not in polynomial space, given that the size of its output may be exponential. In order to solve this problem, we propose a more efficient implementation of the function learner$_{\text{RPNI}} \circ$ pn, the algorithm tRPNI, a variant of RPNI.

Lets us recall the RPNI-algorithm [20, 19, 16]. RPNI inputs a sample of positive and negative examples. It first computes a deterministic automaton which recognizes the set of positive examples in the sample. It then merges states exhaustively in some fixed order. A merging operation applies to the recent deterministic automaton A and two states $q_1, q_2 \in$ states(q) and returns a deterministic automaton det_merge(A, q_1, q_2). A deterministic merge is a merge followed by recursive merges needed to preserve preserve determinism. For example, merging q_1 and q_2 in an automaton with rules $f(q_1) \to q_3$ and $f(q_2) \to q_4$ requires merging q_3 with q_4. A merging operation is licensed only if det_merge(A, q_1, q_2) is consistent with all negative examples in the sample. The main loop of RPNI thus performs at most quadratically many functionality tests and merging operations.

The algorithm tRPNI behaves as RPNI except that it checks differently whether deterministic merging operation are licenced. It tests whether the language of

$(a, \text{true}) \to 2$
$(a, \text{false}) \to 1$
$(@, \text{false})(2, 2) \to 3$
$(@, \text{false})(3, 1) \to 4$
$(@, \text{false})(2, 4) \to 5$
Final states : $\{5\}$

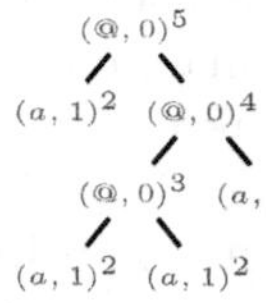

$(@, 0)^5$
$(a, 1)^2 \quad (@, 0)^4$
$(@, 0)^3 \quad (a, 0)^1$
$(a, 1)^2 \quad (a, 1)^2$

$(a, \text{true}) \to 2$
$(a, \text{false}) \to 1$
$(@, \text{false})(2, 2) \to 1$
$(@, \text{false})(1, 1) \to 2$
Final states : $\{1\}$

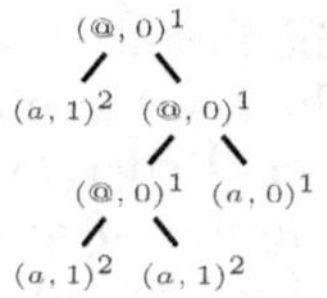

$(@, 0)^1$
$(a, 1)^2 \quad (@, 0)^1$
$(@, 0)^1 \quad (a, 0)^1$
$(a, 1)^2 \quad (a, 1)^2$

Fig. 3. The initial automaton and its run on the example tree.

Fig. 4. The inferred NSTT and its run on the example tree.

det_merge(A, q_1, q_2) is functional. It thereby avoids to enumerate implicit negative examples for functional language once and for all. And fortunately, we can check for functionality in polynomial time in the automaton size (Corollary 1).

Conversely, we compute characteristic samples for NSTTs A as we did before for query$_{L(A)}$ in the proof of Prop. 4: char$(A) = \{t \times \beta \in \text{total}(L(A)) \mid (t \times \beta', b) \in \text{char}_{\text{RPNI}}(A)\}$. Since lan$_{\text{query}_{L(A)}} = \text{total}(L(A))$ it follows that all examples in char(A) are consistent with A or with ony other NSTT in its equivalence class.

5.3 Example

We illustrate how the learning algorithm works in a simplified case. We want to extract leaves that are on an odd level on trees on the alphabet $\Sigma = \{@, a\}$.

The first step of the algorithm is the construction of the initial automaton. This automaton, and its run on the input sample is indicate in Fig. 3. Merges are then being performed following the order of states. det_merge$(A_2, 1, 2)$ is rejected for lack of functionality. Following merge, det_merge$(A_3, 1, 3)$, is then accepted. Then det_merge$(A_4, 1, 4)$ is rejected. det_merge$(A_4, 2, 4)$ is accepted (which implies the merges of states 5 and 1 by propagation of the determinism). This results in the automaton presented in Fig. 4. The example being well chosen, it appears that this NSTT performs the wanted annotation.

6 Application to Web Information Extraction

We have implemented the tRPNI algorithm and started applying it to Web IE. We report first results of this work in progress and discuss some of the problems that arise.

6.1 Modeling HTML Trees

Unranked trees. HTML or XML form *unranked trees.* We encode unranked trees into binary trees. We use the Currying inspired encoding of [3] in order to map to stepwise tree automata, rather than the more frequent first-child next-sibling encoding as in selection automata [8].

The unranked tree TABLE(TR(TD),TR(TD),TR(TD)), for instance, is translated into the binary tree TABLE@(TR@TD)@(TR@TD)@(TR@TD) with a single binary symbol @. Completely annotated examples for unranked trees are translated into completely annotated examples on ranked encodings, too. Node annotations in unranked trees become leaf annotations in binary encodings. Inner @-nodes in binary encodings correspond to edges in unranked trees. As we do not wish to select edges, we label all @-nodes by false.

Infinite alphabets. Leaves of HTML trees may contain arbitrary texts. So far however, we assumed finite alphabets. In our experiments, we ignore leaf contents completely, by abstracting all texts into a single symbol.

Node attributes. Node attributes are currently ignored. Each HTML tag is abstracted into its corresponding symbol, whatever its attributes are.

6.2 Approaching Problems

A nice feature of RPNI is that does never do wrong generalizations when applied to a characteristic sample. In practice, however, we only dispose small samples that are seldom characteristic.

Wrong generalizations. Lacking negative information is particularly embarrassing, as it leads to wrong generalizations. This may have the consequence that parts of documents cannot be recognized by inferred NSTTs, so that NSTT-queries do not select any nodes from such documents. We have designed two heuristics to deal with that problem.

Typed merging. We use typing as inspired from [13] and forbid states with the different types to be merged. So far, we experiment with a fairly basic typing system: leaves of binary encodings are typed by their corresponding HTML tag, while inner nodes inherit the type of their first child. Types in annotated examples become types in the initial automaton. This prevents many wrong generalization, while allowing most of the meaningful ones. Our typing reflect the structure of encodings of unranked trees and that we do not want to merge nodes with different HTML tags.

Wild-card interpretation. We relax the querying interpretation of inferred NSTTs. Consider a tree $t_1@t_2$. If our deterministic NSTT does not have any run on t_2, but a run for t_1 leading into state q_1 and if there exists a single rule of the form $q_1@q_2 \rightarrow q$ then we permit relaxed runs of $t_1@t_2$ into q that labels all nodes in t_2 by wild-cards. Nodes labeled by wild-cards are never selected.

6.3 Experiments

We have experimented with Okra and Bigbook tasks from the RISE benchmarks(www.isi.edu/info-agents/RISE). Both Okra and Bigbook are computer generated web pages which represent sets of personal informations. The extraction task is to extract e-mail addresses. Results are given Fig.5. In Okra, one example is enough to achieve good results. Without wild-cards, performances are weaker in Bigbook, even though the task does not seem more complex than with Okra. Bigbook illustrates the problem of wrong generalizations. At the end of each document, every letter of the alphabet is indicated, either as a link or as standard text. With few examples, tRPNI fails to infer a NSTT that recognizes this part of the document, which is totally irrelevant to the querying task. At the same time, other relevant part of the document are properly labelled. Permitting wild-card interpretations helps in this case.

Okra				
# of Examples	Accuracy	size of initial NSTT	size of inferred NSTT	Learning time
1	100 %	72	24	1.02 s
2	100 %	82	24	1.24 s
3	100 %	85	24	1.34 s
Bigbook				
1	76% / 100 %*	162	37	4.14 s
2	85% / 100 %*	172	42	7.12 s
3	100 %	179	48	9.52 s

Fig. 5. Experimental results on Okra and Bigbook benchmarks. (* indicates results without and with the use of wild-cards).

Experiments with more complex tasks so far often yield poor results, because of lack of informations in pure structure and wrong generalizations.

6.4   Possible Improvements

Better text abstraction. The conversion of HTML node information into symbols could be improved using text-based information extraction techniques. For instance, instead of using one generic symbol for leaves, one could classify leafs in several clusters such as names, dates, numbers, etc.

Better merging orders. A crucial parameter of RPNI (and tRPNI) is the order in which state merges are performed. The technique of *evidence driven state merging* [17] could be applied here. The distance between nodes in the encoded unranked trees should be taken into account in this order.

7   Conclusion

We have presented node selecting tree transducer to represent node queries in trees. We have proposed a variant of RPNI that can identify NSTTs in polynomial time from annotated examples. We have started applying our learning algorithm to Web information extraction and could report first encouraging results.

In follow up work [3], we have shown that all regular queries in trees can be represented by NSTTs. On open theoretical question is, whether deterministic NSTTs with a total languages can be identified in polynomial time.

In future work, we plan to continue improving our learning algorithms in practice. The open challenge remains, to built feasible and reliable learning based systems for Web information extraction.

References

1. R. Baumgartner, S. Flesca, and G. Gottlob. Visual web information extraction with lixto. In *The VLDB Journal*, pages 119–128, 2001.
2. J. Carme, A. Lemay, J. Niehren, and A. Terlutte. Learning regular node queries in trees from completely annotated examples. Forthcoming. 2004.

3. J. Carme, J. Niehren, and M. Tommasi. Querying unranked trees with stepwise tree automata. Intenational Conf. on Rewriting Techniques and Applications, 2004.
4. B. Chidlovskii. Wrapping web information providers by transducer induction. In *Proc. ECML*, volume 2167 of *LNAI*, p 61 – 73, 2001.
5. W. W. Cohen, M. Hurst, and L. S. Jensen. A flexible learning system for wrapping tables and lists in html documents. In *Web Document Analysis: Challenges and Opportunities*, MPAI, WSP 2003.
6. F. Coste and D. Fredouille. Efficient ambiguity detection in c-nfa. In *Grammatical Inference: Algorithms and Applications, LNAI 1891*, 2000.
7. C. de la Higuera. Characteristic sets for polynomial grammatical inference. *Machine Learning*, 27:125–137, 1997.
8. M. Frick, M. Grohe, and C. Koch. Query evaluation on compressed trees. In *Proc. LICS 2003*, 2003.
9. E. Gold. Language identification in the limit. *Inform. Control*, 10:447–474, 1967.
10. G. Gottlob and C. Koch. Monadic queries over tree-structured data. In *LICS*, 2002.
11. M. Gruhe and G. Turan. Learnability and definability in trees and similar structures. In *STACS'02, LNCS 2285*, p 645–658. 2002.
12. P. Garcia. J. Oncina and E. Vidal. Learning subsequential transducers for pattern recognition and interpretation tasks. *IEEE Trans. Patt. Anal. and Mach. Intell.*, 15:448–458, 1993.
13. C. Kermorvant and C. de la Higuera. Learning language with help. In *ICGI 2002*.
14. R. Kosala, M. Bruynooghe, J. V. den Bussche, and H. Blockeel. Information extraction from web documents based on local unranked tree automaton inference. In *(IJCAI-2003)*.
15. N. Kushmerick. *Wrapper Induction for Information Extraction*. PhD thesis, Univ. of Washington, 1997.
16. K. Lang. Random DFA's can be approximately learned from sparse uniform examples. In *Workshop on Comput. Learning Theory*, p 45–52. ACM Press, 1992.
17. K. J. Lang, B. A. Pearlmutter, and R. A. Price. Results of the Abbadingo one DFA learning competition and a new evidence-driven state merging algorithm. In *ICGI 98, LNAI 1433*.
18. F. Neven and T. Schwentick. Query automata over finite trees. *TCS*, 275(1-2):633–674, 2002.
19. J. Oncina and P. Garcia. Inferring regular languages in polynomial update time. In *Pattern Recognition and Image Analysis*, p 49–61, 1992.
20. J. Oncina and P. García. Inference of recognizable tree sets. Tech. report, Universidad de Alicante, 1993. DSIC-II/47/93.
21. H. Seidl, T. Schwentick, and A. Muscholl. Numerical document queries. In *Proceedings of the Symposium on Principles Of Database Systems*, p 155–166, 2003.
22. S. Soderland. Learning information extraction rules for semi-structured and free text. *Machine Learning*, 34(1-3):233–272, 1999.
23. J. W. Thatcher and J. B. Wright. Generalized finite automata with an application to a decision problem of second-order logic. *Mathematical System Theory*, 1968.

Identifying Clusters from Positive Data[*]

John Case[1], Sanjay Jain[2], Eric Martin[3], Arun Sharma[4], and Frank Stephan[2]

[1] Computer and Information Sciences Department, University of Delaware,
Newark, DE 19716-2586, United States of America
case@cis.udel.edu
[2] School of Computing, National University of Singapore, Singapore 117543
{sanjay,fstephan}@comp.nus.edu.sg
[3] School of Computer Science and Engeniering, UNSW Sydney NSW 2052, Australia
emartin@cse.unsw.edu.au
[4] Queensland University of Technology, Division of Research and Commercialization,
GPO Box 2434, Brisbane QLD 4001, Australia
arun.sharma@qut.edu.au

Abstract. The present work studies clustering from an abstract point of view and investigates its properties in the framework of inductive inference. Any class S considered is given by a numbering $A_0, A_1, \ldots$ of nonempty subsets of $\mathbb{N}$ or $\mathbb{Q}^k$ which is also used as a hypothesis space. A clustering task is a finite and nonempty set of indices of pairwise disjoint sets. The class S is said to be clusterable if there is an algorithm which, for every clustering task I, converges in the limit on any text for $\cup_{i \in I} A_i$ to a finite set J of indices of pairwise disjoint clusters such that $\cup_{j \in J} A_j = \cup_{i \in I} A_i$. A class is called semiclusterable if there is such an algorithm which finds a J with the last condition relaxed to $\cup_{j \in J} A_j \supseteq \cup_{i \in I} A_i$.

The relationship between natural topological properties and clusterability is investigated. Topological properties can provide sufficient or necessary conditions for clusterability but they cannot characterize it. On one hand, many interesting conditions make use of both the topological structure of the class and a well-chosen numbering. On the other hand, the clusterability of a class does not depend on the decision which numbering of the class is used as a hypothesis space for the clusterer.

These ideas are demonstrated in the context of geometrically defined classes. Clustering of many of these classes requires besides the text for the clustering task some additional information: the class of convex hulls of finitely many points in a rational vector space can be clustered with the number of clusters as additional information. Similar studies are carried out for polygons with and without holes.

Furthermore, the power of oracles is investigated. The Turing degrees of maximal oracles which permit to solve all computationally intractable aspects of clustering are determined. It is shown that some oracles are trivial in the sense that they do not provide any useful information for clustering at all. Some topologically difficult classes cannot be clustered with the help of any oracle.

[*] J. Case is supported in part by NSF grant number CCR-0208616 and USDA IFAFS grant number 01-04145. S. Jain is supported in part by NUS grant number R252-000-127-112. A. Sharma and F. Stephan have done most of this research while they were working at National ICT Australia which is funded by the Australian Government's Department of Communications, Information Technology and the Arts and the Australian Research Council through Backing Australia's Ability and the ICT Centre of Excellence Program. A full version of this paper is available as a technical report [3].

G. Paliouras and Y. Sakakibara (Eds.): ICGI 2004, LNAI 3264, pp. 103–114, 2004.

1   Introduction

The purpose of the paper is to study the role of computation and topology in the clustering process. To this aim, the following topics are investigated in an abstract model of clustering:

1. necessary or sufficient topological conditions for clustering;
2. various relationships between clustering, learning and hypothesis spaces;
3. clusterability of many natural classes of geometrically defined objects;
4. oracles as a method to distinguish between topological and computational aspects of clustering.

Clustering has been widely studied in several forms in the fields of machine learning and statistics [2, 5, 15, 17]. However abstract treatments of the topic are rare. Kleinberg [13] provides an axiomatic approach to clustering, but, in his settings, computability per se is not an issue. In contrast, the present work investigates clustering from the perspective of Gold style learning theory [9, 11] where limitations also stem from uncomputable phenomena.

The basic setting is that a class of potential clusters is given. This class is recursively enumerable. A finite set I of (indices of) pairwise disjoint clusters from the given class is called a *clustering task*. Given such a task, the clusterer – which might be any algorithmic device – receives a text containing all the data occurring in these clusters and is supposed to find in the limit a set J of (indices of) pairwise disjoint clusters which cover all the data to be seen. There are two variants with respect to a third condition: if one requires that the union of the clusters given by I is the same as the union of the clusters given by J, then one refers to this problem as *clustering*; if this condition is omitted, then one refers to this problem as *semiclustering*.

Clustering is in some cases more desirable than semiclustering: for example the clustering tasks from the class $S_{\text{conv},k}$ defined in Definition 8.1 are collections of convex sets having a positive distance from each other. The solution to such a clustering task is unique since each of these sets corresponds to a cluster. A clusterer has to identify these sets while a semiclusterer can just converge to the convex hull of all data to be seen. Such a solution is legitimate for semiclustering since it is again a member of the class $S_{\text{conv},k}$. But it fails to meet the intuition behind clustering since it does not distinguish the data from the various clearly different clusters.

Note that in the process of clustering, it is sufficient to find the set J of indices mentioned above. From this J one can find for every data-item x in the set $\cup_{j \in J} A_j$ of all permitted data the unique cluster where x belongs to. One just enumerates the sets with the indices in J until the data-item appears in one of them and then uses the index of this set as a description for the cluster to which this data-item belongs. So, from a recursion-theoretic point of view, finding the set J is the relevant part of a given clustering problem.

For every indexed class of recursively enumerable sets there is a canonical translation from these indices to type-0 grammars in the Chomsky hierarchy which generate the corresponding sets. This links the current setting of clustering to grammatical inference although there is no need herein to exploit the detailed structure of the grammars obtained by such a translation.

1. A class has the Finite Containment Property iff any finite union of its members contains only finitely many other members. In Section 5 it is shown that classes satisfying this natural property separate the basic notions of clusterability, semi-clusterability and learnability. There is no purely topological characterization of clusterable classes: if a class contains an infinite set C and all singleton sets disjoint from C then the class is clusterable iff C is recursive. Proposition 6.1 gives a further characterization which depends on the numbering: a class of disjoint sets is clusterable iff it has a numbering where every set occurs only finitely often. Section 6 provides some further sufficient criteria for clusterability which take into account topological aspects as well as properties of the given hypothesis space. These criteria are refinements of the Finite Containment Property.

2. Clusterable classes are learnable but not vice versa. Although clusterable classes are by definition uniformly recursively enumerable, the set of clustering tasks might fail to be. Proposition 3.2 shows that a class that can be clustered using a class comprising hypothesis space, that is a hypothesis space which enumerates the members of a superclass, can be clustered using a hypothesis space which enumerates the members of the class only. But by Example 3.3 a clusterable class might not be clusterable with respect to some class comprising hypothesis space.

3. In Sections 7 and 8 it is demonstrated how one can map down concrete examples into this general framework. These concrete examples are geometrically defined subsets of $\mathbb{Q}^k$: affine sets, classes of sets with distinct accumulation points and convex hulls of finite sets. This third example is not clusterable but it turns out to be clusterable if some additional information about the task given to the clusterer is revealed. While there are several natural candidates for the additional information in the case of convex hulls of finite sets, this approach becomes much more difficult when dealing with clusters of other shapes. In the case of polygons in the 2-dimensional space, the additional information provided can consist of the number of clusters plus the overall number of vertices in the polygons considered. Still this additional information is insufficient for clustering classes of geometrical objects some of which have holes. But the k-dimensional area is a sufficient additional information as long as one rules out that the symmetric difference of two clusters has the k-dimensional area 0.

4. Oracles are a way to distinguish between topological and computational difficulty of a clustering problem. In Section 4 the relationship between an oracle E and the classes clusterable relative to E is investigated. For example, every 1-generic oracle E which is Turing reducible to the halting problem is trivial: every class which is clusterable relative to E is already clusterable without any oracle. On the other hand, some classes are even not clusterable relative to any oracle. Proposition 4.2 characterizes the maximal oracles which permit to cluster any class which is clusterable relative to *some* oracle; in particular it is shown that such oracles exist.

2   The Basic Model

Most of the notation follows [11, 16]. The next paragraph summarizes the most important notions used in the present work.

Basic Notation 2.1. A class S is assumed to consist of recursively enumerable subsets of a countable underlying set $\mathbb{U}$ where in Sections 3–6, $\mathbb{U}$ is the set of natural numbers $\mathbb{N}$ and in Sections 7 and 8, $\mathbb{U}$ is a rational vector space of finite positive dimension. Mostly, S is even required to be *uniformly recursively enumerable* which means that there is a sequence $A_0, A_1, \ldots$ of subsets of $\mathbb{U}$ such that $S = \{A_0, A_1, \ldots\}$ and $\{(i, x) \in \mathbb{N} \times \mathbb{U} : x \in A_i\}$ is recursively enumerable. Such a sequence $A_0, A_1, \ldots$ is called a *numbering* for S.

The letters I, J, H always range over finite subsets of $\mathbb{N}$. Define A_I as $\cup_{i \in I} A_i$. Let disj(S) contain all finite sets I such that $A_i \cap A_j = \emptyset$ for all different $i, j \in I$. The sets in disj(S) are called *clustering tasks*.

For any set A let $|A|$ be the cardinality of A. Let A^* be the set of all finite sequences of members of A and $|\sigma|$ be the length of a string $\sigma \in A^*$.

A text for a nonempty set $A \subseteq \mathbb{U}$ is any infinite sequence containing all elements but no nonelements of A. Clusterers and semiclusterers are recursive functions from $\mathbb{U}^*$ to finite subsets of $\mathbb{N}$, learners are recursive functions from $\mathbb{U}^*$ to $\mathbb{N}$.

The sequence $W_0, W_1, \ldots$ denotes an acceptable numbering of all recursively enumerable sets and W_e can be interpreted as the domain of the e-th partial-recursive function φ_e. The set $K = \{e : e \in W_e\}$ is called the halting problem and this notion can be generalized to computation relative to oracles: A' is the halting problem relative to A; in particular K' is the halting problem relative to K and K'' the one relative to K'. For more information on iterated halting problems see [16, page 450].

Definition 2.2. A class $S = \{A_0, A_1, \ldots\}$ of clusters is called *clusterable* iff there is a clusterer M which, for every $I \in$ disj(S), converges on every text for A_I to a $J \in$ disj(S) with $A_J = A_I$. Such an M is called a *clusterer for S*.

S is called *semiclusterable* if one replaces $A_J = A_I$ by the weaker condition that $A_J \supseteq A_I$.

S is called *learnable in the limit from positive data with respect to the hypothesis space* $A_0, A_1, \ldots$ iff there is a learner M which for every $i \in \mathbb{N}$ converges on every text for A_i to a $j \in \mathbb{N}$ with $A_j = A_i$. In the following "*learnable*" stands for "learnable in the limit from positive data with respect to the hypothesis space $A_0, A_1, \ldots$".

Remark 2.3. A clusterer M for $S = \{A_0, A_1, \ldots\}$ might also use a different hypothesis space instead of the default one. Here a numbering $B_0, B_1, \ldots$ is called the *hypothesis space of M* iff for every clustering task I and any text for A_I, M converges on this text to a finite set J such that $B_J = A_I$ and $B_i \cap B_j = \emptyset$ for all different $i, j \in J$. The hypothesis space is *class preserving* if $S = \{B_0, B_1, \ldots\}$ and *class comprising* if $S \subseteq \{B_0, B_1, \ldots\}$. Nevertheless, in light of Proposition 3.2, it is assumed that a clusterer uses the default numbering $A_0, A_1, \ldots$ as its hypothesis space unless explicitly stated otherwise.

3   Numberings and Clustering

The main topic of this section is to investigate the role of numberings in clustering. A natural question is whether clustering is independent of the numbering chosen as the hypothesis space. Another important issue is the relationship between numberings of the class of clusters and numberings of the class of finite disjoint unions of clusters. The latter, which represents the clustering tasks, might not have a numbering despite of the fact that the former does, as shown in the next example. The class of sets representing the clustering tasks in this example cannot be made recursively enumerable by changing the numbering of the class of clusters.

Example 3.1. *Let $A_0 = \{0\}$ and let, for every $i \in \mathbb{N}$ and $j \in \{1, 2\}$,*

$$A_{2i+j} = \begin{cases} \{2i + j\} & \text{if } i \notin K; \\ \{0, 2i + j\} & \text{if } i \in K. \end{cases}$$

The class $S = \{A_0, A_1, \ldots\}$ is uniformly recursively enumerable but the class $\{A_I : I \in disj(S)\}$ is not since

$$i \notin K \Leftrightarrow (\exists I \in disj(S)) [\{2i + 1, 2i + 2\} \subseteq A_I].$$

This connection holds for all numberings of S but fails for any numbering of the superclass of all finite sets.

Thus there are clusterable classes where the corresponding class of all clustering tasks does not have a numbering. Nevertheless, a fundamental result of de Jongh and Kanazawa [4] carries over to clustering: whenever a class is clusterable with respect to a class comprising hypothesis space then the class is also clusterable with respect to every class preserving hypothesis space. An application of the next result is that every uniformly recursively enumerable class consisting only of finite sets is clusterable.

Proposition 3.2. *Let $A_0, A_1, \ldots$ be a numbering of a class S and $B_0, B_1, \ldots$ be another numbering (of a possibly different class) such that for every $I \in disj(S)$ there is a J with $A_I = B_J$. If there is a clusterer for S using the hypothesis space $B_0, B_1, \ldots$ then there is another clusterer that uses the original numbering $A_0, A_1, \ldots$ as its hypothesis space.*

Example 3.3. *The converse of Proposition 3.2 does not hold: there is a clusterable class S and a numbering of a superclass of S such that no clusterer for S can use this numbering as a hypothesis space.*

Although there are classes $S = \{A_0, A_1, \ldots\}$ such that $\{A_I : I \in disj(S)\}$ is not uniformly recursively enumerable, the superclass $\{A_I : I \subseteq \mathbb{N} \wedge |I| \text{ is finite}\}$ is uniformly recursively enumerable. A clusterer is at the same time a learner for S using the hypothesis space given by the numbering $B_0, B_1, \ldots$ which satisfies $B_{norm(I)-1} = A_I$ for all nonempty sets I. But learnability of uniformly recursively enumerable classes does not depend on the hypothesis space; following a result of de Jongh and Kanazawa [4] there is also a learner for S which uses $A_0, A_1, \ldots$ as its hypothesis space. So every clusterable class is learnable although the converse direction does not hold.

Property 3.4. *Every clusterable class is learnable.*

Examples 3.5. (a) *The class S_{gold} consisting of $\mathbb{N}$ and all its finite subsets is neither learnable nor clusterable. But S_{gold} is semiclusterable.*

(b) *The class S_{sing} consisting of all singletons and the set $\mathbb{N}$ is learnable and semiclusterable but not clusterable.*

(c) *Let C be infinite and recursively enumerable. The class S_C consisting of C and all singletons disjoint from C is learnable. Furthermore, S_C is clusterable iff S_C is semiclusterable iff C is recursive.*

The classes S_{sing} and S_C where C is nonrecursive are learnable but not clusterable. Both have the property that they are not closed under disjoint union. The next result shows that this property is essential for getting examples which are learnable but not clusterable.

Property 3.6. *Let a class S be closed under disjoint union, that is, $A \cup B \in S$ for all disjoint $A, B \in S$. Then S is clusterable iff S is learnable.*

A learner M for a class S is called *prudent* if it only outputs indices of sets it learns. One can enumerate all possible hypotheses $e_0, e_1, \ldots$ of M and so obtain a numbering $B_0, B_1, \ldots$ with $B_i = W_{e_i}$ of a learnable superclass of S. Fulk [8] showed that every learnable class has a prudent learner. Therefore, it is sufficient to consider only uniformly recursively enumerable classes for learning. So Fulk's result can be stated as follows.

Property 3.7 [11, Proposition 5.20]. *Every learnable class has a prudent learner. In particular, every learnable class is contained in some learnable and uniformly recursively enumerable class.*

So every learnable class can be extended to one which is learnable and uniformly recursively enumerable. But in contrast to learning in the limit, this requirement turns out to be restrictive for clustering. Most interesting results are based on Definition 2.2 with the consequence that only countably many classes are clusterable. The more general notion below expands the collection of clusterable classes to an uncountable one. Although the latter collection contains many irregular classes of limited interest, it still gives some fundamental insights. In this case one uses the acceptable numbering $W_0, W_1, \ldots$ of all recursively enumerable sets as the hypothesis space for the clusterer.

Definition 3.8. A class S of recursively enumerable sets is *clusterable in the general sense* iff there is a machine M which converges on every text for the union of finitely many disjoint sets $L_0, L_1, \ldots, L_n \in S$ to a finite set J of indices of pairwise disjoint members of S such that $L_0 \cup L_1 \cup \ldots \cup L_n = \cup_{e \in J} W_e$.

Proposition 3.9. *Let F be a $\{0,1\}$-valued function which is not computable relative to the oracle K''. For all $x, y \in \mathbb{N}$ and $z \in \{0,1\}$ let $A_{x,z} = \{\langle x, u, z \rangle : u \in \mathbb{N}\}$ and $B_{x,y} = \{\langle x, y, 0 \rangle, \langle x, y, 1 \rangle\}$. Then the class S containing all sets $A_{x,z}$ and $B_{x,y}$ with $x, y \in \mathbb{N}$ and $z = F(x)$ is clusterable in the general sense but not contained in any clusterable class which is uniformly recursively enumerable.*

4   Clustering and Oracles

Oracles are a method to measure the complexity of a problem. Some classes are clusterable with a suitable oracle while others cannot be clustered with any oracle. So the use of oracles permits to distinguish between problems caused by the computational difficulty of the class involved from those which are unclusterable for topological reasons. This is illustrated in the following remark.

Remark 4.1. Recall the classes S_C and S_{gold} from Examples 3.5. The class S_C is clusterable iff the set C in its definition is recursive. It is easy to see that supplying C as an oracle to the clusterer resolves all computational problems in the case that C is not recursive. But the class S_{gold} is unclusterable because of its topological structure and remains unclusterable relative to every oracle.

Oracles have been extensively studied in the context of inductive inference [1, 6, 12, 14]. Call an oracle E *maximal for clustering* if every uniformly recursively enumerable class which is clusterable relative to some oracle is already clusterable relative to E. Call an oracle E *trivial for clustering* if every uniformly recursively enumerable class which is clusterable relative to E is already clusterable without any oracle.

The next result shows that in contrast to the case of clustering in the general sense there are maximal oracles for clustering. It turns out that for an oracle E below K the following three conditions are equivalent: E is trivial for clustering, E is trivial for learning sets, E is trivial for learning functions; see [6] for the equivalence of the last two statements.

Proposition 4.2. *For every oracle E the following statements are equivalent:*

1. *$E \geq_T K$ and $E' \geq_T K''$;*
2. *the oracle E is maximal for learning from positive data – every uniformly recursively enumerable class is either not learnable with any oracle or learnable with oracle E;*
3. *the oracle E is maximal for clustering – every uniformly recursively enumerable class is either not clusterable with any oracle or clusterable with oracle E.*

An oracle G is k-generic if for every Σ_k^0-set T of strings there is a prefix $\eta \preceq G$ such that either $\eta \in T$ or $\eta' \notin T$ for all $\eta' \succeq \eta$. There are 1-generic sets but no 2-generic sets below K. Nevertheless, k-generic sets exist for all $k \in \{1, 2, \ldots\}$.

Proposition 4.3. *Let E be a nonrecursive oracle with $E \leq_T K$.*

1. *If E has 1-generic degree then E is trivial and permits only to cluster classes which can already be clustered without any oracle.*
2. *If E does not have 1-generic degree then there is a uniformly recursively enumerable class which can be clustered using the oracle E but not without any oracle.*

The same characterizations hold for learning in place of clustering.

The following example shows that trivial oracles can also be incomparable to K.

Example 4.4. *Every 2-generic oracle is trivial for clustering.*

5 The Finite Containment Property

The main topic of this section is to investigate the relationship between the topological structure of the class S and the question whether S is clusterable. Recall that the classes S_{gold} and S_{sing} are not clusterable for topological reasons: they contain a cluster which is the disjoint infinite union of some other clusters. So one might impose the following natural condition in order to overcome this problem.

Definition 5.1. A class $S = \{A_0, A_1, \ldots\}$ has the *Finite Containment Property* if every finite union of clusters contains only finitely many clusters. That is, for all i there are only finitely many sets $B \in S$ with $B \subseteq A_{\{0,1,\ldots,i\}}$.

Note that the Finite Containment Property is not necessary for clusterability. The class $\{\,\{i, i+1, \ldots\} : i \in \mathbb{N}\}$ is learnable and clusterable but does not satisfy the Finite Containment Property.

It is easy to see that the Finite Containment Property implies Angluin's condition: for every set A_I there are only finitely many sets A_J with $A_J \subset A_I$. If one takes D to be a set which contains for each A_J with $A_J \subset A_I$ the minimum of $A_I - A_J$, then D is finite and there is no A_J left with $D \subseteq A_J \subset A_I$.

Property 5.2. *If $S = \{A_0, A_1, \ldots\}$ has the Finite Containment Property then S is clusterable relative to every oracle E with $E \geq_T K$ and $E' \geq_T K''$.*

Although the Finite Containment Property guarantees clusterability from the topological point of view, it fails to guarantee clusterability from the recursion-theoretic point of view. Instead there are classes satisfying the Finite Containment Property which are clusterable only with the help of a maximal oracle.

Property 5.3. *There is a class satisfying the Finite Containment Property which is learnable but neither clusterable nor semiclusterable. Furthermore, clusterability cannot be characterized in topological terms only.*

Proposition 5.4. *Every class has a semiclusterer using the halting problem as an oracle. Furthermore, a class $S = \{A_1, A_2, \ldots\}$ is semiclusterable without any oracle if the representation of the class is a uniformly recursive family, that is, if $\{(i, x) \in \mathbb{N}^2 : x \in A_i\}$ is recursive and not only recursively enumerable.*

By Property 5.3 one can separate learnability from clusterability and semiclusterability by a class satisfying the Finite Containment Property. The next results show that there are no implications between the notions of learnability, clusterability and semiclusterability except the following two: "clusterable $\Rightarrow$ semiclusterable" and "clusterable $\Rightarrow$ learnable". All nonimplications are witnessed by classes satisfying the Finite Containment Property.

Proposition 5.5. *Let the class S consist of the clusters $A_{3i} = \{\langle i, x \rangle : x \in \mathbb{N}\}$ and $A_{3i+j} = \{\langle i, x \rangle : x \equiv j+1 \text{ modulo } 2 \text{ and } x < 2 + |W_i|\}$ where $i \in \mathbb{N}$ and $j \in \{1, 2\}$. The class S satisfies the Finite Containment Property. Furthermore, S is semiclusterable and learnable but not clusterable.*

Example 5.6. *Assume that $W_0 = \mathbb{N}$. The class $\{\{\langle i, x \rangle : x \in W_j\} : j \le i\}$ is neither learnable nor clusterable. But it is semiclusterable and satisfies the Finite Containment Property.*

6 Numbering-Based Properties

Every uniformly recursively enumerable class of pairwise disjoint sets is learnable: the learner just waits until it finds $x \in \text{range}(\sigma)$ and $i \le |\sigma|$ such that x is enumerated into A_i within $|\sigma|$ steps; from then on the learner outputs the index i. But for nonrecursive sets C, the class S_C witnesses that such a class is not clusterable. So one has to consider not only properties of the class but also properties of some of its numberings. A class $\{A_0, A_1, \ldots\}$ has the *Numbering-Based Finite Containment Property* if for every I there are only finitely many j with $A_j \subseteq A_I$.

Proposition 6.1. *A class of pairwise disjoint sets has the Numbering-Based Finite Containment Property iff it is clusterable.*

The class given in Example 5.6 satisfies the Numbering-Based Finite Containment Property but is not clusterable. The next two results present more restrictive sufficient conditions.

Proposition 6.2. *Assume that $A_i \not\subseteq \cup_{j \ne i} A_j$ for all i and that it is decidable whether two sets A_i, A_j intersect. Then $S = \{A_0, A_1, \ldots\}$ is clusterable.*

Proposition 6.3. *Assume that $S = \{A_0, A_1, \ldots\}$ satisfies the following three conditions:*

1. *every A_i is infinite;*
2. *if $i \ne j$ then $A_i \cap A_j$ is finite;*
3. *S is uniformly recursive, that is, $\{(i, x) : x \in A_i\}$ is recursive.*

Then S is clusterable. But no two of these three conditions are sufficient for being clusterable.

7 Geometric Examples

The major topic of the last two sections is to look at sets of clusters which are characterized by basic geometric properties. Therefore the underlying set is no longer $\mathbb{N}$ but the k-dimensional rational vector space $\mathbb{Q}^k$, where $k \in \{1, 2, \ldots\}$ is fixed. The classes considered consist of natural subsets of $\mathbb{Q}^k$. Except for the class $S_{\text{accu},k}$ in Proposition 7.2 below, the following holds: the clusters are built from finitely many parameter-points in $\mathbb{Q}^k$; the clusters are connected sets; every task consists of clusters having a positive distance from each other. So there is a unique natural way of breaking down a task into clusters.

  Recall that a subset $U \subseteq \mathbb{Q}^k$ is affine iff for every fixed $x \in U$ the set $V = \{y \in \mathbb{Q}^k : x + y \in U\}$ is a rational vector space, that is, closed under scalar multiplication and addition. The dimension of U is the dimension of V as a vector space.

Example 7.1. *Let $S_{aff,k}$ be the class of all affine subspaces of $\mathbb{Q}^k$ which have dimension $k-1$. The class $S_{aff,k}$ is clusterable but the class $S_{aff,k} \cup \{\mathbb{Q}^k\}$ is not.*

Proposition 7.2. *Let k be a positive natural number and $S_{accu,k}$ be a class $\{A_0, A_1, \ldots\}$ of bounded subsets of $\mathbb{Q}^k$ for which there is a recursive and one-one sequence $a_0, a_1, \ldots$ of points in $\mathbb{Q}^k$ satisfying the following: (1) every A_i has exactly one accumulation point which is a_i; (2) no accumulation point of the set $\{a_0, a_1, \ldots\}$ is contained in this set. Then the class $S_{accu,k}$ is clusterable.*

8   Clustering with Additional Information

Freivalds and Wiehagen [7] introduced a learning model where the learner receives in addition to the graph of the function to be learned an upper bound on the size of some program for this function – this additional information increases the learning power and enables to learn the class of all recursive functions.

Similarly, a machine receiving adequate additional information can solve every clustering task for the class $S_{conv,k}$ defined below. But without that additional information, $S_{conv,k}$ is not clusterable. So the main goal of this section is to determine which pieces of additional information are sufficient to cluster certain geometrically defined classes where clustering without additional information is impossible.

Definition 8.1. For a given positive natural number k, the class $S_{conv,k}$ contains all subsets of $\mathbb{Q}^k$ which are the rational points in the convex hull of a finite subset of $\mathbb{Q}^k$.

Proposition 8.2. *The class $S_{conv,k}$ is semiclusterable but not clusterable.*

Proposition 8.3. *The class $S_{conv,k}$ is clusterable with additional information if for any task I one of the following pieces of information is also provided to the machine M:*

- *the number $|I|$ of clusters of the task;*
- *a positive lower bound for $\min(\{1\} \cup \{d(A_i, A_j) : i, j \in I \wedge i \neq j\})$;*
- *the minimal number of points which are needed to generate all the convex sets A_i with $i \in I$.*

The last results of the present work deal with conditions under which nonconvex geometrical objects can be clustered. The first approach is to look at unions of convex objects which are still connected. For $k = 1$, this class is the same as $S_{conv,1}$. But for $k = 2$, this class is larger. There the type of additional information used for clustering $S_{conv,k}$ is no longer sufficient. Given both the number of clusters and the number of vertices as additional information, it is possible to cluster the natural subclass $S_{polygon,2}$ of all classes considered. But if one permits holes inside the clusters, this additional information is no longer sufficient. An alternative parameter is the k-dimensional area covered by a geometric object. In Example 8.7 a natural class $S_{\text{area},k}$ is introduced which can be clustered with the area of a clustering task given as additional information. The class $S_{\text{area},2}$ contains $S_{\text{polygon},2}$ and the class from Example 8.6 as subclasses.

Definition 8.4. A polygon is given by n vertices $q_1, q_2, \ldots, q_n \in \mathbb{Q}^2$ and is the union of n sides which are the convex hulls of $\{q_1, q_2\}, \{q_2, q_3\}, \ldots, \{q_n, q_1\}$. The sides do not cross each other and exactly two sides contain one vertex. Every side has positive length and the angle between the two sides meeting at a vertex is never 0, 180 or 360 degrees. Let $p_0, p_1, \ldots$ be an enumeration of the polygons and let P_i be the set of all points in $\mathbb{Q}^2$ which are on the polygon p_i or in its interior. Let n_i denote the minimum number of vertices to define the polygon p_i and $S_{\text{polygon},2}$ be the class $\{P_0, P_1, \ldots\}$.

Proposition 8.5. *The class $S_{polygon,2} = \{P_0, P_1, \ldots\}$ is clusterable with additional information in the sense that it is clusterable from the following input provided to a clusterer for task I in addition to a text for P_I: the cardinality $|I|$ and the number $\sum_{i \in I} n_i$. Clustering is impossible if only one of these two pieces of information is available.*

Example 8.6. *Let $B_{i,j} = p_j \cup (P_i - P_j)$ and $m_{i,j} = n_i + n_j$ if $P_j \subseteq P_i - p_i$; otherwise let $B_{i,j} = P_i$ and $m_{i,j} = n_i$. Let $S_{hole,2}$ consist of all sets $B_{i,j}$. Then it is impossible to cluster $S_{hole,2}$ if besides a text the only pieces of additional information supplied are $|I|$ and $\sum_{(i,j) \in I} m_{i,j}$.*

Example 8.7. *Let $S_{area,k} = \{A_0, A_1, \ldots\}$ be the class of finite unions of members of $S_{conv,k}$ which are connected and have a positive k-dimensional area. Without loss of generality the set $\{(i, x) : x \in A_i\}$ and the function mapping i to the area of A_i are recursive. Then there is a clusterer for $S_{area,k}$ which uses the area of the members of a cluster as additional information. But $S_{area,k}$ cannot be clustered without additional information.*

9   Conclusion

Clustering is a process which makes important use of prior assumptions. Indeed, not every set of points in an underlying space is a potential cluster; geometric conditions for instance play an important role in the definition of the class of admissible clusters. Whereas such conditions have been taken into account in previous studies, none of those has investigated the consequences of the more fundamental requirement that clustering is a computable process. This paper shows that recursion-theoretic and geometric conditions can both yield substantial insights on whether or not clustering is possible. It also explores to which extent clustering depends on computational properties, by characterizing the power of oracles for clustering. It is expected that further studies of the interaction between topological, recursion-theoretic and geometrical properties will turn out to be fruitful.

References

1. Leonard Adleman and Manuel Blum. Inductive inference and unsolvability. *Journal of Symbolic Logic*, 56:891–900, 1991.
2. Michael R. Anderberg. *Cluster Analysis for Applications*. Academic Press, 1973.
3. John Case, Sanjay Jain, Eric Martin, Arun Sharma and Frank Stephan. Identifying clusters from positive data. Technical Report TRA7/04, School of Computing, National University of Singapore, 2004.
4. Dick de Jongh and Makoto Kanazawa. Angluin's theorem for indexed families of r.e. sets and applications. In *Proceedings 9th Annual Conference on Computational Learning Theory*, pages 193–204. ACM Press, New York, NY, 1996.
5. Richard Duda, Peter Hart and David Stork. *Pattern Classification*. Wiley, second edition, 2001.
6. Lance Fortnow, William Gasarch, Sanjay Jain, Efim Kinber, Martin Kummer, Stuart A. Kurtz, Mark Pleszkoch, Theodore A. Slaman, Robert Solovay and Frank Stephan. Extremes in the degrees of inferability. *Annals of Pure and Applied Logic*, 66:231–276, 1994.
7. Rūsiņš Freivalds and Rolf Wiehagen. Inductive inference with additional information. *Elektronische Informationsverarbeitung und Kybernetik* 15:179–185, 1979.
8. Mark Fulk. Prudence and other conditions on formal language learning. *Information and Computation*, 85:1–11, 1990.
9. E. Mark Gold. Language identification in the limit. *Information and Control*, 10:447–474, 1967.
10. Anil K. Jain and Richard C. Dubes. *Algorithms for Clustering Data*. Prentice-Hall, 1988.
11. Sanjay Jain, Daniel Osherson, James Royer and Arun Sharma. *Systems that Learn: An Introduction to Learning Theory*. MIT Press, second edition, 1999.
12. Sanjay Jain and Arun Sharma. On the non-existence of maximal inference degrees for language identification. *Information Processing Letters*, 47:81–88, 1993.
13. Jon Kleinberg. An impossibility theorem for clustering. *Advances in Neural Information Processing Systems 15* (NIPS 2002), MIT Press, pages 446–453, 2003.
14. Martin Kummer and Frank Stephan. On the structure of the degrees of inferability. *Journal of Computer and System Sciences*, 52:214–238, 1996.
15. Pitu B. Mirchandani and Richard L. Francis (editors). *Discrete Location Theory*. Wiley, 1990.
16. Piergiorgio Odifreddi. *Classical Recursion Theory*. North-Holland, 1989.
17. Sergios Theodoridis and Konstantinos Koutroumbas. *Pattern Recognition*. Academic Press, 1998.

Introducing Domain and Typing Bias
in Automata Inference

François Coste[1], Daniel Fredouille[2],
Christopher Kermorvant[3], and Colin de la Higuera[4]

[1] IRISA, Campus de Beaulieu, Rennes, France
Francois.Coste@irisa.fr
[2] The Robert Gordon University, Aberdeen, UK
df@comp.rgu.ac.uk
[3] Dept. IRO, Université de Montréal, Canada
kermorvc@iro.umontreal.ca
[4] EURISE, Université Jean Monnet, St Etienne, France
cdlh@univ-st-etienne.fr

Abstract. Grammatical inference consists in learning formal grammars for unknown languages when given sequential learning data. Classically this data is raw: Strings that belong to the language and eventually strings that do not. In this paper, we present a generic setting allowing to express domain and typing background knowledge. Algorithmic solutions are provided to introduce this additional information efficiently in the classical state-merging automata learning framework. Improvement induced by the use of this background knowledge is shown on both artificial and real data.

Keywords: Automata Inference, Background Knowledge.

Toward Grammatical Inference with Background Knowledge. Grammatical inference consists in learning formal grammars for unknown languages when given sequential learning data. Classically this data is raw: Strings that belong to the language and eventually strings that do not. If no extra hypothesis is taken, state merging algorithms have shown to be successful for the case of *deterministic finite automata* (DFA) learning. One of the most representative and simplest algorithm in this family is RPNI [14]. Convergence of DFA learning algorithms depends on the presence of characteristic elements in the learning sets. In real applications some of these elements may be missing, but could be compensated by other sources of information. For instance if the learner is allowed to ask questions about the unknown language the setting is that of *active learning*: In the case of learning DFA, algorithm L^* [1] has been proposed. In the absence of a source of reliable counter-examples, the class of learnable languages is more restricted. Either subclasses of the regular languages are used, or statistical regularities can be used to help the inference. Then, with the hypothesis that not only the language but also the distribution is regular, one can hope to learn a *stochastic deterministic finite state automaton*, as with algorithm ALERGIA [4].

   In other areas of machine learning, successful techniques have been invented to be able to learn with more additional information and especially with the

G. Paliouras and Y. Sakakibara (Eds.): ICGI 2004, LNAI 3264, pp. 115–126, 2004.

capacity of including expert knowledge: A typical example is that of *inductive logic programming* (ILP) [13]. ILP is concerned with learning logic programs from data that is also presented as facts. Furthermore some *background knowledge* can be presented to the system using the same representation language (first order logics) as the data or the program to be learned.

In grammatical inference, specific knowledge relative to the application is often included by *ad hoc* modification of the algorithm (see for instance [10]). Very few automata inference algorithms allow the user to express a bias to guide the search. In this article, we propose a method enabling to integrate two kinds of background knowledge into inference: First, *domain bias* which is a knowledge on the language recognised by the target automata, and second *typing bias* which considers semantic knowledge embedded in the structure of the automata.

Domain and Typing Background Knowledge.

Domain bias is often available and may sometimes supply the lack of counter-examples. In [15], domain information may be provided for learning subsequential transducers. The domain is the set of sequences such that translating them make sense, *i.e.*: Those sequences that belong to the original language model. If the exact domain is given, (partial) subsequential transducers may be identified in the limit. In classification tasks performed by automata, the domain may be the set of sequences of interest to be classified inside or outside the concept to learn. Take for instance a task involving well formed boolean expressions: The sequence "¬)" should not appear. But it will neither appear in the correctly labelled examples (those that will evaluate to true), nor in those that will evaluate to false. If – as would be the case with a typical state merging algorithm – one depends on the presence of a counter-example containing "¬)" in the characteristic set for identification to be possible, then we would really have no hope to identify. If on the other hand we can express as domain background knowledge that no string can contain "¬)" as a substring, then identification could take place even when some counter-example cannot be given due to the intrinsic properties of the problem. We propose in section 2 an algorithm which allows to introduce this kind of background knowledge into automata inference.

Typing Bias: In [10], the authors add types to the states of the inferred automaton such as to introduce semantics on the symbols of the alphabet. These types are then used to constraint the structure of the inferred automaton, therefore embedding the type semantic in its structure. In [11], two of the authors proposed a formalism to represent the typing information. However, in this framework, the conditions to be met by the typing information are restrictive. Section 3 proposes an algorithm enabling to get rid of the limitations of this previous framework.

The remainder of the paper is structured as follows: First we review the basics of automata inference by state merging methods. Then, we apply the ideas presented in [5] to take specifically into account some *domain* bias in the inference process. The same algorithmic ideas are then applied for tackling more expressive *typing* functions than in [11]. We end this study by two particular cases allowing a more efficient treatment: We revisit the results of [11] under the formulation of the specialisation of a (type) automaton and we study the practical case when the sole information available is a typing of the sequences.

1   State Merging Inference of Automata

Languages and Automata. An alphabet Σ is a finite nonempty set of symbols. Σ^* denotes the set of all finite strings over Σ. A language L over Σ is a subset of Σ^*. In the following, unless stated otherwise, symbols are indicated by $a, b, c \ldots$, strings by $u, v, \ldots$, and the empty string by λ. A *finite state automaton* (FSA) A is a tuple $\langle \Sigma, Q, Q_0, F, \delta \rangle$ where Σ is an alphabet, Q is a finite set of *states*, $Q_0 \subseteq Q$ is the set of initial states, $F \subseteq Q$ is the set of final states, $\delta : Q \times \Sigma \to 2^Q$ is the transition function. The transition function δ is classically extended to sequences by: $\forall q \in Q, \delta(q, \lambda) = \{q\}$, $\forall q \in Q, \forall w \in \Sigma^*, \forall a \in \Sigma, \delta(q, aw) = \bigcup_{q' \in \delta(q,a)} \delta(q', w)$. The language $L(A)$ recognized by A is $\{w \in \Sigma^* : \exists q_0 \in Q_0, \delta(q_0, w) \cap F \neq \emptyset\}$. Languages recognized by FSA are called regular. For a given state q, the prefix and the suffix sets of q are respectively $P(q) = \{w \in \Sigma^* : \exists q_0 \in Q_0, q \in \delta(q_0, w)\}$ and $S(q) = \{w \in \Sigma^* : \exists q_f \in F, q_f \in \delta(q, w)\}$. The above definitions allow FSA to have inaccessible states or useless states (from which no string can be parsed) but we will not consider such automata in this paper, *i.e.*: In the sequel, we will assume that $\forall q \in Q, P(q) \neq \emptyset$ and $S(q) \neq \emptyset$. A *deterministic finite automaton* (DFA) is an FSA verifying $|Q_0| = 1$ and $\forall q \in Q, \forall a \in \Sigma, |\delta(q, a)| \leq 1$. An automaton is *unambiguous* if there exists at most one accepting path for each sequence. DFA are trivially unambiguous. For each regular language L, the canonical automaton of L is the smallest DFA accepting L; It is denoted $A(L)$.

State Merging Algorithm. Regular languages form the sole class in the Chomsky Hierarchy to be efficiently identifiable from given data [7]. The most popular approach is the state merging scheme used to learn FSA but also applied to the inference of sub-sequential transducers, probabilistic automata and more expressive grammars. This approach relies on the state merging operation which consists in unifying the states (or for grammars, the non-terminals). This operation increases the number of accepted sequences and is thus a generalisation operation. The general framework of state merging inference is given by algorithm 1. It consists in first building from the set I_+ of example strings a *maximal canonical automaton*, in short MCA, that recognizes only these strings, and then in applying the state merging operation iteratively while preserving a "compatibility" property used to avoid over-generalisation. When a set I_- of counter-example strings is available, the compatibility condition prevents over-generalisation by rejecting automata accepting at least one string of I_-. The search may be restricted to deterministic (respectively unambiguous) automata by using a *merging for determinisation* (respectively for disambiguisation) operation after each `merge()` [9, 6].

Two functions are likely to be modified to introduce an application based bias. The function `choose_states()` allows to introduce search heuristics while the function `compatible()` controls the generalization and restricts the search space. In this article, we will focus on the latter to integrate background knowledge.

Algorithm 1 Generic State Merging Algorithm

Require: training set I_+ (set of example strings)
Ensure: $A = \langle \Sigma, Q, F, \delta, Q_0 \rangle$ is compatible
  $A \leftarrow \text{MCA}(I_+)$
  while $\langle q_1, q_2 \rangle \leftarrow$ choose_states(Q) **do**
    $A' \leftarrow$ merge$(A, \langle q_1, q_2 \rangle)$
    if compatible(A') **then** $A \leftarrow A'$

---

2 Using Domain Bias

A first natural way to give information helping the inference is to force the hypothesis language, denoted hereafter by L, to be included in a more general one, denoted by L_G. In practice, this more general language may be defined according to the knowledge of the *maximal domain* of the sequences such that classifying them (as being positive or negative) makes sense. One can also consider that this general language is simply an *over general hypothesis*, obtained from a machine learning system or from an expert, which has to be specialized. Since $L \subseteq L_G \Leftrightarrow L \cap (\Sigma^* - L_G) = \emptyset$, learning a language included in L_G may also be seen as the inference of a language given an (eventually) *infinite set of counter-examples* defined by a language $L_- = \Sigma^* - L_G$ instead of (or in addition to) the traditional finite set I_-. Obviously these three interpretations (L_G, L_- and I_-) are not exclusive and may be combined to obtain a more general language L_G from the expert knowledge on each of these aspects.

The boolean formulae example given in introduction, or a known constraint on the lenghts of the strings of the target language are both instances of domain bias. We give in this section a practical algorithm to ensure during the inference that the hypothesis language L remains included in L_G. More precisely, we take the equivalent "counter-example language" point of view, *i.e.*: We assume that we are given an automaton A_- such that $L(A_-) = L_- = (\Sigma^* - L_G)$, and we propose to ensure that $L \cap L_- = \emptyset$. If we are given the (deterministic) canonical automaton $A(L_G)$, A_- can be easily computed by completing $A(L_G)$ before inverting final and non final states. One can remark that no assumption of determinism is required on A_- allowing a compact representation, if available, of L_-. In particular, A_- can easily be defined as the union of different (non deterministic) automata representing different sources of information without needing a potentially costly determinization. In return, we have to note that this is not true for L_G since a non deterministic automaton of this language would have to be determinized before complementation.

If we denote by A the current automaton representing the current language hypothesis L, a direct way to handle this problem would be to build the intersection product of A and A_- to check whether the intersection language is empty at each step of the inference. The algorithm presented hereafter can be seen as a simulation of this intersection product to detect incrementally non emptiness by introducing and maintaining a *common prefix* relation between the states of each automata defined as follow: Let $A_1 = \langle \Sigma, Q_1, Q_{01}, F_1, \delta_1 \rangle$ and

---

Algorithm 2 Computation and incremental update of common prefix relation
(using the notations $A_1 = \langle \Sigma, Q_1, Q_{01}, F_1, \delta_1 \rangle$ and $A_2 = \langle \Sigma, Q_2, Q_{02}, F_2, \delta_2 \rangle$)

Function common_prefix(A_1, A_2)
$\mathcal{E}_p \leftarrow \emptyset$ {common prefix relation storage}
for all $q_1 \in Q_{01}, q_2 \in Q_{02}$ **do**
    add_to_common_prefix($A_1, A_2, q_1, q_2, \mathcal{E}_p$)
return $\mathcal{E}_p$
Procedure add_to_common_prefix($A_1, A_2, q_1, q_2, \mathcal{E}_p$)
if $\langle q_1, q_2 \rangle \notin \mathcal{E}_p$ **then**
    $\mathcal{E}_p \leftarrow \{\langle q_1, q_2 \rangle\} \cup \mathcal{E}_p$
    propagate_forward($A_1, A_2, q_1, q_2, \mathcal{E}_p$)
Procedure propagate_forward($A_1, A_2, q_1, q_2, \mathcal{E}_p$)
for all $a \in \Sigma, q_1' \in \delta_1(q_1, a), q_2' \in \delta_2(q_2, a)$ **do**
    add_to_common_prefix($A_1, A_2, q_1', q_2', \mathcal{E}_p$)
Procedure update_after_state_merging($A_1, A_2, q, q', \mathcal{E}_p$)
Require: q is the resulting state of merging q and q' in A_1
for all $q_2 : \langle q, q_2 \rangle \in \mathcal{E}_p$ **do**
    propagate_forward($A_1, A_2, q, q_2, \mathcal{E}_p$) {handling new transitions added to q}
for all $q_2 : \langle q', q_2 \rangle \in \mathcal{E}_p$ **do**
    add_to_common_prefix($A_1, A_2, q, q_2, \mathcal{E}_p$) {reporting relations of q'}

$A_2 = \langle \Sigma, Q_2, Q_{02}, F_2, \delta_2 \rangle$. Two states q_1, q_2 in $Q_1 \times Q_2$ *share a common prefix* iff $P(q_1) \cap P(q_2) \neq \emptyset$. It is easy to see that the intersection of $L(A_1)$ and $L(A_2)$ is not empty *iff* there exists a couple of final states $q_1, q_2 \in F_1 \times F_2$ in common prefix relationship. Thus to apply this detection to A and A_-, it is sufficient to compute the set of states of A and A_- in common prefix relationship and to test whether two final states are in relation.

Moreover, since common prefixes are preserved by state merging, this relation may be maintained incrementally during the inference process. The sketch of the algorithm computing and incrementally updating the common prefix relation (algorithm 2) is then the following. At the initialization step, the common prefix relation between A and A_- can be computed by the common_prefix() function. Then, after each merge in A, new common prefixes created by the state merging are propagated using the update_after_state_merging() procedure. Detection of the constraint violation may be done simply by checking when a new common prefix relation is detected between a final state of the current automata A and a final state of A_-. At the initialization step, this violation means that the problem cannot be solved with the given data (*e.g.*: L_- includes a sequence of I_+). During the inference, it allows to detect that the last state merging is invalid and should not be done (involving a backtrack).

The theoretical complexity of function common_prefix() is in $O(|A| \times |A_-| \times t_A \times t_{A_-})$, where t_A and t_{A_-} are the maximum number of outgoing transitions by the same symbol from states of A and A_-. In practice, a maximum sequence of $|A|$ successful state-mergings can be achieved during inference. During such a sequence of state-mergings the complexity of the naïve approach (*i.e.*: Recom-

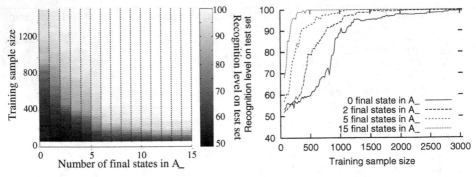

Fig. 1. Recognition level on the test set (*i.e.*: The number of correctly classified words of the test set divided by the test set size) of the solution given by RPNI [14] (extended with common prefix relation). The left plot shows how the recognition level improves (grey level) when considering an increasing "quantity" of domain bias (abscissa), and an increasing training sample size (ordinate). The right plot represents vertical sections of the left plot. The experimental setting is the following: A 31 states target automata, a training and a testing set have been generated by the GOWACHIN server (http://www.irisa.fr/Gowachin/). The complementary A_- of the target automata has been computed to provide progressively domain information by considering an increasing number of its 15 final states. Each point in a plot is a mean of nine executions with different training sets and different choices for the final states of A_-. Even if only illustrative, on can remark that the size of the training sample needed for RPNI to converge is strongly reduced when introducing domain bias (even for "small" bias) but that using only this information without providing a sample of a reasonable size does not enable the algorithm to converge.

puting relations after each merge with function `common_prefix()`) is therefore $O(|A|^2 \times |A_-| \times t_A \times t_{A_-})$. Using the incremental `update_after_state_merging()` procedure improves this complexity by a $|A|$ factor. Indeed, the worst case complexity of this procedure is achieved when $|A| \times |A_-|$ relations are stored from the beginning in $\mathcal{E}_p$. Next $|A|$ calls to `update_after_state_merging()` during the inference process have a complexity of $O(|A_-| \times t_A \times t_{A_-})$. Indeed, the `update_after_state_merging()` procedure try to propagate the $|A_-|$ relations existing on the merged state, but all propagations stop since the set of relations is already complete. This leads to a global complexity of $O(|A| \times |A_-| \times t_A \times t_{A_-})$.

We have presented here the introduction of domain bias in a state merging inference algorithm. The proposed approach is generic enough to be adapted to other inference algorithms whenever they proceed by automaton generalization. In particular, since DeLeTe2 generalization operations [8] preserve common prefix relations, this approach could be easily applied to this algorithm. An experiment on artificial data showing the interest of using domain bias during automata inference is provided figure 1.

In the next section, we propose to use the common prefix relation to take into account typing prior knowledge in the inference process.

3 Using Typing Information

In applications, information on the symbols of the examples is often available. For instance, in genomics, the secondary structure to which the amino acid belongs in the protein is often known. In linguistics, one can have the result of the part of speech tagging or chunking of the sequences. This information may be considered as a typing of the symbols in the sequences and may have been given either by an unknown machine or an expert (in this case, only the result of the typing of example sequences is available) or by a typing machine provided by the expert as background knowledge (in this case, the typing is known for the examples but also for all the sequences in the domain of the machine). In sections 3.1 and 3.2, we will focus on the second case and will assume that we are given a typing machine by the expert. The first case will be studied specifically in section 3.3.

3.1 Inference of Compatible Type Automata

Formalisation of the Expert Knowledge: If we designate by Σ the symbol alphabet and by S the sort alphabet, a *symbol typing function* τ is defined from $\Sigma^* \times \Sigma \times \Sigma^*$ to S. We then designate by $\tau(u, a, v)$ the sort associated to symbol a in string uav. From this definition, the sort can depend both on u, called the *left context*, on v, called the *right context*, and on the typed symbol itself a. The expert knowledge on sorts can be represented as a typing function τ provided to the inference process. Therefore, the sorts returned by the τ function have a semantic meaning on the basis of the expert knowledge.

Since we are considering the inference of FSA, we will assume here that the typing function provided is somehow "rational", *i.e.*: That the typing could have been generated by a finite state machine. Thus, following [11], we consider that the typing function τ provided by the expert can be encoded in a *type automaton*: A finite state type automaton T is a tuple $\langle \Sigma, Q, Q_0, F, \delta, S, \sigma \rangle$ where $\Sigma, Q, Q_0, F, \delta$ are the same as in classical FSA, S is a finite set of sorts and $\sigma : Q \rightarrow S$ is the state typing function. A type automaton T represents a typing application τ from $\Sigma^* \times \Sigma \times \Sigma^*$ to 2^S defined by $\tau(u, a, v) = \{\sigma(q) / \exists q_0 \in Q_0, \exists q_f \in F, q \in \delta(q_0, ua)$ and $q_f \in \delta(q, v)\}$. Such as to consider typing functions (*i.e.*: From $\Sigma^* \times \Sigma \times \Sigma^*$ to S) instead of typing applications, we will restrict ourself to type automata such that $\forall u, v \in \Sigma^*, \forall a \in \Sigma : |\tau(u, a, v)| \leq 1$. As improvments on [11], we authorize type automata to be non-deterministic to handle typing functions depending on the left context but also on the right context of the word. We also authorize incompletely specified typing functions as it is often the case in practice. Figure 2 gives an example of a type automaton.

Integration of the Expert Knowledge in Inference: To integrate the typing information in the learned automaton, this one has to embed this information in its structure. To achieve this goal, one associate a sort to each state of the learned automaton, which can therefore be considered as a type automaton. The idea is that the typing function embedded in the structure of the inferred automaton has to be *compatible* with the typing function provided as expert knowledge.

Fig. 2. Expert knowledge on proteins family is available in the PROSITE database (http://au.expasy.org/prosite/). This type automaton has been constructed from the PROSITE pattern PS00142 (ZINC_PROTEASE). Σ is the amino acids alphabet, the state typing function may be defined to return the state number on significative states. Knowledge embedded in this pattern is for instance the presence of the two amino acids H (Histidine) in the pattern because of their good properties to fix Zinc molecules.

We denote by $\mathcal{D}_\tau$ the domain of a typing function τ which is the set of tuple $\langle u, a, v \rangle$ such that $\tau(u, a, v)$ is defined. Thanks to our distinction between the domain and the typing knowledge, we use a weaker definition of the compatibility of two typing functions than the one proposed in [11]: Two typing functions τ and τ' are *compatible* iff $\forall \langle u, a, v \rangle \in \mathcal{D}_\tau \cap \mathcal{D}_{\tau'}$, $\tau(u, a, v) = \tau'(u, a, v)$.

In the following, two type automata will be considered compatible if their typing functions are compatible. We propose to ensure the compatibility of the learned automaton A with the provided type automaton A_T during the inference process by a similar scheme to the one presented in section 2. But, since left and right contexts are considered for typing, common prefix relation is not sufficient. To propagate the acceptance information backward to the states, the *common suffix* relation is also used. It is defined as follow: Let $A_1 = \langle \Sigma, Q_1, Q_{01}, F_1, \delta_1 \rangle$ and $A_2 = \langle \Sigma, Q_2, Q_{02}, F_2, \delta_2 \rangle$. Two states q_1, q_2 in $Q_1 \times Q_2$ are said to share a *common suffix* iff $S(q_1) \cap S(q_2) \neq \emptyset$. This definition is completely symmetric to the the definition of the common prefix relation and share the same properties. Thus computation and incremental maintenance of this relation can be done by similar functions to those given in algorithm 2 simply by replacing the set of initial states by the set of final states and by propagating the relations backward instead of forward by using the inverse function of transition.

The common prefix and common suffix relations are used during the inference process to ensure the compatibility between the inferred automaton A and the automaton embedding the expert typing function A_T. This is done by assigning to each state q of A sharing both a common prefix and a common suffix with a state q_T of A_T the sort of q_T and by prohibiting assigning different sorts to the same state. At the initialization step, this projection of the sorts allows to initialize the state typing function of A. A failure at this point (*i.e.*: Trying to assign two different types to one state) shows that the typing function of A_T is not functional or, in the deterministic case when the prefix tree acceptor is used as MCA [9], that the typing can not be realized by a DFA. During the inference, a failure detection allows to detect that the last state merging is invalid and should not be done (involving a backtrack). As for domain background knowledge, an experiment on artificial data showing the interest of typing bias during automata inference is provided (figure 3).

It may be easily shown that states of A with different sorts will always fail to be merged and that trying to merge them is useless. In figure 4, we show that the initial typing of the states is not sufficient, even for deterministic type automata, to ensure compatibility and that propagation of relations has to be

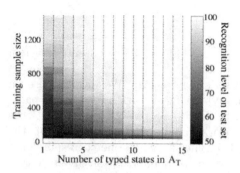
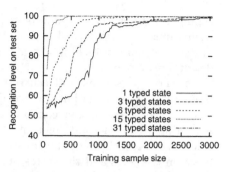

Fig. 3. Recognition level when given a type automaton A_T. The same experimental setting and the same automaton than in figure 1 is used except that instead of giving final states information, typing information is given progressively (here, between 1 and 31 typed states of A_T chosen randomly, all the states are final, the left plot is truncated at 15 typed states). Convergence is faster since the given typing information is richer than the domain one.

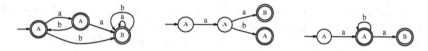

Fig. 4. A_T, deterministic MCA for $I_+ = \{aa, ab\}$ and A obtained by merging source and target state of the transition by b. Although the merged states have the same sort A, in A_T $\tau(ab, a, \lambda) = A$ whereas in the merged automaton $\tau(ab, a, \lambda) = B$ (and the problem remains even if we consider a complete sample wrt to A_T, e.g.: $\{aa, ab, ba, bb\}$).

done after state merging to ensure that new accepted sequences are correctly typed. We will study in the next sections two special cases such that avoiding to merge states with different sorts is sufficient to ensure the compatibility.

3.2 Specialization of a Regular Grammar

In the setting of [11], typing is feasible only if: 1. The expert type automaton is deterministic, 2. It has a completely defined state typing function, 3. It accepts at least all words of I_+, 4. It has different sorts for all its states (*i.e.* $\forall q, q' \in Q_T, q \neq q' : \sigma_T(q) \neq \sigma(q')$), and 5. The inferred automaton is deterministic. The setting presented in section 3.1 removes all these constraints to the cost of a more important complexity. If we consider these restrictions, [11] show that the initial typing of the MCA can be realised in $O(|\,\text{MCA}\,|)$, and the maintenance of types can be realized in $O(1)$ after each state merging.

In fact, the determinism restrictions 1. and 5. can be removed while keeping the $O(1)$ type managment after each state merging. This is done by realizing the initial typing as proposed in subsection 3.1. The maintenance of types along inference is realized in $O(1)$ by preventing to merge states with different state typing functions. The formal proof follows the same lines as the one provided in [11]. This extension is interesting because it allows to handle efficiently some typing functions that cannot be represented by deterministic type automata with different sorts for all states (typing functions τ such that $\tau(u, a, bv) = \tau(u', a', bv')$ and $\tau(ua, b, v) \neq \tau(u'a', b, v')$) but that can be represented by non deterministic ones.

In [11], the semantic of the restrictions stays unclear. We discuss here an interpretation and the links between this typing framework and domain background knowledge. Under constraints 2. to 4., all compatible automata of the search space in the state-merging framework can be seen as *specializing* the structure of A_T. Indeed, the constraint 4. implies a one to one correspondence between the sorts and the states of A_T and thus the information given by typing is the structure of A_T. Let A'_T be the sub-automaton of A_T obtained by discarding useless states for the acceptance of I_+. We can show that A'_T can be obtained by merging states of any compatible automaton of the search space. Therefore these automata are specializations of A_T.

By inferring automata A specializing the structure of A_T, we also specialize the recognized language, *i.e.* $L(A) \subseteq L(A_T)$. Then, by constraining the structure, the domain is also constrained. We obtain a setting such that both the structure and the language of the automaton A_T are specialized and we should rather consider that this setting corresponds to the *specialization of an automaton* (not necessarily typed). In particular, it should be noticed that in this setting some automata verifying the language constraint, but not the structural one, can be excluded from the search space.

3.3 Inference Given Typed Examples

A practical case such that updating common prefix and common suffix relations is not necessary is when we are given only typed examples. A type automaton A_T could easily be constructed from the typed examples and would verify $L(A_T) = I_+$. In that case, no typing constraint is given about sequences outside the training set and the sole remaining constraint is to avoid creating two acceptance paths leading to different typing for a sequence of I_+ (to ensure compatibility) what can be avoided by considering the inference of DFA or more generally of unambiguous type automata [6] (allowing also to ensure functionality of the learned type automaton). Then, one can show that the initial projection of the sorts to the MCA and forbidding merging states with different sorts is sufficient to ensure the compatibility. But it should be noticed that some complementary state merging (for determinization or for disambiguisation) may have to be done before detecting the failure. This case should rather be considered factually as a case such that the typing information can be directly encoded in the automata A and does not need a second automata A_T besides it.

Inference given typed examples is interesting when no type automaton is given and only a tagging of the examples is available. This setting is also interesting if a typing function that cannot be converted into a typing automaton is available. In this case, the function can be used at least to type the examples. We illustrate this by an experiment on the ATIS task using Part-Of-Speech Tagger typing information (figure 5).

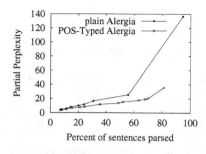

Fig. 5. We have tested the use of type information for automaton inference on the Air Travel Information System (ATIS) task [12]. This corpus has been widely used in the speech recognition community to test various language models. The type information was composed of Part-Of-Speech (POS) tags provided by the Brill tagger [2]. Here we inferred stochastic automata using Alergia inference algorithm [4] with and without the POS-tag information. Each word was tagged with its most probable POS-tag, disregarding the context-rules in the tagger. In this task, a usual quality measure is the *perplexity* of the test set S (ordinate) given by $P = 2^{-\frac{1}{|S|}\sum_{w \in S} \log_2 P(w)}$, where $P(w)$ is the probability given by the stochastic automaton to the word w. The smaller the perplexity the better the automaton can predict the next symbol. The sentences with 0 probability are ignored in this score (the presence of one of these sentence would lead to an infinite perplexity). So to evaluate the results, we also have to represent the percentage of sequences accepted, *i.e*: With non 0 probability (abscissa). In the Alergia algorithm, generalisation is controled by one parameter. Different values for this parameter provided the different points of the figure. The best results are situated in the bottom right corner as they correspond to high coverage and small perplexity. For a given number of sentences parsed, the use of POS-tag based type reduces the partial perplexity and provides better models.

Discussion, Conclusion and Perspectives

We have proposed a generic setting to use domain and/or typing knowledge for the inference of automata. This setting includes the non deterministic and incomplete knowledge cases and allows different degrees of efficiency. In particular, two practical cases have been identified such that the expert knowledge can be taken into account with a small over-cost. Experiments on real applications are now needed to validate the approach and to quantify (experimentally, but also theoretically) the amount of the given help.

As pointed by one of the reviewers the presented models have to be compared to existing models to learn in helpful environments. A starting point of that research for the domain bias could be a comparison with inference being allowed *membership queries* [1]. Indeed a language of counter-examples provided as an automaton A_- can answer some of the membership queries (the ones concerning words in the language of A_-). For the typing bias, a comparison with the work of [3] has to be realised. We also have to explore the fact that the comportement of our algorithms is unclear when the provided knowledge is erroneous. In this case, a solution could be to use this knowledge as a heuristic instead a pruning constraint.

Another promising perspective is to study the extension of this work to more powerful grammars. In particular, coupling non terminals with typing could provide an interesting framework to include semantic background knowledge in the inference of context-free grammars and should be compared to the parsing skeleton information used with success by Sakakibara [16].

References

1. D. Angluin. Learning regular sets from queries and counterexamples. *Information and Control*, 39:337–350, 1987.
2. E. Brill. Some advances in rule-based part of speech tagging. In *Proc. National Conference on Artificial Intelligence*, 1994.
3. A. Cano, J. Ruiz, and P. García. Inferring subclasses of regular languages faster using RPNI and forbidden configurations. In *Proc. Int. Coll. on Gram. Inference*, volume 2484 of *LNCS*, pages 28–36. Springer, 2002.
4. R. Carrasco and J. Oncina. Learning stochastic regular grammars by means of a state merging method. In *Proc. Int. Coll. on Gram. Inference*, number 862 in LNCS, pages 139–150. Springer Verlag, 1994.
5. F. Coste and D. Fredouille. Efficient ambiguity detection in c-nfa, a step toward inference of non deterministic automata. In *Proc. Int. Coll. on Gram. Inference*, pages 25–38, 2000.
6. F. Coste and D. Fredouille. Unambiguous automata inference by means of state-merging methods. In *European Conference on Machine Learning*, pages 60–71, 2003.
7. C. de la Higuera. Characteristic sets for polynomial grammatical inference. *Machine Learning*, 27:125–138, 1997.
8. F. Denis, A. Lemay, and A. Terlutte. Learning regular languages using *rfsa*. In *Proc. Int. Conf. on Alg. Learning Theory*, LNCS, pages 348–363. Springer-Verlag, 2001.
9. P. Dupont, L. Miclet, and E. Vidal. What is the search space of the regular inference? In *Proc. Int. Coll. on Gram. Inference*, number 862 in LNCS, pages 25–37. Springer Verlag, 1994.
10. T. Goan, N. Benson, and O. Etzioni. A grammar inference algorithm for the world wide web. In *Proc. of AAAI Spring Symposium on Machine Learning in Information Access*. AAAI Press, 1996.
11. C. Kermorvant and C. de la Higuera. Learning languages with help. In *Proc. Int. Coll. on Gram. Inference*, volume 2484 of *LNCS*, pages 161–173. Springer, 2002.
12. C. Kermorvant, C. de la Higuera, and P. Dupont. Improving probabilistic automata learning with additional knowledge. In *Proc. of the IAPR International Workshops SSPR and SPR*, 2004.
13. S. Muggleton. Inductive Logic Programming. In *The MIT Encyclopedia of the Cognitive Sciences (MITECS)*. MIT Press, 1999.
14. J. Oncina and P. García. Identifying regular languages in polynomial time. In H. Bunke, editor, *Advances in Structural and Syntactic Pattern Recognition*, volume 5, pages 99–108. World Scientific, 1992.
15. J. Oncina and M. A. Varó. Using domain information during the learning of a subsequential transducer. In *Proc. Int. Coll. on Gram. Inference*, volume 1147 of *LNCS*, pages 301–312. Springer, 1996.
16. Y. Sakakibara and H. Muramatsu. Learning context-free grammars from partially structured examples. In *Proc. Int. Coll. on Gram. Inference*, number 1891 in LNCS, pages 229–240. Springer-Verlag, 2000.

Analogical Equations in Sequences: Definition and Resolution

Arnaud Delhay and Laurent Miclet*

IRISA – Projet CORDIAL
6, rue de Kerampont – BP 447
F-22305 Lannion Cedex
arnaud.delhay@univ-rennes1.fr, miclet@enssat.fr
http://www.irisa.fr/cordial/

Abstract. We present a definition of analogy on sequences which is based on two principles: the definition of an analogy between the letters of an alphabet and the use of the edit distance between sequences. Our definition generalizes the algorithm given by Lepage and is compatible with another definition of analogy in sequences given by Yvon.

1 Introduction: Learning Sequences by Analogy

We study in this paper a lazy method of supervised learning in the universe of sequences. We assume that there exists a learning set of sequences, composed of sequences associated with class labels. When a new sequence is introduced, a supervised learning algorithm has to infer which label to associate with this new sequence.

Lazy learning makes no parametric assumption on the data and uses only the learning set. The simplest lazy learning technique is the *nearest neighbor* algorithm: the label attributed to the new sequence is that of the nearest sequence in the learning set. It requires a definition of a distance (or at least a dissemblance) between sequences.

Analogy is a more complex lazy learning technique, since it is necessary to find three sequences in the learning set and to use a more sophisticated argument. Let X be the sequence to which we want to give a label. We have to find three sequences A, B and C in the learning set, with labels $L(A)$, $L(B)$ and $L(C)$, such that "A *is to* B *as* C *is to* X". Then the label of X will be computed as "$L(X)$ *is to* $L(C)$ *as* $L(B)$ *is to* $L(A)$". This is for example the way that we can guess the past of the verb "to grind" knowing that the past of the verb "to bind" is "bound".

Learning by analogy requires to give a definition to the terms "is to" and "as". This is the primary goal of this paper, which is organized as follows. In section 2,

---

* The research reported here was supported by CNRS interdisciplinary program TCAN Analangue and some of its ideas have been elaborated during its meetings. We especially thank Nicolas Stroppa and François Yvon at ENST Paris for their comments and help in formalizing Section 3.3

G. Paliouras and Y. Sakakibara (Eds.): ICGI 2004, LNAI 3264, pp. 127–138, 2004.

we will define more precisely what is analogy, especially on sequences. We present our approach, based on the edit distance and on the resolution of analogical equations on letters. In section 3, we remind what is the edit distance and we give a formal framework firstly to solve analogical equations on letters, secondly to compute all the solutions of analogical equations on sequences. Finally, in section 4, we will compare our proposition with related works and show that it generalizes previous algorithms. We then conclude and give some possible extensions to our work.

2   What Is Analogy on Sequences

2.1   Analogy

Analogy is a way of reasoning which has been studied throughout the history of philosophy and has been widely used in Artificial Intelligence and Linguistics. Lepage ([1], in French, or [2], in English) has given an extensive description of the history of this concept and its application in science and linguistics.

An analogy between four objects or concepts: A, B, C and D is usually expressed as follows: "A is to B as C is to D". Depending on what the objects are, analogies can have very different meanings. For example, natural language analogies could be: "a crow is to a raven as a merlin is to a peregrine" or "vinegar is to bordeaux as a sloe is to a cherry". These analogies are based on the *semantics* of the words. By contrast, in the formal universe of sequences, analogies such as "abcd is to abc as abbd is to abb" or "g is to gg as gg is to ggg" are *syntactic*.

Whether syntactic or not, the examples above show the intrinsic ambiguity in defining an analogy. Some would have good reasons to prefer: "g is to gg as gg is to gggg". Obviously, such ambiguities are inherent in semantic analogies, since they are related to the meaning of words (the concepts are expressed through natural language). Hence, it seems easier to focus on formal syntactic properties. And resolving syntactic analogies is also an operational problem in several fields of linguistics, such as morphology and syntax, and provides a basis to learning and data mining by analogy in the universe of sequences.

The first goal of this paper is therefore to give a definition of a syntactic analogy between sequences of letters.

2.2   Analogies and Analogical Equations on Sequences

In this section, we focus on concepts that are sequences of letters in a finite alphabet and we are interested in studying what is an analogy on these concepts.

Our development will be based on two basic ideas. Firstly, we will formalize the comparison of sequences through the classical notion of *edit distance* between sequences; we will give a method in section 3 which will be proved to transform the problem of analogy between *sequences* into that of analogy between *letters*.

We will also introduce an algebraic definition of the analogy between letters, or more generally between the elements of a finite set (section 3.2).

Unlike D. Hofstadter *et al.* [3], we will not *a priori* consider as correct the following analogy: "abc *is to* abd *as* ghi *is to* ghj", since we assume that the alphabet of the sequences is simply a finite set of letters, with no order relation. In that, we will stick to the classical definition of an alphabet in language theory. Of course, adding properties on an alphabet increases the possible number of ambiguities in resolving analogies. If we want to give an algorithmic definition, we have to focus our interest on problems with the lowest number of free parameters.

We denote now "A *is to* B *as* C *is to* D" by the equation $A : B \doteq C : D$ and we say informally that *solving an analogical equation* is finding one or several values for X from the relation $A : B \doteq C : X$. We will give a more precise definition at the end of this section.

The classical definition of $A : B \doteq C : D$ as an analogical equation requires the satisfaction of two axioms, expressed as equivalences of this primitive equation with two others equations [2]:

Symmetry of the 'as' relation: $C : D \doteq A : B$

Exchange of the means: $A : C \doteq B : D$

As a consequence of these two basic axioms, five other equations are easy to prove equivalent to $A : B \doteq C : D$:

Inversion of ratios: $B : A \doteq D : C$

Exchange of the extremes: $D : B \doteq C : A$

Symmetry of reading: $D : C \doteq B : A$

$B : D \doteq A : C$

$C : A \doteq D : B$

Another possible axiom (*determinism*) requires that one of the following trivial equations has a unique solution (the other being a consequence):

$$A : A \doteq B : X \Rightarrow X = B$$
$$A : B \doteq A : X \Rightarrow X = B$$

We can give now a definition of a solution to an analogical equation which takes into account the axioms of analogy.

Definition 1 X *is a* correct solution *to the analogical equation* $A : B \doteq C : X$ *if X is a solution to this equation and is also a solution to the two others equations:*

$$C : X \doteq A : B \quad and \quad A : C \doteq B : X$$

3   A Formal Framework for Solving Analogies

As our approach is based on the edit distance, we firstly remind what it is. In the second part of this section, we give sufficient (algebraic) arguments to justify the resolution of all analogical equations on letters. Then we present a formal way to characterize the solutions of equations on sequences by using transducers and finite state automata. We have derived an algorithm [4] from these formal approaches.

3.1   The Edit Distance Between Two Sequences

We give here notations and definitions of elementary language theory [5] and we recall what is the *edit distance* between sequences.

Basic Definitions About Sequences. Let Σ be a finite set that we will call an *alphabet*. We call *letters* $a, b, c, \ldots$ the elements of Σ. We denote $u, v, \ldots$ or $A, B, \ldots$ the elements of Σ^*, called *sequences* or *sentences* or *words*. A sequence $u = u_1 u_2 \ldots u_{|u|}$ is an ordered list of letters of Σ ; its length is denoted $|u|$. ϵ, the *empty sequence*, is the sequence of null *length*. We use the classical notion of concatenation: if $u = u_1 u_2 \ldots u_{|u|}$ and $v = v_1 v_2 \ldots v_{|v|}$, their concatenation is $uv = u_1 u_2 \ldots u_{|u|} v_1 v_2 \ldots v_{|v|}$.

Alignments as a Particular Case of Transformation.   To compute the edit distance, we have to give more definitions and quote a theorem, demonstrated by Wagner and Fischer in [6]. We first have to introduce the notion of edition between sequences. This edition is based on three edit operations between letters: the insertion of a letter in the target sequence, the deletion of a letter in the source sequence and the substitution, replacing a letter in the source sequence by another letter in the target sequence. Each of these operations can be associated to a cost C. We denote $C_{a \to b}$ the cost of substitution from a into b, $C_{a \to \epsilon}$ the cost of deletion of a and $C_{\epsilon \to b}$ the cost of insertion of b. The cost of the edition between sequences is the sum of the costs of the operations between letters required to transform the source sequence into the target one.

Definition 2 *The edit distance is the minimum cost of all possible transformations between two sequences.*

Definition 3 *An* alignment *between to words $x, y \in \Sigma^*$, which respective length is m and n, is a word z on the alphabet $(\Sigma \cup \{\epsilon\}) \times (\Sigma \cup \{\epsilon\}) \setminus \{(\epsilon, \epsilon)\}$ which projection on the first compound is x and which projection on the second compound is y.*

Informally, an alignment represents a sequence of edit operations. The substitution (ϵ, ϵ) is not an edit operation. It can be presented as an array of two rows, one for x and one for y, each word completed with some ϵ, both resulting in words having the same length.

For instance, here is an *alignment* between $x = abgef$ and $y = acde$:

$$
\begin{array}{ccccccc}
x^1 = & a & b & \epsilon & g & e & f \\
 & | & | & | & | & | & | \\
y^1 = & a & c & d & \epsilon & e & \epsilon
\end{array}
$$

In the following, we will denote $x^1 = ab\epsilon gef$ and $y^1 = acde\epsilon e$ the two sentences created by the optimal alignments between x and y. The sentences x and x^1, on one hand, and y and y^1, on the other hand, have the same semantics in language theory, since ϵ is the empty word.

The following theorem [6], states that the only transformations to be considered for computing the edit distance are the alignments. In this theorem, $\mathcal{C}$ denotes the cost of transformation from a letter into another ($\mathcal{C}$ is either $\mathcal{C}_{a \to b}$, $\mathcal{C}_{\epsilon \to b}$ or $\mathcal{C}_{a \to \epsilon}$.

Theorem 1 *If $\mathcal{C}$ is a distance on Σ, then the* edit distance *D can be computed as the cost of an* alignment *with the lowest cost that transforms x into y.*

An alignment corresponding to the edit distance, that of lowest cost, is often called *optimal*. It is not necessarily be unique.

It is now possible to use the classical dynamic programming Wagner and Fischer algorithm [6] which computes the edit distance and the optimal alignment. A consequence of this algorithm is the following remarkable result [7], which justifies the name of edit *distance*:

Theorem 2 *If $\mathcal{C}$ is a distance on $(\Sigma \cup \{\epsilon\})$ then D is also a distance on Σ^*.*

This algorithm can be completed to construct x^1 and y^1 from x and y and to produce the optimal alignment, or all the optimal alignments if there are more than one. This is done by memorizing more information during the computation and by backtracking on an optimal path in the final matrix [8] computed by the Wagner ans Fischer algorithm.

3.2   Analogical Equations on Alphabets and Finite Groups

In this section, we give a method for solving analogical equations on sequences based on the edit distance. This approach is composed of two steps. The first one is to give a correct solution to an analogical equation on a set composed of a finite alphabet Σ plus the empty string ϵ. The aim of this section is to give an algebraic definition of what is analogy between letters and to find a link between this algebraic structure and the distance δ on $\Sigma \cup \{\epsilon\}$ (*cf* section 3.1).

An Algebraic Definition of Analogy. In a vector space, the analogy $\overrightarrow{OA}$: $\overrightarrow{OB} \doteq \overrightarrow{OC} : \overrightarrow{OX}$ is quite naturally solved by choosing X as the fourth summit of the parallelogram built on A, B and C (Fig. 1). Obviously, this construction verifies all the axioms of a correct solution to the analogical equation.

A parallelogram has two equivalent definitions: either

$$\overrightarrow{AB} = \overrightarrow{CX} \ \text{(or: } \overrightarrow{AC} = \overrightarrow{BX}), \quad \text{or} \quad \overrightarrow{OA} + \overrightarrow{OX} = \overrightarrow{OB} + \overrightarrow{OC}$$

Let us firstly consider the second definition (we will come back to the first one later). If we want to transfer it into an alphabet Σ, we have to define in the same manner an operator $\oplus$ from $\Sigma \cup \{\epsilon\} \times \Sigma \cup \{\epsilon\}$ to a set F such that:

$$a \oplus x = b \oplus c \Leftrightarrow a : b \doteq c : x$$

It is not important what F is for the moment. We want to define what such an operator $\oplus$ can be and what structure it would give to the set $\Sigma \cup \{\epsilon\}$.

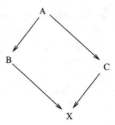

Fig. 1. Analogy in a vector space.

Properties of Analogy According to the Operator $\oplus$. We have given in section 2 the axioms of analogy as described by Lepage. Let us rewrite them with the operator $\oplus$. For each axiom, we exhibit a corresponding algebraic property and this will allow us to determine more precisely what properties the operator $\oplus$ must have.

Symmetry: $a : b \doteq c : d \Rightarrow c : d \doteq a : b$ that is $a \oplus d = b \oplus c \Rightarrow c \oplus b = d \oplus a$

Exchange of the means: $a : b \doteq c : d \Rightarrow a : c \doteq b : d$ that is $a \oplus d = b \oplus c \Rightarrow a \oplus d = c \oplus b$

From this, we can deduce that our operator $\oplus$ must be commutative, since $c \oplus b = b \oplus c$ if $a : b \doteq c : d$. Moreover, we notice that the equation concerning the symmetry of analogy is always true because of the commutativity of the operators $\oplus$ and $=$.

Determinism: $a : a \doteq c : x \Rightarrow x = c$ and $a : b \doteq a : x \Rightarrow x = b$. It can be expressed with $\oplus$ as: $a \oplus x = a \oplus c \Rightarrow x = c$ and $a \oplus x = b \oplus a \Rightarrow x = b$

The first equation expresses the algebraic property of *left regularity*. Because of the commutativity, we can say that $\oplus$ must be *regular*.

Construction of an Operator and a Distance

The alphabet as a finite group. We already know that the operator $\oplus$ must be commutative and regular. In addition to these properties, we would like to solve some cases in analogy that Lepage cannot handle.

One of these cases is to find a solution to the analogical equation: $a : \epsilon \doteq \epsilon : x$, which can be expressed as: $a \oplus x = \epsilon \oplus \epsilon$. If we consider that $\oplus$ is an internal composition operator and that ϵ is the null element of $\Sigma \cup \{\epsilon\}$ for $\oplus$, then we transform the above expression into: $a \oplus x = \epsilon \oplus \epsilon = \epsilon = x \oplus a$.

Since every element in $\Sigma \cup \{\epsilon\}$ has a symmetric, every equation of this form has a solution which is the symmetric of a. Assuming that $(\Sigma \cup \{\epsilon\}, \oplus)$ is a *group* [9] is sufficient to get these properties. Moreover, this group is *abelian* since $\oplus$ is commutative.

An example: the additive cyclic group We take as an example the cyclic finite abelian group. The table that describes $\oplus$ in this case is given in [4] and in Fig. 2. This algebraic structure is sufficient to solve every analogical equation on letters, but it is only one solution between others. This table, where each line is a circular permutation of the others, brings the unique solution to every analogical equation on letters. The case quoted at the beginning of section 3.2, $a : \epsilon \doteq \epsilon : x$ also has a solution.

$\oplus$	ϵ	a	b	c	d	e	f
ϵ	ϵ	a	b	c	d	e	f
a	a	b	c	d	e	f	ϵ
b	b	c	d	e	f	ϵ	a
c	c	d	e	f	ϵ	a	b
d	d	e	f	ϵ	a	b	c
e	e	f	ϵ	a	b	c	d
f	f	ϵ	a	b	c	d	e

$\mathcal{C}$	ϵ	a	b	c	d	e	f
ϵ	0	α	β	γ	γ	β	α
a	α	0	α	β	γ	γ	β
b	β	α	0	α	β	γ	γ
c	γ	β	α	0	α	β	γ
d	γ	γ	β	α	0	α	β
e	β	γ	γ	β	α	0	α
f	α	β	γ	γ	β	α	0

Fig. 2. A table for an analogical operator on an alphabet of 6 elements plus ϵ, seen as the additive cyclic group $\mathcal{G}_7$, and the corresponding discrete distance $\mathcal{C}$.

A distance on the additive cyclic group. We also have to build a distance on the alphabet, since it is necessary to compute the edit distance between strings of letters when using the Wagner and Fischer algorithm [6]. In the case of the additive cyclic group, we have a well defined table ([4] and Fig. 2). For a quadruplet (x, y, z, t) that defines an analogy, we have the equation: $((x : y \doteq z : t) \Leftrightarrow (x \oplus t = y \oplus z)) \Rightarrow \mathcal{C}_{x \to y} = \mathcal{C}_{z \to t}$. This equation is coherent with the first characterization of a parallelogram, as given in section 3.2. Our aim is to guess a particular structure for the corresponding distance table, if there is one, by using the analogy table. Considering all the equations deduced from analogical equations given by this particular analogy table, we can deduce the distance related to the analogy defined by table. The distance table has only $\lfloor \frac{n}{2} \rfloor$ different values and has a constrained structure (see [4]).

We have a way to construct a distance table under these constraints: by using a geometrical representation in $\mathbb{R}^2$, in which the letters are regularly placed on a circle (see Fig. 3) and by defining the distance between letters as the euclidian distance in $\mathbb{R}^2$. This distance table is coherent with the distance related to analogy that we have just defined. But, of course, other solutions can be devised[1].

3.3   Using Transducers for Computing Analogical Solutions

We have now to find how to compose these elementary equations from the first three sequences of the analogical equation on sequences $X : Y \doteq Z : T$, T

---

[1] Another useful case is when the letters of the alphabet are defined as sets of binary features [10]. This is for example the case of the phonemes of a language. The resolution is done by solving analogies between sets of features and a natural distance is the Hamming distance (the distance is given by the difference between phonemes in term of features). In that case, some analogical equations on the alphabet may have no solution.

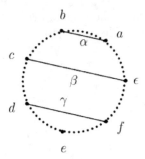

Fig. 3. Representing $\mathcal{G}_7$, the additive cyclic finite group with 7 elements, and defining a distance on $\mathcal{G}_7$.

being the solution to find. The first problem is to characterize the relation "is to" in the analogical equation. Our idea is to use the notion edit distance to represent the transformation of a sequence into another. In this subsection, we will explain how to formalise this transformation with a transducer. The second problem is to characterize the relation "as" that represents a relation between the two transformations. This relation will be formalized with an automaton. The use of transducers is inspired from the work of Stroppa and Yvon[11].

About Finite State Tranducers and Automata. A finite automaton A is a 5-tuple $(\Sigma, Q, q^0, F, \delta)$, where Σ is a finite alphabet, Q a finite set of states, $q^0 \in Q$ the initial state, $F \subset Q$ the set of final states, and Δ the transition function. The langage accepted by A is noted $L(A)$; denoting δ^* the transitive closure of δ we have $L(A) = \{w, \delta^*(q^0, w) \in F\}$. A_L denotes the canonical automaton for L whenever L is a rational language.

A finite-state transducer T is a finite automaton with two tapes (an input and an output tape); transitions are labeled with pairs $a : b$ with a in the input alphabet Σ_1, and b in the output alphabet Σ_2. In the rest of this paper, we will only consider the case where $\Sigma_1 = \Sigma_2$. A thorough introduction to finite-state transducers and their use in the context of natural language processing is given in [12].

An Edit Transducer for the Relation "Is to". The idea is to define a weighted transducer that can copy with a null cost, that can substitute, insert or delete with costs that are defined by the distance table proposed in section 3.2. This transducer is represented in Fig. 4. We assume that $\mathcal{C}_{a \to b}$ is the cost of the substitution of a into b. If a is ϵ then it concerns the insertion of b, if b is ϵ then it concerns the deletion of a.

The edit transducer is $T_{EDIT} = (\Sigma_1 \cup \Sigma_2, Q, q_0, \delta)$, the 1-state weighted transducer defined as: $Q = \{0\}$, $I = 0$, $F = \{0\}$, and δ is defined as $\forall a \in \Sigma_1$ and $\forall b \in \Sigma_2$, $\delta(0, a : b/\mathcal{C}_{a \to b}) = 0$; $\delta(0, a : \epsilon/\mathcal{C}_{a \to \epsilon}) = 0$; $\delta(0, \epsilon : b/\mathcal{C}_{\epsilon \to b}) = 0$; $\forall a = b, \delta(0, a : b/0) = 0$.

Let T_X (*resp.* T_Y) be the transducer that copies X (*resp.* Y). The alignment between two sequences X and Y is then the result of the composition $T_X \circ$

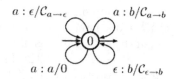

$$a : \epsilon/\mathcal{C}_{a \to \epsilon} \qquad a : b/\mathcal{C}_{a \to b}$$

$$a : a/0 \qquad \epsilon : b/\mathcal{C}_{\epsilon \to b}$$

Fig. 4. The edit transducer.

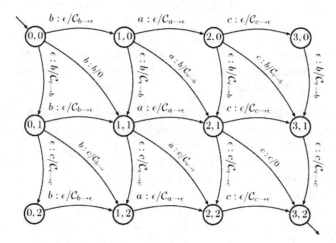

Fig. 5. The automaton that recognizes all the alignments between bac and bc.

$T_{EDIT} \circ T_Y$. The result is very similar to the edit tables built by the Wagner and Fischer algorithm (Fig. 5).

An Automaton for the Relation "as". The next step is to use the relation between edit transformations to "align" the transformation of X into Y and of X into Z. The principle of our approach is arrange the alignments found during the former step so as to produce all possible solutions by solving elementary equations.

The composition produces a transducer that recognizes the language of the alignments between two sequences. This transducer has transitions that correspond either to substitution (including identity), to deletion or insertion. Each state of the transducer is a compound state built from the edit transducer and the copy transducers. It is therefore numbered by a couple of indices taken from both copy transducers (see Fig. 5).

We propose to build an automaton which recognizes the language of the solutions of the analogical equation. The idea is to synchronise the transitions in this automaton on the letters of X, the first string of the analogical equation $X : Y \doteq Z : T$. That is why we consider that in every situation (state), we always are in the same position in X^1 (aligned with Y^1) and in X^2 (aligned with Z^1).

This automaton takes into account compound transducers that produces the alignments between X^1 and Y^1 in one hand, and the alignments between X^2 and Z^1 in the other hand. A state of the automaton is designed by a couple of indices of the transducers, that is $((i,j),(i',j'))$ and the first state is $((0,0),(0,0))$. Considering that we come from a state $((i,j),(i,j'))$ (as $i=i'$), we can go to several possible states, incrementing i or j or j'. Each transitions corresponds to a case where, from X to Y and from X to Z, there is a deletion on both sides, an insertion on one side and nothing on the other side, *etc.* Remark that going from state $((i,j),(i,j'))$ to state $((i,j+1),(i,j'+1))$, that would represent two insertions at the same time, is impossible. A transition of this automaton therefore corresponds to the solution of an elementary analogical equation.

Finally the automaton that recognizes the language of analogical solutions is $A=(\Sigma,Q,q_0,\delta)$, defined as:

- Q, the set of states, numbered by the indices of states of both transducers that produces alignements between X and Y and between X and Z;
- $I=((0,0),(0,0))$, the initial state;
- $F=\{(i,j),(i',j')\}$ the final state where $i=i'=j=j'$. These indices are equal to the length of the optimal alignments;
- δ is defined as $\forall t \in \Sigma$
  - $\delta(((i,j),(i,j')),t)=((i+1,j),(i+1,j'))$, where $X[i]:\epsilon \doteq \epsilon:t$;
  - $\delta(((i,j),(i,j')),t)=((i+1,j),(i+1,j'+1))$, where $X[i]:\epsilon \doteq \epsilon:t$;
  - $\delta(((i,j),(i,j')),t)=((i,j+1),(i,j'))$, where $\epsilon:Y[j] \doteq \epsilon:t$;
  - $\delta(((i,j),(i,j')),t)=((i+1,j+1),(i+1,j'))$, where $X[i]:Y[j] \doteq \epsilon:t$;
  - $\delta(((i,j),(i,j')),t) = ((i+1,j+1),(i+1,j'+1))$, where $X[i]:Y[j] \doteq Z[j']:t$;
  - $\delta(((i,j),(i,j')),t)=((i,j),(i,j'+1))$, where $\epsilon:\epsilon \doteq Z[j']:t$;
  - $\delta(((i,j),(i,j')),t)=((i,j+1),(i,j'))$, where $\epsilon:Y[j] \doteq \epsilon:t$.

The solution to each elementary equation is found in the analogy table defined in section 3.2. The combination of the edit transducers and the automaton produce a graph with weighted edges. The path from the initial state to the final state that have the minimum cost describe the solutions of the analogical equation.

We have proposed a direct algorithm for finding a set of solution to any analogical equation on sequences, based on the same concepts that we have presented in the precedent section. This algorithm has been presented in full details in [4]. It can be considered as a heuristic algorithm since it only considers the optimal alignments to solve the analogy. On the contrary, our formal approach takes every possible alignment into account, solves the analogy on letters and a preference measure can then be applied to chose the best solutions.

4   Related Work

Solving analogical equations between strings has only drawn little attention in the past. Most relevant to our discussion are the works of Lepage, especially [13] and [14], presented in full details in [1] and more recent work of Yvon[15] and Stroppa[11].

Like in studies of Lepage, Yvon considers in [15] that comparing sequences for solving analogical equations must be based only on insertions and deletions of letters[2], and must satisfy the axioms of Lepage. Yvon introduces the notion of *shuffle* [16, 17], and of *complementary set* to contruct a finite-state transducer to compute the set of a solutions to any analogical equation on strings. He produces also a refinement of this finite state machine able to rank these analogies so as to recover an intuitive preference towards "simple" analogies, that preserve large chunks of the original objects.

Lepage [13] details the implementation of a analogy solver for words, based on a generalisation of the algorithm computing the longest common subsequence between strings. Given the equation $u : v \doteq w : x$, this algorithm proceeds as follows: it alternatively scans v and w for symbols in u; when one is found, say in w, it outputs in x the prefix of w which did not match, while extending as much as possible the current match; then exchange the roles of v and w. If u has been entirely matched, then output if necessary in x the remaining suffixes of v and w; otherwise the analogical equation does not have any solution.

In the framework of Yvon, our approach is equivalent to computing the longest common subsequence (and not all the common subsequences). Thus we can consider that we propose an extension that uses one supplementary editing operator: the substitution of a letter by a different letter. Moreover, Yvon says himself in [15] that his work is very similar to Lepage's work.

5   Conclusion and Extension

In this paper, we propose a new approach for solving analogy between sequences as a first step to learning by analogy. This approach is built on a formal framework based on transducers using edit distance in the "is to" relation and an automaton for solving elementary equations on letters.

We have given an algebraic structure so as to get a unique solution of all possible combinations of analogical equations with symbols chosen in an alphabet. We have shown that a finite additive cyclic group is a sufficient structure and we give an example of the corresponding operator $\oplus$ on a given set $\Sigma \cup \{\epsilon\}$. We also have shown how to build a distance on this group, needed for alignments at the first step of the algorithm.

An extension to this work could focus on several points. Firstly we could examine if there less restrictive algebraic forms than the cyclic finite group for respecting the desired properties of an analogy. We could also study the influence of the analogical operator on the distance table. For example, is there an algorithm to give a general solution for building a distance for every alphabet given an analogical table? Is there an algorithm to transform an *a priori* distance into an analogical distance or to built an analogical distance that is *close* to the given distance? Finally, we have to focus on learning by analogy.

---

[2] This assumption is called the **inclusion** property.

References

1. LEPAGE, Y.: De l'analogie rendant compte de la commutation en linguistique, Grenoble (2003) Habilitation à diriger les recherches.
2. LEPAGE, Y., ANDO, S.I.: Saussurian analogy: a theoretical account and its application. In: Proceedings of COLING-96, København (1996) 717–722
3. HOFSTADTER, D., the Fluid Analogies Research Group: Fluid Concepts and Creative Analogies. Basic Books, New York (1994)
4. MICLET, L., DELHAY, A.: Analogy on sequences: a definition and an algorithm. Technical Report 4969, INRIA (2003)
5. AHO, A., ULLMAN, J.: The Theory of Parsing, Translation and Compiling, Vol 1: Parsing. Prentice-Hall (1972)
6. WAGNER, R., FISCHER, M.: The string-to-string correction problem. JACM (1974)
7. CROCHEMORE, M., et al.: Algorithmique du texte. Vuibert (2001)
8. SANKOFF, D., KRUSKAL, J., eds.: Time Warps, String Edits and Macromolecules: the Theory and Practice of Sequence Comparison. Addidon-Wesley (1983)
9. ROWLAND, T.: Group. Technical report, Mathworld, Wolfram (2004) http://mathworld.wolfram.com/Group.html.
10. MICLET, L., DELHAY, A.: Relation d'analogie et distance sur un alphabet défini par des traits. Technical Report 5244, INRIA (2004) in French.
11. STROPPA, N., YVON, F.: Analogie dans les séquences: un solveur à états finis. In: TALN 2004. (2004)
12. ROCHE, E., SCHABES, Y. In: Introduction to finite-state devices in natural language processing. The MIT Press (1997)
13. LEPAGE, Y.: Solving analogies on words: an algorithm. In: Proceedings of COLING-ACL'98, Vol 1, Montréal (1998) 728–735
14. LEPAGE, Y.: Analogy and formal languages. In: Proceedings of FG/MOL 2001, Helsinki (2001) 373–378
15. YVON, F.: Analogy-based NLP: Implementation issues. Technical report, Ecole Nationale Supérieure des Télécommunications (2003)
16. SAKAROVITCH, J.: Eléments de théorie des automates. Vuibert (2003)
17. KOZEN, D.: Automata and Computability. Springer (1996)

Representing Languages
by Learnable Rewriting Systems*

Rémi Eyraud, Colin de la Higuera, and Jean-Christophe Janodet

EURISE, Université Jean Monnet de Saint-Etienne,
23 rue Paul Michelon, 42023 Saint-Etienne, France
{remi.eyraud,cdlh,janodet}@univ-st-etienne.fr

Abstract. Powerful methods and algorithms are known to learn regular languages. Aiming at extending them to more complex grammars, we choose to change the way we represent these languages. Among the formalisms that allow to define classes of languages, the one of string-rewriting systems (SRS) has outstanding properties. Indeed, SRS are expressive enough to define, in a uniform way, a noteworthy and non trivial class of languages that contains all the regular languages, $\{a^n b^n : n \geq 0\}$, $\{w \in \{a,b\}^* : |w|_a = |w|_b\}$, the parenthesis languages of Dyck, the language of Lukasewitz, and many others. Moreover, SRS constitute an efficient (often linear) parsing device for strings, and are thus promising and challenging candidates in forthcoming applications of Grammatical Inference. In this paper, we pioneer the problem of their learnability. We propose a novel and sound algorithm which allows to identify them in polynomial time. We illustrate the execution of our algorithm throughout a large amount of examples and finally raise some open questions and research directions.

Keywords: Learning Context-Free Languages, Rewriting Systems.

1 Introduction

Whereas for the case of learning regular languages there are now a number of positive results and algorithm, things tend to get harder when the entire class of context-free languages is considered [10, 17]. Typical approaches have consisted in learning special sorts of grammars [20], by using genetic algorithms or artificial intelligence ideas [16], and by compression techniques [13]. Yet more and more attention has been drawn to the problem: One example is the OMPHALOS context-free language learning competition [19].

An attractive alternative when blocked by negative results is to change the representation mode. In this line, little work has been done for the context-free case: One exception is pure context-free grammars which are grammars where both the non-terminals and the terminals come from a same alphabet [8].

---

* This work was supported in part by the IST Programme of the European Community, under the PASCAL Network of Excellence, IST-2002-506778. This publication only reflects the authors' views.

G. Paliouras and Y. Sakakibara (Eds.): ICGI 2004, LNAI 3264, pp. 139–150, 2004.

In this paper, we investigate string-rewriting systems (SRS). Invented in 1914 by Axel Thue, the theory of SRS (also called semi-Thue systems) and its extension to trees and to graphs was paid a lot of attention all along the 20th century (see [1,3]). Rewriting a string consists in replacing substrings by others, as far as possible, following laws called rewrite rules. For instance, consider strings made of a and b, and the single rewrite rule $ab \to \lambda$. Using this rule consists in replacing a substring ab by the empty string, thus in erasing ab. It allows to rewrite $abaabbab$ as follows:

$$abaab\underline{ab} \to aba\underline{ab}b \to \underline{ab}ab \to \underline{ab} \to \lambda$$

Other rewriting derivations may be considered but they all lead to λ. Actually, it is rather clear on this example that a string will rewrite to λ *iff* it is a "parenthetic" string, *i.e.*, a string of the Dyck language. More precisely, the Dyck language is completely characterized by this single rewrite rule and the string λ, which is reached by rewriting all other strings of the language. This property was first noticed in a seminal paper by Nivat [14] which was the starting point of a large amount of work during the three last decades.

We use this property, and others to introduce a class of rewriting systems which is powerful enough to represent in an economical way all regular languages and some typical context-free languages: $\{a^n b^n : n \geq 0\}$, $\{w \in \{a,b\}^* : |w|_a = |w|_b\}$, the parenthesis languages of Dyck, the language of Lukasewitz, and many others. We also provide a learning algorithm called LARS (Learning Algorithm for Rewriting Systems) which can learn systems representing these languages from string examples and counter-examples of the language.

In section 2 we give the general notations relative to the languages we consider and discuss the notion of learning. We introduce our rewriting systems and their expressiveness in section 3 and develop the properties they must fulfill to be learnable in section 4. The general learning algorithm is presented and justified in section 5. We report in section 6 some experimental results and conclude.

2   Learning Languages

An *alphabet* Σ is a finite nonempty set of symbols called *letters*. A *string* w over Σ is a finite sequence $w = a_1 a_2 \ldots a_n$ of letters. Let $|w|$ denote the length of w. In the following, letters will be indicated by $a, b, c, \ldots$, strings by $u, v, \ldots, z$, and the empty string by λ. Let Σ^* be the set of all strings. We assume a fixed but arbitrary total order $\leq$ on the letters of Σ. As usual, we extend $\leq$ to Σ^* by defining the *hierarchical order* [15], denoted $\trianglelefteq$, as follows:

$$\forall w_1, w_2 \in \Sigma^*, w_1 \triangleleft w_2 \text{ } iff \begin{cases} |w_1| < |w_2| \text{ or} \\ |w_1| = |w_2| \text{ and } \exists u, v_1, v_2 \in \Sigma^*, \exists x_1, x_2 \in \Sigma \\ \text{such that } w_1 = u x_1 v_1, w_2 = u x_2 v_2 \text{ and } x_1 < x_2. \end{cases}$$

By a language we mean any subset $L \subseteq \Sigma^*$. Many classes of languages were investigated in the literature. In general, the definition of a class $\mathbb{L}$ relies on a class $\mathbb{R}$ of abstract machines, here called *representations*, that characterize all and only the languages of $\mathbb{L}$: (1) $\forall R \in \mathbb{R}, \mathcal{L}(R) \in \mathbb{L}$ and (2) $\forall L \in$

$\mathbb{L}, \exists R \in \mathbb{R}$ such that $\mathcal{L}(R) = L$. Two representations R_1 and R_2 are *equivalent*
iff $\mathcal{L}(R_1) = \mathcal{L}(R_2)$. In this paper, we will investigate the class REG of *regular*
languages characterized by the class DFA of *deterministic finite automata (dfa)*,
and the class CFL of *context-free languages* represented by the class CFG of
context-free grammars (cfg).

We now turn to our learning problem. The *size* of a representation R, denoted
by $\|R\|$, is polynomially related to the size of its encoding.

Definition 1. *Let $\mathbb{L}$ be a class of languages represented by some class $\mathbb{R}$.*

1. *A sample S for a language $L \in \mathbb{L}$ is a finite set of ordered pairs $\langle w, label(w) \rangle \in$*
   $\Sigma^* \times \{+, -\}$ such that if $label(w) = +$ then $w \in L$ and if $label(w) = -$ then
   $w \notin L$. The size of S is the sum of the lengths of all strings in S.
2. *An $(\mathbb{L}, \mathbb{R})$-learning algorithm is a program that takes as input a sample of*
   labeled strings and outputs a representation from $\mathbb{R}$.

Finally, let us recall what "learning" means. We choose to base ourselves
on the paradigm of polynomial identification, as defined in [6,2], since many
authors showed that it was both relevant and tractable. Other paradigms are
known (*e.g.* PAC-learnability), but they are often either similar to this one or
inconvenient for Grammatical Inference problems.

In this paradigm we first demand that the learning algorithm has a running time polynomial in the size of the data from which it is learning from.
Next we want the algorithm to converge in some way to a chosen target. Ideally
the convergence point should be met very quickly, after having seen a polynomial number of examples. As this constraint is usually too hard, we want the
convergence to take place in the limit, *i.e.*, after having seen a finite number
of examples. The polynomial aspects then correspond to the size of a minimal
learning or *characteristic* sample, whose presence should ensure identification.
For more details on these models we refer the reader to [6,2].

3   Defining Languages with String-Rewriting Systems

String-rewriting systems are usually defined as sets of rewrite rules. These rules
allow to replace factors by others in strings. However, as we feel that this mechanism is not flexible enough, we would like to extend it. Indeed, a rule that one
would like to use at the beginning (prefix) or at the end of a string could also
be used in the middle of this string and then have undesirable side effects.

Therefore, we introduce two new symbols $ and £ that do not belong to
the alphabet Σ and will respectively mark the beginning and the end of each
string. In other words, we are going to consider strings from the set $\$\Sigma^*\pounds$. As
for the rewrite rules, they will be *partially* marked (and thus belong to $\overline{\Sigma^*} =$
$(\lambda + \$)\Sigma^*(\lambda + \pounds)$). Their forms will constrain their uses either to the beginning,
or to the end, or to the middle, or to the string taken as a whole. Notice that this
solution is an intermediate approach between the usual one and string-rewriting
systems with variables introduced in [11].

Definition 2 (Delimited SRS).

- *A delimited rewrite rule is an ordered pair of strings* (l, r), *generally written* $l \rightarrow r$, *such that l and r satisfy one of the four following constraints:*
  1. $l, r \in \$\Sigma^*$ *(used to rewrite prefixes) or*
  2. $l, r \in \$\Sigma^*\pounds$ *(used to rewrite whole strings) or*
  3. $l, r \in \Sigma^*$ *(used to rewrite factors) or*
  4. $l, r \in \Sigma^*\pounds$ *(used to rewrite suffixes).*

  Rules of type 1 and 2 will be called \$-rules and rules of type 3 and 4 will be called non-\$-rules.
- *By a delimited string-rewriting system (DSRS), we mean any finite set $\mathcal{R}$ of delimited rewrite rules.*

Let $|\mathcal{R}|$ be the number of rules of $\mathcal{R}$ and $\|\mathcal{R}\|$ the sum of the lengths of the strings $\mathcal{R}$ is made of: $\|\mathcal{R}\| = \sum_{(l \rightarrow r) \in \mathcal{R}} |lr|$.

Given a DSRS $\mathcal{R}$ and two strings $w_1, w_2 \in \overline{\Sigma^*}$, we say that w_1 *rewrites in one step into* w_2, written $w_1 \rightarrow_{\mathcal{R}} w_2$ or simply $w_1 \rightarrow w_2$, *iff* there exists a rule $(l \rightarrow r) \in \mathcal{R}$ and two strings $u, v \in \overline{\Sigma^*}$ such that $w_1 = ulv$ and $w_2 = urv$. A string w is *reducible iff* there exists w' such that $w \rightarrow w'$, and *irreducible* otherwise. *E.g.*, the string $\$aabb\pounds$ rewrites to $\$aaa\pounds$ with rule $bb\pounds \rightarrow a\pounds$ and $\$aaa\pounds$ is irreducible. We get immediately the following property:

Proposition 1. *The set* $\$\Sigma^*\pounds$ *is stable w.r.t.* $\rightarrow_{\mathcal{R}}$.

In other words, $\$$ and $\pounds$ cannot disappear or move in a string by rewriting.

Let $\rightarrow_{\mathcal{R}}^*$ (or simply $\rightarrow^*$) denote the reflexive and transitive closure of $\rightarrow_{\mathcal{R}}$. We say that w_1 *reduces to* w_2 or that w_2 *is derivable from* w_1 *iff* $w_1 \rightarrow_{\mathcal{R}}^* w_2$.

Definition 3 (Language Induced by a DSRS). *Given a DSRS $\mathcal{R}$ and an irreducible string $e \in \Sigma^*$, we define the language $\mathcal{L}(\mathcal{R}, e)$ as the set of strings that reduce to e using the rules of $\mathcal{R}$:*

$$\mathcal{L}(\mathcal{R}, e) = \{w \in \Sigma^* : \$w\pounds \rightarrow_{\mathcal{R}}^* \$e\pounds\}.$$

Deciding whether a string w belongs to a language $\mathcal{L}(\mathcal{R}, e)$ or not consists in trying to obtain e from w by a rewriting derivation. However, w may be the starting point of numerous derivations and so, such a task may be really hard. (Nevertheless, remember that we introduced $\$$ and $\pounds$ to allow some control...) We will tackle these problems in next section but present some examples first.

Example 1. Let $\Sigma = \{a, b\}$.

- $\mathcal{L}(\{ab \rightarrow \lambda\}, \lambda)$ is the Dyck language. Indeed, this single rule erases factors ab, so we get the following example of derivation:

$$\$aabb\underline{ab}\pounds \rightarrow \$a\underline{ab}b\pounds \rightarrow \$\underline{ab}\pounds \rightarrow \$\pounds$$

- $\mathcal{L}(\{ab \rightarrow \lambda; ba \rightarrow \lambda\}, \lambda)$ is the language $\{w \in \Sigma^* : |w|_a = |w|_b\}$, since every rewriting step erases one a and one b.

- $\mathcal{L}(\{aabb \to ab; \$ab\pounds \to \$\pounds\}, \lambda) = \{a^n b^n : n \in \mathbb{N}\}$. For instance,

$$\$aa\underline{aabbbb}\pounds \to \$a\underline{aabbb}\pounds \to \$\underline{aabb}\pounds \to \$\underline{ab}\pounds \to \$\pounds$$

Notice that the rule $\$ab\pounds \to \$\pounds$ is necessary for λ to belong to the language.
- $\mathcal{L}(\{\$ab \to \$\}, \lambda)$ is the regular language $(ab)^*$. Indeed,

$$\$\underline{ab}abab\pounds \to \$\underline{ab}ab\pounds \to \$\underline{ab}\pounds \to \$\pounds$$

Actually, all regular languages can be induced by a DSRS:

Theorem 1. *For each regular language L, there exist a DSRS $\mathcal{R}$ and a string e such that $L = \mathcal{L}(\mathcal{R}, e)$.*

Proof (Hint). A DSRS that is only made of $\$$-rules defines a *prefix grammar* [5]. It has been shown that this kind of grammars generates exactly the regular languages.

4 Shaping Learnable DSRS

As already mentioned, a string w belongs to a language $\mathcal{L}(\mathcal{R}, e)$ *iff* one can build a derivation from w to e. However this raises many difficulties. Firstly, one can imagine a DSRS such that a string can be rewritten indefinitely[1]. In other words, an algorithm that would try to answer the problem may loop. Secondly, even if all the derivations induced by a DSRS are finite, they could be of exponential lengths and thus computationally intractable[2].

We first extend the hierarchical order $\trianglelefteq$ to the strings of $\overline{\Sigma^*}$, by defining the *extended hierarchical order*, denoted $\preceq$, as follows: $\forall w_1, w_2 \in \Sigma^*$, if $w_1 \triangleleft w_2$ then $w_1 \prec \$w_1 \prec w_1\pounds \prec \$w_1\pounds \prec w_2$. Therefore, if $a < b$, then $\lambda \triangleleft a \triangleleft b \triangleleft aa \triangleleft ab \triangleleft ba \triangleleft bb \triangleleft aaa \triangleleft \ldots$, so $\lambda \prec \$ \prec \pounds \prec \$\pounds \prec a \prec \$a \prec a\pounds \prec \$a\pounds \prec b \prec \ldots$ The following technical definition ensures that all the rewriting derivations are finite and tractable in polynomial time.

Definition 4 (Hybrid DSRS). *We say that a rule $l \to r$ is*
(i) length-reducing iff $|l| > |r|$ and (ii) length-lexicographic iff $l \succ r$.
A DSRS $\mathcal{R}$ is hybrid iff (i) all $\$-rules (whose left hand sides are in $\$\Sigma^*(\lambda + \pounds)$) are length-lexicographic and (ii) all non-$\$-rules (whose left hand sides are in $\Sigma^*(\lambda + \pounds)$) are length-reducing.

Theorem 2. *All the derivations induced by a hybrid DSRS $\mathcal{R}$ are finite. Moreover, every derivation starting from a string w has a length that is $\leq |w| \cdot |\mathcal{R}|$.*

---

[1] Consider the derivations induced by $\{a \to b; b \to a; c \to cc\} \ldots$

[2] Consider the DSRS $\{1\pounds \to 0\pounds; 0\pounds \to c1d\pounds; 0c \to c1; 1c \to 0d; d0 \to 0d; d1 \to 1d; dd \to \lambda\}$. All the derivations it induces are finite; Indeed, assuming that $d > 1 > 0 > c$, the left hand side l is lexicographically greater than the right hand side r for all rules $l \to r$, so this DSRS is strongly normalizing [3]. However, it induces the derivation $\$1111\pounds \to \$1110\pounds \to^* \$1101\pounds \to \$1100\pounds \to^* \$1011\pounds \to \ldots \to^* \$0000\pounds$

Proof. Let $w_1 \to w_2$ be a single rewriting step. There exists a rule $l \to r$ and two strings $u, v \in \overline{\Sigma}^*$ such that $w_1 = ulv$ and $w_2 = urv$. Notice that if $|l| > |r|$ then $l \succ r$. Moreover, if $l \succ r$, then we deduce that $w_1 \succ w_2$. So if one has a derivation $w \to u_1 \to u_2 \to \ldots$, then $w \succ u_1 \succ u_2 \succ \ldots$. As $\preceq$ is a good order, there is no infinite and strictly decreasing chain of the form $w \succ u_1 \succ u_2 \succ \ldots$. So every derivation induced by $\mathcal{R}$ is finite. Now let $n \in \mathbb{N}$. Assume that for all strings w' such that $|w'| < n$, the lengths of the derivations starting from w' are at most $|w'| \cdot |\mathcal{R}|$. Let w be a string of length n. We claim that the maximum length of a derivation that would preserve the length of w cannot exceed $|\mathcal{R}|$ rewriting steps. Indeed, all rules that can be used along such a derivation are of the form $\$l \to \$r$, with $|l| = |r|$ and $l \succ r$; When such a rule is used once, then it cannot be used a second time in the same derivation. Otherwise, there would exists a derivation $\$lu\pounds \to \$ru\pounds \to \ldots \to \$lv\pounds$ with $|u| = |v|$ (since the length is preserved). As $\$ru\pounds \to^* \$lv\pounds$ and $|l| = |r|$ and $|u| = |v|$, we deduce that $r \succeq l$ which is impossible since $r \prec l$. So there are at most $|\mathcal{R}|$ rewriting steps that preserve the length of w, and then the application of a rule produces a string w' whose length is $< n$. So by induction hypothesis, the length of a derivation starting from w is no more than $|\mathcal{R}| + |w'| \cdot |\mathcal{R}| \leq |w| \cdot |\mathcal{R}|$.   □

We saw that a hybrid DSRS induces finite and tractable derivations. Nevertheless, many different irreducible strings may be reached from one given string by rewriting. Therefore, answering the problem "$w \in \mathcal{L}(\mathcal{R}, e)$?" will require to compute *all* the derivations that start with w and check if one of them ends with e. In other words, such a DSRS is a kind of "undeterministic" (thus inefficient) parsing device. An usual way to circumvent this difficulty is to impose our hybrid DSRS to be also Church-Rosser [3].

Definition 5 (Church-Rosser DSRS). *We say that a DSRS $\mathcal{R}$ is Church-Rosser iff for all strings $w, u_1, u_2 \in \overline{\Sigma}^*$ such that $w \to^* u_1$ and $w \to^* u_2$, there exists $w' \in \overline{\Sigma}^*$ such that $u_1 \to^* w'$ and $u_2 \to^* w'$.*

In the definition above, if $w \to^* u_1$ and $w \to^* u_2$ and u_1 and u_2 are irreducible strings, then $u_1 = u_2(= w')$. So given a string w, there is no more than *one* irreducible string that can be reached by a derivation starting with w, whatever the derivation is considered. However, the Church-Rosser property is undecidable in general [3], so we constrain our DSRS to fulfill a restrictive condition:

Definition 6 (ANo DSRS). *A DSRS $\mathcal{R}$ is almost nonoverlapping (ANo) iff for all rules $R_1 = l_1 \to r_1$ and $R_2 = l_2 \to r_2$ of $\mathcal{R}$:*

   i. if $l_1 = l_2$ then $r_1 = r_2$;
  ii. if l_1 is strictly included in l_2: $\exists u, v \in \Sigma^*, ul_1v = l_2, uv \neq \lambda$, then $ur_1v = r_2$;
 iii. if a strict suffix of l_1 is a strict prefix of l_2:
     $\exists u, v \in \Sigma^*, l_1u = vl_2, 0 < |v| < |l_1|$, then $r_1u = vr_2$.

Notice that if R_1 does not overlap R_2, then R_2 may still overlap R_1.

Theorem 3. *Every ANo DSRS is Church-Rosser. Moreover, every subsystem of an ANo DSRS is an ANo DSRS, and thus Church-Rosser.*

Proof. Let us show that an ANo DSRS $\mathcal{R}$ induces a rewriting relation $\to_{\mathcal{R}}$ that is *subcommutative* [7]. Let us write $w_1 \to_\varepsilon w_2$ *iff* $w_1 \to_{\mathcal{R}} w_2$ or $w_1 = w_2$. We claim that for all w, u_1, u_2, if $w \to_{\mathcal{R}} u_1$ and $w \to_{\mathcal{R}} u_2$, then there exists a string w' such that $u_1 \to_\varepsilon w'$ and $u_2 \to_\varepsilon w'$. Indeed, assume that $w \to_{\mathcal{R}} u_1$ uses a rule $R_1 = l_1 \to r_1$ and $w \to_{\mathcal{R}} u_2$ uses a rule $R_2 = l_2 \to r_2$. If both rewriting steps are independent, *i.e.*, $w = x l_1 y l_2 z$ for some strings x, y, z, then $u_1 = x r_1 y l_2 z$ and $u_2 = x l_1 y r_2 z$; Obviously, $u_1 \to_{\mathcal{R}} w'$ and $u_2 \to_{\mathcal{R}} w'$ with $w' = x r_1 y r_2 z$. Otherwise, R_1 overlaps R_2 (or vice-versa), and so $u_1 = u_2$, since $\mathcal{R}$ is ANo. An easy induction allows to generalize this property to derivations: If $w \to_{\mathcal{R}}^* u_1$ and $w \to_{\mathcal{R}}^* u_2$ then there exists w' such that $u_1 \to_\varepsilon^* w'$ and $u_2 \to_\varepsilon^* w'$, where $\to_\varepsilon^*$ is the reflexive and transitive closure of $\to_\varepsilon$. Finally, as $u_1 \to_\varepsilon^* w'$ and $u_2 \to_\varepsilon^* w'$, we deduce that $u_1 \to_{\mathcal{R}}^* w'$ and $u_2 \to_{\mathcal{R}}^* w'$. □

Finally, we get the following properties with our DSRS: (1) For all strings w, there is no more than *one* irreducible string that can be reached by a derivation which starts with w, whatever the derivation is considered. This irreducible string will be called the *normal form* of w and denoted $w \downarrow$. (2) No derivation can be prolonged indefinitely, so every string w has at least one normal form. And whatever the way a string w is reduced, the rewriting steps produce strings that are ineluctably closer and closer to $w \downarrow$. An important consequence is that one has an immediate algorithm to check whether $w \in \mathcal{L}(\mathcal{R}, e)$ or not: One only needs to (i) compute the normal form $w \downarrow$ of w and (ii) check if $w \downarrow$ and e are *syntactically* equal. As all the derivations have polynomial lengths, this algorithm is polynomial in time.

5   Learning Languages Induced by DSRS

In this section we present our learning algorithm and its properties. The idea is to enumerate the rules following the order $\preceq$. We discard those that are useless or inconsistent *w.r.t.* the data, and those that break the ANo condition.

The first thing LARS does is to compute all the factors of S_+ and to sort them *w.r.t.* $\preceq$. Left and right hand sides of the rules will be chosen in this set since it is reasonable to think that the positive examples contain all information that is needed to learn the target language. This assumption reduces dramatically the search space. LARS then enumerates the elements of this set thanks to two "for" loops, which allows to build the candidate rules.

Function `is_useful` discards the rules that cannot be used to rewrite at least one string of the current set I_+ (and are thus useless). Function `type` returns an integer in $\{1, 2, 3, 4\}$ and allows to check if the candidate rule is syntactically correct according to Def.2. Function `is_ANo` avoids the rules that would produce non ANo DSRS. Notice that a candidate rule that passes all these tests with success ensures that the DSRS will be syntactically correct, hybrid and ANo. The last thing to check is that the rule is consistent with the data, *i.e.*, that it does not produce a string belonging to both I_+ and I_-. This is easily performed by computing the normal forms of the strings of I_+ and I_-, which is the aim of function `normalize`.

Algorithm 1: LARS (Learning Algorithm for Rewriting Systems)

Data : a sample $\langle S_+, S_- \rangle$

Result : $\langle \mathcal{R}, e \rangle$ where $\mathcal{R}$ is a hybrid ANo DSRS and e is an irreducible string

begin

    $\mathcal{R} \longleftarrow \emptyset;\ I_+ \longleftarrow S_+;\ I_- \longleftarrow S_-;$

    $F \longleftarrow \mathtt{sort}_{\preceq} \{v : \exists u, w \in \overline{\Sigma}^*, uvw \in I_+\};$

    for $i = 1$ **to** $|F|$ **do**

        if $\mathtt{is\_useful}(F[i], I_+)$ **then**

            for $j = 0$ **to** $i - 1$ **do**

                if $\mathtt{type}(F[i]) = \mathtt{type}(F[j])$ **then**

                    $\mathcal{S} \longleftarrow \mathcal{R} \cup \{F[i] \to F[j]\};$

                    if $\mathtt{is\_ANo}(\mathcal{S})$ **then**

                        $E_+ \longleftarrow \mathtt{normalize}(I_+, \mathcal{S});\ E_- \longleftarrow \mathtt{normalize}(I_-, \mathcal{S});$

                        if $E_+ \cap E_- = \emptyset$ **then**

                            $\mathcal{R} \longleftarrow \mathcal{S};\ I_+ \longleftarrow E_+;\ I_- \longleftarrow E_-;$

    $e \longleftarrow \min_{\preceq} I_+;$

    foreach $w \in I_+$ **do**

        if $w \neq e$ **then** $\mathcal{R} \longleftarrow \mathcal{R} \cup \{w \to e\};$

    return $\langle \mathcal{R}, e \rangle;$

end

Theorem 4. *Given a sample $\langle S_+, S_- \rangle$ of size m, algorithm LARS returns a hybrid ANo DSRS $\mathcal{R}$ and an irreducible string e such that $S_+ \subseteq \mathcal{L}(\mathcal{R}, e)$ and $S_- \cap \mathcal{L}(\mathcal{R}, e) = \emptyset$. Moreover, its execution time is a polynomial of m.*

Proof (Hint). The termination and polynomiality of LARS is straightforward. Moreover, the following four invariant properties are maintained all along the double "for" loops: (1) $\mathcal{R}$ is a hybrid ANo DSRS, (2) I_+ contains all and only the normal forms of the strings of S_+ w.r.t. $\mathcal{R}$, (3) I_- contains all and only the normal forms of the strings of S_- w.r.t. $\mathcal{R}$ and (4) $I_+ \cap I_- = \emptyset$. Clearly, these properties remain true before the "foreach" loop. Now at the end of the last "foreach" loop, it is clear that: (1) $\mathcal{R}$ is a hybrid ANo DSRS, (2) e is the normal form of all the strings of S_+, so $S_+ \subseteq \mathcal{L}(\mathcal{R}, e)$ and (3) the normal forms of the strings of S_- are all in I_- and $e \notin I_-$, so $S_- \cap \mathcal{L}(\mathcal{R}, e) = \emptyset$. $\quad\square$

We now establish an identification theorem for LARS. This theorem focuses on languages that may be defined thanks to special DSRS that we define now. We begin with the notion of consistent rule that characterizes the rules that LARS will have to find.

Definition 7 (Consistent Rule). *We say that a rule $R = l \to r$ is consistent w.r.t. a language $L \subseteq \Sigma^*$ iff $\forall u, v \in \overline{\Sigma}^*$, if $ulv \notin \$L\pounds$, then $urv \notin \$L\pounds$.*

Definition 8 (Closed DSRS). *Let* $L = \mathcal{L}(\mathcal{R}, e)$ *be a language and* R_{max} *the greatest*[3] *rule of* $\mathcal{R}$ *w.r.t.* $\preceq$*. We say that* $\mathcal{R}$ *is closed iff: (i)* $\mathcal{R}$ *is hybrid and ANo, and (ii) for all length-lexicographic \$-rules and all length-decreasing non-\$-rules* S*, if* $S \preceq R_{max}$ *and* $S \notin \mathcal{R}$*, then* S *is not consistent with* L*.*

We do not know whether this property is decidable or not. This is a work in progress. Nevertheless, this notion allows to get the following result:

Theorem 5. *Given a language* $L = \mathcal{L}(\mathcal{R}, e)$ *such that* $\mathcal{R}$ *is closed, there exists a finite characteristic sample* $\langle CS_+, CS_- \rangle$ *such that, on* $\langle S_+, S_- \rangle$ *with* $CS_+ \subseteq S_+$ *and* $CS_- \subseteq S_-$*, algorithm LARS finds* e *and returns a hybrid ANo DSRS* $\mathcal{R}'$ *such that* $\mathcal{L}(\mathcal{R}', e) = \mathcal{L}(\mathcal{R}, e)$*.*

Notice that the polynomiality of the characteristic sets is not established.

Proof (Hint). Let $L = \mathcal{L}(\mathcal{T}, e)$ be the target language. $\mathcal{T}$ is assumed closed. Let us first define CS_+ and CS_-:

1. For all $\mathcal{R} \subseteq \mathcal{T}$ and all $R \in \mathcal{T}$ such that $\mathcal{L}(\mathcal{R}, e) \neq L$ but $\mathcal{L}(\mathcal{R} \cup \{R\}, e) = L$, there exists $w = ulv \in \$L\pounds \setminus \$\mathcal{L}(\mathcal{R}, e)\pounds$ such that $w \in CS_+$, where $R = l \rightarrow r$. (Notice that if $\mathcal{L}(\mathcal{R}, e) \neq L$, then $\mathcal{L}(\mathcal{R}, e) \subset L$ since $\mathcal{R} \subseteq \mathcal{T}$.)
2. For all rules $l \rightarrow r \in \mathcal{T}$, there exists $u, v \in \overline{\Sigma}^*$ such that $ulv \in \$L\pounds \cap CS_+$ and $urv \in \$L\pounds \cap CS_+$.
3. For all length-lexicographic \$-rules and all length-decreasing non-\$-rules $R = l \rightarrow r \notin \mathcal{T}$, if $\mathcal{T} \cup \{R\}$ is ANo, then there exists $u, v \in \overline{\Sigma}^*$ such that $ulv \in (\overline{\Sigma}^* \setminus \$L\pounds) \cap CS_-$ and $urv \in \$L\pounds \cap CS_+$.

We now prove that if $S_+ \supseteq CS_+$ and $S_- \supseteq CS_-$ LARS returns a correct system. By construction of the characteristic set, F contains all the left and right hand sides of the rules of the target. Assume now that LARS has been run during a certain number of steps; Let $\mathcal{R}$ be the current hybrid ANo DSRS. As I_+ is not empty, let $m = \min_{\preceq} I_+$ and $\widehat{\mathcal{R}} = \mathcal{R} \cup \{w \rightarrow m : w \in I_+, w \neq m\}$. Notice that $\widehat{\mathcal{R}}$ is also a hybrid ANo DSRS. Finally let $\widehat{L} = \mathcal{L}(\widehat{\mathcal{R}}, m)$.

Let $R = l \rightarrow r$ be the next rule to be checked, *i.e.*, $l = F[i]$ and $r = F[j]$. We assume that R is well-typed and $\mathcal{R} \cup \{R\}$ is ANo, otherwise R does not belong to $\mathcal{T}$ and LARS discards it. There are two cases:

1. If R is inconsistent, then there exists $m = ulv \in (\overline{\Sigma}^* \setminus \$L\pounds) \cap CS_-$ and $m' = urv \in \$L\pounds \cap CS_+$. So $m \downarrow_{\widehat{\mathcal{R}}} \in I_-$, $m' \downarrow_{\widehat{\mathcal{R}}} \in I_+$ and LARS discards R.
2. If R is consistent, then consider system $\mathcal{S} = \widehat{\mathcal{R}} \cup \{T \in \mathcal{T} : R \prec T\}$. Either $\mathcal{L}(\mathcal{S}, e) = L$ and then rule R is not needed (but can be added with no harm). Or $\mathcal{L}(\mathcal{S}, e) \neq L$ and then there is a string $w = ulv$ in CS_+ (where $R = l \rightarrow r$). As $w \downarrow_{\widehat{\mathcal{R}}} \in I_+$ and $w \downarrow_{\widehat{\mathcal{R}}} = u'lv'$ (because $\widehat{\mathcal{R}} \cup \{R\}$ is Church-Rosser), this means that l is a factor of a string I_+, which is consistent, so LARS adds R to $\mathcal{R}$. $\square$

---

[3] $\preceq$ is basically extended to ordered pairs of strings, thus to rules, as follows: $\forall u_1, u_2, v_1, v_2 \in \overline{\Sigma}^*, (u_1, u_2) \preceq (v_1, v_2)$ *iff* $u_1 \prec v_1$ or $(u_1 = v_1$ and $u_2 \preceq v_2)$

6   Experimental Results

We present in this section some specific languages for which rewriting systems exist, and on which the algorithm LARS has been tested. In each case we describe the task, the learning set from which the algorithm has worked. We do not report any runtimes here as all computations took less than one second: Both the systems and the learning sets were small.

Dyck Languages. The language of all bracketed strings or balanced parentheses is classical in formal language theory. It is usually defined by the rewriting system $\langle\{ab \to \lambda\}, \lambda\rangle$. The language is context-free and can be generated by the grammar $\langle\{a, b\}, \{S\}, P, S\rangle$ with $P = \{S \Rightarrow aSbS; S \Rightarrow \lambda\}$. The language is learned in [18] from all positive strings of length up to 10 and all negative strings of length up to 20. In [12] the authors learn it from all positive and negative strings within a certain length, typically from five to seven. Algorithm LARS learns the correct grammar from both types of learning sets but also from much smaller sets of about 20 strings. Alternatively [16] have tested their GRIDS system on this language, but when learning from positive strings only. They do not identify the language. It should also be noted that the language can be modified to deal with more than one pair of brackets and remains learnable.

Language $\{a^n b^n : n \in \mathbb{N}\}$. Language $\{a^n b^n : n \in \mathbb{N}\}$ is a language often used as a context-free language that is not regular. The corresponding system is $\langle\{aabb \to ab; \$ab\pounds \to \$\pounds\}, \lambda\rangle$. Variants of this language are $\{a^n b^n c^m : m, n \in \mathbb{N}\}$ which is studied in [18], or $\{a^m b^n : 1 \le m \le n\}$ from [12]. In all cases algorithm LARS has learned the intended system from as few as 20 examples, which is much less than for previous methods.

Regular Languages. We have run algorithm LARS on benchmarks for regular language learning tasks. There are several such benchmarks. Those related to the ABBADINGO [9] tasks were considered too hard for LARS: As we have constructed a deterministic algorithm (in the line for instance of RPNI [15]) results when the required strings are not present are bad. We turned to smaller benchmarks, as used in earlier regular inference tasks [4]. These correspond to small automata, and thus to from 1 to 6 rewriting rules. In most cases LARS found a correct system, but when it did not the error was important.

Other Languages and Properties. Languages $\{w \in \{a, b\}^* : |w|_a = |w|_b\}$ and $\{w \in \{a, b\}^* : 2|w|_a = |w|_b\}$ are used in [12]. In both cases the languages can be learned by LARS from less than 30 examples.

Language of Lukasewitz is generated by grammar $\langle\{a, b\}, \{S\}, P, S\rangle$ with $P = \{S \Rightarrow aSS + b\}$. The intended system is $\langle\{abb \to b\}, b\rangle$ but what LARS returned was $\langle\{\$ab \to \lambda; aab \to a\}, b\rangle$, which is correct.

Language $\{a^m b^m c^n d^n : m, n \in \mathbb{N}\}$ is not linear (but then Dyck isn't either) and is recognized by system $\langle\{aabb \to ab; ccdd \to cd\}, abcd\rangle$.

On the other hand the language of palindromes ($\{w : w = w^R\}$) does not admit a DSRS, unless the centre is some special character. [12] learn this language whereas LARS cannot.

System $\langle\{ab^k \to b\}, b\rangle$ requires an exponential characteristic sample so learning this language with LARS is a hard task.

The system has also been tested on the OMPHALOS competition training sets without positive results. There are two explanations to this: On one hand LARS being a deterministic algorithm needs a restrictive learning set to converge (data or evidence driven methods would be more robust and still need to be investigated), and on the other hand, there is no means to know if the target languages admit rewriting systems with the desired properties.

7   Conclusion and Future Work

In this paper, we have investigated the problem of learning languages that can be defined with string-rewriting systems (SRS)[4]. We have first tailored a definition of "hybrid almost nonoverlapping delimited SRS", proved that they were efficient (often linear) parsing devices and showed that they allowed to define all regular languages as well as famous context-free languages (Dyck, Lukasewitz, $\{a^n b^n : n \geq 0\}$, $\{w \in \{a, b\}^* : |w|_a = |w|_b\}$, ...). Then we have provided an algorithm to learn them, LARS, and proved that it could identify, in polynomial time (but not data), the languages whose SRS had some "closedness" property. Finally, we have shown that LARS was capable of learning several languages, both regular and not.

However, much remains to be done on this topic. On the one hand, LARS suffers from its simplicity, as it failed in solving the (hard) problems of the Omphalos competition. We think that we could improve our algorithm either by pruning our exploration of the search space, or by studying more restrictive SRS (*e.g.*, special or monadic SRS [1]), or by investigating more sophisticated properties (such as *basicity*). On the other hand, other kind of SRS can be used to define languages, such as the CR-languages of McNaugthon [11], or the DL0 systems (that can generate deterministic *context-sensitive* languages). All these SRS may be the source of new attractive learning results in Grammatical Inference.

References

1. R. Book and F. Otto. *String-Rewriting Systems*. Springer-Verlag, 1993.
2. C. de la Higuera. Characteristic sets for polynomial grammatical inference. *Machine Learning Journal*, 27:125–138, 1997.
3. N. Dershowitz and J. Jouannaud. Rewrite systems. In J. van Leeuwen, editor, *Handbook of Theoretical Computer Science : Formal Methods and Semantics*, volume B, chapter 6, pages 243–320. North Holland, Amsterdam, 1990.

---

[4] We thank Géraud Sénizergues from LaBRI (Bordeaux, France) for providing us with pointers to the rewriting systems literature.

4. P. Dupont. Regular grammatical inference from positive and negative samples by genetic search: the GIG method. In R. C. Carrasco and J. Oncina, editors, *Grammatical Inference and Applications, Proceedings of ICGI '94*, number 862 in LNAI, pages 236–245, Berlin, Heidelberg, 1994. Springer-Verlag.
5. M. Frazier and C.D. Page Jr. Prefix grammars: An alternative characterisation of the regular languages. *Information Processing Letters*, 51(2):67–71, 1994.
6. E. M. Gold. Complexity of automaton identification from given data. *Information and Control*, 37:302–320, 1978.
7. J. W. Klop. Term rewriting systems. In S. Abramsky, D. Gabbay, and T. Maibaum, editors, *Handbook of Logic in Computer Science*, volume 2, pages 1–112. Oxford University Press, 1992.
8. T. Koshiba, E. Mäkinen, and Y. Takada. Inferring pure context-free languages from positive data. *Acta Cybernetica*, 14(3):469–477, 2000.
9. K. Lang, B. A. Pearlmutter, and R. A. Price. The Abbadingo one DFA learning competition. In *Proceedings of ICGI'98*, pages 1–12, 1998.
10. S. Lee. Learning of context-free languages: A survey of the literature. Technical Report TR-12-96, Center for Research in Computing Technology, Harvard University, Cambridge, Massachusetts, 1996.
11. R. McNaughton, P. Narendran, and F. Otto. Church-Rosser Thue systems and formal languages. *Journal of the Association for Computing Machinery*, 35(2):324–344, 1988.
12. K. Nakamura and M. Matsumoto. Incremental learning of context-free grammars. In P. Adriaans, H. Fernau, and M. van Zaannen, editors, *Grammatical Inference: Algorithms and Applications, Proceedings of ICGI '02*, volume 2484 of *LNAI*, pages 174–184, Berlin, Heidelberg, 2002. Springer-Verlag.
13. C. Nevill-Manning and I. Witten. Identifying hierarchical structure in sequences: a linear-time algorithm. *Journal of Artificial Intelligence Research*, 7:67–82, 1997.
14. M. Nivat. On some families of languages related to the dyck language. In *Proc. 2nd Annual Symposium on Theory of Computing*, 1970.
15. J. Oncina and P. García. Identifying regular languages in polynomial time. In H. Bunke, editor, *Advances in Structural and Syntactic Pattern Recognition*, volume 5 of *Series in Machine Perception and Artificial Intelligence*, pages 99–108. World Scientific, 1992.
16. G. Petasis, G. Paliouras, V. Karkaletsis, C. Halatsis, and C. Spyropoulos. E-grids: Computationally efficient grammatical inference from positive examples. *to appear in Grammars*, 2004.
17. Y. Sakakibara. Recent advances of grammatical inference. *Theoretical Computer Science*, 185:15–45, 1997.
18. Y. Sakakibara and M. Kondo. Ga-based learning of context-free grammars using tabular representations. In *Proceedings of 16th International Conference on Machine Learning (ICML-99)*, pages 354–360, 1999.
19. B. Starkie, F. Coste, and M. van Zaanen. Omphalos context-free language learning competition. http://www.irisa.fr/Omphalos, 2004.
20. T. Yokomori. Polynomial-time identification of very simple grammars from positive data. *Theor. Comput. Sci.*, 1(298):179–206, 2003.

A Divide-and-Conquer Approach to Acquire Syntactic Categories*

Pablo Gamallo, Gabriel P. Lopes, and Joaquim F. Da Silva

CITI, Faculdade de Ciências e Tecnologia, Universidade Nova de Lisboa, Portugal
{gamallo,jfs,gpl}@di.fct.unl.pt

Abstract. In this paper we propose an unsupervised strategy for learning syntactic information that proceeds in several steps. First, we identify, cluster, and classify function words from unannotated corpora. Then, the acquired information is used in two different learning processes. On the one hand, it is used to learn morpho-syntactic categories of nouns and, on the other, it turns out to be useful to also induce syntactic/semantic relationships between content words. Experiments performed on Portuguese and English corpora are reported.

1 Introduction

In this paper we present a strategy to induce some syntactic categories of words and syntactic dependencies using only distributional information. The method proceeds in various steps. First, we aim at identifying and automatically tagging various subcategories of function words. Then, we use the previously tagged function words to both induce classes of nouns and extract syntactic/semantic dependencies between content words (i.e., selection restrictions).

Classical methods of syntactic category acquisition from large corpora are based on the following processes [2, 8, 1]. First, they select the set of target words, for instance, the $1,000$ most frequent words or those that occur more than N times in the corpus. Second, they characterize the contexts of the target words. For instance, [8] defines 4 contexts for a word occurrence w_i: the two words immediately appearing at its left and the two words immediately appearing at its right. Third, they Compute similarity between pairs of words on the basis of their context distributions. Forth, they cluster words with similar distribution. Unlike classical approaches to learn syntactic categories, we do not attempt to define a global method to induce categories of both function and content words at the same time. As in [9], we propose a "divide and conquer" approach which starts separating the most frequent function words, which are distributed in very small closed classes, from content words, which are organized in enormous open classes. This split enables us to focus first the analysis on function words in order to define a specific strategy to deal with some of their syntactic properties. Once the basic categories of function words have been identified, they can be used to

---

* Research supported by Program POSI, FCT/MCT, Portugal; ref: SFRH/BPD/ 11189/2002

G. Paliouras and Y. Sakakibara (Eds.): ICGI 2004, LNAI 3264, pp. 151–162, 2004.

cluster content words into morpho-syntactic categories. For instance, a closed class of particles like {those, the, these, such} may be useful to identify the open class of plural nouns. In addition, identifying basic categories of particles will enable us to extract more elaborate linguistic patterns: for instance, we can learn syntactic/semantic patterns like $< word_i, particle_j, W >$, where W is the class of semantically related words that can appear after $word_i$ and $particle_j$. We will use the terms "function words" and "particles" as synonyms.

This paper is organized in following sections. Section 2 describes the method for acquiring and automatically labeling syntactic categories of function words. Section 3 describes how the function categories acquired are used to extract subcategories of nouns: singular and plural nouns in English, and singular-masculine, singular-feminine, plural-masculine, and plural-feminine, in Portuguese. Then, Section 4 shows the results of evaluation. Finally, in Section 5, we also use the function categories to identify patterns of syntactic/semantic dependencies.

2 Inducing Categories of Function Words and Automatic Tagging

We divide the learning method in several steps. First, a list of function words is identified (Subsection 2.1). Indeed, we are interested in discovering the statistical properties of the main function words in order to induce their basic categories. In a second step, The list of function words is automatically sorted in such a way that words behaving as elliptic modifiers (e.g., determiners) are put on the bottom of the list, while words behaving as connectors (prepositions and conjunctions) are put on the top. This separation will be useful to provide words with meaningful tags, in particular we will automatically distinguish modifiers from connectors (Subsection 2.2). Then, we cluster separately words situated on the top and on the bottom of this ranked list. As a result, the generated clusters contain words representing the prototypes of different syntactic categories: e.g., typical singular determiners, typical prepositions, etc. (Subsection 2.3). Finally, we use these typical clusters for classifying new function words, for instance, those that convey some kind of grammatical ambiguity (2.4).

2.1   Separating Function from Content Words

Most function words tend to be the more frequent words in a corpus. Generally, about 50% word total frequency is considered as a reasonable first approximation for selecting a significant number of function words [9]. However, two problems arise when one acts like that and selects the k most frequent words. First, content words generically associated with the topic of the corpus may be more frequent than an important number of function words. Moreover, some function words may be as rare as most content words In order to solve these two problems, we propose the following strategy. First, the k most frequent words are selected. Then, we compute their *similarity* with regard to the rest of words. Both the most frequent words and those that are more similar to them are considered as a first approximation to characterize the set of function particles. This allows us to identify function words that are not frequent but are similar to the most frequent ones. However, the set of particles extracted so far still includes several frequent content words. In order to filter out these content words, we follow the strategy described in [9]. A new set of potential function words is extracted from a different corpus addressing different subject matters. As a consequence, frequent content words tend to be different. So, the intersection of the two sorts of most frequent words does not contain any topic-dependent word. Table 1 shows the lists extracted from Portuguese and English text corpora.

Table 1. English function words were extracted from E.C. (European Commission) corpus and the novel The Quixote. Portuguese particles were extracted from E.C. and CETEMPublico corpora.

English Particles:
such these been on and in of a any have are which have are which from that as those the being not with by to at or this for may under has be is
Portuguese Particles:
as de suas uma com e estas este os para se sua o por essa ou esta foi será outros a um ser seu são qualquer que foram seus pode não outras esse em

2.2 Ranking Functional Words

The next step is to sort the set of words by following some basic ideas. We assume that it is possible to distinguish two large meta-categories of function words: those somehow playing the role of modifiers of content words, and those playing the role of connectors between content words. An important property of modifiers is that they can be removed without affecting the main syntactic structure of the phrase. By contrast, connectors such as prepositions and conjunctions are the scaffolding for building syntactic structures. They cannot be removed. According to these ideas, function words are ranked within a scale of obligatoriness, ranging from higher $(+)$ to lower values $(-)$. Each word is assigned a weight representing its tendency to be omitted or not between two adjacent words. For instance, preposition "of" cannot be omitted from an expression like "president of Ireland", since the bigram "president Ireland" does not occur in the corpus. Given a function word w, a measure (Obl) that gives us an idea about how much is w compelled to be part of their contexts, is computed as follows:

$$Obl(w) = \frac{1}{|(x,y) : \exists(x,w,y)|} \sum_{(x,y):\exists(x,w,y)} \frac{f(x,w,y)}{f(x,w,y) + f(x,y)} \tag{1}$$

where $f(x,w,y)$ denotes the frequency of w in a context constituted by the words, x and y, immediately before and after w, and where $|(x,y) : \exists(x,w,y)|$ is the number of unique contexts of w. Moreover, $f(x,y)$ represents the frequency of word x occurring immediately before y. The higher the sum of values in the denominator of (1), the lower is the overall probability, and so, particle w is likely to be a modifier. Equation (1) assigns lower weights to words that are not entirely obligatory. Conversely, obligatory words have higher probabilities and so, should not be omitted. Table 2 shows function words ordered according to the $(+ - obligatory)$ feature. The most obligatory particles are put at the top of the list because of their high OBL values. As the 10 top particles can be considered as typical connectors, they are provided with tag CON(nector). On the other hand, optional particles are at the bottom of the list. We select the 10 most optional particles as typical MOD(ifiers).

Table 2. lists of English and Portuguese particles sorted according to the *obligatory* feature.

ENGLISH			PORTUGUESE		
Tag	**Word**	**OBL**	**Tag**	**Word**	**OBL**
CON	of	0.95	CON	de	0.93
CON	to	0.89	CON	em	0.87
CON	or	0.89	CON	com	0.86
CON	and	0.89	CON	por	0.85
CON	for	0.88	CON	para	0.85
CON	in	0.88	CON	e	0.82
CON	with	0.88	CON	pode	0.81
CON	may	0.87	CON	será	0.79
CON	by	0.87	CON	ou	0.78
CON	on	0.86	CON	que	0.78
CON	from	0.86	CON	são	0.77
-	is	0.80	-	ser	0.73
-	at	0.80	-	a	0.71
-	under	0.79	-	não	0.69
-	as	0.78	-	foi	0.69
-	has	0.77	-	foram	0.65
-	are	0.76	-	uma	0.64
-	that	0.71	-	se	0.63
-	have	0.69	-	as	0.62
-	be	0.65	-	um	0.60
MOD	which	0.61	MOD	este	0.37
MOD	being	0.57	MOD	esta	0.37
MOD	not	0.55	MOD	estas	0.36
MOD	the	0.54	MOD	essa	0.34
MOD	a	0.50	MOD	esse	0.33
MOD	any	0.47	MOD	outras	0.31
MOD	this	0.46	MOD	outros	0.27
MOD	such	0.44	MOD	sua	0.13
MOD	those	0.40	MOD	seu	0.11
MOD	these	0.39	MOD	seus	0.11
MOD	been	0.35	MOD	suas	0.11

2.3 Clustering

Typical Modifiers and Connectors are then aggregated into clusters using a hierarchical algorithm based on group average. Similarity between words is computed over their context distribution. Two words are similar if they share a large proportion of contexts and they do not occur as part of the contexts of each other. Similarity Sim between two words is computed by (2)

$$Sim(w_1, w_2) = \frac{\sum_{x,y}(f(x, w_1, y) + f(x, w_2, y))}{\sum_{x,y,v,z}(f(x, w_1, y) + f(v, w_2, z)) + F(w_1, w_2)} \qquad (2)$$

were $f(x, w_i, y)$ denotes the frequency of word w_i in a context defined as a position between words x and y. In addition, $F(w_1, w_2)$ is defined as:

$$F(w_1, w_2) = f(w_1, w_2) + f(w_2, w_1) \qquad (3)$$

It computes the frequency of w_1 occurring both immediately before w_2 and immediately after w_2. This type of frequency is used in (2) to generate low similarity values if the two compared words co-occur many times in the same sequence or phrase. Two words that may co-occur are likely to belong to different syntactic categories. So, not only paradigmatic information but also syntagmatic information is used to tune similarity between two words. One of the aims of taking into account syntagmatic information is to be sure that the clustering algorithm will not put in the same cluster ambiguous particles behaving as both modifiers and connectors.

Results of the clustering process are plotted in Table 3. Note that in both languages, typical connectors are aggregated into two clusters constituted by prepositions and coordinate conjunctions. On the other hand, typical modifiers are aggregated into clusters constituted by determiners sharing the same agreement features: for instance, in Portuguese, cluster MOD_1 contains singular feminine determiners. Clusters of only one member are removed. So far, typical clusters do not include ambiguous particles. Classification, explained in the next subsection, will allow to assign ambiguous words to different classes.

Table 3. Clusters of typical connectors and modifiers.

English basic clusters
MOD_1 a any the this
MOD_2 such these those
CON_1 by for in of on to with
CON_1 and or
Portuguese basic clusters
MOD_1 essa esta sua
MOD_2 esse este
MOD_3 estas outras suas
MOD_4 outros seus
CON_1 com de em para por
CON_2 e ou

2.4 Classification

Basic clusters are now used to classify more particles. Classification operates on 500 potential particles previously selected using the strategy described above in section 2.1. A particle is classified and then integrated into a cluster if the similarity between the particle and the cluster is higher than an empirically set threshold. Similarity between a word and a cluster is computed as the average the similarity between this word and each one of clustered words. To calculate word similarity we use a version of coefficient (2), defined without syntagmatic frequencies, i.e., without F. As Table 4 shows, classification procedure turns out to be useful to put in various clusters those words that convey some grammatical ambiguity. Note that determiners "the" and "qualquer" are aggregated into both the singular and plural clusters. The ambiguous Portuguese particle "a" is correctly classified as a connector and a modifier. Results shown in Table 4 display the extension of the basic subcategories shown above in Table 3. However, it is not always pertinent to distinguish several subcategories of modifiers and connectors. As we will see later in Section 5, the distinction of two generic categories, such as for instance modifiers and connectors, may suffice to perform specific NLP tasks, such as identify basic chunks and some syntactic dependencies. Table 5 shows the results of classifying particles in two large categories of function words: MOD and CON.

Table 4. Clusters generated after classification.

English clusters
MOD_1 a any each that the this
MOD_2 such the these those
CON_1 before by during for in of on to under with within
CON_2 and or

Portuguese clusters
MOD_1 a essa esta mesma qualquer sua uma
MOD_2 aquele esse este o qualquer tal um
MOD_3 as estas novas outras suas
MOD_4 novos os outros seus vários
CON_1 com de durante em para por sobre
CON_2 e ou

3   Inducing Subcategories of Nouns

Learned classes of function words (shown above in Table 4) may be used to identify morpho-syntactic subcategories of content words. For instance, words often appearing to the right of MOD_2 particles are, in general, masculine and singular nouns in Portuguese, and plural nouns in English. However, we find not only nouns to the right of MOD_2 particles, but also many adjectives. A more reliable pattern would be the trigram:

Table 5. Particles classified in two generic clusters.

Two English generic clusters of particles
MOD a all any each this its one some such that the their these this those
CON after and at before between by during for from if in of on or that to under when where with within
Two Portuguese generic clusters of particles
MOD a as cada essa esse esta estas este o outras outros qualquer seus sua suas tal um uma
CON a com de durante e em entre ou para por quando segundo sobre

$$< MOD\_i, w, CON > \qquad (4)$$

This pattern represents a word w appearing between a modifier of type MOD_i and any type of connector, where $i = 1, \ldots, 4$. This grammatical pattern should be adequate for those languages that place determiners before nouns. A word will be categorized as a noun of type i, $NOUN\_i$, if it is likely to appear in pattern (4). Table 6 shows the different morpho-syntactic categories of nouns extracted by computing the probability of appearing in patterns like (4). We define the probability of word w occurring in pattern (4) as the number of different modifiers of category MOD_i occurring before w and any connector divided by the total number of modifiers of category MOD_i. So, those words occurring immediately to the right of different modifiers of category MOD_i and before any connector are a high probability of being members of the category

Table 6. Nouns organized in morpho-syntactic categories (excerpt of nouns whose first letter is "a").

English clusters of nouns
NOUN_1 abuse according affair afternoon aid amendment animal answer application applications art article
NOUN_2 activities agreements animals arrangements
Portuguese clusters of nouns
NOUN_1 aceitação actividade acção adaptação admissão análise aplicação apresentação aprovação associação autoridade avaliação
NOUN_2 abandono abuso acordo acto aditivo anexo ano apoio artigo aspecto assunto aumento auxílio
NOUN_3 actividades acções administrações alterações associações autoridades
NOUN_4 accionistas acessórios acidentes activos aderentes aditivos adubos aeroportos agentes agrupamentos alimentos anexos aparelhos argumentos arrendatários artefactos artigos aspectos aviões aços

$NOUN\_i$. In order to improve accuracy, ambiguous particles are removed from the patterns used for extraction.

If we are interested in separating just nouns independently of their morphological features (gender and number), it may be possible to relax specific patterns like (4), by using:

$$< MOD, w, CON >$$ (5)

This coarse-grained pattern enables to extract a single set of nouns, regardless of the values of their gender and number. The size of the set extracted using this pattern is larger than the coverage obtained using fine-grained patterns like (4). For instance, the set of English nouns starting with letter "a" is the following:

> ability abode absurdities abuse acceptance account achievements activities activity adventures advice affair ages agreements aid aim allocation amendment amendments animals answer anxiety apparatus appearance application applications approval arm armour arms arrangements arrival art *as* ass assessment attention authority

4   Evaluation of Results

Concerning the English experiments, we used 1,5 million words of the English EC corpus as training data[1]. In order to extract a list of potential particles (see Section 2), we intersected the particles extracted from EC with those extracted from the novel "The Quixote". As regards as Portuguese is concerned, we used 3 millions words of the Portuguese EC corpus. The extracted particles were intersected with those selected from the CETEMPúblico corpus[2].

Table 7 displays the evaluation results for function words and nouns. *Precision* is defined as the number of different words (i.e., word types) that have been correctly extracted and classified in a particular category divided by the total number of word types that have been classified in that category. Concerning recall, we considered that it was necessary to follow a different strategyy. As far as we know, no work on syntactic category acquisition uses any type of coverage or recall as a measure to evaluate their results. To compute recall, we count the frequency of word tokens instead of the frequency of word types. So, *Recall* is defined as the frequency count of the correct word tokens that have been correctly classified by our system in a particular category divided by the total frequency of all word tokens of that category in the corpus. We claim that counting the token frequencies of a particular category gives a more accurate idea of recall than counting the number of different words (i.e. the number of word types) belonging to that category. Indeed, given a particular category, the word types of that category that have not been extracted by our system can

---

[1] E.C. (European Commission) contains documents on different legislative aspects (legislation in force, social policy, environment, etc.) of the European Commission. This corpus is in: http://europa.eu.int/eur-lex/X/index.html, with X = {pt,en}.

[2] CETEMPúblico is a heterogeneous corpus constituted by articles out of the newspaper Público.

be more than 50% of the total number of different members of that category. However, they may represent less than 5% of the total token frequency of the category through the corpus. To calculate the recall, we need to know the total frequency of tokens belonging to the categories that will be evaluated. To do it, first we automatically tagged the training English corpus with standard software[3]. Then, we obtained the frequency of nouns and function words (we counted together the frequency of connectors and modifiers-determinants). As a result, we observed that connectors and modifiers are about 38% of the total frequencies of a given corpus, whereas nouns, including proper names, are 23%. So, given this information, the recall of the cluster of nouns we have extracted is the total frequency of those words clustered and classified as nouns $(223, 000)$ divided by the rate of nouns (0.23) occurring in a corpus of $1, 5$ million words. The result is 0.63.

Table 7. Precision and recall of the acquired word classes.

	Precision	Recall
Eng. particles	100	84.39
Port. particles	100	85.10
Eng. nouns	95.30	63.36
Port. nouns	98.78	63.51

The scores plotted in Table 7 shows a high precision even for the open-class of nouns. These values are higher than in related work. In [5], they report that the word cluster manually declared as a Noun group reaches 85% precision. In [7], the $1, 000$ most frequent words in the corpus were organized in several disjoint clusters, and the syntactic labels for each of these clusters were appropriate for around 95% of the words in each cluster. On the other hand, note that the recall of particles is much higher than that for nouns. This difference is caused by the fact that function words are organized in relatively small closed-sets while nouns define a large open-class. In related work, we did not find any evaluation protocol on recall. Yet, we simulated a simple experiment to measure the recall of the nouns extracted in, at least, two different works: [7] and [9]. Their clustering strategy takes as input the $1, 000$ most frequent words. So, given our corpus, we computed the frequency of the nouns that are part of the $1, 000$ most frequent words. This results in $244, 758$ noun occurrences. As the corpus is constituted by $431, 860$ noun occurrences, which are the 23% of the total word frequency, recall would achieve 56.67%, which is still lower than our results.

Note also that the values are very similar in the two tested languages. This means that our strategy cannot be considered as totally language-dependent. We aim at extending the strategy acquisition to Slavic languages.

---

[3] The software used was TreeTagger, available in http://www.ims.uni-stuttgart.de/ projekte/corplex/TreeTagger/DecisionTreeTagger.html

5   Work in Progress:
Learning Syntactic/Semantic Relations

Besides the acquisition of morpho-syntactic categories such as nouns, we also attempt to use the function categories to identify other kind of higher-level linguistic regularities. In particular, we aim at identifying candidate syntactic dependencies between pairs of content words, which will be clustered giving rise to specific syntactic-semantic relations. At this level of linguistic induction, we only need information of some coarse-grained tags: both MOD and CON.

In order to identify candidate syntactic dependencies, the syntactic information learned in previous steps is used to associate a particular tag to each word in the corpus. For this purpose, the lexicon is divided in four large categories: Modifiers (MOD), Connectors (CON), Other-Function-Words (OFW), i.e. those particles appearing in Table 2 that have not been clustered, and Non-Function-Words (NFW), i.e. every word that does not appear in Table 2. The latter category corresponds to possible content words. Each word occurrence is automatically assigned one of these tags. We assume that they are useful for identifying possible dependencies between content words. Note that, for this generic tagging application, we do not need fine-grained subcategories of connectors or modifiers. Table 8 shows different cases of candidate syntactic dependencies that will be taken as input of the clustering process.

Table 8. Dependencies extracted from tagged text.

european_NFW community_NFW
(L_european, community)
(R_community, european)
ratify_NFW the_MOD law_NFW
(L_ratify, law)
(R_law, ratify)
ratification_NFW of_CON the_MOD law_NFW
(L_ratification_of, law)
(R_of_law, ratification)
have_OFW made_NFW
***

The process of extracting syntactic dependencies simulates a partial parsing based on Right Association strategy. It proposes attachments between immediate content words. Note that in other frameworks, such attachments can only be proposed after having tagged and parsed the text using language-dependent computational tools [4].

A syntactic dependency between two content words convey semantic information on the selection restrictions imposed by the two related words. For instance, taking "ratification of law", dependency ($L\_ratification\_of, law$) means that word *law* is required to appear following "ratification of". That is, "ratification of" is the L(eft) context of *law*. Conversely, we also use the dependency $(R\_of\_law, ratification)$, representing the opposite requirement: *ratification* is required to appear before "of law". So "of law" is the R(ight) context of *ratification*. Proposing two complementary co-requirements is in accordance with the assumption on semantic subcategorization made in [3], assumption which is somehow related to the notion of "co-composition" introduced in [6].

In order to induce syntactic/semantic relations, we use the clustering algorithm defined in [3]. The work described in that paper uses dependent-language software to annotate the training corpus. Here, however, we use a very basic annotation that does not require any *a priori* linguistic knowledge.

Table 9 shows some learned clusters of dependencies. Each cluster consists of both a set of content words and a set of interchangeable contexts. For instance, in the third cluster, words "exports", "imports", and "sales" are interchangeable in contexts like $L\_applicable\_to$, L_german, or $R\_of\_textile$. Intuitively, these contexts are semantically similar because they impose the same semantic requirements. Content words appearing in those contexts satisfy such requirements. These results still need to be evaluated. This can be done using the same strategy than that described in [3], where the clusters of syntactic/semantic dependencies were evaluated by measuring their adequacy to solve word attachment in a parsing task.

Table 9. Excerpt of word classes and their syntactic contexts.

Words:	agreement annex appendix article articles chapter community contract convention council directive marginal paragraph paragraphs point points protocol regulation section
Contexts:	L_appendix_to L_as_in L_attached_to L_compatible_with L_conditions_of L_contained_in L_criteria_in L_indicated_in L_interpretation_of L_listed_in L_meaning_of L_required_under L_scope_of L_see R_i R_ii R_iii R_iv
Words:	commission complainant european member mr ombudsman president
Contexts:	L_addressed_to L_adopted_by L_attention_of L_commission_and L_information_from L_letter_to L_received_from
Words:	exports imports sales
Contexts:	L_applicable_to L_german L_greek L_problem_of L_restrictions_on L_subsidized L_value_of R_of_products R_of_textile
Words:	accept meet pay provide sell supply
Contexts:	L_failed_to L_obliged_to L_position_to L_prepared_to L_refused_to L_unable_to L_willing_to R_copies R_to_contracting

6   Future Work and Final Remarks

The general objective of our work is to learn Human Languages without requiring no *a priori* linguistic knowledge. In particular, we intend to define new strategies for learning syntactic categories, grammatical patterns, and semantic classes, even of unknown languages. to do it, our current and future work aims at automatically characterize the properties of the syntactic/semantic dependencies as those shown in last section. Patterns as those plotted in Table 9 can be used as restrictions on word attachments in a parsing task. Moreover, they may help further identification of syntactic regularities underlying the behavior of various syntactic categories. We claim that learning syntactic categories and grammatical patterns must be perceived as an incremental procedure that involves the interaction of morphological, syntactic, and semantic information. Basic morpho-syntactic information carries significant regularities underlying the process of learning typical semantic classes, while these typical classes turn out to be useful to identify irregular lemmas, exceptions in morphological rules, and more elaborate syntactic categories. In turn, this new information will allow to tune the acquisition of more reliable semantic classes.

References

1. A Clark. Inducing syntactic categories by context distribution clustering. In Proceedings of CoNLL-2000, pages 91–94, 2000.
2. S. Finch and N. Chater. Bootstrapping syntactic categories. In 14th Annual Meeting of the Cogntive Science Society, pages 820–825, 1992.
3. Pablo Gamallo, A. Agustini, and Gabriel P. Lopes. Learning subcategorisation information to model a grammar with co-restrictions. Traitement Automatique de la Langue, 44(1):93–117, 2003.
4. Gregory Grefenstette. Explorations in Automatic Thesaurus Discovery. Kluwer Academic Publishers, USA, 1994.
5. J. Hughes and E. Atwell. The automated evaluation of inferred word classifications. In Proceedings of ECAI'94: 11th European Conference on Artificial Intelligence, pages 535–540, 1994.
6. James Pustejovsky. The Generative Lexicon. MIT Press, Cambridge, 1995.
7. M. Redington, N. Chater, and S. Finch. Distributional information adn the acquisition of linguistic categories: A statistical approach. In 15th Anual Conference of the Cognitive Science Society, pages 848–853, Hillsdale, NJ:Erlbaum, 1993.
8. H. Schutze. Part-of-speech induction from scratch. In ACL-93, Ohio State, 1993.
9. T.C. Smith and I.H. Witten. Probability-driven lexical classification: A corpus-based approach. In PACLING-95, 1995.

Grammatical Inference Using Suffix Trees

Jeroen Geertzen[1] and Menno van Zaanen[2]

[1] ILK, Computational Linguistics
Tilburg University
Tilburg, The Netherlands
J.Geertzen@uvt.nl

[2] ILK, Computational Linguistics
Tilburg University
Tilburg, The Netherlands
M.M.vanZaanen@uvt.nl

Abstract. The goal of the Alignment-Based Learning (ABL) grammatical inference framework is to structure plain (natural language) sentences as if they are parsed according to a context-free grammar. The framework produces good results even when simple techniques are used. However, the techniques used so far have computational drawbacks, resulting in limitations with respect to the amount of language data to be used. In this article, we propose a new alignment method, which can find possible constituents in time linear in the amount of data. This solves the scalability problem and allows ABL to be applied to larger data sets.

1   Introduction

Alignment-Based Learning (ABL) is a symbolic grammar inference framework that structures plain text according to an implicit context-free grammar. The result of the process is a treebank based on the plain input text. The structure should be linguistically relevant, hence the comparison against linguistically motivated data. The framework consists of several phases, which each need to be instantiated with a specific algorithm. Previous work has shown that even ABL systems based on simple phase instantiations yield state-of-the-art results [1].

The main problem with the previous implementation of the ABL systems is that the time complexity of the first phase, that finds possible constituents, is quadratic in the size of the corpus [2]. Even though ABL can learn structure from only a few sentences, scalability is a major problem. We expect that when more data is used, more possible constituents can be found, and hence a higher accuracy can be achieved. Furthermore, when more possible constituents are found, more precise counts are available, which results in more specific statistics in the disambiguation phase.

Here, we present a completely new alignment phase, that is linear in the size of the corpus with respect to time and space complexity. This allows for grammatical induction from much larger corpora. In this article, we first give a brief overview of the ABL grammatical inference framework. Next, we describe

G. Paliouras and Y. Sakakibara (Eds.): ICGI 2004, LNAI 3264, pp. 163–174, 2004.

the new alignment learning instantiations based on suffix trees. We conclude with the results of the suffix trees instantiation applied to the ATIS and WSJ corpora and compare them against the previous implementations.

2   Alignment-Based Learning

The ABL framework consists of three distinct phases. The *alignment learning* phase tries to find possible constituents by searching for regularities within the data. The *clustering* phase groups non-terminals that occur within the same context together. The *selection learning* phase selects the best constituents among all possible constituents generated by the alignment learning phase. All of these phases will be described in some detail below.

2.1   Alignment Learning

The alignment learning phase is based on Harris' [3] linguistic notion of substitutability, which (in terms of syntax) states that if two constituents are of the same type then they can be substituted by each other. The reversed reading of Harris' implication: "if parts of sentences can be substituted by each other then they are constituents of the same type" allows us to find possible constituents, called *hypotheses*, by aligning sentences. If parts of sentences occur in the same context, they can be seen as substitutable and hence are stored as hypotheses.

Previous implementations [4] are based on the well known edit distance algorithm [5]. Each sentence from the plain text corpus is aligned to each other sentence using the edit distance algorithm. This uncovers the substitutable parts of the sentences, which are stored as hypotheses.

2.2   Clustering

The alignment learning phase introduces hypotheses with each of them having a set of non-terminal type labels attached. The clustering phase analyzes the non-terminals and clusters together (merges) non-terminals of hypotheses that occur in the same context. The current implementation of the clustering phase is relatively simple and is fast in practice.

The clustering of non-terminals is not always correct, but so far the accuracy of the non-terminal type assignment has not been researched extensively. In the future, more complex clustering phases may be devised, but the impact of the clustering phase on the rest of the system is minimal; only one selection learning instantiation may make different choices depending on the results of this phase.

2.3   Selection Learning

The selection learning phase selects the best hypotheses of those that were found by the alignment learning phase. The existing alignment learning phases generate overlapping pairs of brackets, which are unwanted if the underlying grammar is considered context-free. The selection learning phase makes sure that overlapping pairs of brackets are removed, resulting in tree structures that are comparable to derivations of a context-free grammar.

2.4   Problems

The main problem of the previous implementations of ABL is scalability [2]. The alignment learning phase compares each sentence in the corpus to all other sentences. Adding more sentences to the corpus greatly increases the execution time. This poses no problem for small corpora (of roughly up to 10,000 sentences), but learning from much larger corpora is currently not feasible.

Previous work [6] showed that ABL outperforms the EMILE grammatical inference system [7] on small corpora. However, EMILE was designed to work on larger corpora (say $> 100,000$ sentences). When we want to compare the two systems on such corpora, the scalability problem of ABL needs to be tackled.

3   Grammatical Inference with Suffix Tree Alignment

To solve the problem of complexity of the previous alignment learning instantiations, we introduce a completely new alignment learning phase, based on aligning sentences using a suffix tree as an alternative to the edit distance algorithm. Where the edit distance alignment uses a two-dimensional matrix as data structure to store information on two sentences, suffix tree alignment uses a suffix tree as an efficient data structure to represent all sentences of a corpus. By using a suffix tree, we avoid pairwise comparison of sentences and, consequently, reduce the complexity in corpus size from quadratic to linear time and space.

3.1   Suffix Trees

A suffix tree is a compact representation of all suffixes of a string in the form of a tree structure. The most apparent use of a suffix tree is in applications of string matching. For example, a substring T of length n can be matched in $O(n)$ time in a string S of length m by constructing a suffix tree for S first. This preprocessing will only take linear $O(m)$ time (and only needs to be done once). Since searching only depends on the length of the search string, suffix trees are a preferred option when S needs to be searched repeatedly. A suffix tree can be defined informally as in Definition 1.

Definition 1. *A suffix tree T for a string S (with $n = |S|$) is a rooted, labeled tree with a leaf for each non-empty suffix of S. Furthermore, a suffix tree satisfies the following conditions:*

- *Each internal node, other than the root, has at least two children;*
- *Each edge leaving a particular node is labeled with a non-empty substring of S for which the first symbol is unique among all first symbols of the edge labels of the edges leaving the node;*
- *For any leaf in the tree, the concatenation of the edge labels on the path from the root to the leaf, exactly spells out a non-empty suffix of S.*

When searching for regularities in a corpus or, more specifically, searching for substitutable parts of sentences, we are particularly interested in a suffix tree that represents the suffixes of the sentences of a complete corpus. In other words, we use a *generalized suffix tree*, which is a suffix tree representing the suffixes of a set $\{S_1, S_2, \ldots, S_n\}$ of sentences.

An example of a generalized suffix tree for the sentences S_1=[she, was, walking], S_2=[she, is, walking, away], S_3=[she, runs, away] is depicted in Figure 1. Parts of sentences that share the same context can be identified by taking the topology of the suffix tree into account. Using this knowledge, we can introduce a new alignment method based on suffix trees, which consist on two linear steps:

1. Construct the generalized suffix tree for the corpus;
2. Employ an algorithm that finds possible constituents by taking the suffix tree topology into account.

We will describe step 1 briefly and study step 2 in more detail.

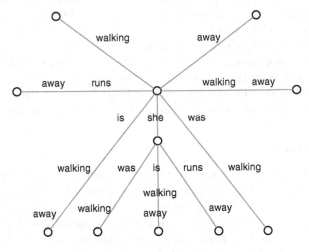

Fig. 1. Generalized suffix tree

3.2   Constructing a Generalized Suffix Tree

Currently, there are three basic algorithms to build a suffix tree: Weiner's [8], McCreight's [9], and Ukkonen's [10]. Weiner presented the first linear time suffix tree construction algorithm. McCreight gave a simpler and less space consuming version, which became the standard in research on suffix trees. In this paper, we consider Ukkonen's algorithm. In contrast to the algorithm of McCreight, it builds the tree incrementally from left to right instead of vice versa.

All m suffixes of string $S = a_1, \ldots, a_m$ with $m = |S|$ need to be present in the suffix tree. To accomplish this, each prefix ending at $S[i]$ of S, starting with $i = 1$ and incrementing i until $i = m$, is processed. For each prefix $S[1..i]$, every suffix $S[j..i]$ where $1 \le j \le i$ is considered. This results in algorithm 1 in pseudo-code.

Algorithm 1 Ukkonen simplified

Require:
  α : string
  p : point
1: **for** i **from** 1 **to** m **do** { prefix phase }
2:   **for** j **from** 1 **to** i **do** { suffix phase }
3:     $\alpha = S[j..i - j]$
4:     $p = $ Find_end_of_path(α)
5:     Apply_suffix_extension_rules(p, $S[i]$)
6:   **end for**
7: **end for**

The routine *Find_end_of_path()* finds the *point* p in the current tree that indicates the end of the path from the root to the maximum prefix of α that can be represented in the tree.

Once p is determined, the routine *Apply_suffix_extension_rules()* checks whether α can be represented completely. This is the case when point p marks a leaf node and the current tree does not need to be expanded. When p marks either an internal node or a position in an edge, α cannot be represented completely and subsequently the current tree needs to be expanded to represent α as well.

For Algorithm 1 to be linear, both routines should have constant time complexity. One of the essential "tricks" to achieve this is the introduction of *suffix links*. The routine *Find_end_of_path_from_root()* traverses, for each suffix phase, through the suffix tree and considers the edge labels on the way until a path is found to the point where the suffix extension rules can be applied. Using suffix links, we only need to traverse from the root node to the leaf node in the first suffix phase of a particular prefix phase. The remaining suffixes in the prefix phase can be found efficiently by following the suffix links.

3.3   Finding Hypotheses

Now we know how to construct a suffix tree, the question arises how to extract hypotheses from this suffix tree. Due to space restrictions, we will describe the algorithms in an informal way, which will illustrate how the actual algorithms work[1].

Let us consider a mini-corpus consisting of the following sentences:

S_1=[she, is, walking, away],
S_2=[she, was, walking],
S_3=[she, runs, away]

A generalized suffix tree of these sentences is depicted in Figure 1.

---

[1] [11] gives more formal descriptions of the alignment learning algorithms and discusses them in more detail.

From Definition 1 it follows that words or word groups that are used in more than one sentence *and are followed by disjoint words* have a joint edge. This can also be found when examining the topology of the generalized suffix tree. The location where one edge branches into multiple edges marks the position in the sentences involved where hypotheses can start. Since it is less obvious where the hypotheses should end, we assume the pair of brackets to close at the end of the sentences for now. This algorithm can be summarized as follows:

1. Use the joint edges in the suffix tree to place all *opening* brackets;
2. Close every opening bracket at the end of the sentence;
3. Assign non-terminal labels to brackets, creating labeled hypotheses.

From now on, we will refer to this algorithm as ST:s (Suffix Tree:suffix). Using ST:s on the generalized suffix tree of S_1, S_2 and S_3 will result in the following bracketing:

> she $[_a$ is walking away $]_a$
> she $[_a$ was walking $]_a$
> she $[_a$ runs away $]_a$

One of the major limitations of ST:s is that only *suffix hypotheses* are presented. In other words, we only see where joint words are followed by distinct words, but not the other way around. To find distinct words followed with joint words (e.g. "away" in the first and third sentence in the example), we construct a generalized suffix tree for sentences *with reversed word order*. We refer to this kind of suffix tree as a *prefix tree*. A generalized prefix tree for the three example sentences is depicted in Figure 2.

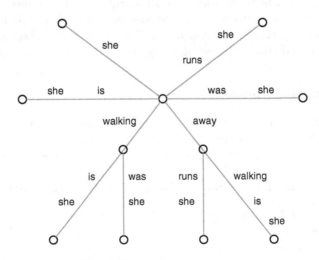

Fig. 2. Generalized prefix tree

By analyzing the prefix tree similarly to the analysis of the suffix tree, we are able to place closing brackets. Since the opening brackets cannot be read from the prefix tree we assume prefix hypothesis to start at the beginning of the sentence, as we did with the closing brackets in the suffix tree analysis. We can generate both suffix and prefix hypothesis by an algorithm summarized as follows:

1. Use the joint edges in the suffix tree to place all *opening* brackets;
2. Close every opening bracket introduced in the previous step at the end of the sentence;
3. Use the joint edges in the prefix tree to place all *closing* brackets;
4. Open every closing bracket introduced in the previous step at the beginning of the sentence;
5. Label brackets belonging to each other with a non-terminal type label.

We will refer to this algorithm as ST:ps1 (Suffix Tree:prefix suffix version 1). Using ST:ps1 on the generalized suffix tree of S_1, S_2 and S_3 will result in the following bracketing:

$[_b \ [_c$ she $[_a$ is $]_c$ walking $]_b$ away $]_a$
$[_c$ she $[_a$ was $]_c$ walking $]_a$
$[_b$ she $[_a$ runs $]_b$ away $]_a$

Although ST:ps1 will capture more hypotheses than ST:s, there is still the limitation that hypotheses *either* start at the beginning of the sentence and stop somewhere in the middle of the sentence *or* start somewhere in the sentence and stop at the end of the sentence. To capture hypotheses that start somewhere in the sentence and stop somewhere later in the sentence as well, we introduce ST:ps2, which uses both prefix and suffix trees but additionally matches opening and closing brackets:

1. Use the joint edges and suffix links in the suffix tree to place all *opening* brackets;
2. Use the joint edges and suffix links in the prefix tree to place all *closing* brackets;
3. Match each opening bracket with each closing bracket appearing later in the sentence to form hypotheses;
4. Label brackets belonging to each other with non-terminals.

An illustration of how ST:ps2 matches opening brackets with closing brackets to induce hypotheses is depicted in Figure 3. The opening and closing brackets are inserted according to information from the trees. The table in the middle of the figure represents the storage that contains the joint identifier for each unique pair of brackets. The sentences in the right part of the figure contain proper hypotheses. The storage is used to replace the identifier of the brackets in one pair with the joint identifier. In this way, each opening bracket (introduced by using the suffix tree) is paired with each closing bracket (introduced by using the prefix tree) to form hypotheses[2].

---

[2] For the sake of simplicity, we omit placing an initial opening and a closing bracket at the beginning and the end of each sentence.

she $[_a$ is $]_b$ walking $]_c$ away   she $[_e$ $[_d$ is $]_d$ walking $]_e$ away
she $[_a$ was $]_b$ walking   she $[_d$ was $]_d$ walking
she $[_a$ runs $]_c$ away   she $[_e$ runs $]_e$ away

$$a \leftrightarrow b \mid d$$
$$a \leftrightarrow c \mid e$$

Fig. 3. Matching opening and closing brackets in hypotheses generation

4   Results

4.1   Evaluation Methodology

To evaluate the performance of the learning systems, we extract plain natural language sentences from a treebank, that is considered the *gold standard*. These sentences are used as input of the grammar induction system. We compare the output of the grammar induction system, the learned treebank, against the gold standard. This is done using the unlabeled version of the PARSEVAL metrics: recall (measuring completeness of the structure), precision (correctness), and f-score (geometric mean of recall and precision). Additionally, we examine the number of constituents present in the treebanks.

As we are interested in comparing the performance of alignment learning given different instantiations, we have to keep the performance of the selection learning phase constant. We do this by assuming the *perfect selection learning*. This means that from the hypotheses in its input, the selection learning process selects only those hypotheses that are also present in the original treebank. Since only correct hypotheses are selected from the learned treebank, the precision in these kind of experiments is 100% and the recall indicates the proportion of correct constituents that is introduced by the alignment learning phase. The selection learning can never improve on these values[3].

4.2   Performance on the ATIS Treebank

The English ATIS (Air Traffic Information System) treebank, taken from the Penn treebank [12], contains mostly questions and imperatives on air traffic. It contains 568 sentences with a mean length of 7.5 words per sentence and the lexicon size is 358 words. Examples of sentences from the ATIS are:

How much would the coach fare cost
I need to return on Tuesday
Does this flight serve dinner

The results of applying the different alignment learning phases to the ATIS treebank using ten fold cross-validation and selecting only the hypotheses that are also present in the original treebank can be found in Table 1. The results marked with *rnd* are used as a baseline. They are generated by randomly selecting a right-branching or left-branching tree structure on top of the sentence. *Def*

---

[3] Considering only perfect selection learning does not show the differences in bias of the different alignment learning algorithms. More research needs to go into the actual effect of this influence.

is the default alignment method based on the edit distance algorithm, with the standard longest common subsequence edit costs [1][4], while the other algorithms are based on suffix trees.

Table 1. Results for alignment learning on the ATIS treebank

		recall	f-score	learned	best	% left
	rnd	28.90 (0.85)	44.83 (0.70)	4,353 (0.0)	1,851 (25.6)	42.5
ED	def	48.08 (0.09)	64.94 (0.08)	12,692 (8.8)	4,457 (4.4)	35.1
ST	s	31.56 (0.00)	47.98 (0.00)	4,194 (0.0)	2,290 (0.0)	54.6
	ps1	34.85 (0.00)	51.68 (0.00)	8,527 (0.0)	2,750 (0.0)	32.3
	ps2	46.85 (0.00)	63.81 (0.00)	25,740 (0.0)	7,277 (0.0)	28.3

The recall and f-score metrics are self explanatory (standard deviation is given between brackets). The *learned, best* and *% left* give an overview of the number of hypotheses in the learned treebank at two moments in the learning process. The number of hypotheses present (including overlapping hypotheses) after the alignment learning phase are given in *learned*. The number of remaining hypotheses after the "perfect" selection learning phase are given in *best*. Comparing the two counts indicates how productive the alignment learning is and how many correct hypotheses are left after removing the incorrect ones. *% left* shows the percentage of hypotheses that remain after selection.

To be able to relate the counts of hypotheses, the original ATIS treebank contains 7,017 constituents. Also, note that the performance of the edit distance methods depends on the order of the sentences in the corpus whereas the performance of the suffix tree methods is invariant (hence their zero standard deviation).

When looking at the recall and f-score of the suffix tree methods, the ST:ps2 generates best results, as expected. Comparing them against the baseline, we see that all generate better results. The main reason for ST:s, which is closest to the baseline, to do poorly is that not enough hypotheses are generated (as indicated by the low learned measure). Although ST:ps2 performs reasonably well, the edit distance method performs slightly better. We do not have a clear explanation for this, especially when we consider the fact that ST:ps2 produces substantially more hypotheses, but we expect that adding more data will be in the benefit of ST:ps2.

Taking another look at the number of learned hypotheses, we observe a larger difference between method ST:s and ST:ps1 than difference between ST:ps1 and ST:ps2. This can be explained by considering the right-branching nature of the English language. Since prefix hypotheses implicitly have a left-branching nature, the effect of including prefix hypotheses (ST:ps1) will not result in a high increase in recall. In the same line of thought, we predict that method ST:s performs worse on corpora of left-branching languages such as Japanese.

---

[4] [1] uses a slightly different ATIS version of 577 sentences. Here we use the original Penn treebank 2 ATIS version of 568 sentences.

4.3   Performance on the WSJ Treebank

The Wall Street Journal (WSJ) treebank consists of newspaper articles. It contains more complex sentences than the questions and imperatives of the ATIS treebank and the lexicon is much larger. The treebank is divided into numbered sections. We shall use section 23, which has informally developed as a test section of the WSJ treebank[5]. It contains 1,904 sentences with an average sentence length of > 20 words. The lexicon of section 23 contains 8,135 distinct words and the section has 65,382 constituents. Some examples of sentences from section 23 of the WSJ treebank are:

> Big investment banks refused to step up to the plate to support the beleaguered floor traders by buying big blocks of stock.
> Once again the specialists were not able to handle the imbalances on the floor of the New York Stock Exchange.
> When the dollar is in a free-fall, even central banks can't stop it.

For the WSJ, we only compare the edit distance alignment method (default) and the best suffix tree alignment method (ST:ps2). The results of applying these algorithms to section 23 of the WSJ are shown in the upper part of Table 2.

Table 2. Results for alignment learning on section 23 and sections 2–21+23 of WSJ

Section			recall	f-score	learned	best	% left
23	ED	def	53.26 (0.07)	69.50 (0.12)	186,593 (94.3)	34,835 (19.7)	18.7
	ST	ps2	67.81 (0.00)	80.82 (0.00)	431,432 (0.0)	58,115 (0.0)	13.5
2–21+23	ST	ps2	65.98 (0.00)	79.47 (0.00)	10,759,549 (0.0)	1,353,022 (0.0)	12.6

It is interesting to see that, even though the corpus is considered more complex, the results seem to be better compared to the ATIS treebank. This is perhaps not entirely true, since many more hypotheses are found and less than 20% of the learned hypotheses remain after perfect selection learning. (This is still over 28% with the ATIS treebank.) However, the upper bound is quite high, and ST:ps2 performs significantly better than the edit distance method.

One of the main reasons to develop the suffix tree alignment method was to reduce the scalability problem. To show that this has indeed been removed, we have applied the system to a large part of the WSJ corpus. For this purpose, we use sections 02–21 (standard training set sections) and 23 together. With a corpus of this size (38,009 long sentences), edit distance alignment learning is computationally not feasible anymore. Therefore, we only present the results for the suffix tree alignment learning (lower part of Table 2). The treebank fragment has 1,355,210 constituents and the lexicon contains 40,982 distinct words.

As can be observed, the recall has dropped slightly. Compared to the performance on the previous treebanks, these results are in the line of expectation.

---

[5] See e.g. [13, 14, 1].

The proportion of selected hypotheses (*best*) to the learned hypotheses (*learned*) seems to be correlated to the sentence complexity, because this proportion is considerably smaller for WSJ 2–21/23 than it is for ATIS.

4.4   Performance on Execution Time

Apart from the numerical results on actual natural language corpora, we are also interested in the execution times of the systems. Table 3 gives an overview of the time systems takes to learn on several corpora[6]. This clearly shows the benefits of suffix tree alignment over the edit distance variant.

Table 3. Timing results (in seconds) on several corpora

	edit distance	suffix tree
ATIS	4.05 (0.04)	0.37 (0.03)
WSJ23	283.00 (0.73)	6.08 (0.39)
WSJ2–21+23	n.a. n.a.	124.86 (0.11)

On the ATIS corpus, suffix tree alignment is approximately a factor 11 faster than edit distance alignment. On WSJ section 23, this is already a factor 46 and on WSJ section 02–21+23, suffix tree alignment needed about 2 minutes whereas the edit distance alignment learning was aborted after some 14 hours of computation (resulting in a factor >400).

5   Conclusion

In this article, we introduced a new alignment learning instantiation that is to be used in the ABL grammatical inference framework. Instead of using the edit distance algorithm (as all other alignment learning methods), this method is based on suffix trees. When applying the systems to real natural language corpora, we see that the results of the suffix tree alignment methods are comparable or significantly better. However, the main advantage of the new systems is that it solves the scalability problem inherent in the edit distance systems. Where the complexity of the edit distance based alignment learning is squared in the size of the corpus, the complexity of the suffix tree based system is linear. This greatly improves the usability of this approach.

One main aspect of comparing different alignment learning instantiations is the influence of the bias of the algorithms on the selection learning phase. The difficulty is that the specific selection learning instances themselves probably have a preferred bias. Future work should look into the complex interaction between the separate phases.

---

[6] These results were generated on a AMD Athlon XP 2200, 1800MHz with 1GB internal memory.

References

1. van Zaanen, M.: Bootstrapping Structure into Language: Alignment-Based Learning. PhD thesis, University of Leeds, Leeds, UK (2002)
2. van Zaanen, M.: Theoretical and practical experiences with Alignment-Based Learning. In: Proceedings of the Australasian Language Technology Workshop; Melbourne, Australia. (2003) 25–32
3. Harris, Z.S.: Structural Linguistics. 7th (1966) edn. University of Chicago Press, Chicago:IL, USA and London, UK (1951) Formerly Entitled: Methods in Structural Linguistics.
4. van Zaanen, M.: Implementing Alignment-Based Learning. In Adriaans, P., Fernau, H., van Zaanen, M., eds.: Grammatical Inference: Algorithms and Applications (ICGI); Amsterdam, the Netherlands. Volume 2482 of Lecture Notes in AI., Berlin Heidelberg, Germany, Springer-Verlag (2002) 312–314
5. Wagner, R.A., Fischer, M.J.: The string-to-string correction problem. Journal of the Association for Computing Machinery **21** (1974) 168–173
6. van Zaanen, M., Adriaans, P.: Alignment-Based Learning versus EMILE: A comparison. In: Proceedings of the Belgian-Dutch Conference on Artificial Intelligence (BNAIC); Amsterdam, the Netherlands. (2001) 315–322
7. Adriaans, P.: Language Learning from a Categorial Perspective. PhD thesis, University of Amsterdam, Amsterdam, the Netherlands (1992)
8. Weiner, P.: Linear pattern matching algorithms. In: Proceedings of the 14th Annual IEEE Symposium on Switching and Automata Theory, Los Alamitos, Calif., USA, IEEE Computer Society Press (1973) 1–11
9. McCreight, E.M.: A space-economical suffix tree construction algorithm. Journal of the Association for Computing Machinery **23** (1976) 262–272
10. Ukkonen, E.: On-line construction of suffix trees. Algorithmica **14** (1995) 249–260
11. Geertzen, J.: String alignment in grammatical inference: what suffix trees can do. Technical Report ILK-0311, ILK, Tilburg University, Tilburg, The Netherlands (2003)
12. Marcus, M.P., Santorini, B., Marcinkiewicz, M.A.: Building a large annotated corpus of English: the Penn treebank. Computational Linguistics **19** (1993) 313–330
13. Charniak, E.: Statistical parsing with a context-free grammar and word statistics. In: Proceedings of the Fourteenth National Conference on Artificial Intelligence, American Association for Artificial Intelligence (AAAI) (1997) 598–603
14. Collins, M.: Three generative, lexicalised models for statistical parsing. In: Proceedings of the 35th Annual Meeting of the Association for Computational Linguistics (ACL) and the 8th Meeting of the European Chapter of the Association for Computational Linguistics (EACL); Madrid, Spain, Association for Computational Linguistics (ACL) (1997) 16–23

Learning Stochastic Finite Automata[⋆]

Colin de la Higuera[1] and Jose Oncina[2]

[1] EURISE, Université de Saint-Etienne, 23 rue du Docteur Paul Michelon,
42023 Saint-Etienne, France
`cdlh@univ-st-etienne.fr`
[2] Departamento de Lenguajes y Sistemas Informaticos,
Universidad de Alicante, Alicante, Spain
`oncina@dlsi.ua.es`

Abstract. Stochastic deterministic finite automata have been introduced and are used in a variety of settings. We report here a number of
results concerning the learnability of these finite state machines. In the
setting of identification in the limit with probability one, we prove that
stochastic deterministic finite automata cannot be identified from only
a polynomial quantity of data. If concerned with approximation results,
they become PAC-learnable if the L_∞ norm is used. We also investigate
queries that are sufficient for the class to be learnable.

1 Introduction

Probabilistic finite state automata [1] have been introduced to describe distributions over strings. They have been successfully used in several fields, including
pattern recognition [2], computational biology [3] or linguistics [4].

Learning stochastic finite state automata has been an important issue in
grammatical inference [5], with several algorithms already developed and used
[6, 7]. Even though the subject has received increasing attention over the past
years a systematic study of the different paradigms of learning in this context,
with the land stone results, was still missing. It is the ambition of this paper to
contribute to this issue.

In section 2 we give the main notations used in this paper: These concern
stochastic finite automata and distances. We then visit the different learning
paradigms. A first result (section 3) concerns identification in the limit with
probability one: We argue that if the definition only requires that the algorithm
runs in polynomial update time then even a simple enumerative algorithm is sufficient. On the other hand, if we want identification to be achieved in polynomial
time, this is impossible due to the fact that probabilities need to be encoded in
some binary scheme.

We then explore the approximation setting (section 4) and recall that if the
distance is computed following the L_∞ norm, then even a simple algorithm that

---

[⋆] This work was supported in part by the IST Programme of the European Community, under the PASCAL Network of Excellence, IST-2002-506778. This publication
only reflects the authors' views.

G. Paliouras and Y. Sakakibara (Eds.): ICGI 2004, LNAI 3264, pp. 175–186, 2004.

just returns the learning sample is going to PAC-learn automata or any other recursively enumerable family of distributions. Another sort of results (section 5) concerns learning deterministic stochastic finite automata with queries: We introduce various new types of queries and examine learning results with these queries. We conclude in section 6.

2   Notations and Definitions

Let Σ be a finite alphabet and Σ^* the (infinite) set of all strings that can be built from Σ. λ will denote the empty string.

A *language* is a subset of Σ^*. By convention, symbols from Σ will be denoted by letters from the beginning of the alphabet $(a, b, c, ...)$ and strings from Σ^* will be denoted by the end of alphabet letters $(..., x, y, z)$. The size of a string $x \in \Sigma^*$ is written $|x|$. Given a string x, $\mathrm{Pref}(x) = \{u : uv = x\}$ and $\mathrm{Suf}(x) = \{v : uv = x\}$. Pref and Suf are extended to sets as $\mathrm{Pref}(X) = \cup_{x \in X} \mathrm{Pref}(x)$ and $\mathrm{Suf}(X) = \cup_{x \in X} \mathrm{Suf}(x)$.

Let $\equiv$ denote an equivalence relation on a set X, then by $[x]$ we are going to denote the class of equivalence of the element x, that is $[x] = \{y \in X : y \equiv x\}$. A *stochastic language* L is a probability distribution over Σ^*. The probability of a string $x \in \Sigma^*$ under the distribution L is denoted as $p_L(x)$. If the distribution is modelled by some syntactic machine A, the probability of x according to the probability distribution defined by A is denoted $p_A(x)$.

We denote by log the base 2 logarithm.

From formal language theory [8] we introduce deterministic finite automata (DFA):

Definition 1. *A Deterministic Finite Automaton (*DFA*) A is a tuple $(Q, \Sigma, \delta, q_0, F)$, where: Q is a finite set of* states; *q_0 is the* initial state; *Σ is the alphabet; $\delta : Q \times \Sigma \to Q$ is a transition function; $F \subset Q$ is the set of final states.*

We extend in the usual way [8] the transition function to a function $\delta : Q \times \Sigma^* \to Q : \delta(q, \lambda) = q, \delta(q, aw) = \delta(\delta(q, a), w)$.

We now adapt this definition to the stochastic setting:

Definition 2. *A Stochastic Deterministic Finite Automaton (*SDFA*) A is a tuple $(Q, q_0, \Sigma, \delta, \pi)$, where Q, Σ, δ, q_0 are as in* DFA *and π is a function with two profiles: $\pi : Q \times \Sigma \to \mathbb{Q}^+$ (transition probabilities) and $\pi : Q \to \mathbb{Q}^+$ (final-state probabilities).*

Function π is recursively extended to $\pi : Q \times \Sigma^* \to \mathbb{Q}^+$ such that $\pi(q, \lambda) = 1$ and $\pi(q, ax) = \pi(q, a)\pi(\delta(q, a), x)$.

The probability of a string x starting from the state q is defined as $p(q, x) = \pi(q, x)\pi(\delta(q, x))$. The probability of a string x is $p(x) = p(q_0, x)$. Let X be a set of strings, $p(X) = \sum_{x \in X} p(x)$.

We are going to say that a probability distribution L is a *Stochastic Deterministic Regular Language* (SDRL) if it is produced by a SDFA.

As the stochastic languages define probability distributions over Σ^*, it is required that $0 \leq p(x) \leq 1\ \forall x$ and $p(\Sigma^*) = 1$ (*consistence condition*).

Usually $\sum_{a \in \Sigma} \pi(q, a) + \pi(q) = 1, \forall q \in Q$ is also required. This condition is not strictly necessary, as the SDFA $(\{q_0, q_1\}, q_0, \{a\}, \{\delta(q_0, a) = q_1, \delta(q_1, a) = q_0\}, \{\pi(q_0, a) = 27, \pi(q_1, a) = 0.5/27, \pi(q_0) = 0.5, \pi(q_1) = 0\})$ is consistent and does not fulfil the condition. In theorem 5 we describe a method to transform a SDFA that does not fulfil the condition into one that does.

For combinatorial purposes such as needing to compute the complexity of an algorithm, the size of a SDFA must be polynomially linked with the number of bits needed to encode it in a reasonable way. This only makes sense if the probabilities themselves can be encoded; Therefore rational probabilities will be used. In the case of SDFA the number n of states, the size $|\Sigma|$ of the alphabet and the number of bits needed to encode the probabilities are needed. We denote by $\|A\|$ the size of a SDFA A.

When concerned with measuring how close one distribution can be from another, or from a sample, it will be of interest to compare these through distances:

$$d_n(\mathcal{D}, \mathcal{D}') = \sqrt[n]{\sum_{w \in \Sigma^*} |p_{\mathcal{D}}(w) - p_{\mathcal{D}'}(w)|^n}$$

$$d_\infty(\mathcal{D}, \mathcal{D}') = \max_{w \in \Sigma^*} |p_{\mathcal{D}}(w) - p_{\mathcal{D}'}(w)|$$

This last distance allows favourable convergence bounds, through the use of the following lemma due to Angluin [9]:

Lemma 1. *Let $\mathcal{D}$ be any distribution on Σ^*, let $a > 1$ and let $I(n) = \sqrt{\frac{6a(\log n)}{n}}$.*
Then,

- *with probability at least $1 - n^{-a}$,*
- *with probability 1 and for all but a finite number of values of n,*

$$d_\infty(\mathcal{D}, \mathcal{D}\langle n \rangle) \leq I(n)$$

where $\mathcal{D}\langle n \rangle$ is the empirical distribution built from a sample of size n.

3   About Polynomial Identification in the Limit with Probability One

Even if grammatical inference is usually considered to be dealing with learning languages, it is clearer to define things in terms of learning grammars or automata. In this paper, we are concerned with automata, and therefore all definitions shall be given in this setting.

We consider a class of languages $\mathcal{L}$ and a class $\mathcal{R}$ of representations for these languages. We are going to denote by $r_{\mathcal{R}}(L)$ (and simplify to $r(L)$ in non ambiguous contexts) the smallest representation in $\mathcal{R}$ of a language L and by $\|r_{\mathcal{R}}(L)\|$ its size. $L(r)$ denotes the language represented by the description r.

In order to learn we are going to suppose that the data to identify a stochastic language is obtained following the probability distribution and that successive draws are independent. The probability of a sequence of draws is the product of the probabilities of each draw.

Definition 3 (Identification in the limit with probability 1). *A class of stochastic languages $\mathcal{L}$ is learnable[1] with probability 1 in terms of a representation class $\mathcal{R}$ if there exists an algorithm $\phi(\cdot)$ that given any language L in $\mathcal{L}$, for any increasing sequence $\langle s_n \rangle$ drawn according to L, $\phi(s)$ returns some representation r. Moreover, with probability 1, for all but a finite number of values of n, $\phi(s)$ returns r such that $L(r) = L$.*

The previous definition has led to the implicit definition of polynomial identification that has been mainly used in the literature [6]. It basically states that identification has to be obtained by using an algorithm that has polynomial runtime. This does not mean that a polynomial number of examples may be sufficient, as discussed in [10]. We will refer to this definition as weak polynomial identification:

Definition 4 (Weak polynomial identification in the limit with probability 1). *A class of stochastic languages $\mathcal{L}$ is weak polynomially learnable with probability 1 in terms of a representation class $\mathcal{R}$ if there is an algorithm $\phi(\cdot)$ and a polynomial p for which for any language L in $\mathcal{L}$, and any increasing sequence $\langle s_n \rangle$ of strings drawn according to L:*

1. *$\phi(\cdot)$ identifies L in the limit with probability 1;*
2. *$\phi(\cdot)$ works in time in $p(\|\langle s_n \rangle\|)$.*

Under this criterion it has been established that algorithm ALERGIA [6] could learn SDFA, but also that stochastic deterministic linear grammars [10] could be identified.

Nevertheless this definition has a serious flaw:

Theorem 1. *Let $\mathcal{L}$ be a class of recursivelly enumerable languages that admits a representation class $\mathcal{R}$ for which distance d_∞ is computable. $\mathcal{L}$ when represented by $\mathcal{R}$ can be weakly polynomially learned with probability 1.*

Proof. We follow in this proof arguments from [11] and [9] and use a simple enumerative algorithm that would find the first language consistent (in the sense of lemma 1) in the enumeration identifies in the limit. To make the algorithm fit with the complexity constraints, we just make the algorithm compute the time it is entitled to from the current examples. The algorithm then computes as far as it can go with that time and returns whatever solution it has reached at that point. There is a point where the algorithm will converge.   □

Corollary 1. SDRL *when represented by* SDFA *can be weakly polynomially identified in the limit with probability 1.*

---

[1] We will write learnable for identifiable in the limit.

An alternative definition which would bound the overall time is as follows:

Definition 5 (Strong polynomial identification in the limit with probability 1). *A class of stochastic languages $\mathcal{L}$ is strongly polynomially learnable with probability 1 in terms of a representation class $\mathcal{R}$ if there is an algorithm $\phi(\cdot)$ and two polynomials p and q for which for any language L in $\mathcal{L}$ and any $\delta > 0$, and any increasing sequence $\langle s_n \rangle$ of strings drawn according to L:*

1. *$\phi(\cdot)$ identifies L in the limit with probability 1;*
2. *$\phi(\cdot)$ works in time in $p(\|\langle s_n \rangle\|, \frac{1}{\delta})$;*
3. *If $n \geq q(\|r(L)\|, \frac{1}{\delta})$, $\phi(\cdot)$ computes with probability at least $1 - \delta$ a representation h such that $L(h) = L$.*

The above definition takes into account three aspects: As before, the algorithm is required to identify in the limit and to work in polynomial time; Furthermore, with high probability, identification is expected from a polynomial number of examples only.

Because probabilities can be encoded in very different ways it may seem that results will depend on the way they are encoded. Nevertheless a reasonable encoding of the probabilities means that the size of the encodings will be logarithmic in the number of different probabilities that need encoding.

We prove here that even in the case where we have only to choose one probability out of n, identification requires a number of strings that is too high. To do so we do not make any assumption on the way the learning algorithm is to use the information it receives. To do so we consider n languages $L_1, L_2, .., L_n$ such that they just have 2 strings that are different, x and y: namely $p_{L_i}(x) = p_i$ and $p_{L_i}(y) = 1 - p_i$. We have also $\forall i, j \leq n, p_i \neq p_j$.

Proposition 1. *Let $\mathcal{L}$ be a class of languages that contains $\{L_1, L_2, .., L_n\}$ as above, let $\mathcal{R}$ be any representation class for $\mathcal{L}$, let $\phi(\cdot)$ be any learning algorithm for the class $\mathcal{L}$ in terms of the representation class $\mathcal{R}$ and m be an integer. Then there is an L_i in $\mathcal{L}$ such that for any sequence s of size at most m, $p_{L_i}(\phi(s) = L_i) \leq \frac{(m+1)(m+2)}{2n}$.*

Proof. Let us suppose (for contradiction) that there exists such an algorithm $\phi(\cdot)$.

Consider the sets S_j of all possible sequences of length m over strings $\{x, y\}$. With each sequence s we associate value $v(s) = |s|_x$, the number of times string x appears in the sequence. The set of sequences of S_j with value $v(s) = i$ will be denoted S_j^i.

Lemma 2. *Let $m > 0$, there is a language L in $\mathcal{L}$ such that for each $j : 0 \leq j \leq m$ and each $i : 0 \leq i \leq j$*

$$\frac{|\{s \in S_j^i : \phi(s) = L\}|}{|S_j^i|} = \frac{|\{s : \phi(s) = L \wedge |s| = j \wedge v(s) = i\}|}{|\{s : |s| = j \wedge v(s) = i\}|} \leq \frac{(m+1)(m+2)}{2n}$$

As the sequences s of each S_j^i have all the same probability, using lemma 2 for such a language L the sum of all probabilities of sequences drawn according to L is less than $\frac{(m+1)(m+2)}{2n}$. □

Proof (of lemma 2). Suppose this is not true. Then for each of the n languages L in $\mathcal{L}$ there are $i, j : 0 \leq i \leq j \leq m$ with more than $\frac{(m+1)(m+2)}{2n}$ sequences for which $\phi(s) = L$. But such associations can only be produced less than $\frac{(m+1)(m+2)}{2n} \cdot n$ times. Hence this cannot be true for each language L. □

If now we restrict ourselves to reasonable representations we have:

Corollary 2. *Let $\mathcal{L}$ be a class of languages that contains $\{L_1, L_2, .., L_n\}$ as above, let $\mathcal{R}$ be any representation class for $\mathcal{L}$ such that $\|r(L_i)\| < p(\log n)$ for some polynomial $p(\cdot)$, let $\phi(\cdot)$ be any learning algorithm for the class $\mathcal{L}$ in terms of the representation class $\mathcal{R}$ and let $q(\cdot)$ be a polynomial. Then there is an L_i and a constant k such that for any sequence of size at most $q(\|r(L_i)\|)$,*
$$p_{L_i}(\phi(s) = L_i) \leq \frac{\log^{2k} n}{n}.$$

Proof. As $\|r(L_i)\| < p(\log n)$ and $q(\cdot)$ is a polynomial it is enough to show the existence of L_i for all sequences of length at most $m < \log^k n$ for any fixed k. □

As this applies to regular languages when represented by SDFA as a corollary we have:

Theorem 2. *The class of SDRL is not strongly polynomially learnable with probability 1 by means of SDFA.*

4 Polynomial Approximation of Languages

To be able to identify both the structure and the individual probabilities have to be exactly identified. This may legitimately prove to be a too hard task. An alternative is then to adapt Valiant's PAC-learning model [12] to the stochastic setting. We base ourselves here on the definitions from [7]:

Definition 6 (ϵ-good hypothesis). *Let A be the target SDFA and B be a hypothesis SDFA. We say that B is an ϵ-good hypothesis with respect to A for $\epsilon \geq 0$ if $d(L(A), L(B)) < \epsilon$.*

A learning algorithm is now asked to learn a grammar given a *confidence* parameter δ and an *approximation* parameter ϵ. The algorithm can also be given an upper bound on the size of the target grammar and has access to a learning sample.

Definition 7 (Polynomial Pac-learnable). *A class of stochastic languages $\mathcal{L}$ is polynomially PAC-learnable in terms of a representation class $\mathcal{R}$ (using distance d) if there exists an algorithm $\phi(\cdot)$ and a polynomial $p()$ such that for any language L in $\mathcal{L}$ if ϕ is given a learning sample s of size $p(\|r(L)\|)$ it returns a representation r such that $L(r)$ is an ϵ-good hypothesis with respect to L with probability at least $1-\delta$ in time polynomial in $\frac{1}{\epsilon}, \frac{1}{\delta}, |\Sigma|, \|r(L)\|$ and the length of the longest example in s.*

This definition depends strongly on the distance measure that is chosen:

Proposition 2. SDRL *when represented by* SDFA *is polynomially* PAC-*learnable using distance* d_∞.

Proof. This is a consequence of lemma 1. Let us consider a simple algorithm that we will call RETURNPTA which given a learning sample constructs a SDFA that represents exactly the empirical distribution given by the sample. Obviously RETURNPTA is no good at identifying SDFA. Nevertheless RETURNPTA will polynomially PAC-learn SDFA as with high probability the distance according to norm L_∞ between the empirical distribution and the target distribution converges very fast.   □

On the other hand, it can easily be shown that the above result is no longer true when the distance is taken according to another norm. For instance for the norms L_1 and L_2, a language which shares the mass of probabilities in a uniform way over an exponential number of strings will not be closely approximated by the empirical distribution drawn from only a polynomial number of strings.

5   Polynomial Learning with Queries

Queries have been used in order to provide an alternative learning setting, a more favourable one, but also one that can be better controlled. Typical queries include equivalence and membership queries [13] and extended membership queries [14]. An *extended membership query* is built from a string x. The oracle has to return the probability of x. An *equivalence query* is built from a represetation r. The oracle has to return "yes" if $L(r)$ is the target language or a counterexample if not. Angluin [13] gives the following definition of learning with queries:

Definition 8. *A class of grammars is learnable with queries of type T if*

1. *It works in polynomial update time (in the size of the target and of the longest counter-example);*
2. *The number of queries always is polynomial (in the size of the target).*

5.1   Extended Membership Queries

It is easy to show that SDRL (represented by SDFA) are learnable from extended membership queries only if regular languages (represented by DFA) are learnable from membership queries, which is known not to be the case [15].

Theorem 3. *The class of* SDRL *when represented by* SDFA *is not learnable from extended membership queries only.*

Proof. If not DFA would be identifiable from membership queries. We construct from a completed DFA $A = (Q, \Sigma, \delta, q_0, F)$ a SDFA $B = (Q', \Sigma', \delta', q_0', \pi)$ as follows:

- $Q' = Q \cup \{q_f\}$; $\Sigma' = \Sigma \cup \{+, -\}$; $q_0' = q_0$;
- $\forall q \in Q$, $\delta'(q, +) = q_f$, $\delta'(q, -) = q_f$; $\forall q \in Q, \forall a \in \Sigma$, $\delta'(q, a) = \delta(q, a)$;
- $\forall q \in Q, \forall a \in \Sigma$, $\pi(q) = 0, \pi(q_f) = 1, \pi(q, a) = \frac{1}{2 \cdot |\Sigma|}, \pi(q_f, a) = 0$
- $\forall q \in Q, q \in F \Rightarrow \pi(q, +) = \frac{1}{2}, \pi(q, -) = 0; q \notin F \Rightarrow \pi(q, +) = 0, \pi(q, -) = \frac{1}{2}$

The above construction is made from a completed DFA, *i.e.* a DFA to which eventually an extra non final state has been added and is reached by all absent transitions. This ensures that through the construction we have $w \in L_A \Leftrightarrow p_B(w+) = \frac{(2 \cdot |\Sigma|)^{-|w|}}{2}$ and $w \notin L_A \Leftrightarrow p_B(w-) = \frac{(2 \cdot |\Sigma|)^{-|w|}}{2}$. An extended membership query therefore gives us the same information on the underlying SDFA as a membership query would. □

The reasons explaining the above result are that some transition, or some state in the automaton can be barely reachable. *Lock automata*, introduced by Angluin [15] in the DFA setting, are hard to learn. In these automata one long string is going to be the *lock* to the automaton, and only by guessing this string is learning possible.

5.2   Extended Membership Queries and Equivalence Queries

To avoid the problem due to lock automata there are usually three possibilities:

- Accept to make a small (ϵ) error and therefore to learn in a PAC setting;
- Give the algorithm a specific learning set (called a *teaching set* or *complete set*) of strings indicating that certain strings will have to be specifically checked;
- Introduce equivalence queries.

Carrasco and Oncina [16] showed that given a SDRL L, the minimal SDFA A such that $L(A) = L$ fulfils that

$$\delta(q_0, x) = \delta(q_0, y) \iff \frac{p(xv)}{p(x\Sigma^*)} = \frac{p(yv)}{p(y\Sigma^*)} \; \forall v \in \Sigma^*$$

Then, if two strings (x, y) reach two non equivalent states, there are two strings (u,v) such that $\frac{p(xu)}{p(xv)} \neq \frac{p(yu)}{p(yv)}$. Then, the following definition makes sense:

Definition 9. *A set of examples I is* complete *if every probability in the automaton is exercised and if all pairs of states can be separated:*

1. $\forall q, q' \in Q, \forall a \in \Sigma : \delta(q, a) = q', \exists uav \in I : \delta(q_0, u) = q$.
2. $\forall q, q' \in Q, q \neq q', \exists xu, xv, yu, yv \in I :$
   $\delta(q_0, x) = q, \delta(q_0, y) = q', \frac{p(xu)}{p(xv)} \neq \frac{p(yu)}{p(yv)}$

Theorem 4. *The class of SDRL when represented by SDFA is learnable from extended membership queries and a complete set.*

Proof. The algorithm is based on the construction of a 2 entries table (T) indexed respectively by the prefixes and the suffixes of the learning set I. Each cell of the table is filled by making an extended membership query, with the probability of the concatenation of its indexes. That is, $T(x, y) = p_T(xy)$.

Let us define the following equivalence relation:

$$x \equiv y \iff \exists \alpha > 0 : \forall w \in \text{Suf}(I) \ T(x, w) = \alpha T(y, w)$$

From the table, the structure of an automaton A is built: $Q = \{[x] : x \in \text{Pref}(I)\}$, $q_0 = [\lambda]$, $\delta([x], a) = [xa]$.

By construction of the complete set, all the states of the target automaton can be reached by a prefix of a string in I, and for all pairs of non equivalent states in the target automaton we know that there exists a pair of strings that makes the equivalence false. Obviously, if two states are equivalent in the target automaton, they are also equivalent in the hypothesis automaton.

Then we have the structure of the hypothesis automaton. Now the remaining problem is how to assign the probabilities of the hypothesis automaton. We are going to follow some ideas from [17].

On the following, subscript T will denote items related to the target autonaton, while subscript A will denote items related to the hipothesis automaton.

Let w_i be a string such that $\delta(q_0, w_i) = q_i$ (we force $w_0 = \lambda$) and let v_i be such that $p_T(w_i v_i) \neq 0$.

We are going to assign

$$\pi_A(q_i) = p_T(w_i); \qquad \pi_A(q_i, a) = \frac{p_T(w_i a v_j)}{p_T(w_j v_j)} \qquad \text{where } q_j = \delta(q_i, a)$$

This automaton does not fulfil the condition $\pi_A(q_i) + \sum_{a \in \Sigma} \pi_A(q_i, a) = 1$ but we are going to show that $p_A(w) = p_T(w) \ \forall w$.

As $p_T(w_i v_i) = \pi_T(q_0, w_i) p_T(q_i, v_i)$, and let $q_j = \delta(q_i, w)$, we can write

$$\pi_A(q_i, a) = \frac{\pi_T(q_0, w_i)}{\pi_T(q_0, w_j)} \pi_T(q_i, a); \qquad \pi_A(q_i, w) = \frac{\pi_T(q_0, w_i)}{\pi_T(q_0, w_j)} \pi_T(q_i, w)$$

Let now $q_i = \delta(q_0, w)$. Then $p_A(w) = \pi_A(q_0, w) \pi_A(q_i)$
$= \frac{\pi_T(q_0, \lambda)}{\pi_T(q_0, w_i)} \pi_T(q_0, w) p_T(w_i) = \pi_T(q_0, \lambda) \pi_T(q_0, w) \pi_T(q_i) = p_T(w)$

$\square$

Theorem 5. *There is an algorithm that given any* SDFA *A constructs a* SDFA *B such that $L(A) = L(B)$ and $\pi_B(q_i) + \sum_{a \in \Sigma} \pi_B(q_i, a) = 1 \ \forall q_i \in Q_B$.*

Proof. From SDFA A define a row vector F, a column vector S, and a matrix M_a for each $a \in \Sigma$ as:

$$S = (1, 0, \ldots, 0); \quad F_i = \pi_A(q_i); \quad (M_a)_{i,j} = \begin{cases} \pi(q_i, a) & \text{if } q_j = \delta(q_i, a) \\ 0 & \text{otherwise} \end{cases}$$

Then, the probability of a string $a_1 \ldots a_n$ can be computed as $p(a_1 \ldots a_n) = S M_{a_1} \ldots M_{a_n} F$. Let $M_{a_1 \ldots a_n} = M_{a_1} \ldots M_{a_n}$ and let $M = \sum_{a \in \Sigma} M_a$.

Let us define the automaton B with the same structure that A but with the function π defined as follows:

$$\pi_B(q_i) = \frac{p_A(w_i)}{p_A(w_i \Sigma^*)}; \qquad \pi_B(q_i, a) = \frac{p_A(w_i a \Sigma^*)}{p_A(w_i \Sigma^*)}$$

where w_i are arbitrary strings such that $\delta(q_0, w_i) = q_i$. Note that $p(w\Sigma^*) = SM_w \sum_{i=0}^{\infty} M^i F = SM_w (I - M)^{-1} F$ where I is the unity matrix.

It is easy to verify that B fulfils the normalisation condition. It remains to be shown that $\forall x, p_A(x) = p_B(x)$. First note that, $\forall x, y : \delta(q_0, x) = \delta(q_0, y) = q_i$,

$$\frac{p(xav)}{p(xv)} = \frac{\pi(q_0, x) p(q_i, av)}{\pi(q_0, x) p(q_i, v)} = \frac{\pi(q_0, y) p(q_i, av)}{\pi(q_0, y) p(q_i, v)} = \frac{p(yav)}{p(yv)}$$

then $\frac{Ap(xa\Sigma^*)}{p(x\Sigma^*)} = \frac{p(ya\Sigma^*)}{p(y\Sigma^*)}$ and similarly $\frac{p(x)}{p(x\Sigma^*)} = \frac{p(y)}{p(y\Sigma^*)}$.

Let us now consider a string $a_1 \ldots a_n$, let we call $q_i = \delta(q_0, a_1 \ldots a_i)$, then

$$p_B(a_1 \ldots a_n) = \frac{p_A(w_0 a_1 \Sigma^*)}{p_A(w_0 \Sigma^*)} \frac{p_A(w_1 a_2 \Sigma^*)}{p_A(w_1 \Sigma^*)} \cdots \frac{p_A(w_{n-1} a_n \Sigma^*)}{p_A(w_{n-1} \Sigma^*)} \frac{p_A(w_n)}{p_A(w_n \Sigma^*)} =$$

$$\frac{p_A(a_1 \Sigma^*)}{p_A(\Sigma^*)} \frac{p_A(a_1 a_2 \Sigma^*)}{p_A(a_1 \Sigma^*)} \cdots \frac{p_A(a_1 \ldots a_{n-1} a_n \Sigma^*)}{p_A(a_1 \ldots a_{n-1} \Sigma^*)} \frac{p_A(a_1 \ldots a_n)}{p_A(a_1 \ldots a_n \Sigma^*)} = p_A(a_1 \ldots a_n)$$

$\square$

It is reasonable to use equivalence queries instead of a complete set, as in both cases the construction of the SDFA from the table can be done in the same way. We thereby claim that:

Theorem 6. *The class of* SDRL *when represented by* SDFA *is polynomially learnable from extended membership queries and equivalence queries.*

5.3   Extended Prefix Language Queries

An extended prefix language query is made by submitting to the oracle a string w. The oracle then returns the probability $p(w\Sigma^*)$. It can be noticed that an extended membership query can easily be simulated through $|\Sigma|$ extended prefix language queries.

Theorem 7. *The class of* SDRL *when represented by* SDFA *is not polynomially learnable from extended prefix language queries.*

Proof. Let $w \in \Sigma^n$ and consider the following language L_w: $\forall x \in \Sigma^n, x = w \Rightarrow p(x) = 0, x \neq w \Rightarrow p(x) = \frac{1}{2^n}$, $p(wa) = \frac{1}{2^n}$ This language is recognised by a SDFA with at most $2n + 2$ states. Call L_n the set of all languages L_w with $w \in \Sigma^n$. Now let the oracle answer to each extended prefix language query "x" with the quantity $\frac{1}{2^{|x|}}$ if $|x| \leq n$, 0 if not. Then it is straightforward that in the worse case at least 2^n queries are needed. $\square$

Since extended membership queries can be simulated by extended prefix language queries, it follows that:

Theorem 8. *The class of* SDRL *when represented by* SDFA *is polynomially learnable from extended prefix language queries and equivalence queries.*

6   Open Questions and Conclusions

From this point, a number of alternative routes are open. We mention two problems and research directions that deserve in our view to be investigated, and conclude.

- Extended membership queries were introduced in [14]: The learning algorithm may ask for the value $p(x)$ on strings x of its choice.
  We refine the concept to the case where the answer to the query can be an approximate answer: A *specific sampling* query is made by submitting a pattern: The oracle draws a string matching pattern sampled according to the distribution $\mathcal{D}$. Specific sampling queries are intended to fit the idea that the user can ask for examples matching some pattern he is interested in.
  For example specific sampling $a\Sigma^*b$ requires an example starting with a and ending with b, sampled following the distribution induced by $\mathcal{D}$.
  We conjecture that these queries should be able to help us learn the class of SDFA.
- In the previous sections we have shown that both identification and PAC-learning are hard because of the infinite number of probability values that can be reached. So, we suggest to limit the set of probabilities of the automaton. The idea here is to learn SDFA but where the probabilities are predefined, *i.e.* come from a fixed set. We would typically consider $K - $ SDFA built from a set $\mathcal{P}_K = \{\frac{i}{K} : 0 \leq i \leq K\}$ of predefined probabilities, and taking all transition probabilities from $\mathcal{P}_K$.
  We believe that that the identification of the probabilities becomes easier in this setting, and that the class of $K - $ SDFA can now be learnable. We conjecture the class to be PAC-learnable using distances d_1 and d_2.

We have proved that when considering identification the problem of learning SDFA was in most cases intractable.

We have suggested 2 options in order to obtain new positive results: The first consisted in allowing the sampling to be directed. We believe that positive PAC-learning results are possible in this case.

A second, and possibly more practical approach, is to severely reduce the class of stochastic languages under consideration, not by taking a smaller support class, but by simplifying the expression of the probabilities. This is a a way of adding bias to the problem and might allow SDFA to be better fitted for language modeling tasks.

Acknowledgement

The authors thank Franck Thollard for pointing out to them the result from section 4.

References

1. Paz, A.: Introduction to probabilistic automata. Academic Press, NY (1971)
2. Lucas, S., Vidal, E., Amari, A., Hanlon, S., Amengual, J.C.: A comparison of syntactic and statistical techniques for off-line OCR. [18] 168–179
3. Lyngsø, R.B., Pedersen, C.N.S., Nielsen, H.: Metrics and similarity measures for hidden Markov models. In: Proceedings of ISMB'99. (1999) 178–186
4. Mohri, M.: Finite-state transducers in language and speech processing. Computational Linguistics **23** (1997) 269–311
5. Kearns, M.J., Mansour, Y., Ron, D., Rubinfeld, R., Schapire, R.E., Sellie, L.: On the learnability of discrete distributions. In: Proc. of the 25th Annual ACM Symposium on Theory of Computing. (1994) 273–282
6. Carrasco, R.C., Oncina, J.: Learning stochastic regular grammars by means of a state merging method. [18] 139–150
7. Ron, D., Singer, Y., Tishby, N.: On the learnability and usage of acyclic probabilistic finite automata. In: Proceedings of COLT 1995. (1995) 31–40
8. Harrison, M.H.: Introduction to Formal Language Theory. Addison-Wesley Publishing Company, Inc., Reading, MA (1978)
9. Angluin, D.: Identifying languages from stochastic examples. Technical Report YALEU/DCS/RR-614, Yale University (1988)
10. de la Higuera, C., Oncina, J.: Identification with probability one of stochastic deterministic linear languages. In: Proceedings of ALT 2003. LNCS, Berlin, Heidelberg, Springer-Verlag (2003) 134–148
11. Pitt, L.: Inductive inference, DFA's, and computational complexity. In: Analogical and Inductive Inference. Number 397 in LNAI. Springer-Verlag, Berlin, Heidelberg (1989) 18–44
12. Valiant, L.G.: A theory of the learnable. Communications of the Association for Computing Machinery **27** (1984) 1134–1142
13. Angluin, D.: Queries and concept learning. Machine Learning Journal **2** (1987) 319–342
14. Bergadano, F., Varricchio, S.: Learning behaviors of automata from multiplicity and equivalence queries. SIAM Journal of Computation **25** (1996) 1268–1280
15. Angluin, D.: A note on the number of queries needed to identify regular languages. Information and Control **51** (1981) 76–87
16. Carrasco, R.C., Oncina, J.: Learning deterministic regular grammars from stochastic samples in polynomial time. RAIRO (Theoretical Informatics and Applications) **33** (1999) 1–20
17. Carlyle, J.W., Paz, A.: Realizations by stochastic finite automata. Journal of Computation and System Sciences (1971) 26–40
18. Carrasco, R.C., Oncina, J., eds.: Grammatical Inference and Applications, Proceedings of ICGI '94. In Carrasco, R.C., Oncina, J., eds.: Grammatical Inference and Applications, Proceedings of ICGI '94. Number 862 in LNAI, Berlin, Heidelberg, Springer-Verlag (1994)

Navigation Pattern Discovery
Using Grammatical Inference

Nikolaos Karampatziakis[1], Georgios Paliouras[2],
Dimitrios Pierrakos[2], and Panagiotis Stamatopoulos[1]

[1] Department of Informatics and Telecommunications, University of Athens, Greece
[2] Institute of Informatics and Telecommunications, NCSR "Demokritos", Greece

Abstract. We present a method for modeling user navigation on a web site using grammatical inference of stochastic regular grammars. With this method we achieve better models than the previously used first order Markov chains, in terms of predictive accuracy and utility of recommendations. In order to obtain comparable results, we apply the same grammatical inference algorithms on Markov chains, modeled as probabilistic automata. The automata induced in this way perform better than the original Markov chains, as models for user navigation, but they are considerably inferior to the automata induced by the traditional grammatical inference methods. The evaluation of our method was based on two web usage data sets from two very dissimilar web sites. It consisted in producing, for each user, a personalized list of recommendations and then measuring its recall and expected utility.

1 Introduction

In this work we are concerned with modeling the behavior of users on the web. We are specifically interested in discovering interesting navigation patterns by means of grammatical inference methods. When a user requests a page from a specific web site, this transaction is recorded in various places like the browser's history, the web server log file and intermediary devices such as proxies. These transactions are generally called web usage data and the research discipline whose purpose is the discovery of patterns in these data is called Web Usage Mining. In our scenario we examine web usage data in the form of a web server log file. From these data we try to discover interesting patterns by assuming that the user's navigation is governed by the rules of an unknown formal language. To infer the language's grammar, each sequence of web pages that a user requests during an interaction with the web site, is treated as a positive example of a string belonging to the unknown language.

The motivation in choosing a grammar to model the navigation behavior of the users of a web site lies in the sequential nature of browsing. The users usually begin from a page, spend some time reading it and then select the link which they think will satisfy their informational needs. The process is then repeated, producing a sequence of pages that each user has requested. Thus, the use of formal languages seemed natural since they are very well suited for modeling

G. Paliouras and Y. Sakakibara (Eds.): ICGI 2004, LNAI 3264, pp. 187–198, 2004.
© Springer-Verlag Berlin Heidelberg 2004

sequences and also because of their strong theoretical foundation. For example, formal languages have already been used to model biological sequences with very good results [13]. To our knowledge, existing techniques towards our direction have not so far utilized grammatical inference methods to build the model of user navigation behavior. Popular approaches include Markov models, usually of first order [2–4, 8, 16, 17], or ad-hoc methods [18]. However, these approaches result either in difficult to interpret models or they do not have a sound theoretical background.

The rest of the paper is organized as follows. In the next section we summarize the major research directions in the field of user modeling and web usage mining. In section 3 we analyze the inference methods that were used and the necessary adaptations that were made for this specific problem. In section 4, we describe the framework in which the experiments were conducted and we interpret the results. Finally, in section 5 we draw our conclusions and suggest some directions for further work.

2   Related Work

Web Usage Mining is a relatively new research field inspired by the recent growth in the WWW and on-line information sources. Web usage mining, aims at discovering interesting usage patterns, by analyzing Web usage data such as those kept in the log file of a web server. The research work on Web Usage Mining is very extensive and covers aspects both related to traditional data mining issues as well as difficulties inherent in this specific area, such as the reliability of the usage data. Two thorough surveys on the field of Web Usage Mining can be found in [15] and [19].

An approach that has been employed for extracting patterns from web usage data is sequential pattern discovery. Markov chains have been extensively used for this purpose due to their ability to model sequential processes, such as browsing a web site. One of the earliest approaches was presented in [4]. In this work, a first order Markov model was employed in order to predict the subsequent link that a user might follow. A more elaborate approach is proposed in [2] in which the previous model is enhanced with the use of a hybrid prediction model. This model consults four simple Markov chains to select which document the user might request. In [17] first order Markov chains are used to accomplish four tasks: prediction of HTTP requests, adaptive navigation, automatic tour generation and locating personalized "hubs" and "authorities". In addition, the method presented in [8] exploits a mixture of first order Markov models, each one corresponding to the navigational behavior of users with similar behavior. This work is extended in [3] where an algorithm that recommends shortcut links to the user is presented. This can help users find the information they are looking for more quickly, which is especially interesting in the case of users with low bandwidth devices. Finally, in [16], the authors try to reduce the complexity of the previously used Markov model while maintaining a comparable predictive accuracy. This is achieved by calculating the most important navigation patterns and removing everything else which is considered as noise. Generally, Markov chains produce simplistic models for the users navigation behavior, simply aggregating the information in the data, without involving any inference procedure.

Except from Markov models, a few other techniques have been used to discover sequential patterns in web usage data. In [18], a system called Web Utilization Miner is presented. This system provides an SQL-like language that can be used to set the constraints that the mined patterns should satisfy. These constraints can be highly elaborate since the language is very expressive. Unfortunately, setting the right constraints requires a human expert which makes the mining procedure semi-automatic. In [14] a method to discover interesting sequences using clustering is discussed. According to this method, the transitions between pages, which were performed during a user's single interaction with the site are clustered to produce models, which correspond to the navigational behavior of users. Finally, the Clementine tool of SPSS also employs sequential pattern discovery algorithm, known as CAPRI. CAPRI (Clementine A-Priori Intervals) is an association rule discovery algorithm that apart from discovering relationships between items, also finds the order in which these items have been traversed. However, all these methods are generally ad-hoc and they usually do not have any theoretical foundations.

3   Grammatical Inference Methods for Sequence Mining

In our work, we model user navigation on a web site as being governed by an unknown stochastic regular language L. Each interaction of a user with the web site can equivalently be expressed as a sequence of web pages the user requests from the web site. These sequences are represented as strings belonging to L. Thus, each web page that appears in the web server logs is represented by a unique terminal symbol. A web site visitor is then implicitly providing a string belonging to L by following the links on the web pages until the desired information is found or the user leaves the web site.

In order to infer the language L, from the usage data, we applied the widely used ALERGIA algorithm using the Hoeffding statistical test [9], and a slight modification of it, using the proportions test [11]. Our contribution lies primarily in the initial hypothesis with which these algorithms work. We tried starting from the standard probabilistic prefix tree automaton (PPTA) as well as the so called hypertext probabilistic automaton (HPA) [6]. The latter type of automaton has been previously used in web usage mining to locate the most frequently accessed paths in a web site [5] but not within the paradigm of grammatical inference.

The hypertext probabilistic automaton (HPA) was proposed as a compact way to model the users' interaction with a web site. This interaction is initially recorded in the web server's log file. Then, the sequence of web pages that each user requests within a certain period of time, which is called a user session, is extracted from it (see table 1) . Given a set of user sessions, a HPA is constructed in the following way: For each page A_i that appears in the sessions a unique state is created in the HPA. If a user requests the page A_j right after the page A_i,

Table 1. Sample user session set.

Session	Page Sequence
1	$A_1 \rightarrow A_2 \rightarrow A_3 \rightarrow A_4$
2	$A_1 \rightarrow A_5 \rightarrow A_3 \rightarrow A_4 \rightarrow A_1$
3	$A_5 \rightarrow A_2 \rightarrow A_4 \rightarrow A_6$
4	$A_5 \rightarrow A_2 \rightarrow A_3$
5	$A_5 \rightarrow A_2 \rightarrow A_3 \rightarrow A_6$
6	$A_4 \rightarrow A_1 \rightarrow A_5 \rightarrow A_3$

a transition is created in the HPA from A_i to A_j, labeled with the symbol A_j. Furthermore there is a starting state S and transitions from S to the states that correspond to pages which appear first in at least one user session. Each transition's probability, as well as each state's probability to be an accepting one, is estimated straightforwardly from frequency data of the given set of user sessions. For example, the HPA which models the sessions of table 1, is shown in figure 1. The numbers inside each state denote the number of requests of each page and the number of times this page was last in the session set. The number on each transition $A_i \rightarrow A_j$ denotes the number of times the users followed a link from A_i towards A_j. From this figure and the above description, it becomes apparent that the HPA is equivalent to first order Markov chains, which have been previously used for modeling the user behavior on the web. In the rest of this work we will refer to HPAs and Markov chains interchangeably.

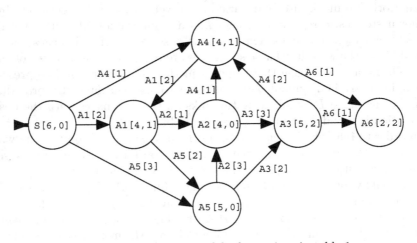

Fig. 1. The HPA that models the sessions in table 1.

The HPA approach reduces the space in which the search for the target automaton is conducted. Furthermore, the HPA can be derived from a PPTA, by merging together the states that correspond to the same web pages. As a result, the HPA is a generalization of the corresponding PPTA. This means that a large portion of the original search space, containing more general automata than the PPTA but less general than the HPA, is excluded from the search when using the HPA. Additionally, some automata that are more general than the HPA may also be excluded from the new search space. In the next section the overall quality of the hypotheses in this smaller search space will be illustrated.

Therefore, it is interesting to compare the effect of grammatical inference starting from a HPA, rather than a PPTA. However, applying the existing stochastic regular grammar inference algorithms, which were designed for the PPTA, on an arbitrary automaton is not always feasible. This is due to assumptions about the structure of the automaton in each step of the inference procedure. For example, the ALERGIA algorithm, shown in table 2, avoids the possibility of infinite recursion by specifying a sequence for the merging operations which ensures that one of the states is always the root of a subtree of the PPTA. As a result, ALERGIA cannot be applied as is to an arbitrary automaton. However, the HPA has an interesting property that allows the algorithm to be applied despite the automaton's structure. As can be seen in figure 1, each symbol A_i labeling a transition fully defines the destination state, independently of the current state. The first consequence of this property is that state merging cannot result in a non-deterministic automaton. Non-determinism can in principal occur when merging two states which have transitions with the same symbol s towards different states. The merged state will then be non-deterministic because there will be two states to which s can lead. In order to remove non-determinism, the states causing it are repeatedly merged together. In the case of the HPA, transitions with the same symbol always lead to the same state, so non-determinism cannot occur. The other effect of the above property is that the compatibility test is greatly simplified. To test for the compatibility of two states it is no longer necessary to test the compatibility of all subsequent states, since these states are now identical and thus guaranteed to be compatible.

4   Experiments

Two data sets were used for the evaluation of our method. The first set was the MSWeb[1] data and the second was usage data from the web site "Information Retrieval in Chemistry"[2], hosted at NCSR "Demokritos". The data used in the experimental evaluation of our work were already split into sessions and some amount of "denoising", for example from bot sessions, had already taken place [14]. This prevented any experimentation with different session timeouts. Recent work that addresses the issue of session timeout can be found in [12]. In order to distinguish between different sessions of the same user, the sessions of the second data set were produced by constraining the time between two consecutive requests from the same IP to sixty minutes. If the time between two consecutive requests exceeded sixty minutes, the second request was considered as the beginning of a new session. The MSWeb data were grouped according to the identity of the user, rather than simply the IP address. As a result the constraint on the time between consecutive requests was not required. The MSWeb data set

---

[1] Publically available from http://www.ics.uci.edu/~mlearn/MLRepository.html
[2] http://macedonia.chem.demokritos.gr

Table 2. The original ALERGIA algorithm. $C(k)$ denotes the number of times state k was visited while parsing the user sessions. $C(k, \#)$ denotes the number of times state k was last in the user sessions. $C(k, x)$ is the number of times that the terminal symbol x was encountered in the sample when the automaton was in state k and $\delta(k, x)$ denotes the state in which the automaton goes when it is in state k and x in encountered.

ALERGIA(S, α)
   $A = \text{PPTA}(S)$
   for $j = 2$ to $|A|$ do
      for $i = 1$ to $j - 1$ do
         if COMPATIBLE(i, j, α)
            MERGE(i, j)
            DETERMINIZE(A)

COMPATIBLE(i, j, α)
   if DIFFERENT$(C(i), C(j), C(i, \#), C(j, \#), \alpha)$
      return false
   for each terminal t do
      if DIFFERENT$(C(i), C(j), C(i, t), C(j, t), \alpha)$
         return false
      if not COMPATIBLE$(\delta(i, t), \delta(j, t), \alpha)$
         return false
   return true

DIFFERENT$(n_i, n_j, f_i, f_j, \alpha)$
   return $\left| \frac{f_i}{n_i} - \frac{f_j}{n_j} \right| > \sqrt{\frac{1}{2} \ln \frac{2}{\alpha}} \left(\frac{1}{\sqrt{n_i}} + \frac{1}{\sqrt{n_j}} \right)$

contained around 38000 sessions while the chemistry data set contained 4500 sessions. For the experiments, two thirds of the sessions were used to infer the automaton and the rest were used for its evaluation.

The tasks in which the inferred automata were assessed, were designed to capture their ability as predictors of the user's behavior and their ability as good recommenders for the next page a user would request. After the training phase, we hid the last page of each session in the test set and gave the automaton the rest of the pages in each session. That would lead the automaton in a specific state from which we could then construct a list of recommendations based on the most probable transitions from that state. A successful prediction occurs when the hidden page is among the most probable pages to request from the current state.

For the assessment of a list of recommendations we used the metric of expected utility [7]. The expected utility of a recommended page is simply the probability of requesting the page times the page's utility. As in [7], the utility v_{aj} of a page j for a user a is one if j belongs in the pages of the session and zero otherwise. The probability of requesting the ith page in a list was set to decay exponentially with i. Thus the expected utility of a list of pages (sorted in decreasing order of transition probability) is:

$$R_a = \sum_{j=0}^{l} \frac{v_{aj}}{2^{j/h}}$$

where l is the ordinal number of the last page in the list and h is the viewing halflife. Similar to other exponentially decaying phenomena, the viewing halflife is the ordinal number of the page which has a 50-50 chance to be requested. In our experiments, following [7], we set this chance to occur in the fifth page. Finally, for a set of user sessions with the corresponding recommendation lists, the expected utility is:

$$R = 100\frac{\sum_a R_a}{\sum_a R_a^{max}}$$

where R_a^{max} is the maximum achievable utility if the top of the list contained only pages with v_{aj} equal to one. For example, if a recommended list of items for a user a is the one shown in the second row of table 3 then the expected utility is:

$$R_a = \frac{1}{2^{0/4}} + \frac{1}{2^{2/4}} + \frac{1}{2^{5/4}} + \frac{1}{2^{6/4}} = 2.48$$

where only items A, C, E and F belong in the user session (item utility one). Furthermore, if we assume that there is one more item H whose utility equals one then the maximum achievable utility is:

$$R_a^{max} = \frac{1}{2^{0/4}} + \frac{1}{2^{1/4}} + \frac{1}{2^{2/4}} + \frac{1}{2^{3/4}} + \frac{1}{2^{4/4}} = 3.64$$

since H also contributes to the maximum achievable utility.

Table 3. A sample recommendation list.

ordinal	0	1	2	3	4	5	6
item	A	B	C	D	E	F	G
utility	1	0	1	0	0	1	1

The predictive accuracy of an inferred automaton is measured using the recall of the list it recommends. The recall of an information retrieval system is defined as the proportion of the totally available relevant documents retrieved by it. In this case, the hidden page is considered to be a relevant one. To calculate the recall, we compute the percentage of the user sessions in which the hidden page belongs in the recommended list as a function of the length of the list. The graph of this function gives a hint for the appropriate size of the list of pages that should be recommended to the user.

In figures 2 and 3 the recall of the best automata is drawn. The legend shows for each curve the initial hypothesis that was used, the algorithm that was applied and the chosen value of α. With the term "prop test" we mean the ALERGIA algorithm with the statistical test proposed in [11]. On the other hand the term "alergia" refers to the original algorithm using the Hoeffding test.

From these graphs, the models that were induced with the PPTA as initial hypothesis are clearly superior over the models that were induced from a Markov chain. The graph shows that traditional grammatical inference methods

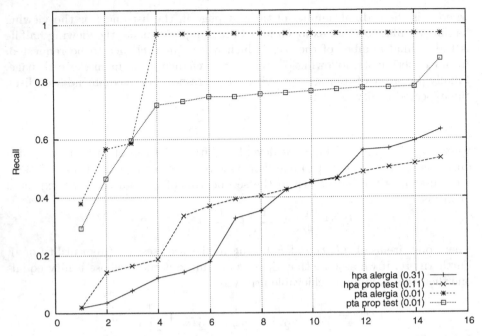

Fig. 2. Recall of some automata induced from the chemistry data set. The x axis represents the length of the recommendation list.

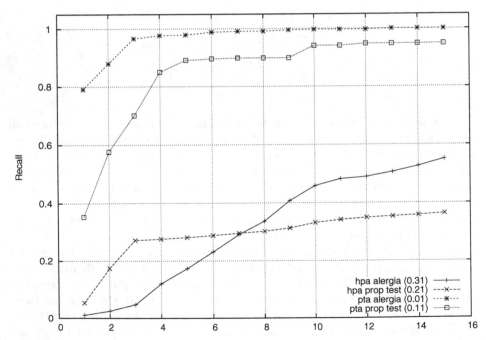

Fig. 3. Recall of some automata induced from the MSWeb data set. The x axis represents the length of the recommendation list.

can produce models with more than 90% recall in the top 4 pages of the recommendation list. On the other hand, the automata induced from Markov chains have poor recall which increases steadily with the length of the list. This implies that their recommendations are actually guesses of the user behavior.

The expected utility of automata induced with different values of the α parameter is shown in figures 4 and 5. By inspecting the recall graphs, it was decided to set the maximum length of the produced recommendation list to ten items. As α increases, fewer states are merged and the automaton is less general. This means that the expected utility should decrease when α increases. Again the automata induced from Markov chains yield inferior models compared to the automata induced from the conventional algorithms. Regarding the automata inferred from the Markov chains, their expected utility seems to be greater from what the initial Markov chain would produce. This conclusion is drawn because for α equal to one we get the initial hypothesis, since no merging operations will be done, and also because the expected utility is decreasing as α increases. However, the expected utility in the case of these automata is much lower than that of the automata inferred from PPTAs and it also very sensitive to the changes of α. The latter observation is evidence that good models are excluded from the search space.

5   Conclusions

We evaluated two models for the navigation behavior of users in a web site. Both can be seen as stochastic regular grammars, but one is inferred from the traditional prefix tree automaton while the other from the first order Markov chain that has been previously used to model this navigation behavior. In this work we present the results produced by the well known ALERGIA algorithm suitably adapted to work with Markov chains as initial hypotheses. Two statistical tests were used to decide if two states of the automaton should be merged, the Hoeffding test and the proportions test. The difference between the two tests is that the latter is stricter than the former, leading to fewer state merging operations and larger automata. This has two effects. On one side the Hoeffding test leads to automata with better generalization ability which is reflected in the higher recall and expected utility that it achieves. On the other side, the proportions test is less likely to perform a bad merging, due to the inevitable presence of noise in the data. When two incompatible states are merged, the resulting automaton can be very different from the target. This can lead to results that are very sensitive to the value of α. This is the reason why the expected utility in figures 4 and 5 is predictably decreasing in the case of the proportions test. In the case of the Hoeffding test however, the curve is very sensitive to the value of α.

We have used data from two very different web sites. In both data sets the automata that were induced from the prefix tree automaton achieved better performance with respect to the metrics of recall and expected utility. This suggests that, even though stochastic regular languages have not been previously used in modeling the user navigation on the web, they are better suited for

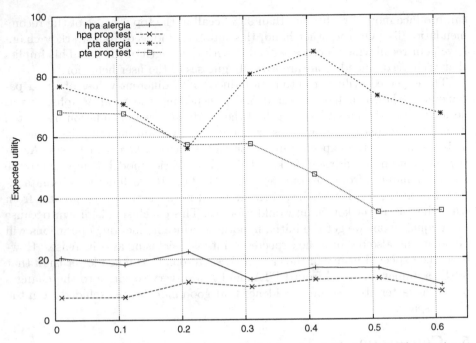

Fig. 4. The expected utility as a function of α for the chemistry data set. The maximum length of the recommendation list was set to 10.

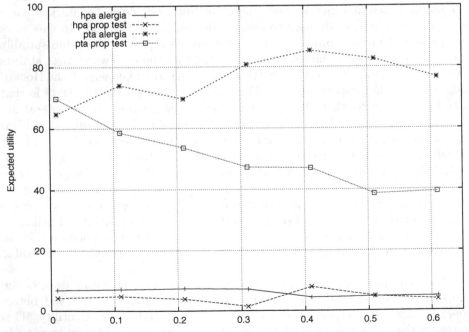

Fig. 5. The expected utility as a function of α for the MSWeb data set. The maximum length of the recommendation list was set to 10.

this task than the previously used Markov chains. This is attributed to the expressiveness of stochastic regular languages.

In addition to further empirical evaluation, we are interested in utilizing the inferred automata in different ways. The merged states are virtually sets of web pages that could be viewed as a clustering of the pages of a web site. Preliminary experiments with the Msweb data set are promising since they have shown the emergence of meaningful clusters. We are also looking into different criteria with which the states could be merged. Since merging the web pages according to their transition probabilities seems at first awkward, we are trying to adopt criteria that would provide a more intuitive meaning to a merged state. Finally, we plan to compare our results with those of well known sequential pattern discovery algorithms [1, 10].

Acknowledgments

We would like to thank the members of the team "Information Retrieval in Chemistry" of NCSR "Demokritos" (E. Varveri, A. Varveris and P. Telonis) for providing the chemistry data.

References

1. R. Agrawal and R. Srikant. *Mining sequential patterns.* In Proceedings of the Eleventh International Conference on Data Engineering, 1995.
2. D. Albrecht, I. Zukerman and A. Nicholson. *Pre-sending documents on the WWW: A comparative study.* Proceedings of the Sixteenth International Joint Conference on Artificial Intelligence, pp. 1274-1279, 1999.
3. C. Anderson, P. Domingos, and D. Weld. *Adaptive Web Navigation for Wireless Devices.* Proceedings of the 17th International Joint Conference on Artificial Intelligence, 2001.
4. A. Bestavros. *Using speculation to reduce server load and service time on the www.* Proceedings of the fourth ACM International Conference on Information and Knowledge Management, 403-410, 1995.
5. J. Borges and M. Levene. *Data Mining of User Navigation Patterns.* Lecture Notes in Computer Science, Vol. 1836, pp. 92-111, 1999.
6. J. Borges. *A Data Mining Model to Capture User Web Navigation Patterns.* PhD dissertation, 2000.
7. J. S. Breese, D. Heckerman and C. Kadie. *Empirical Analysis of Predictive Algorithms for Collaborative Filtering.* Proceedings of the Fourteenth Conference on Uncertainty in Artificial Intelligence, 1998.
8. I. Cadez, D. Heckerman, C. Meek, P. Smyth, and S. White. *Visualization of Navigation Patterns on a Web Site Using Model Based Clustering.* Technical Report MSR-TR-00-18, 2000.
9. R. Carrasco and J. Oncina. *Learning Regular Grammars by Means of a State Merging Method.* Proceedings of the ICGI, 1994.
10. R. Cooley, B. Mobasher, and J. Srivastava. *Web Mining: Information and Pattern Discovery on the World Wide Web.* In Proceedings of the 9th IEEE International Conference on Tools with Artificial Intelligence, 1997.

11. A. Habrard, M. Bernard and M. Sebban. *Improvement of the State Merging Rule on Noisy Data in Probabilistic Grammatical Inference.* Proceedings of the Fourteenth European Conference on Machine Learning (ECML 2003), 2003.

12. R. Kohavi and R. Parekh. *Ten supplementary analyses to Improve E-commerce Web Sites.* In Proceedings of the Fifth WEBKDD workshop, 2003.

13. S.H. Muggleton, C. H. Bryant and A. Srinivasan. *Learning Chomsky-like grammars for biological sequence families.* In Proceedings of the Seventeenth International Conference on Machine Learning, 2000.

14. G. Paliouras, C. Papatheodorou, V. Karkaletsis and C. D. Spyropoulos. *Clustering the Users of Large Web Sites into Communities.* Proceedings of International Conference on Machine Learning (ICML), 2000.

15. D. Pierrakos, G. Paliouras, C. Papatheodorou and C. D. Spyropoulos. *Web Usage Mining as a Tool for Personalization: a survey.* User Modeling and User-Adapted Interaction Journal, vol. 13, issue 4, pp. 311-372, 2003.

16. J. Pitkow and P. Pirolli. *Mining longest repeating subsequences to predict WWW surfing.* Proceedings of the 1999 USENIX Annual Technical Conference, 1999.

17. R. Sarukkai. *Link Prediction and Path Analysis Using Markov Chains.* Proceedings of the 9th World Wide Web Conference, 2000.

18. M. Spiliopoulou, L. C. Faulstich, and K. Wilkler. *A data miner analyzing the navigational behavior of Web users.* In Proceedings of the Workshop on Machine Learning in User Modeling of the ACAI99, 1999.

19. J. Srivastava, R. Cooley, M. Deshpande, and P. T. Tan. *Web Usage Mining: Discovery and Applications of Usage Patterns from Web Data.* SIGKDD Explorations, 1(2), pp. 12-23, 2000.

A Corpus-Driven Context-Free Approximation of Head-Driven Phrase Structure Grammar

Hans-Ulrich Krieger

German Research Center for Artificial Intelligence (DFKI)
Stuhlsatzenhausweg 3, D-66123 Saarbrücken, Germany
krieger@dfki.de

1 Introduction

We present a simple and intuitive unsound corpus-driven approximation method
for turning unification-based grammars (UBGs), such as HPSG [1] or PATR-II
[2], into context-free grammars (CFGs). The method is unsound in that it does
not generate a CFG whose language is a true superset of the language accepted
by the original UBG. It is a corpus-driven method in that it relies on a corpus
of parsed sentences and generates broader CFGs when given more input samples. Our open approach can be fine-tuned in different directions, allowing us to
monotonically come close to the original parse trees by shifting more information
into the CF symbols. The approach has been fully implemented in JAVA.

Due to space limitations, the interested reader might further consult [3].
This report discusses several orthogonal adjusting parameters, additional post-
processing steps and motivate that the extracted CFGs can be tuned to deliver
a meaningful semantic output.

1.1 Motivation

Since unification-based parsers usually rely on a context-free backbone of unification rules (or rule schemata, to borrow the broader HPSG term), it should
not be that difficult to extract a context-free grammar. In fact, relatively specific
unification-based rules (e.g., ANLT, LFG), should result in approximated CFGs
of good quality [4]. However, lexicalized grammar theories such as HPSG are of
a different kind: rule schemata in these frameworks are usually so general that
the resulting CFGs are worthless, meaning that they accept nearly everything.
Proper recognition of utterances in lexicalized theories is realized by shifting
the great amount of information into the lexicon and by applying a specific
descriptive means in rule schemata: coreferences or reentrancies.

Our attempt thus does *not* operate on the rules of a grammar (as do, e.g., [5]
in their sound HPSG approximation), but instead on valid rule *instantiations*
of a special kind, viz., passive edges of the unification chart, resulting from
parsing a corpus. In order to access such passive edges, we have defined an
universal external exchange format for representing a chart (see section 3.1).
Since passive edges directly encode their immediate daughters, a passive edge
can be seen as a tree of depth 1. From such a tree and with the help of the feature

G. Paliouras and Y. Sakakibara (Eds.): ICGI 2004, LNAI 3264, pp. 199–210, 2004.
© Springer-Verlag Berlin Heidelberg 2004

structure directly associated with each passive edge, it is possible to create an annotated context-free rule of arbitrary specificity (section 3). Terminal and nonterminal symbols in our framework are equipped with information from the related feature structure of the passive edge, similar to annotated symbols in the GPSG framework (see section 2.2). When taking deeper nested daughters into account, we can even escape the flat domain of context-free rules, resulting in various forms of context-free tree grammars [6].

In order to predict probabilities for CF parse trees, we provide each rule with a frequency counter, telling us how often the rule has been successfully applied during parsing of the corpus. Given these counters, it is then easy to move from the extracted CFG to the associated PCFG which might be employed during Viterbi parsing in order to disambiguate context-free readings. Assuming that the extracted CFG does not produce too many additional readings, the PCFG can thus be seen as an indirect probability model for the UBG. The trick goes as follows. Since every CF rule is related by its rule name to a unification rule, we first let the PCFG parse a given input, predicting probabilities for CF parse trees. In a second phase, the ranked parsing trees can be deterministically replayed one after another by the UBG (processing the most probable CFG trees first), establishing an order of best UBG parsing trees. Obviously, the two-step parsing approach also speeds up unification-based parsing, since most of the original UBG rule applications are filtered out by the (P)CFG. [5] have shown that two-stage parsing is feasible, even with large approximated CF grammars of more than 600,000 rules, resulting in a speedup of 41%–62%.

Since the form and size of an approximated CFG is determined by the training corpus, our approach makes it easy to compute domain-specific subgrammars from general large-scale unification grammars. Thus this approach might gain importance in information extraction and related tasks.

1.2   Structure of Paper

The structure of this paper is as follows. In the next section, we first introduce some basic inventory (types, type hierarchy, typed feature structures, unification) and discuss the objects which are constructed and manipulated during the extraction of the CFG (symbols, rules). After that, section 3 presents the interface to the chart of the HPSG parser and describes the basic extraction algorithm, together with a variation that produces smaller, although more general CFGs. The section also has a few words on the quick-check paths of the UBG which serve as the starting point for finding the proper annotations of the context-free symbols. In section 4, we elaborate on how the size of the training corpus and the size of the annotation change the language of the approximated CFG w.r.t. the two variations of the basic algorithm. Finally, section 5 present first measurements for different grammars.

2   Objects of Interest

The goal of this section is a description of the objects which are built and manipulated by the extraction algorithm (section 3). The section furthermore defines important relations between symbols and rules. It also has a few introductory remarks concerning typed feature structures.

2.1 Typed Feature Structures

This subsection introduces some fundamental theoretical concepts which are used throughout the paper. A more thorough investigation can be found in, e.g., [2], [7], and [8].

Definition 1 (TYPE HIERARCHY)
Let $\mathcal{T}$ be a finite set of type symbols. We refer to a type hierarchy by a pair $\langle \mathcal{T}, \preceq \rangle$, such that $\preceq \subseteq \mathcal{T} \times \mathcal{T}$ is a decidable partial order [9]. I.e., $\preceq$ is reflexive, antisymmetric and transitive. We assume that $\mathcal{T}$ contains three special symbols: $\top$ (the most general type), $\bot$ (the most specific type), and U (expressing undefinedness), such that $\bot \preceq t$ and $t \preceq \top$, for all $t \in \mathcal{T}$. Furthermore, U is a direct subtype of $\top$ and is incompatible with every type in $\mathcal{T} \setminus \{\top, \mathsf{U}\}$, i.e., U does not have any subtype, except $\bot$. We will use the undef type U later to express the fact that a certain feature is not appropriate for a given type.

We also need the notion of a typed feature structure (TFS) and will frequently talk about the finite set of features $\mathcal{F}$ and the already mentioned finite set of types $\mathcal{T}$. However, we will not present a definition here and only note that there exist orthogonal, although precise definitions of what TFSs are (the enumeration is, of course, not complete): (i) a kind of deterministic finite state automaton [7]; (ii) an extension of Aït-Kaci's ψ/ϵ terms [8]; (iii) syntactic sugar/expressions in a *designer logic* which can be transformed into definite equivalences [9]; (iv) elements of the least solution of a certain recursive domain equation [5].

From an implementation point of view, TFSs are not that different from records in imperative programming languages or classes in object-oriented languages. They can also be seen as a generalization of unnamed tuples and fixed-arity terms (as, e.g., in PROLOG). TFSs possess an interesting descriptive means, viz., coreferences or reentrancies. This helps to state the fact that the values under several features within a TFS are identical (and not merely structural equal).

We close this subsection by defining the notion of a path. Putting it simply, a path is a sequence of features $f_1, f_2, \ldots, f_n \in \mathcal{F}$ which helps us to access information from deeper levels of a TFS. We depict such a path as $f_1 | f_2 | \ldots | f_n$. One specific path stands out, viz., the empty path ϵ, referring to the TFS itself.

2.2 Symbols

Symbols bear a *name* and an *annotation* vector. The name of a terminal refers to the full surface string of this terminal word and its annotation vector is empty. A nonterminal also has a name, encoding the HPSG rule name (e.g., hcomp or measure_np), whereas the annotation groups several types, originating from (possibly deep-nested) values under pre-specified paths (the so-called annotation paths) within the instantiated rule TFS. Thus an annotation is quite similar to a feature specification in GPSG [10] or a quick-check vector [11].

Definition 2 (SYMBOL)
We refer to a symbol s by a pair $[n, a]$, consisting of a name n and an annotation a. We write $N(s)$ to depict the first projection of s (the name) and $A(s)$ to access the annotation part of s. We often use the more GPSGish notation n[a].

Definition 3 (ANNOTATION)
An annotation $a = [t_1, \ldots, t_n]$ is a n-tuple of type names or type IDs $t_i \in \mathcal{T}$, $i \in \{1, \ldots, n\}$. We write $\pi_i(a)$ to denote value t_i of the i-th projection of a.

Definition 4 (SYMBOL SUBSUMPTION)
Let s_1 and s_2 be CF symbols. s_1 is said to be subsumed by s_2 (written as $s_1 \preceq s_2$) iff $N(s_1) = N(s_2)$ and $\pi_i(A(s_1)) \preceq \pi_i(A(s_2))$, for all $i \in \{1, \ldots, n\}$.

Let us give an example. Assume the CF symbols N[sg, fem], N[pl, fem], N[num, fem], and let sg $\preceq$ num and pl $\preceq$ num. Then N[sg, fem] $\preceq$ N[num, fem] and N[pl, fem] $\preceq$ N[num, fem] holds. However, N[sg, fem] and N[pl, fem] are not related by subsumption, so we say that these symbols are incompatible.

2.3 Rules

Context-free grammar rules consist of a left-hand side nonterminal symbol and a sequence of right-hand side symbols. A rule also possesses a frequency counter, telling us how often that rule has been applied during parsing. It is worth noting that rule frequency will later gain importance when we move from the extracted CFG to the associated PCFG which will predicts probabilities for CF trees.

Definition 5 (CONTEXT-FREE GRAMMAR RULE)
Let $l, r_1, \ldots, r_n$ be CF symbols and let furthermore l be a nonterminal symbol. We then call the expression $l \rightarrow r_1 \ldots r_n$ a context-free grammar rule. l is usually referred to as the left-hand side (LHS) of the rule, whereas the sequence $r_1 \ldots r_n$ is called the right-hand side (RHS). Given a CF rule α, the projection L yields the LHS of α, i.e., $L(\alpha) = l$. R delivers the RHS: $R(\alpha) = r_1 \ldots r_n$.

Definition 6 (RULE SUBSUMPTION)
Let $\alpha = (l_\alpha \rightarrow r_{1\alpha} \ldots r_{n\alpha})$ and $\beta = (l_\beta \rightarrow r_{1\beta} \ldots r_{n\beta})$ be two context-free grammar rules. We say that α is subsumed by β and write $\alpha \preceq \beta$ iff $l_\alpha \preceq l_\beta$, $n_\alpha = n_\beta$, and $r_{i\alpha} \preceq r_{i\beta}$, for all $1 \leq i \leq n_\alpha$. We say that two CF rules α and β are equivalent iff they both subsume each other: $\alpha \equiv \beta \iff \alpha \preceq \beta$ and $\beta \preceq \alpha$. Let $\alpha \npreceq \beta$ abbreviate $\neg(\alpha \preceq \beta)$. Two rules are said to be incompatible iff they are not related by rule subsumption: $\alpha \bowtie \beta \iff \alpha \npreceq \beta$ and $\beta \npreceq \alpha$.

Assume $\alpha = ($NP[sg,fem] -> N[sg,fem]$)$, $\beta = ($NP[pl,fem] -> N[pl,fem]$)$, and $\gamma = ($NP[num,fem] -> N[num,fem]$)$. Then $\alpha \preceq \gamma$ and $\beta \preceq \gamma$, but $\alpha \bowtie \beta$.

3   Extracting a Context-Free Grammar

This section centers around the offline extraction of a context-free grammar from a given corpus, originally parsed by the deep HPSG parser of the PET system [12]. We first describe the textual interface between our extraction component and PET. After this, we motivate that the annotation values of context-free symbols for a recognition grammar are related to the quick-check paths, originally introduced within the context of deep HPSG parsing [11]. Given this background, we then describe the basic extraction algorithm in pseudo code. Finally, we argue for an extension of the original algorithm, which helps to compute smaller grammars and describe how the probabilities for the CF rules are obtained.

feat	::= *integer*		*type*	::= *integer*
coref	::= "#" *integer*		*fvpair*	::= *feat* ({*coref*} *tfs* | *coref*)
tfs	::= "[" *type fvpair* "]"*		*id*	::= *integer*
edgename	::= *id* | *string*		*rulename*	::= *string*
imdtrs	::= "(" *edgename*+ ")"*		*edge*	::= *id rulename imdtrs tfs*

Fig. 1. The external exchange format of an edge as delivered by a modified version of the PET system. *rulename* serves as the main category symbol. *imdtrs* refers to the immediate daughters of an edge. Since the delivered passive edges are topologically sorted, it is not necessary to reencode an edge that has already been introduced earlier. Thus the immediate daughters *imdtrs* of an edge are referred to by integer numbers *id*. The only exception are terminal symbols (the surface form) which are written as pure strings.

3.1   Interface to HPSG

The interface to HPSG is established via the creation of text files: for every input sentence of the training corpus, a new file is created that contains exactly the passive edges produced by PET. Although not every deep passive edge contributes to a deep reading, we have decided to take all passive edges into account (one can think of other options as well). Due to the fact that features and types are represented as integers in PET, it is important that both PET and the extraction process operate on the same *TDL* [13] grammar.

Because HPSG requires all relevant information to be contained in the SYNSEM feature of the mother structure, the unnecessary daughters (which are part of the TFS) only increase the size of the overall feature structure without constraining the search space. Due to the *Locality Principle* of HPSG, they can therefore be legally removed in fully instantiated items, i.e., passive edges. To be independent from a certain grammatical theory, we use *restrictors* similar to [14] as a flexible and easy-to-use specification to perform this deletion. In case we are trying to work with a larger tree context and not limiting ourselves to context-free rules (= trees of depth 1), the restrictor is the right means to accomplish this.

3.2   Quick-Check Paths

Quick-check paths are used during unification-based parsing to quickly and correctly filter out failing unifications without applying the costly unification operation [11]. Such a filter is extremely important since most of the unifications usually fail (95–99% of all unifications). The quick-check filter exploits the fact that unification fails more often at certain points in feature structures than at others. In order to determine the most prominent failure points, we parse a test corpus in an offline stage, using a special unification engine that records all failures instead of exiting after the first failing unification. These failure points constitute the quick-check (QC) vector. When executing unification during parsing, the points are efficiently accessed and checked using type unification prior to the rest of the structure. QC filtering heavily relies on type unification being very fast, which in fact is the case since it can be cached or even precompiled. Figure 2 displays the ten most prominent failure paths for the English HPSG.

SYNSEM|LOCAL|CAT|HEAD
SYNSEM|NON-LOCAL|QUE
SYNSEM|LOCAL|CAT|HEAD|MOD
SYNSEM|LOCAL|CAT|VAL|COMPS|FIRST|OPT
SYNSEM|LOCAL|CAT|HEAD|MOD|FIRST|LOCAL|CAT|HEAD

SYNSEM|LOCAL|CAT|MC
SYNSEM|LOCAL|CONJ
SYNSEM|LOCAL|KEYS|KEY
SYNSEM|NON-LOCAL|SLASH|LIST
SYNSEM|LOCAL|CAT|HEAD|VFORM

Fig. 2. The ten most prominent failure points for the English HPSG grammar, developed at CSLI, Stanford.

```
01  local result = ∅;
02  for each file ∈ D do
03    local edges = makeEdges(file);
04    for i = 1 to |edges| do
05      local e = edges[i];
06      local lhs = [getName(e), getAnnotation(e, Q)];
07      local rhs = makeArray(|e|);
08      local dtrs = getImmediateDaughters(e);
09      for j = 1 to |dtrs| do
10        local d = dtrs[j];
11        rhs[j] = [getName(d), getAnnotation(d, Q)];
12      result = result ∪≅ {lhs → rhs};
13  return result;
```

Fig. 3. The overall structure of the extraction algorithm.

As already said in subsection 2.2, the annotation of a CF symbol bears a close resemblance to a QC vector – an annotation is a subvector of a QC vector. The reason for using (parts of) the QC vector is due to the fact that we are interested in fast and modestly overgenerating context-free *recognition* grammars. Exactly the failure points in a QC vector are of this property, viz., heavily contributing to failures which rule out parts of the search space during unification-based parsing. We note here that not every QC path has to be present in every feature structure, since only certain features are appropriate for certain TFSs. Let us give an example. Given the above set of QC paths, it turns out that the original head-complement rule schema [1] hcomp is undefined for the ninth QC path. To account for this problem, we use the type U introduced in subsection 2.1 to express such undefinedness. Consequently, we obtained instantiations such as

    hcomp[verb*, na, ..., U, bse] --> bse_verb_infl[...] bare_np[...]

3.3   Algorithm

The idea behind the context-free extraction is relatively straightforward and is given in pseudo code in figure 3.

As we already said, the HPSG parser produces for each input sentence an output file that contains the passive edges of the chart for this sentence, encoded in the format given by figure 1. The extraction of a CFG then proceeds as follows. Given a directory D and a vector of quick check paths Q, we iterate over the files in D (line 2). For each file, we construct a vector edges of internal edges (i.e., JAVA objects) for the set of external passive edges stored in this file using *makeEdges* (line 3). This includes the in-memory reconstruction of the TFSs for the mother structures (the LHSs). For each vector position, i.e., for each edge e, we build up a LHS symbol (i.e., a pair), consisting of a name field (via *getName*) and an annotation vector (via *getAnnotation*), given the quick-check paths Q (line 6). The same is done for every RHS symbol, but since we usually have more than one symbol, we collect them in an array dtrs of length equal to the number of the immediate daughters of the passive chart edge (lines 7–11). For every passive edge, we finally generate a context-free rule object, given the LHS and the RHS (line 12). The new CF rules are adjoined to the result set (line 12). After we have processed all files in directory D, the result set is returned at last (line 13).

The subscript $\equiv$ of the union operator in line 12 should indicate that new rules are added to the result set using rule equivalence. I.e., a new rule only contributes to the final CFG if no structural equivalent rule has already been introduced earlier during the extraction process. Even for a small corpus, a large number of structural equivalent rules are generated, resulting from either reappearing words or from reappearing linguistic constructions. The non-astonishing observation is that the smaller the annotation gets, the larger the number of equivalent rules becomes. Clearly, by using more quick-check paths, we obtain more specific CF grammars. In the next subsection, we will slightly modify line 12, replacing the rule equivalence test by rule subsumption.

3.4   A Variation

Rule subsumption, defined in section 2.3, now comes into play to scale down generated grammars. We apply this operation online during the extraction process in that we replace line 12 of the algorithm by

12   result = result $\cup_{\preceq}$ {lhs → rhs};

The intention behind $\cup_{\preceq}$ is that a new rule is only added to the result set iff it is more general than at least one rule already in the set. If so, the old rule and perhaps further other rules are removed. If it is more specific, the new rule is clearly not added. The application of $\cup_{\preceq}$ guarantees that the rules from the result set result are pairwise incompatible, i.e.,

$$\forall \alpha, \beta \in \text{result} . \ \alpha \bowtie \beta, \text{ for all } \alpha \neq \beta$$

$\cup_{\preceq}$ is somewhat related to the specialized union operation $\cup_{\sqsubseteq}$ in [5]. However, $\cup_{\sqsubseteq}$ operates over feature structures representing context-free symbols, whereas our operation is directly applied to annotated CF rules.

Of course, $\cup_{\preceq}$ does change the context-free language $\mathcal{L}_{\preceq}$ when compared to the language $\mathcal{L}_{\equiv}$, resulting from the application of $\cup_{\equiv}$, viz., $\mathcal{L}_{\equiv} \subseteq \mathcal{L}_{\preceq}$. Given the number of rules for the grammars $\mathcal{G}_{\preceq}$ and $\mathcal{G}_{\equiv}$, we have $| \mathcal{G}_{\preceq} | \leq | \mathcal{G}_{\equiv} |$.

A simple example clearly shows this. Assume that the temporary result set contains the following three CF rules

$$\{ \alpha = (A \rightarrow \ldots B_1 \ldots), \ \ \beta_1 = (B_1 \rightarrow \ldots), \ \ \beta_2 = (B_2 \rightarrow \ldots), \ \ \ldots \}$$

and assume that the new rule $(\beta = B \rightarrow \ldots)$ subsumes both β_1 and β_2. $\cup_{\preceq}$ would thus delete β_1 and β_2 from the result set and will add β to it. Furthermore, since B_1 and B_2 are no longer valid (β_1 and β_2 have been deleted!), we must replace every occurrence of B_1 and B_2 by the new nonterminal B, introduced in production β. This, however, has the effect that at least the modified rule $(\alpha' = A \rightarrow \ldots B \ldots)$, derived from α, overgenerates.

Our approach keeps track of such rule deletions by implementing a rule subsumption maintenance graph. In the above example, we establish two associations between B_1, B_2 and B: $(B_1 \mapsto B)$, $(B_2 \mapsto B)$. Given the example, it is possible that the new rule β might even be deleted by a newer, more general rule $B' \rightarrow \ldots$ later. In this case, we have to further specify a new association: $(B \mapsto B')$. In the end, such substitution chains will be dereferenced, so that we can immediately substitute a dead RHS symbol by its correct and existing LHS counterpart. In the example, for instance, we must then know that B_1 should not be substituted by B, but instead by B'.

We also have to make associations for the converse case – if a new special rule γ is not added due to an existing more general rule γ', we must record this fact by creating the association $(L(\gamma) \mapsto L(\gamma'))$, since $L(\gamma)$ might occur on the RHS of final CF rules.

3.5   Computing Start Productions

One point in the algorithm is still missing, viz., the generation of start productions. We have decided to employ only a single synthetic start symbol s in our grammars. This symbol has to be fresh, i.e., for all symbols $[n, a]$ of the extracted grammar, we demand that $N(\mathsf{s}) \neq n$. In the implementation, the user must specify a non-empty list of start types, types which subsume original rule definitions, and thus subsumes potential rule instantiations. Now let T be the set of all start types, R the set of extracted CF rules so far, and s the new top-level start symbol. Computing such start rules then reduces to

> **local** S = ∅;
> **for each** type ∈ T **do**
>   **for each** α ∈ R **do**
>   **if** type $\succeq N(L(\alpha))$
>   S = S ∪ {s → $L(\alpha)$};
>   **return** S;

In the English HPSG grammar developed at CSLI, sentential phrases are subsumed by the type *root_strict*, and thus a start symbol in the extracted CFG can be determined by checking whether the name of a LHS symbol is subsumed by this start type. Non-sentential saturated phrases in this grammar (e.g., PPs and NPs) are characterized by *root_phr*, thus if we want find all saturated phrases in the approximated CFG, we have to declare these two types to be start types.

3.6   Rule Probability

As we said in section 2.3, rule objects possess a frequency field which will gain importance when we move from the generated CFG to the corresponding PCFG which predicts probability distributions over CFG trees. Exactly the frequency counter is set to 1 during the creation of a rule and is incremented by 1 in case a structural equivalent new rule has been detected.

Concerning the frequency field f of a new rule α that has replaced more specific rules $\alpha_1, \ldots, \alpha_n$, we have

$$f(\alpha) := \left(\sum_{i=1}^{n} f(\alpha_i) \right) + 1, \text{ for all } \alpha_i \prec \alpha$$

since the more general rule now acts as a representative for the deleted specialized rules. The frequency counter of more general rules α_i ($1 \leq i \leq n$) are incremented by 1 when penalizing α, i.e., $f(\alpha_i) := f(\alpha_i) + 1$, for all $\alpha_i \succeq \alpha$.

Considering the unary start productions from section 3.5, the frequency counter of a start production $s \rightarrow l$ is set to the sum of the frequencies of those rules $\alpha \in R$, whose LHS is exactly l, given the set of all CF rules R:

$$f(s \rightarrow l) := \sum_{\alpha \in R} f(\alpha), \text{ where } \alpha = l \rightarrow r_1 \ldots r_n$$

In order to obtain a proper probability distribution, we have to normalize the rule frequency counter in the standard way. Let R be the set of all extracted CF rules, $f(r)$ be the value of the frequency counter for rule $r \in R$, and n be the total number of all passive edges for a given parsed corpus as delivered by the unification-based parser. We then compute the probability $p(r)$ for a context-free rule r as $p(r) := f(r)/n$, which gives us $p(R) := \sum_{r \in R} p(r) = 1$.

4   Discussion

As already explained in the paper, the corpus-driven approximation method is *unsound*, that is, given a corpus C of training sentences and a set of annotation paths A (from which we determine the annotation of a context-free symbol), the approximated CF language is usually *not* a superset (but also *not* a subset) of the language accepted by the HPSG (see figure 4). This is due to the fact that not all linguistic constructions licensed by the HPSG are covered by the training corpus, but also because not every piece of information from the TFS is encoded in the annotation of a CF symbol:

$$\forall C, A \,.\, \mathcal{L}(\text{HPSG}) \not\subseteq \mathcal{L}(\text{CFG}, C, A)$$

It is easy to see that more training samples C' result in a broader language:

$$\forall C', C \subseteq C' \,.\, \mathcal{L}(\text{CFG}, C, A) \subseteq \mathcal{L}(\text{CFG}, C', A)$$

The subset relation turns around with more annotations:

$$\forall A', A \subseteq A' . \mathcal{L}(\text{CFG}, C, A) \supseteq \mathcal{L}(\text{CFG}, C, A')$$

In both cases, more training sentences and/or more annotation paths result in more rules. Overall, we can say that the more information from the feature structure is put into the annotations of the context-free symbols, the better the CFG approaches the HPSG in terms of the number of readings and the less it overgenerates. Remember, annotated CF rules approximate HPSG (passive) chart edges, and the existence of more specific CF symbols and rules helps to better mimic the behavior of the HPSG during CF parsing. Finding the right CF annotation, of course, depends on the application domain in which the extracted CFG is employed.

The correlation between UBGs and the family of approximated CFGs w.r.t. a given corpus and a set of annotation paths is depicted in figure 4.

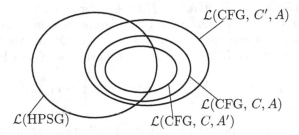

Fig. 4. The correlation between the language accepted by the HPSG $\mathcal{L}(\text{HPSG})$ and the approximated context-free language $\mathcal{L}(\text{CFG}, C, A)$, given a corpus C and a set of annotation paths A. The approximated language $\mathcal{L}(\text{CFG}, C', A)$ monotonically grows when given a larger corpus $C' \supseteq C$. The language $\mathcal{L}(\text{CFG}, C, A')$ usually shrinks when given a larger set of annotation paths $A' \supseteq A$ (but the *number* of rules grows).

As motivated in section 3.4, when fixing a corpus C and a set of annotation paths A, the language obtained under $\cup_{\equiv}$ is always a subset of the language resulting from the application of $\cup_{\preceq}$, given the same HPSG source grammar:

$$\mathcal{L}_{\equiv}(C, A) \subseteq \mathcal{L}_{\preceq}(C, A)$$

However, the more general grammar has less rules due to the fact that $\cup_{\preceq}$ might delete more than one specialized rule when favoring a more general rule. Further aspects of our method, e.g., elimination of useless rules, folding/unfolding of rules, automatic lexicon extension, or construction of meaningful output, are discussed in detail in [3]

(see also http://www.dfki.de/~krieger/approximation.html).

5 Experiments

Due to space limitations, we hasten to mention that we have conducted measurements with four different grammars at this point of writing. We took these grammars from [5]. The first three grammars are small-size UBGs, used primarily for showing interesting properties of the approximation method. The fourth grammar is an HPSG encoding of John Dowding's mid-size unification grammar, written in the Gemini/CLE formalism.

A grammar for $a^n b^n$. This binary branching grammar consists of three rules, together with two lexicon entries (for a and b). With a training corpus of only one sentence, viz., "$a\,a\,a\,b\,b\,b$", we obtained the same six CF rules as reported in [5]. Even a non-wellformed sentence such as "$a\,a\,a\,b\,b$" yields the same result. Our approximation is even correct, yielding the same language as the UBG.

A grammar with Coreferences. Our second grammar employs coreferences in an extremely ambiguous grammar to show the variation of the CAT feature in the annotated CF rule between the mother and the two daughters. Again, we obtained the same 12 rules as have been found by [5] during their grammar-driven approximation. Our test corpus consisted of only a few sentences.

Shieber's Grammar. The third grammar is a reencoding of a PATR-II grammar that licenses verb phrase construction such as *Uther persuades knights to storm Cornwall*. The grammar consists of three relatively general rule schemata, together with 13 lexicon entries. We made several tests, varying the number of quick-check paths, both under equivalence and subsumption. We derived 20/21 CF rules with zero/one quick check path (SUBCAT|REST). When adding more paths, e.g., HEAD|FORM, the CF grammar grows to 25 rules. Additional quick check paths had no further effects. We have chosen a training corpus of 12 positive and negative sentences. Overall, we obtained a grammar of 25 CF rules, again the same rules which were reported in [5].

Dowding's Grammar. The Gemini grammar consisted of 57 unification rules which were approximated by 400–500 CF rules, depending on the number of annotation paths (0, 2, 3, 5, 10, 17). The following table gives a summary of the quality of the approximated CFGs under equivalence, when compared to the original UBG. When taking the best 17 quick-check paths of the UBG into account, we obtain a moderately overgenerating grammar (factor: 1.23), resulting in a speedup by a factor of about 66.

	#rules	#passive edges	#readings	runtime[s]	overgeneration	speedup
HPSG	57	19716	666	6.59	1.00	1.00
CFG-0	401	24815	4028	0.23	6.05	28.65
CFG-2	401	24662	1376	0.20	2.07	32.95
CFG-3	454	23364	982	0.16	1.47	41.19
CFG-5	455	23379	982	0.15	1.47	43.93
CFG-10	505	21327	975	0.11	1.46	54.92
CFG-17	525	21007	819	0.10	**1.23**	**65.90**

Compared to the results reported in [5], it is clear that our grammars are much smaller, since they are derived from a corpus, and not merely by the UBG alone. Of course, the approximated CFGs in [5] cover a greater variety of linguistic constructions.

Acknowledgments

First of all, my thanks go to Bernd Kiefer for providing me with the modified HPSG parser and for helping me adapting the grammars. I have also benefited from many discussions with him. I am grateful to Hans Uszkoreit and Feiyu Xu for reading a preliminary version of this paper. I would also like to thank the reviewers for their detailed comments. This work was supported by the German BMBF under grant no. 01 IW C02 (QUETAL).

References

1. Pollard, C., Sag, I.A.: Head-Driven Phrase Structure Grammar. Studies in Contemporary Linguistics. University of Chicago Press, Chicago (1994)
2. Shieber, S.M.: An Introduction to Unification-Based Approaches to Grammar. CSLI Lecture Notes, Number 4. Center for the Study of Language and Information, Stanford (1986)
3. Krieger, H.U.: From UBGs to CFGs–a practical corpus-driven approach. Research report, German Research Center for Artificial Intelligence (DFKI), Saarbrücken, Germany (2004)
4. Carroll, J.A.: Practical Unification-based Parsing of Natural Language. PhD thesis, University of Cambridge, Computer Laboratory, Cambridge, England (1993)
5. Kiefer, B., Krieger, H.U.: A context-free approximation of Head-Driven Phrase Structure Grammar. In Oepen, S., Flickinger, D., Tsuji, J., Uszkoreit, H., eds.: Collaborative Language Engineering. A Case Study in Efficient Grammar-based Processing. CSLI Publications (2002) 49–76
6. Neumann, G.: Data-driven approaches to head-driven phrase structure grammar. In Bod, R., Scha, R., Sima'an, K., eds.: Data-Oriented Parsing. CSLI Publications, University of Chicago Press (2003)
7. Carpenter, B.: The Logic of Typed Feature Structures. Tracts in Theoretical Computer Science. Cambridge University Press, Cambridge (1992)
8. Krieger, H.U.: TDL—A Type Description Language for Constraint-Based Grammars. Foundations, Implementation, and Applications. PhD thesis, Universität des Saarlandes, Department of Computer Science (1995)
9. Krieger, H.U.: Greatest model semantics for typed feature structures. Grammars 4 (2001) 139–165 Kluwer.
10. Gazdar, G., Klein, E., Pullum, G., Sag, I.: Generalized Phrase Structure Grammar. Harvard University Press, Cambridge, MA (1985)
11. Kiefer, B., Krieger, H.U., Carroll, J., Malouf, R.: A bag of useful techniques for efficient and robust parsing. In: Proceedings of the 37th Annual Meeting of the Association for Computational Linguistics, ACL-99. (1999) 473–480
12. Callmeier, U.: PET – a platform for experimentation with efficient HPSG processing. Natural Language Engineering 6 (2000) 99–107
13. Krieger, H.U., Schäfer, U.: TDL—a type description language for constraint-based grammars. In: Proceedings of the 15th International Conference on Computational Linguistics, COLING-94. (1994) 893–899
14. Shieber, S.M.: Using restriction to extend parsing algorithms for complex-feature-based formalisms. In: Proceedings of the 23rd Annual Meeting of the Association for Computational Linguistics, ACL-85. (1985) 145–152

Partial Learning Using Link Grammars Data

Erwan Moreau

LINA - FRE CNRS 2729 - Université de Nantes
2 rue de la Houssinière - BP 92208 - 44322 Nantes cedex 3
Erwan.Moreau@lina.univ-nantes.fr

Abstract. Kanazawa has shown that several non-trivial classes of categorial grammars are learnable in Gold's model. We propose in this article to adapt this kind of symbolic learning to natural languages. In order to compensate the combinatorial explosion of the learning algorithm, we suppose that a small part of the grammar to be learned is given as input. That is why we need some initial data to test the feasibility of the approach: link grammars are closely related to categorial grammars, and we use the English lexicon which exists in this formalism.

1 Introduction

In [1], Buszkowski has proposed an algorithm that learns rigid categorial grammars from structures. Kanazawa extended this result, and showed that several non-trivial classes of categorial grammars are learnable in Gold's model of identification in the limit [2]. Since these works, several results have been obtained, concerning learnability or unlearnability (in Gold's model) of some classes of categorial grammars (e.g. [3]). This kind of learning is symbolic, and relies on some properties of categorial grammars, in particular their total lexicalization.

In this article we propose to apply this learning method to natural language data. Such an application faces the problem of efficiency, due to the obviously big complexity of any natural language: actually, the fact that a class of grammars is learnable in Gold's model does not implie that learning can be done in a reasonable time. That is why we propose to learn in the framework of *partial learning*, where it is supposed that a part of the grammar to be learned is already known. This permits both to learn in a quite reasonable time, and without needing other information (like structures).

This idea is rather close from the one presented in [4], where semantic types are used, instead of structures, to learn efficiently. In a different framework, Hockenmaier has obtained good results in acquiring a natural language grammar from structures, using the Penn treebank [5].

Link grammars, introduced in [6], are close to categorial grammars. Thus it is possible to adapt learning algorithms to this formalism, as it has been shown in [7]. Furthermore, the authors Sleator and Temperley have built a link grammars lexicon which covers an important subset of the English language. This data will be very useful, since we need an *initial grammar* in our framework.

G. Paliouras and Y. Sakakibara (Eds.): ICGI 2004, LNAI 3264, pp. 211–222, 2004.

It should be emphasized that the problem is not simple, because the constraints imposed by symbolic learning and the fact that existing algorithms are exponential make it hard to obtain good results with a natural language. For this reason, we only study in this article the efficiency of the partial learning method, which is only one part of the problem. We will also discuss several problems appearing when using symbolic learning with complex data.

2 Link Grammars

Link grammars are defined by Sleator and Temperley in [6]. This is a rather simple formalism which is able to represent in a reliable way natural languages. This can be seen in the modelization that the authors provided for English in this sytem: their grammar deals with most of the linguistic phenomena in English, as it can be verified using their link grammar parser [8]. Their work is very interesting for our objectives for the following reasons:

- There exists a close relation between link grammars and categorial grammars: both are totally lexicalized and based on some kind of dependency notion.
- It is possible to express the link grammars model as a small set of rules using unification. This point is essential because several categorial grammars formalisms share this property, and it seems that this point plays an important role in learning algorithms based on Buszkowski's one.

Informally, a sentence is correct in link grammars if it is possible to *link* all words according to the links needed by each word, defined in the lexicon. Links represent syntactic relations between words.

A link grammar G is a tuple $\langle \Sigma, \mathcal{C}, \triangleright \rangle$, where Σ is the set of words, $\mathcal{C}$ is the set of *connectors*. A *disjunct* is a pair of lists denoted $\mathtt{d}(L,R)$, where L and R are lists of connectors, and $\triangleright$ is the relation assigning disjuncts to words: $w \triangleright d$ means that the disjunct d can be used with the word w.

Given a sentence $w_1, .., w_n$, a *linkage* is a set of links drawn above the sentence, each link connecting two words and being labelled with a connector. A linkage is valid if it satisfies the following conditions:

- *Planarity:* all links can be drawn above the words without crossing.
- *Connectivity:* given any couple of words (w_i, w_j) there exists a path of links between them.
- *Ordering:* for each word w_i there exists a disjunct d_i such that $w_i \triangleright d_i$ and d_i is satisfied. A disjunct $d_i = \mathtt{d}([L_1,..,L_l], [R_1,..,R_r])$ is satisfied if for each connector L_j (resp. R_j) there is a link labelled with the name of the connector coming to w_i from the left (resp. the right), and for any couple of connectors L_j, L_k (resp. R_j, R_k) with $j < k$, the words $w_{j'}, w_{k'}$ respectively connected to them verify $j' > k'$ (resp. $j' < k'$)[1].
- *Exclusion:* No two links may connect the same pair of words.

---

[1] In other words when $j < k$ the word $w_{j'}$ is closer to w_i than $w_{k'}$. Remark: in the original definition the right list is written $[R_r,\ldots,R_1]$. We choose the reverse order to be coherent with the $\mathtt{cons(c,L)/nil}$ notation presented in section 2.1.

These conditions are called the *meta-rules* of link grammars. It is shown in [6] that link grammars are equivalent to context-free grammars.

Example 1. With the following lexicon, the linkage below is valid:

a,the   ▷ d([],[D])
cat, snake ▷ d([D],[S]), d([O,D],[])
chased   ▷ d([S],[O])

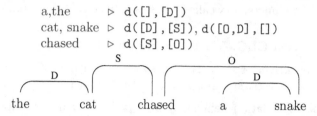

2.1   Categorial Link Grammars

Link grammars are closely related to categorial grammars: both formalisms are totally lexicalized, and share the property to link words or constituents through a binary relation of dependency. However this dependency relation is different in the two systems. In link grammars, dependencies are not directed and apply only to words, contrary to categorial grammars where dependencies are directed and may apply to constituents of the sentence.

Classical Categorial Grammars. AB grammars (or classical categorial grammars) are the most simple formalism in categorial grammars. An AB grammar G is a tuple $\langle \Sigma, Pr, \rhd \rangle$ where Σ is the set of words and Pr the set of primitive types. The set of types Tp is defined as the smallest set such that $Pr \subseteq Tp$ and $A/B, A\backslash B \in Tp$ for all $A, B \in Tp$. The relation $\rhd \subseteq \Sigma \times Tp$ assigns one or several types to each word. The relation $\rightarrow$ is defined with the following universal rules:

$$A/B, \ B \rightarrow A \ \text{(for any } A, B \in Tp)$$
$$B, \ B\backslash A \rightarrow A \ \text{(for any } A, B \in Tp)$$

Let $\Rightarrow$ be the relation defined by $\alpha t_1 t_2 \beta \Rightarrow \alpha t_0 \beta$ if and only if $t_1 t_2 \rightarrow t_0$, and let $\Rightarrow^*$ be the reflexive and transitive closure of $\Rightarrow$. A sentence $x = w_1 w_2...w_n$ is correct for G (denoted $x \in L(G)$) if there is a sequence of types $\langle t_1 t_2...t_n \rangle$ such that $w_i \rhd t_i$ for all i and $t_1 t_2...t_n \Rightarrow^* s$.

CLG: Definition. In order to emphasize the correspondence between link grammars and categorial grammars, we will use an intermediate formalism called *categorial link grammars* (CLG), where dependencies are directed and apply to constituents. This will permit to apply learning methods used with categorial grammars [2] to link grammars in a straightforward way. Actually, the CLG formalism is simply a different interpretation of (usual) link grammars rules. It is shown in [9] that CLG and basic link grammars rules are equivalent under the following restriction: each valid sentence must have a cycle-free linkage.

The CLG formalism takes exactly the same definition for grammars as the one presented above. But the rules governing derivations of sentences are expressed as the rewriting of a sequence of terms into another, like in classical categorial grammars. In order to emphasize that disjuncts are simple terms, we reformulate their definition in the following way: the set of connectors lists CL is defined as the smallest set such that nil $\in CL$ and for all L' $\in CL$ and c $\in \mathcal{C}$, cons(c, L') $\in CL$. The set of disjuncts, now called *types*, is defined as $Tp = \{$d(L,R) $\mid$ L, R $\in CL\}^2$.

Derivations with CLG. The two reduction rules between two types are

d(L, cons(c, R)), d(cons(c, nil), nil) $\rightarrow$ d(L,R) (with c $\in \mathcal{C}$ and L, R $\in CL$)

d(nil, cons(c, nil)), d(cons(c, L), R) $\rightarrow$ d(L,R) (with c $\in \mathcal{C}$ and L, R $\in CL$)

Let $\Rightarrow$ be the relation defined by $\alpha t_1 t_2 \beta \Rightarrow \alpha t_0 \beta$ if and only if $t_1 t_2 \rightarrow t_0$, with $\alpha, \beta \in Tp^*$ and $t_1, t_2, t_0 \in Tp$. $\Rightarrow^*$ is defined as the reflexive and transitive closure of $\Rightarrow$. Let $G = \langle \Sigma, \mathcal{C}, \triangleright \rangle$ be a grammar. A sentence $x = w_1 w_2 ... w_n$ is correct for G (denoted $x \in L(G)$) if there is a sequence of types $\langle t_1, t_2, ..., t_n \rangle$ such that $w_i \triangleright t_i$ for all i and $t_1 t_2 ... t_n \Rightarrow^*$ d(nil, nil).

Example 2. With the lexicon defined in example 1, the sentence "The cat chased a snake" can be derived in the following way[3]:

	the	cat	chased	a	snake
	d([],[D]),	d([D],[S]),	d([S],[O]),	d([],[D]),	d([D,O],[])
$\Rightarrow$		d([],[S]),	d([S],[O]),	d([],[D]),	d([D,O],[])
$\Rightarrow$		d([],[S]),	d([S],[O]),		d([O],[])
$\Rightarrow$		d([],[S]),	d([S],[])		
$\Rightarrow$			d([],[])		

One can notice that a given linkage in basic link grammars can have several equivalent derivation trees in CLG. These ambiguities appear because links are not directed, and no order is required between connectors. The relation between CLG and AB grammars is detailed in [9].

2.2   The Link Grammars English Lexicon

One of the main reasons why link grammars are interesting is that the authors Sleator and Temperley have built such a grammar for English. The lexicon they provide contains approximately 59000 words, distributed into 1350 entries, each entry corresponding to a set of types. The grammar deals with an important number of linguistic phenomena in English, *"indicating that the approach may have practical uses as well as linguistic significance"* [6]. Furthermore, the link parser provided by the authors includes a file containing 928 sentences, labelled as correct or incorrect.

In this section we outline how the link grammars lexicon for English is converted into the formalism of CLG. This transformation must take into account several complex features added to the basis of link grammars by their authors.

---

[2] One can see that this definition is coherent with the first one.

[3] *Remark:* in the following we will keep the notation $[c_1, c_2, .., c_n]$ for connectors lists, easier to read than cons(c_1, cons(c_2, .. cons(c_n, nil)..)). Nevertheless it is important to notice that there is no associativity in these terms.

Multi-connectors. Iterations are represented using *multi-connectors*: Any connector C in a connectors list may be preceded by the operator @, meaning that this connector @C can be connected to several links C. For example, nouns can be given the type d([@A,D],[S]), allowing them to be preceded by any number of adjectives. This feature is included in the same way in CLG, by replacing the "basic rules" with these new ones (where [@] means that @ is optionnal):

$$d(L, cons([@]c, R)) , d(cons([@]c, nil), nil) \rightarrow d(L,R)$$
$$d(nil, cons([@]c, nil)) , d(cons([@]c, L), R) \rightarrow d(L,R)$$
$$d(L, cons(@c, R)) , d(cons([@]c, nil), nil) \rightarrow d(L,cons(@c, R))$$
$$d(nil, cons([@]c, nil)) , d(cons(@c, L), R) \rightarrow d(cons(@c, L),R)$$

Subscripts. Subscripts are used to specialize connectors, in a similar way than feature structures in unification grammars. They are used to make the grammar easier to read and understand. For example, the subscripts s and p are assigned to nouns (and pronouns, determiners, etc.) to distinguish between singular and plural ones. In order to maintain the simplicity of the reduction rules, subscripts are converted into types that do not contain subscripts. This is achieved through a program that classifies all existing connectors (with their subscripts) in such a way that all connectors in a same class match the same set of connectors. When it is possible two classes are merged together, in order to minimize their number. Finally a new type is created for each such class.

The CLG Parser. The correctness of the conversion has been tested by comparing results of parsing the example file using the converted grammar to the ones obtained using the original link parser. The CLG parser is a standard CYK-like parser running in $o(n^3)$, applying the binary reduction rules defined above. The file 4.0.batch provided with the original link parser contains 928 sentences, in which 572 are correct and 356 are not. We extensively used this set of examples as a benchmark to test the CLG parser soundness and completness.

The CLG parser does not handle some "high-level" features of the original parser. Our objective being to provide a simple system based on a little set of rules, we did not translate these abilities into the CLG parser, and consequently modified the set of examples. Therefore sentences needing these features (conjonctions, post-processing rules, cost system and unknown words) have been removed from the example file: after this process, a set of 771 sentences is obtained, in which 221 are incorrect. Another important simplification concerns the problem of cycles. In the experiments detailed in this article, we consider a cycle-free version of the grammar which is simpler than the original one, but does not correctly handle all incorrect sentences: 38 incorrect sentences from the example file are parsed as correct, corresponding to an error rate of 4.9%. More details about the problem of cycles can be found in [9].

Example 3. Here are several sentences taken from the example file (incorrect ones are preceded with an asterisk):

What did John say he thought you should do
*What did John say did he think you should do
To pretend that our program is usable in its current form would be silly
*Is that our program will be accepted likely
The man there was an attempt to kill died

3   Partial Learning

3.1   Background

Buszkowski has proposed in [1] an algorithm, called *RG*, that learns *rigid* classical categorial grammars from *functor-argument structures* in Gold's model. A grammar is said *rigid* if every word in its lexicon is defined by only one type: this is of course a strong constraint on learnable languages. In particular, any slightly complex subset of any natural language does not fit into this definition. A *functor-argument structure* for a given sentence is some kind of parse tree for this sentence, where nodes are only labelled with FA or BA (identifiers for the two universal rules). Thus the nodes indicate which branch (i.e. constituant) should be used as functor (e.g. the left one, A/B, in the FA case) and which should be used as argument (e.g. the right one in the FA case). The fact that RG needs fa-structures as input is also an important drawback, because such structures arc very precise, and therefore hardly available for applications.

Kanazawa has explored several extensions of this algorithm in [2], and has proved learnability in Gold's model of various classes of grammars obtained from these extensions. In particular, Kanazawa proposed an algorithm that learns k-valued[4] AB grammars from strings, and proved its convergence. Clearly, this extension avoids the two main constraints of the original algorithm. However, the problem of learning grammars (even rigid) without structures, as well as the one of learning k-valued grammars (even with structures) are shown by Costa-Florêncio to be NP-hard [10].

3.2   Partial Learning: Idea and Interest

As a consequence, it seems hard to apply this learning method to natural languages: the first algorithm is efficient but needs a lot of information as input and learns only a small class of grammars, and the other one is more general but unefficient. As a compromise between these two cases, We propose what we call *partial learning*: the algorithm takes flat strings as input, but it is also supposed that a part of the grammar to be learned, called the *initial grammar*, is already known (i.e. one knows the types assigned to some words in the lexicon). This information is intended to help building some part of the parse tree for the sentence given as input, thus replacing (to a certain extent) the information previously given in the structure. This information is important to avoid that too many possible trees make the algorithm unefficient.

---

[4] A grammar is k-valued if each word in the lexicon is defined by at most k types.

Several arguments tend to make this hypothese rather plausible and well suited for natural languages applications:

- The total lexicalization of categorial grammars (or link grammars) was already an advantage for this kind of learning algorithms. Furthermore, it permits to consider that some words are known and other are unknown without any difficulty, since there can be no other kind of grammar rules.
- In the viewpoint of applications, the hypothese that a certain subset of the lexicon can be defined by advance seems more realistic than the hypothese that some complex information, like fa-structures, will be available with each sentence given to the algorithm.
- Finally, the efficiency (and the accuracy) of the algorithm in this framework mainly depends on the initial grammar: if there is a large number of known words in the examples, there are less possible parse trees and therefore the process goes faster. Applied to natural languages, Zipf's law says that, among the set of all words in a text, a little number of words covers a big part of the text (counting the number of occurences). Partial learning can benefit from this property in the following way: one has to build the initial grammar with this little set of frequent words, corresponding more or less to grammatical words (determiners, prepositions, etc.). This task is feasible because these words are not too numerous, and above all their number is bounded: for example, there may be new nouns or adjectives appearing in a natural language, but not a new determiner. Thanks to Zipf's law, these words are frequent, so knowing types for these words may be sufficiant to bound the number of possible parse trees for the sentences provided as input to the learning algorithm.

3.3   Algorithm

The fact that AB grammars and link grammars (when expressed in the CLG formalism) depend only on a small set of rules, and that these rules are based on unification is crucial in learning algorithms based on RG. This point is emphasized in the algorithm that we present here. The naive partial learning algorithm would consist in computing all possible parse trees for a sentence, and then see what among them are compatible with the types provided by the known words. Instead, the algorithm can benefit from the unification process by behaving like a parser: in the initialization step, distinct variables are assigned to unknown words. Then the incremental (CYK-like) parser computes, as usual, all possible types for each constituent, taking care of applying all substitutions that allow a reduction to the variables. At the end of the process, analyzing the set of applied substitutions provides all possible types for the unknown words.

The PL (Partial Learning) algorithm takes as input a sentence $w_1, .., w_n$ and an initial grammar G_0. This grammar contains rules of the form $w \triangleright t$, where t is a type that can be used with word w. The algorithm returns the set of *general form grammars*: this means that any other grammar that accept the sentence according to the initial grammar G_0 is an instance of one of these grammars.

$\mathrm{PL}(G_0, [w_1, w_2, .., w_n])$
  $Lex \leftarrow \{(W, T) \mid (W \rhd T) \in G_0\}$
  create an empty matrix $M[1..n, 1..n]$ % Initialization
  for $i \leftarrow 1$ to n do
    if $\exists T$ such that $(w_i \rhd T) \in G_0$ then
      $M[i, i] \leftarrow \{(T, Id) \mid (w_i \rhd T) \in G_0\}$
    else
      create a fresh variable V
      $Lex \leftarrow Lex \cup \{(w_i, V)\}$
      $M[i, i] \leftarrow \{(V, Id)\}$
    end if
  end for
  for $i \leftarrow 2$ to n do   % Partial learning process (incremental parsing)
    for $j \leftarrow i - 1$ to 1 do
      for $k \leftarrow j$ to $i - 1$ do
        for each $(T_l, \sigma_l) \in M[j, k]$ do
          for each $(T_r, \sigma_r) \in M[k + 1, i]$ do
            let $\sigma_u = mgu(\sigma_l, \sigma_r)$
            for each rule $R \in \mathcal{R}$ do
              let $R = A_1 A_2 \rightarrow A_0$ % (where variables in all A_i are fresh)
              if $\exists \sigma_R = mgu(\{\{\sigma_u(T_l), A_1\}, \{\sigma_u(T_r), A_2\}\})$ then
                $M[j, i] \leftarrow M[j, i] \cup \{(\sigma_R(A_0), \sigma_R \circ \sigma_u \circ \sigma_l\}$
              end if
            end for
          end for
        end for
      end for
    end for
  end for
  $Res \leftarrow \emptyset$ % Apply possible substitutions
  for each $(T, \sigma) \in M[1, n]$ do
    if $\exists \tau$ such that $\tau(T) = S$ then
      $Res \leftarrow Res \cup \{(\tau \circ \sigma)(Lex)\}$
    end if
  end for
  return Res
End PL

- Id is the identity substitution. $\circ$ is the composition of two substitutions.
- A unifier for a family of sets $\mathcal{A}$ is a substitution σ such that for every $\mathcal{A}_i \in \mathcal{A}$ and every couple of types $t, t' \in \mathcal{A}_i$: $\sigma(t) = \sigma(t')$. The *most general unifier* (*mgu*) is the (unique) unifier σ_u such that for any other unifier σ there exists a substitution τ such that $\sigma = \tau \circ \sigma_u$.
- Since σ_u is defined as the MGU of σ_l and σ_r, we have $(\sigma_u \circ \sigma_l) = (\sigma_u \circ \sigma_r)$.
- $\mathcal{R}$ is the set of universal rules: in the case of AB grammars, one will obtain for example $A/B = A_1, B = A_2$ and $A = A_0$ for the first rule, FA (variables are A and B). In the case of CLG, one would have $\mathrm{d}(L, \mathrm{cons}(c, R)) = A_1$, $\mathrm{d}(\mathrm{cons}(c, \mathrm{nil}), \mathrm{nil}) = A_2$ and $\mathrm{d}(L, R) = A_0$ for the first rule (with variables L, R, c). This algorithm works for both formalisms.

The "CYK-like" form of this algorithm should not hide that the algorithm remains exponential in the general case. This algorithm describes the process only for one sentence: the question to know what should be done with the whole set of *general form grammars* is discussed in section 4.3.

4   Experiments and Discussion

In this section we explore feasibility of partial learning using link grammars data. A prototype has been implemented (coded in SWI Prolog), and some tests have been realized. The only part of the problem explored here is the possibility to "parse with variables" in a reasonable time.

4.1   The CLG Partial Learning Prototype: Parsing with Variables

The CLG partial learning prototype is based on the CLG parser presented in 2.2. Clearly, the Prolog language is well suited to deal with terms containing variables during the parsing: actually, substitutions are not stored in a data structure like this is presented in the algorithm above, but simply obtained by Prolog unification. The process remains deterministic however: types are copied whenever necesary in order to build lists of types in the matrix, and thus avoiding backtrack through the matrix.

Apart from some non essential optimization, the program has an important feature that avoids a large part of the combinatorial explosion. This feature consists in factorizing types that are "structurally equivalent": two types t_1 and t_2 are structurally equivalent if there exists two substitution σ_1 and σ_2 such that $\sigma_1(t_1) = t_2$ and $\sigma_2(t_2) = t_1$ (i.e. there is only a renaming of variables between the two types). The case where several structurally equivalent types belong to the same cell of the matrix is frequent, so this saves a lot of time and space. But this mechanism also requires that the composition of substitutions be no longer computed along the whole process, otherwise the next level would have to re-develop the types. That is why only the substitution used to transform a type at one level (one reduction) is stored: in order to obtain the composition (which gives what types are possible for unknown words), the program makes a second pass after the incremental parsing.

Some tests have been done using the example file provided with the link grammar parser [8]. First the set of examples has been filtered in order to keep only correct sentences. The tests consist in removing a certain set of words from the lexicon, so that these words will be considered as unknown.

4.2   Results

The sample used contains 537 sentences and 4765 words (size of the sample), but only 1064 different words (size of the lexicon). The most frequent words are *the* (270), *I* (155), *is* (122), *to* (121). In these tests we compare times taken for partial learning for different rates of unknown words in the lexicon and sample.

In this first test[5] we remove randomly a set of words from the lexicon. Results are shown in table 1: one can see that the rate of unknown words in the sample is similar to the rate of unknown (removed) words in the lexicon.

"UW" stands for "unknown words": the second column (lexicon) indicates the number of UW within the set of words, whereas the third one (sample) indicates the number of occurencies of UW in the sentences.

Table 1.

UW (lexicon)	UW (sample)	Total time	UW per sentence (min ; avg ; max)	time per sentence (min ; avg ; max) (sec)
0 (0%)	0 (0%)	27 min	0 ; 0 ; 0	0.1 ; 3.1 ; 14.7
106 (10%)	407 (8.5%)	75 min	0 ; 0.7 ; 4	0.1 ; 8.3 ; 333
211 (20%)	870 (18.2%)	3.5 h	0 ; 1.5 ; 6	0.1 ; 24 ; 1985
264 (25%)	1106 (23.2%)	3.8 h	0 ; 1.8 ; 7	0.1 ; 24.9 ; 1115
317 (30%)	1481 (31.1%)	Failure (out of memory)		

In order to simulate the idea that the initial grammar should be built using a small set of frequent words, in this second test we remove only the less frequent words from the lexicon. Therefore, Zipf's law permits to remove a large part of the lexicon without having too many unknown words in the sample (table 2).

Table 2.

UW (lexicon)	UW (sample)	Total time	UW per sentence (min ; avg ; max)	time per sentence (min ; avg ; max) (sec)
0 (0%)	0 (0%)	27 min	0 ; 0 ; 0	0.1 ; 3.1 ; 14.7
211 (20%)	211 (4.4%)	45 min	0 ; 0.3 ; 4	0.1 ; 5.0 ; 173
422 (40%)	422 (8.8%)	78 min	0 ; 0.6 ; 5	0.1 ; 8.7 ; 620
634 (60%)	727 (15.2%)	2.6 h	0 ; 1.1 ; 7	0.1 ; 17.3 ; 1844
845 (80%)	1302 (27.3%)	5.1 h	0 ; 2.0 ; 9	0.1 ; 34.1 ; 1893

These tests show that the partial learning process can run in an almost reasonable time (and without overloading memory) with up to 25 to 30% unknown words in the sample. It is interesting to see that we only need around 20% of the words defined in the lexicon to obtain such a rate, thanks to Zipf's law.

Of course, the data is a bit too small to consider that these tests guarantee that the algorithm works in any situation with a certain rate of unknown words. However, link grammars data for English are a good approximation of a natural language, and were not intended to serve for this kind of application. So these tests tend to show that the partial learning method can be a realistic approach to apply symbolic learning to natural languages.

---

[5] These tests were done on a PIII 1GHz.

4.3   Problems and Future Work

Although the partial learning part seems to work quite well, we do not have yet "real" learning results to present in this paper. Actually, several problems make hard the adaptation of symbolic learning algorithms to "almost real" applications to natural languages. In a practical viewpoint, the main question is: what do we want to obtain as a result ? Indeed, the algorithm can return a set of grammars, but this set may be too big in complex cases (and therefore take too much time to be computed). It would also be possible to use a different representation for the types, like in the original link grammar where types are logical formulas using some operators (*and*, *or*, etc.). But symbolic learning requires that types be in a normal form, in order to be able to recognize two identical types.

Another (more theoretical) important problem concerns the constraints in Gold's model. Actually, Gold's model require that only one hypothese (grammar) be proposed for any set of examples. Kanazawa has explored this problem for categorial grammars, in a rather theoretical perspective [2]. In the case of AB grammars, as soon as one is interested in learning k-valued grammars with $k > 1$ or in learning without full fa-structures there are (generally) more than one grammar solution. Kanazawa shows that it is possible to compute a minimal grammar, and this is why the classes observed are learnable in Gold's model. But again the algorithm is exponential and unusable in any complex case. In the perspective of application to natural language, one can not use this solution. That is why the algorithm we propose does not really *learn*, in the sense of Gold. However, the reason of this constraint in Gold's model is that it would be too easy for an algorithm to *learn* if it was allowed to make an infinitely growing number of hypotheses.

We propose the following solution to bound the number of solutions without restricting too much the generative power of the learnable classes of grammars in this framework. Following the hypothese that it is rather easy to build an initial grammar containing most possible types but only a small set of words, it is possible to consider that a set of *syntactic classes* is defined: each class contains a set of fixed types, and the role of the learning algorithm would be to correctly assign a class to each word. This method is already used in part-of-speech taggers (like [11]). As the link grammar lexicon is made of 1350 entries, each containing a set of types corresponding to a set of words, one can hope that this method can be adapted in the CLG framework.

5   Conclusion

In conclusion, several important problems must be solved before considering obtaining useful results for a natural language: the form of the data, the formalism itself, the size of the initial grammar are some very important parameters. Also, solutions should be found for some simplifications made in this experiment, for the problem of cycles (due to link grammars formalism) and the one of conjonctions.

Actually, nothing ensures that this learning method will be able to provide valuable results. Nevertheless, this first experiment shows that this hypothese could hold: it seems that a "good" initial grammar, together with Zipf's law, can compensate for the lack of efficiency of existing theoretical algorithms. Furthermore, the fact that this algorithm does not need important information (like fa-structures) in input makes it more suited to real applications. But the main interest in symbolic learning is the accuracy: probably this kind of learning can not be very efficient, but the fact that the correctness of the answer always hold can be an interesting feature for some applications.

References

1. Buszkowski, W., Penn, G.: Categorial grammars determined from linguistic data by unification. Technical Report TR-89-05, Department of Computer Science, University of Chicago (1989)
2. Kanazawa, M.: Learnable classes of categorial grammars. Cambridge University Press (1998)
3. Bonato, R., Retoré, C.: Learning rigid lambek grammars and minimalist grammars from structured sentences. In Popelínský, L., Nepil, M., eds.: Proceedings of the 3d Workshop on Learning Language in Logic, Strasbourg, France (2001) 23–34
4. Sofronie, D.D., Tellier, I., Tommasi, M.: A tool for language learning based on categorial grammars and semantic information. In Adriaans, P., Fernau, H., van Zaanen, M., eds.: Grammatical Inference: Algorithms and Applications; 6th International Colloquium, ICGI 2002. Volume 2484 of LNCS/LNAI., Springer (2002) 303–305
5. Hockenmaier, J.: Data and models for statistical parsing with Combinatory Categorial Grammar. PhD thesis, School of Informatics, The University of Edinburgh (2003)
6. Sleator, D.D.K., Temperley, D.: Parsing english with a link grammar. Technical Report CMU-CS-TR-91-126, Carnegie Mellon University, Pittsburgh, PA (1991)
7. Béchet, D.: k-valued link grammars are learnable from strings. In: Proceedings Formal Grammars 2003. (2003) 9–18
8. Temperley, D., Sleator, D., Lafferty, J.: Link grammar. http://hyper.link.cs.cmu.edu/link/ (1991)
9. Moreau, E.: From link grammars to categorial grammars. In: Proceedings of Categorial Grammars 2004, Montpellier, France. (2004) 31–45
10. Costa Florêncio, C.: Consistent Identification in the Limit of Rigid Grammars from Strings is NP-hard. In Adriaans, P., Fernau, H., van Zaanen, M., eds.: Grammatical Inference: Algorithms and Applications 6th International Colloquium: ICGI 2002. Volume 2484 of Lecture Notes in Artificial Intelligence., Springer-Verlag (2002) 49–62
11. Brill, E.: A Corpus-Based Approach to Language Learning. PhD thesis, Computer and Information Science, University of Pennsylvania (1993)

eg-GRIDS: Context-Free Grammatical Inference from Positive Examples Using Genetic Search

Georgios Petasis[1], Georgios Paliouras[1],
Constantine D. Spyropoulos[1], and Constantine Halatsis[2]

[1] Software and Knowledge Engineering Laboratory,
Institute of Informatics and Telecommunications,
National Centre for Scientific Research (N.C.S.R.) "Demokritos",
P.O BOX 60228, Aghia Paraskevi, GR-153 10, Athens, Greece
{petasis,paliourg,costass}@iit.demokritos.gr
[2] Department of Informatics and Telecommunications,
University of Athens,
TYPA Buildings, Panepistimiopolis, GR-157 84, Athens, Greece
halatsis@di.uoa.gr

Abstract. In this paper we present eg-GRIDS, an algorithm for inducing context-free grammars that is able to learn from positive sample
sentences. The presented algorithm, similar to its GRIDS predecessors,
uses simplicity as a criterion for directing inference, and a set of operators for exploring the search space. In addition to the basic beam search
strategy of GRIDS, eg-GRIDS incorporates an evolutionary grammar
selection process, aiming to explore a larger part of the search space.
Evaluation results are presented on artificially generated data, comparing the performance of beam search and genetic search. These results
show that genetic search performs better than beam search while being
significantly more efficient computationally.

Keywords: grammatical inference, context-free grammars, minimum
description length, genetic algorithms, positive examples

1 Introduction

In this paper we present eg-GRIDS, an algorithm for inducing context free grammars solely from positive sample sentences. This algorithm is an enhancement
of the e-GRIDS algorithm [10], which was based on the GRIDS algorithm as
it appeared in [6], which in turn is based on earlier work by Wolff [18], [19]
and his SNPR system. The presented algorithm, similar to its predecessors, uses
simplicity as a criterion for directing inference, a set of operators for exploring
the search space and a basic beam search strategy. However, eg-GRIDS extends
e-GRIDS by employing additional search operators and an evolutionary grammar selection process in addition to the basic beam search strategy, aiming to
explore a larger part of the search space. Evaluation results on artificially generated data from context-free grammars suggest that eg-GRIDS performs better
than e-GRIDS and that the evolutionary grammar selection process significantly

G. Paliouras and Y. Sakakibara (Eds.): ICGI 2004, LNAI 3264, pp. 223–234, 2004.

improves the processing efficiency and scalability of eg-GRIDS over its previous version.

The majority of grammatical inference algorithms presented in the literature share a common methodology. Based on an initial set of positive training examples, an overly specific grammar is constructed that is able to recognise only these examples. Then, a set of operators generalises this initial grammar, usually with respect to a set of *negative examples*, i.e. sentences that should not be recognised by the grammar. The existence of negative examples is a requirement of many algorithms, due to the need to limit the extent of generalisation. If in a given inference step a grammar is produced whose language is larger than the unknown target language, this is irreversible since no positive example could ever supply information to detect this error. Overly general grammars can be detected if negative examples are available, since the language of such a grammar is likely to include some negative examples. Thus, a learning algorithm that uses negative examples in this manner should primarily prevent *overspecialisation (or over-fitting)*, as overgeneralisation can be controlled by the negative examples. On the other hand, a learning algorithm that has to learn solely from positive examples must prevent both overspecialisation and *overgeneralisation*. However, as the absence of negative evidence often arises in practice, two solutions have been proposed in order to alleviate this problem:

– Restricted classes of formal languages have been proven to be learnable from positive examples, such as reversible languages [1], k-testable languages [3], code regular and code linear languages [2], pure context-free languages [5], [17] and strictly deterministic automata [20].
– Various heuristics aiming to avoid overgeneralisation without the use of negative examples have been proposed [12], [6].

The eg-GRIDS algorithm presented here belongs to the latter category and uses simplicity as a heuristic for directing the inference process, based solely on positive information. Viewing grammars as code, the heuristic utilised in eg-GRIDS, based on Minimum Description Length (*MDL*) [11], seeks to compress the grammar itself, as well as the encoding of the training sentences by the grammar.

Section 2 discusses work related to our approach, whereas section 3 presents the architecture, heuristics, search operators and search strategies employed by eg-GRIDS. Section 4 reports on an evaluation of eg-GRIDS on examples generated from an artificial[1] context-free grammar. Finally, section 5 concludes and outlines plans for future research.

2   Related Work

eg-GRIDS shares some of its central features with earlier work in grammatical inference. We have already mentioned that eg-GRIDS originates from GRIDS

---

[1] The term "artificial grammar" is used to describe a grammar devised solely for evaluation purposes, which does not necessarily correspond to any real-world problem.

[6] which is in turn based on SNPR [18], [19]. Both GRIDS and SNPR are also biased towards "simple" grammars, as they use *MDL* for scoring and selecting the most plausible grammars.

Although the majority of the work in grammatical inference focuses on regular grammars, a significant number of algorithms exist that infer context-free grammars. Stolcke and Omohundro [16], [15] have presented an approach which infers probabilistic context-free grammars. Using a Bayesian framework, their system employs learning operators similar to those employed by eg-GRIDS in order to find a grammar with maximal posterior probability given the training example set, a criterion essentially equivalent to the *MDL*. In [13] an algorithm for inducing context-free grammars from positive and negative structured examples is presented. A structured example is simply an example with parentheses that indicate the shape of the derivation tree of the grammar (structural information). The learning algorithm employs a genetic search and the CYK algorithm [4] for converging to a final grammar. An efficient successor of this algorithm can be found in [7]. A more recent version of this algorithm [14] operates on partially structured examples instead of complete ones and uses a tabular representation, leading to a more flexible and applicable algorithm, compared to its predecessor. The algorithm has been successfully applied to various simple languages as well as to DNA sequence modelling. *Synapse* [8] is another algorithm that is based on CYK. Synapse learns incrementally from positive and negative examples following a top-down search organisation, while preliminary results show that it is able to infer both ambiguous and unambiguous context-free grammars for simple languages in reasonable time.

3   The eg-GRIDS Algorithm

GRIDS [6] infers context-free grammars solely from positive example sets. It incorporates a beam search towards simple grammars with the help of two learning operators. Being based on GRIDS, eg-GRIDS shares some features with its predecessor:

- grammatical knowledge representation (context-free grammars);
- bias towards simple grammars, based on the same principle, i.e. minimum description length (*MDL*);
- two basic learning operators; and
- beam search.

However, eg-GRIDS also has some notable differences with GRIDS:

- it optimises the beam-based search process by using the results of a theoretical analysis of the dynamic behaviour of the learning operators [10];
- it incorporates new learning operators that can lead to more compact grammars; and
- it implements an additional genetic search strategy.

3.1   A Bias Towards "Simple" Grammars

As eg-GRIDS uses no negative evidence, an additional criterion is needed to direct the search through the space of context-free grammars and avoid overly general grammars. As we have mentioned above, this criterion provides a bias towards *simple* grammars. Following the GRIDS algorithm, we adopt the approach of *minimum description length (MDL)*, which directs the search process towards grammars that are compact, i.e., ones that require few bits to be encoded, while at the same time they encode the example set in a compact way, i.e. few bits are required to encode the examples using the grammar.

In order to use *MDL*, we must measure the encoding length of the grammar and of the example set, as encoded by the grammar. Assuming a context-free grammar G and a set of examples (sentences) T that can be recognised (parsed) by the grammar G, the total description length of a grammar (henceforth *model description length*, abbreviated as *ML*) is the sum of two independent lengths:

- The grammar description length (*GDL*), i.e. the bits required to encode the grammar rules and transmit them to a recipient who has minimal knowledge of the grammar representation, and
- the derivations description length (*DDL*), i.e. the bits required to encode and transmit all examples in the set T as encoded by grammar G, provided that the recipient already knows G.

The first component of the *ML* heuristic directs the search away from the sort of trivial grammar that has a separate rule for each training sentence, as this grammar will have a large *GDL*. However, the same component leads to the other sort of trivial grammar, a grammar that accepts all sentences. In order to avoid this, the second component estimates the *derivation power* of the grammar, by measuring the way the *training examples* are generated by the grammar, and helps to avoid overgeneralisation by penalising general grammars. The higher the derivation power of the language, the higher its *DDL* is expected to be. The initial overly specific grammar is trivially best in terms of *DDL*, as usually there is a one-to-one correspondence between the examples and the grammar rules, i.e. its derivation power is low. On the other hand, the most general grammar has the worst score, as it involves several rules in the derivation of a single sentence, requiring substantial effort to track down all the rules involved in the generation of the sentence.

Although *MDL* aims at a minimally compact representation of *both the model and the data* simultaneously, it does not provide means for creating the models, i.e. given a set of models that describe the same example set, *MDL* can only be used as an evaluation metric to decide which model is better. As a result, *MDL* cannot provide any help on how the space of possible models should be searched, in order to converge to a satisfactory model. In grammatical inference, *MDL* simply offers a mechanism for comparing grammars and selecting the one that is more "compact" with respect to both the length of the grammar as well as the encoding of the training set by the grammar.

3.2   Architecture of eg-GRIDS and the Learning Operators

The architecture of eg-GRIDS is summarised in figure 1. Like many other grammar inference algorithms, eg-GRIDS uses the training sentences in order to construct an *initial, "flat" grammar*. This initial grammar is constructed by simply converting each one of the training examples into a grammatical rule[2]. As a result, the number of initial rules corresponds to the number of training examples. This initial grammar is overly specific, as it can recognise only the sentences contained in the training set. After the initial grammar has been created, eg-GRIDS tries to generalise this initial grammar, with one of the two search processes: beam or the genetic search. Both search strategies utilise the same search operators in order to produce more general grammars.

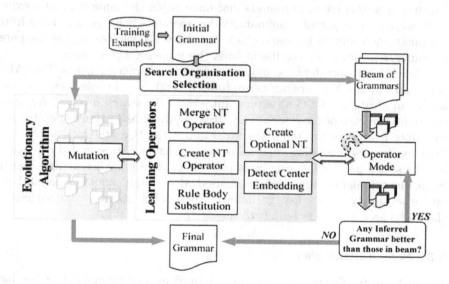

Fig. 1. The architecture of the eg-GRIDS algorithm.

Currently, eg-GRIDS supports five search operators:

Merge NT: merges two non-terminal symbols into a single symbol, thereby replacing all their appearances in the head and the body of rules.

Create NT: creates a new non-terminal symbol X, which is defined as a sequence of two or more existing non-terminal symbols. X is defined as a new production rule that decomposes X into its constituent symbols.

Create Optional NT: duplicates a rule created by the "Create NT" operator and appends an existing non-terminal symbol at the end of the body of the rule, thus making this symbol optional.

---

[2] The body of each rule is a sequence of non-terminal symbols, as each terminal is mapped initially to a unique non-terminal.

Detect Center Embedding: aims to capture the center embedding phenomenon. This operator tries to locate the most frequent four-gram[3] of the form "*AABB*". Once such a four-gram is located, the operator creates a new non-terminal symbol X as the operator "Create NT" would have done. However, *assuming* that this four-gram was created through center embedding involving symbol X, this operator additionally creates a new production rule of the form "$X \rightarrow AAXBB$" and replaces all symbol sequences that match the pattern "$A+ X? B+$" with X.

Rule Body Substitution: examines whether the body of a production rule R is contained in bodies of other production rules. In such a case, every occurrence of the body of rule R in other rule bodies is replaced by the head of rule R.

The five operators create grammars that have either the same or greater expressiveness than their parent grammar. As the operators never remove rules from a grammar, the resulting grammars have at least the same coverage as the parent grammar, i.e. they can recognise at least the same set of sentences.

The choice of operators was motivated mostly by practical needs. The "Merge NT" and "Create NT" operators are fundamental: in principle these two operators can create any CFG structure, subject to the search involved for finding the right sequence of operators. The "Rule Body Substitution" operator helps to reduce redundancy in the grammar. Finally, the "Create Optional NT" and "Detect Center Embedding" operators operate as heuristics, and try to accelerate the search process focusing on important predetermined structures. Clearly, many more similar heuristics can be devised. However, it should be noted that all operators simply *suggest* new grammars. The final choice over what suggestions should be accepted is always left to the *MDL*.

3.3 Search Strategies

Beam Search. The first search strategy implemented by eg-GRIDS is a beam search. Having an initial hypothesis (the initial grammar) in the search beam, eg-GRIDS uses five "modes" (one mode for each search operator) in order to explore the space of context-free grammars.

During learning, eg-GRIDS constantly alternates among the five modes, where each mode is characterised by the repetitive application of the same operator. Each mode initiates with a beam (beam A) containing the current grammars. For each grammar in beam A, all possible ways of applying the operator corresponding to the mode are examined. For example, the mode for the "Create NT" operator considers all ways of creating new symbols from all possible n-grams found in a grammar[4], while the mode for the "Merge NT" considers all

---

[3] Since bigrams and trigrams are quite common (frequent) structures and their presence can be attributed to a large number of phenomena, we assume that four-grams are the smallest n-grams that indicate possible existence of center embedding.

[4] All possible n-grams are examined, with n ranging from two (bigrams) to the length of the longest rule in the grammar.

ways of merging non-terminal symbols by repeatedly applying the "Merge NT" operator. For each operator application, a successor grammar is created and the best grammars according to the *MDL* form the new beam (beam B).

After all grammars in beam A have been examined, beams A and B are compared. If any of the grammars in beam B scores better than a grammar in beam A, beam A is replaced by beam B and the algorithm continues in this mode. However, if none of the grammars in beam B scores better than the grammars in beam A, then beam B is discarded and eg-GRIDS switches to another mode.

The algorithm continues alternating among the five modes until it is unable to produce a successor grammar that scores better than the ones in beam A. At that stage, the learning process terminates.

Genetic Search. The second search strategy implemented by eg-GRIDS is based on genetic algorithms. A genetic algorithm consists of four basic elements:

1. the evolutionary process, describing among other things which individuals should survive, reproduce or die;
2. the representation for individuals;
3. the set of genetic operators; and
4. the objective function for scoring individuals.

Regarding the evolutionary process, a variety of genetic algorithms is available in eg-GRIDS[5]. For the representation of individuals we have chosen to use the context-free grammars directly, rather than a special mapping that converts a grammar into a string. As a result, the choice of objective function was straightforwardly *MDL*. Regarding the set of genetic operators, eg-GRIDS can be considered to perform "informed mutation", using its five search operators.

More specifically, the genetic algorithm selects a grammar and an offspring grammar is produced from it as follows:

1. A search operator is randomly[6] chosen from the five operators.
2. The chosen operator is applied to the selected grammar, producing the offspring.
3. In case the chosen search operator requires additional information, e.g. the two non-terminal symbols that should be merged by the "Merge NT" operator, the required parameter values are randomly chosen from the set of all suitable values, e.g. all non-terminals for the "Merge NT" operator.

4   Experimental Evaluation

In this section we evaluate the eg-GRIDS algorithm experimentally, focusing mainly on its performance on learning from examples generated from artificial context-free grammars.

---

[5] The eg-GRIDS software uses the GAlib genetic algorithm package, written by Matthew Wall at the Massachusetts Institute of Technology. Available from http://lancet.mit.edu/ga/.

[6] All random selections in our experiments were based on a uniform distribution.

4.1   Evaluation Metrics for Artificial Grammars

Evaluation in grammatical inference presents peculiarities and common metrics that are used for supervised learning tasks, like recall and precision, are not directly applicable. Alternatively, in order to evaluate an inferred grammar we have to compare it against the "correct" grammar, so as to identify their similarity. However, even if the "correct" grammar is known, which is not the case in most real-world situations, the problem of determining whether two context-free grammars are equivalent is not an easy task: Given two context-free grammars G_1 and G_2, there exists no algorithm that can determine whether G_1 is more general than G_2 (i.e. $L(G_1) \supseteq L(G_2)$ or if $L(G_1) \cap L(G_2) = \emptyset$, where $L(G)$ the language of grammar G [9], [4].

As a result, during evaluation we mainly focus on measuring three aspects of the inferred grammar [6]:

- errors of omission (failures to parse sentences generated by the "correct" grammar), which indicate that an overly specific grammar has been learned,
- errors of commission (failures of the "correct" grammar to parse sentences generated by the inferred grammar), which indicate that an overly general grammar has been learned, and
- ability of the inferred grammar to parse correctly sentences longer than the sentences used during training, which indicates the additional expressiveness of the learned grammar.

In experiments with artificial context-free grammars, where the "correct" grammar is known, to estimate these figures we use the original (or "correct") grammar G_O and the learned grammar G_L to generate a large number of sentences. Errors of omission can be estimated as the fraction of the number of sentences generated by G_O that are not parsed by G_L to the total number of sentences generated by G_O. Errors of commission can be estimated as the fraction of the number of sentences generated by G_L that are not parsed by G_O to the total number of sentences generated by G_L. Errors of omission and errors of commission measure the *overlap* of the two grammars. In the ideal case, both of these figures must be zero, indicating that all sentences generated by one grammar can be parsed by the other. In order to estimate the third figure, example sentences must be generated from G_O that have greater length than the ones used for training. This figure can then be estimated as the fraction of the number of sentences that were successfully parsed by G_L to the total number of generated sentences.

4.2   The Balanced Parenthesis Language

Our experiments examine the learning behaviour of eg-GRIDS on the Dyck language, not only because it is a context-free language but also because e-GRIDS comes very close into learning it [10], but fails to converge to the correct grammar for a small number of the used training sets. Hence, we evaluate eg-GRIDS using the Dyck language with $k = 1$:

$$S \to S\,S|(S)| \in \qquad\qquad (1)$$

In the experiments that we have conducted, we have generated a large number of unique sentences[7] top-down from the above grammar, using a uniform distribution for selecting randomly when expanding ambiguous non-terminals. The generated example sentences were randomly shuffled. Then, we defined an arbitrary maximum length $L_{max} = 20$ tokens[8] for the examples. The resulting set (subset A) was used for evaluation according to the first two figures, i.e. errors of omission and commission. Thus, a second test set was created (subset B), containing example sentences with lengths greater than L_{max} but lower than a second arbitrary maximum length (25 tokens). This second set is the set that was used in order to calculate the third figure, i.e. the ability to parse sentences longer than the ones used for training. All sets were populated by randomly selecting example sentences from the generated sentences. Special care was taken in order to ensure that the same sentence did not appear both in the training and the test sets.

As the Dyck language with $k = 1$ cannot be used to generate a large number of example sentences if we restrict the maximum sentence length, we have performed a ten-fold cross validation. Thus, subset A is split into ten subsets of equal size and the experiment is repeated 10 times: each time 9 subsets of A are used for training eg-GRIDS and the learned grammar is evaluated on the 10th unused set, augmented with a test set created from subset B.

Figures 2 and 3 show the results of this experiment for the e-GRIDS algorithm (eg-GRIDS' predecessor), as presented in [10]. As it is evident from figure 2, e-GRIDS comes very close to learning the target grammar, as its performance approaches 0.95 with a training set size of 900 example sentences and remains around 0.90 for greater example set sizes. Regarding example sentences longer than the ones used for training (figure 3), e-GRIDS exhibits a similar behaviour. Finally, e-GRIDS never converges to a grammar that could produce ungrammatical sentences, i.e. it has zero errors of commission.

The same experiment was repeated for the eg-GRIDS algorithm, using the extended operator set and the genetic grammar selection strategy, with the "steady-state" genetic algorithm, an algorithm supporting overlapping populations. The first observation from the results was a significant improvement in terms of errors of omission. There were no such errors for sentences with length up to 20 words, even for very small training sets, while the situation is similar even for longer test sentences, as can be seen in figure 4.

An interesting difference between the two algorithms is the fact that eg-GRIDS seems to converge to more general grammars than the target grammar for small training set sizes, thus producing ungrammatical sentences (figure 5). Genetic search allows eg-GRIDS to search a larger space of possible grammars, mainly due to the diversity of the grammars maintained in evolving populations. We believe that this diversity helped eg-GRIDS to converge to "better" grammars than e-GRIDS, even if these grammars are more general than the target one for small training set sizes.

---

[7] All example sets used in our experiments contain unique example sentences, i.e. an example set of size 900 contains 900 distinct example sentences.

[8] A token is either a single left parenthesis "(" or a right one ")".

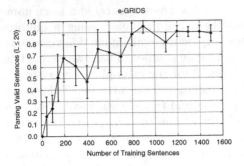

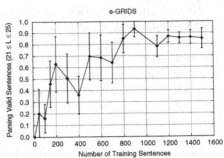

Fig. 2. Probability of parsing a valid sentence of length up to 20 words. (1-errors of omission).

Fig. 3. Probability of parsing a valid sentence of length between 21 and 25 words. (1-errors of omission).

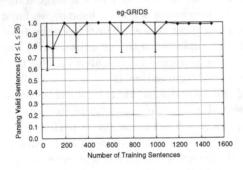

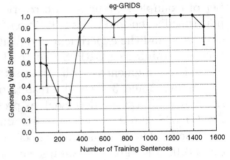

Fig. 4. Probability of parsing a valid sentence of length between 21 and 25 words. (1-errors of omission).

Fig. 5. Probability of generating a valid sentence. (1-errors of commission).

5 Conclusions

In this paper, we presented the eg-GRIDS algorithm for inducing context-free grammars solely from positive evidence. eg-GRIDS utilises a heuristic based on minimum description length to avoid overgeneralisation, a consequence of the absence of negative evidence. Its main advantages are the fact that implements a genetic search strategy and has a richer set of search operators, offering eg-GRIDS the ability to adapt easier to a wider range of tasks and perform better than its predecessors.

Regarding the learning performance of eg-GRIDS, experiments have been conducted with the help of artificially generated examples. Our results have shown that eg-GRIDS is able to infer grammars that perform well, based on relatively small sets of training examples. The addition of the genetic search process, besides the increase in the performance of the algorithm, has also increased significantly the processing efficiency of the algorithm, and thus its scalability to more complex tasks. Preliminary results show that eg-GRIDS is more than an order of magnitude faster than e-GRIDS, due to the less exhaustive nature of its search. Future work will focus on the effect of the newly added search operators. Preliminary results suggest that eg-GRIDS can achieve very good performance on the Dyck language with k=2, a task beyond the capabilities of e-GRIDS.

Concluding, the work presented here has resulted in a new algorithm that alleviates some of the shortcomings of its predecessors, with special attention given to robustness and efficiency. We believe that eg-GRIDS will be useful in modelling various subparts of natural languages and identifying these subparts in texts, a task that cannot be easily modeled by other machine learning approaches, at least those that expect fixed-length vectors as input. Interesting tasks that fit this description include noun phrase chunking, named-entity recognition and information extraction.

References

1. D. Angluin, "Inference of reversible languages", *Journal of ACM*, vol. 29, pp. 741–765, 1982.
2. J. D. Emerald, K. G. Subramanian, D. G. Thomas, "Learning Code regular and Code linear languages", *Proceedings of International Colloquium on Grammatical Inference (ICGI-96)*, Lecture Notes in Artificial Intelligence 1147, Springer – Verlag, pp. 211–221, 1996.
3. P. García, E. Vidal, "Inference of K-testable languages in the strict sense and applications to syntactic pattern recognition", *Journal of IEEE Transactions on Pattern Analysis and Machine Intelligence*, vol. 12(9), pp. 920–925, 1990.
4. J. Hopcroft, J. Ullman, *Introduction to Automata Theory, Languages and Computation*. Addison – Wesley, 1979.
5. T. Koshiba, E. Makinen, Y. Takada, "Inferring pure context-free languages from positive data", *Technical report A-1997-14*, Department of Computer Science, University of Tampere, 1997.
6. P. Langley, S. Stromsten, "Learning Context-Free Grammars with a Simplicity Bias", *Proceedings of the Eleventh European Conference on Machine Learning (ECML 2000)*, Lecture Notes in Artificial Intelligence 1810, Springer – Verlag, pp. 220–228, Barcelona, Spain, 2000.
7. F. Mäkinen, "On the structural grammatical inference problem for some classes of context-free grammars", *Information Processing Letters*, 42, pp. 193–199, 1992.
8. K. Nakamura, T. Ishiwata, "Synthesizing Context Free Grammars from Simple Strings Based on Inductive CYK Algorithm", *Proceedings of the Fifth International Colloquium on Grammatical Inference (ICGI 2000), Grammatical Inference: Algorithms and Applications, Oliveira A. (ed.)*, Portugal, 2000. Springer.
9. R. Parekh, V. Honavar, "Grammar Inference, Automata Induction, and Language Acquisition", R. Dale, H. Moisl, and H. Somers (eds.), *Handbook of Natural Language Processing*, chapter 29, pp. 727–764, Marcel Dekker Inc., 2000.
10. G. Petasis, G. Paliouras, V. Karkaletsis, C. Halatsis and C.D. Spyropoulos, "e-GRIDS: Computationally Efficient Grammatical Inference from Positive Examples," *Grammars*, Special Issue, 2004. Available from http://217.125.102.104/special4.asp.

11. J. Rissanen, *Stochastic Complexity in Statistical Inquiry*, World Scientific Publishing Co, Singapore, 1989.
12. H. Rulot, E. Vidal, "Modelling (sub)string-length-based constraints through grammatical inference methods", Devijer and Kittler (eds.), Springer – Verlag, 1987.
13. Y. Sakakibara, "Efficient learning of context-free grammars from positive structural examples", *Information and Computation*, 97, pp. 23–60, 1992.
14. Y. Sakakibara, H. Muramatsu, "Learning Context-Free Grammars from Partially Structured Examples", *Proceedings of the Fifth International Colloquium on Grammatical Inference (ICGI 2000), Grammatical Inference: Algorithms and Applications, Oliveira A. (ed.)*, Portugal, 2000. Springer.
15. A. Stolcke, "Bayesian Learning of Probabilistic Language Models", *PhD Thesis, University of California at Berkley*, 1994.
16. A. Stolcke, S. Omohundro, "Inducing Probabilistic Grammars by Bayesian Model Merging", *Proceedings of International Colloquium on Grammatical Inference (ICGI-94)*, Lecture Notes in Artificial Intelligence 862, Springer – Verlag, pp. 106–118, 1994.
17. N. Tanida, T. Yokomori, "Inductive Inference of Monogenic Pure Context-free languages", Lecture Notes in Artificial Intelligence 872, Springer – Verlag, pp. 560–573, 1994.
18. G. Wolff, "Grammar Discovery as data compression", *Proceedings of the AISB/GI Conference on Artificial Intelligence*, pp. 375–379, Hamburg, West Germany, 1978.
19. G. Wolff, "Language Acquisition, Data Compression and Generalisation", *Language and Communication*, 2, pp. 57–89, 1982.
20. T. Yokomori, "On Polynomial-Time Learnability in the Limit of Strictly Deterministic Automata", *Journal of Machine Learning*, vol. 19, pp. 153–179, 1995.

The Boisdale Algorithm –
An Induction Method for a Subclass
of Unification Grammar from Positive Data

Bradford Starkie[1,2] and Henning Fernau[2,3]

[1] Telstra Research Laboratories,
770 Blackburn Rd Clayton, Melbourne Victoria, 3127, Australia
Brad.Starkie@team.telstra.com
http://www.cs.newcastle.edu.au/~bstarkie/
[2] University of Newcastle, School of Electrical Engineering and Computer Science,
University Drive, NSW 2308 Callaghan, Australia
[3] Theoretische Informatik, Wilhelm-Schickard-Institut für Informatik,
Universität Tübingen, Sand 13, D-72076 Tübingen, Germany
fernau@informatik.uni-tuebingen.de
http://www-fs.informatik.uni-tuebingen.de/~fernau/

Abstract. This paper introduces a new grammatical inference algorithm called the Boisdale algorithm. This algorithm can identify a class of context-free unification grammar in the limit from positive data only. The Boisdale algorithm infers both the syntax and the semantics of the language, where the semantics of the language can be described using arbitrarily complex data structures represented as key value pairs. The Boisdale algorithm is an alignment based learning algorithm that executes in polynomial time with respect to the length of the training data and can infer a grammar when presented with any set of sentences tagged with any data structure. This paper includes a description of the algorithm, a description of a class of language that it can identify in the limit and some experimental results.

1 Introduction

If an algorithm can identify a class of language in the limit from positive data only, then it is guaranteed to learn a grammar of that class exactly at some finite time when presented with an infinite stream of example sentences generated from that language. In this respect, the ability to identify a class of language in the limit is a measure of the quality of the algorithm if the objective of the learning task is to learn a language exactly. The papers of Gold [5] and Angluin [3] are the quintessential texts on identification in the limit of languages from positive data only. A brief but up-to-date introduction to the state of the art of grammatical inference of context-free grammars can be found in de la Higuera and Oncina [4].

In Starkie [9] a new grammatical inference algorithm for inferring context-free grammars was introduced called the Left-Alignment algorithm. This algorithm has the property that it can identify a class of context-free grammar in the limit from positive data only. The Boisdale algorithm described in this paper is an extension of

G. Paliouras and Y. Sakakibara (Eds.): ICGI 2004, LNAI 3264, pp. 235–247, 2004.
© Springer-Verlag Berlin Heidelberg 2004

the left alignment algorithm that enables the *semantics* of the language to be learnt in addition to the syntax of the language. To this end, we use unification grammars that are similar to Definite Clause Grammars (DCGs) Pereira and Warren [7]; both can be viewed as attributed context-free grammars. Unification grammars can be used to both convert natural language sentences into data structures (represented as key-value pairs) and to convert data structures into natural language sentences. The algorithm can infer a grammar when presented with an arbitrary set of tagged sentences, and can do so in polynomial (update) time. We also add a very brief description of a class of grammar that can be identified in the limit using the Boisdale algorithm (so-called Boisdale grammars); Starkie and Fernau [10] contains a proof showing that all Boisdale grammars can be identified in the limit from positive data only using the Boisdale algorithm. Some experimental results will be presented including an empirical confirmation that the algorithm can infer any Boisdale grammar in the limit from positive data only. Although the Boisdale algorithm can infer any Boisdale grammar in the limit from positive data, there exist some sets of training examples for which no Boisdale grammar exists that can generate those sentences amongst others. In this instance, the Boisdale algorithm still terminates and returns a unification grammar that can generate at least the training examples. The exact characterization of the class of grammars that can be identified in the limit using the Boisdale algorithm is currently an open problem.

2 Background

2.1 Notation

A *unification grammar* is given by a 5-tuple $G = (N,\Sigma,\Pi,S,A)$ where N is the alphabet of non-terminal symbols; Σ is the alphabet of terminal symbols with $N \cap \Sigma = \{\ \}$; S is a special non-terminal called the start symbol; A is the *signature definition* which is an ordered list of key-type pairs (k,t) and Π is a finite set of rewrite rules of the form $r =$ "$N_i(x_1..x_{|A|}) \rightarrow \Omega_1(x_1..x_{|A|}) \ldots \Omega_{|r|}(x_1..x_{|A|})$" where $N_i \in N, \Omega_i \in (\Sigma \cup N)$.

The rewrite rules of G define transformations of sequences of terms to other sequences of terms. A *term* is comprised of a *root* and a *signature*. The *root* is a symbol and the *signature* is an ordered list of symbols. In our definition of unification grammars, all terms in the language have the same number of elements in their *signature* as there are elements in the *signature definition*. For example, the term "City(- ?fm)" has the root "City" and the signature "(- ?fm)". In this paper we will use the symbol '-' to denote an undefined value within a signature. A signature that contains only one or more instances of the symbol "-" within parentheses is referred to as the *empty signature*. For instance, the term "sydney(- -)" has the root "sydney" and the empty signature "(- -)". The notation root(X) denotes the root of X.

If a term does not explicitly show a signature, then it contains the empty signature, i.e., we can write "sydney" in place of "sydney(- -)".

A term Ω is either a terminal term in which case root(Ω) $\in \Sigma$ and begins with a lower case letter, or a non-terminal term in which case root(Ω) $\in N$ and begins with an upper case letter. A terminal term always has the empty signature.

In this paper an uppercase letter is used to represent any non-terminal symbol (*e.g.,* A), a lowercase symbol to represent any terminal symbol *(e.g., a)* and a Greek letter is used to represent a symbol that could be either terminal or non-terminal *(e.g., Ω or Ψ).* The notation A(x) represents a term with an unknown number of symbols in its signature and |x| denotes the *length* of the signature. An italic uppercase letter is used to represent a sequence of zero or more terminals or non-terminal terms (*e.g., A*) and an italic bold uppercase letter represents a sequence of one or more terms, either terminal or non-terminal *(e.g., A).* The notation |*A*| denotes the number of terms in *A*. Lowercase italic letters represent a sequence of zero or more terminal terms (*e.g., a*) and bold italic lowercase letters represent a sequence of one or more terminal terms (*e.g., a*).

2.2 Unification Grammars

An example unification grammar G that is described using the notation employed in this paper is given below. Relating to the formal definition introduced above, for this grammar the non-terminal alphabet is {S,City}, the terminal alphabet is {sydney,perth,perth scotland}and the signature definition is {(fm.fm),(to,fm)}.

```
%slots {fm fm, to fm}
%start S
S(?fm ?to)→S(?fm -)S(- ?to)
S(?fm -)→ from City(?fm -)
S(- ?to)→ to City(?to -)
City(SYD -)→sydney
City(PTH -)→perth
City(SCT -)→perth scotland
```

Fig. 1. An example unification grammar.

The first part in this denotation is the signature definition. This states that all terms in the grammar have two parameters namely a "to" attribute and an "fm" attribute. Both of these attributes are of the same type, specifically the type "fm". As well as defining the length of the signature (two) the signature definition enables a term signature to be converted into a key-value form. For instance, the signature (PTH SYD) can be seen as the attributes {fm=PTH, to=SYD}. The start symbol of G is the non-terminal 'S' and all sentences that are described by this grammar (denoted L(G)) can be generated by expanding the non-terminal S until no non-terminal terms exist in the term sequence. Non-terminals can be expanded using the rewrite rules. Symbols other than '-' that appear in the signature on the left-hand side of the rule and in the signature of a symbol on the right hand side are *variables*. (Prefixed by '?' in this paper). If a rule is *well formed*, then for every variable in the signature of the left hand side of a rewrite rule, there is exactly one instance of that variable contained in the signature of exactly one non-terminal on the right hand side of the rewrite rule. Similarly, for every variable in the signature of a non-terminal on the right hand side of rule, there is exactly one instance of that variable in the signature on the left hand side of the rewrite rule. For instance, the rule "S(?fm ?to)→S(?fm -)S(- ?to)" contains one instance of the variable "?fm" on the left hand side and exactly one instance of "?fm" on the right hand side.

Before each non-terminal is expanded, all variables in the signature on the left-hand side of the rule need to be instantiated to a constant value via a process referred to as *unification*. Two signatures are said to *unify* if there is a set of mappings σ: t → u for the variables in the signatures such that if you replace the variables with their mappings, the two signatures are identical. The notation L^σ denotes the result of applying the substitution σ to L.

For instance, in the above example the signature ("melbourne" "sydney") unifies with (?fm ?to) using the mapping σ =(?fm→"melbourne", ?to→"sydney"). That is, (?fm ?to)$^\sigma$ = ("melbourne" "sydney"). In contrast, the signature ("melbourne" "sydney") does *not* unify with the signature (- ?to).

An important method of expanding the start symbol into a terminal sequence is the *rightmost expansion* (denoted $_{rm,G}$) in which non-terminals are expanded right to left. For example:

S("melbourne"-)S(-"sydney") $_{rm,G}$ S("melbourne"-) to City(-"sydney").

The notation A * B denotes that A can be expanded using zero or more single step expansions to become **B**. A *constituent* is defined as an ordered pair (A , **B**) where A * **B**. Similarly, a string can be converted to a data structure by a process referred to as *reduction* (denoted ⇐), where rewrite rules are applied in reverse. One important method of reduction is the *leftmost reduction* (denoted $_{L,G}$⇐) in which reductions are applied left to right. For example:

to melbourne $_{L,G}$⇐ to City("melbourne"-) $_{L,G}$⇐ S(-"melbourne")

Similarly, the notation **B** ⇐* A denotes that **B** can be transformed to become A via zero or more single step reductions.

To formally describe a leftmost reduction we need to introduce a definition of *uniquely inverted* that can be applied to unification grammar. A unification grammar is uniquely inverted if there are no two rules of the form A(x)→**B** and C(y)→**D** such that root(**B**) = root(**D**). Here the function root is extended to a sequence of terms as follows: root($\Omega_1 \Omega_2 .. \Omega_x$) = root($\Omega_1$) root($\Omega_2$) .. root($\Omega_x$).

Formally a leftmost reduction can be described as follows: if G is uniquely inverted and A B C $_{L,G}$⇐ A D(x) C then there exists a substitution ζ and a rule D(y) → Q such that Q^ζ = B and D(y) $^\zeta$ = D(x) and there does not exist any rule of the form E(x)→F such that for some substitution ρ, A B C = H F$^\rho$ J ⇐ H E(x)$^\rho$ J and H F$^\rho$ is a proper prefix of A B. For any uniquely inverted unification grammar, the normal form achieved from a leftmost reduction is deterministic Otto [6]. It can be seen that if **B** $_L$⇐* N(x) then N(x) $^*_{rm,G}$ **B**.

To describe the Boisdale algorithm, some additional notation is required. If N(y) is a term, then val(y) denotes the unordered list of values (either constants or variables) in y other than '-'. Let pattern(y) be a sequence of 0's and 1's that denotes whether each element of the signature is either '-' or not '-' respectively. Let const(y) denote the unordered list of constants in y; e.g., if y = ("melbourne" - ?action 6), then val(y) = { "melbourne", ?action, 6 }, pattern(y)=(1011) and const(y)={ "melbourne", 6 }.

The function val can be extended to terms and term sequences as follows: val(A(x))=val(x) and val(A(x) B) = val(A(x)) $\cup$ val(B). The functions const can be similarly expanded to reference terms and term sequences.

2.3   The Typed Leftmost Reduction

We will now introduce the concept of the *typed leftmost reduction*. Given a set of rewrite rules, a starting term sequence and a set of constants, a typed leftmost reduction defines a deterministic set of reductions. A typed leftmost reduction is similar to a leftmost reduction in that rewrite rules are applied in a left to right sequence with the following important distinction: the definition of a typed leftmost reduction includes a set of constants c such that a rule R can only be used if const(R) $\subseteq$ c. This is reflected by the notation $_{L(c),G}\Leftarrow$. The function typed_leftmost(I,G,c) shown in Figure 2 calculates the typed leftmost reduction B such that $I_{L(c),G}\Leftarrow^*B$.

```
Function typed_leftmost(I,G,c)
//I     a sequence of terms,G a set of rewrite rules
//c     a set of constants
{i=0;while(i < |I|){
  shift I[i] onto stack;i++;
  while(∃ A(x)→ B, ∃σ such that Bσ = top |B| of stack,const(x)⊆ c){
    pop |B| symbols off stack;push A(x)σ onto stack;}}
```

Fig. 2. An algorithm for calculating a typed leftmost reduction.

Formally, given a target set of constants c, a uniquely inverted set of rewrite rules G and a starting sequence I a typed leftmost reduction denoted $I_{L(c),G}\Leftarrow^* B$ is a sequence of reduction steps such that if $I_{L(c)}\Leftarrow^* A D C_{L(c)} \Leftarrow A$ F(x) $C_{L(c)}\Leftarrow^* B$ then there exists a substitution ζ and a rule F(x)$^\zeta \rightarrow D^\zeta$ such that const(x) $\subseteq$ c and there does not exist any rule of the form E(y)$\rightarrow$F and a substitution σ such that $A D C = H$ $F^\sigma J \Leftarrow H$ E(y)$^\sigma J_L\Leftarrow^* B$ and $H F^\sigma$ is a proper prefix of $A D$, const(y) $\subseteq$ c.

Although the definition of a typed leftmost reduction is stated in terms of a uniquely inverted grammar, we will extend the definition to enable it to be used as part of the inference process as follows: If two rules R_1 and R_2 can be applied at any point in a typed leftmost reduction sequence then if $|$const(R_1)$| > |$const(R_2)$|$, the sequence is reduced by R_1; otherwise, the sequence is reduced by R_2.

2.4   The Working Principle of the Boisdale Algorithm

It can be seen that for all unification grammars, if $B_{L(c),G}\Leftarrow^*A(c)$ then A(c) $^*_{rm,G} B$. The Boisdale algorithm has been designed to infer grammars where for each rule there exists at least one terminal sequence, whose typed leftmost reduction recreates a rightmost derivation in reverse, i.e., for each rule of the form A(d)→E there exists **at least one** terminal string b such that A(c) $_{rm,G}$ E^σ $^*_{rm,G}$ b and $b_{L(c),G} \Leftarrow^*$ $E^\sigma_{L(c),G} \Leftarrow$A(c).

The Boisdale algorithm takes as its input a set of positive training examples each tagged with key value pairs representing the meaning of those sentences. The constituents of these sentences are then guessed by aligning sentences with common prefixes from the left. In Starkie and Fernau [10] it is proven that a class of grammar exists such that aligning sentences from the left either identifies the correct constituents of the sentence, or if it incorrectly identifies constituents then those constituents will be deleted by the time the algorithm has completed.

The Boisdale algorithm is believed to be one example of a class of alignment based learning algorithms that can identify classes of unification grammar in the limit from positive data only. A related algorithm could be constructed to infer grammars for which **all** sentences can be reconstructed using a typed leftmost reduction, i.e.,

$$\forall A(c) \quad _{rm,G} E \quad ^*_{rm,G} b \; , \; b_{L(c),G} \Leftarrow^* E_{L(c),G} \Leftarrow A(c).$$

Similarly the concept of a typed rightmost reduction can be introduced that is identical to a typed leftmost reduction with the exception that reductions occur in a right to left manner. This variant of course gives rise to another class of learnable languages.

3   The Boisdale Algorithm

The Boisdale algorithm begins with a set T of positive examples of the language L(G) where each $s \in$ T can include a set of key value pairs (denoted *attributes(s)*) that describe the semantics of s. Although this algorithm uses unstructured key value pairs to describe the semantics of sentences, arbitrarily complex data structures can be mapped into assignment functions and therefore simple key-value pairs as described in Starkie [8]. (eg date.hours= "4" date.minutes="30").

The algorithm creates a set of constituents C and hypothesis grammar H with rule set Π. The algorithm is comprised of the following 7 steps.

Step 1. (Incorporation Phase)
For each sentence $s \in$ T, *attributes(s)* =x a rewrite rule of the form S(x) → s is added to H.

Step 2. (Alignment Phase)
<u>Rule 1.</u> If there exists two sentences c x_1 and c x_2 with a common prefix c and with attributes y_1 and y_2, respectively, for which the same attribute keys are defined, i.e., *pattern*(y_1)=*pattern*(y_2), then a new non-terminal X_1 is introduced and two rules of the form $X_1(y_5) \rightarrow x_1$ and $X_1(y_6) \rightarrow x_2$ are created. The signatures of these rules (y_5 and y_6) are constructed such that val(y_5) = val(y_1) – val(y_2) and val(y_6) = val(y_2) – val(y_1).

Example: When presented with the sentences "from sydney" {fm=SYD} and "from perth" {fm=PTH}, the non-terminal X_{48} is constructed and the rules

X_{48}(SYD -)→sydney   and X_{48}(PTH -)→perth

are added to the hypothesis grammar.

Rule 2. If there exists a sentence c x_7 that is a prefix of another sentence c x_7 x_8 with attributes y_7 and y_8, respectively, for which the same attribute keys are defined, i.e., *pattern*(y_7)=*pattern*(y_8) such that there exists at least one key value pair in y_7 that is not in y_8 then a new non-terminal X_7 is created and two rules of the form $X_7(y_{10}) \rightarrow$ x_7 and $X_7(y_{11}) \rightarrow x_7$ x_8 are constructed.

Example: When presented with the sentences "from perth" {fm=PTH} and "from perth scotland" {fm=SCT} the non-terminal X_{48} is formed and the rules "X_{48}(PTH-) →perth" and "X_{48}(SCT -)→perth scotland" are constructed.

At this point the right hand side all of the rewrite rules of the hypothesis grammar contain only terminals. The set of constituents C is then created by copying the hypothesis grammar H, i.e., C ={ (A(x),**B**) | "A(x)→**B**"∈ H }. Continue to step 3.

Step 3. (Substitution Phase)

The substitution phase consists of two sub phases: normalisation and completion.

In both subphases, merging of non-terminals may occur. Merging non-terminals in the Boisdale algorithm involves the relabelling of some non-terminals as well as the reordering of the signatures of non-terminals. A *reordering* r is an array of length l where l is the number of attributes per term in the grammar. Each element of r (denoted r_i) is set to either '-' or an integer k such that k < l. When a signature s is reordered using a reordering r, a signature u is created such that u_i = '-' if r_i = '-', otherwise $u_i = s_k$ where k= r_i. After u has been constructed s is replaced by u. We will use the notation y $|\text{-}|_\varsigma$ z to denote that y is reordered using the reordering ς to become z.

Example: The signature (- SYD) can be reordered using the reordering (1 -) to become (SYD –).

When the non-terminals A and C are merged using the reordering r, all signatures attached to A are reordered using r. A well-founded linear ordering $<_r$ (not defined here) is used to determine the name of the newly merged non-terminal. Specifically, if A$<_r$ C then all instances of C are renamed as A, otherwise all instances of A are renamed as C. For any non-terminal N_i other than 'S' 'S'$<_r$ N_i. This ensures that H always contains at least one rule with the start symbol on its left hand side.

Example: If a grammar contains the rules

X_1(- SYD)→sydney and X_2(PTH -)→perth

and the non-terminal X_2 is merged with X_1 using the reordering (- 1) then after merging these rules become; X_1(- SYD)→sydney and X_1(- PTH)→perth.

Normalisation.
During normalization for each rule of the form $N_i(y) \rightarrow E$ in H the right hand side E is reduced using a typed leftmost reduction and y (i.e., using the function of Figure 2.) That is the value K is calculated where $E_{L(y)} \Leftarrow^* K$.

a) If $N_i \neq$ 'S' and a term sequence is encountered while reducing E that begins with N_i, then the rule $N_i(y) \rightarrow E$ is deleted.

b) Otherwise if $K \neq N_i(y)$ and $|K| \neq 1$ and each constant in const(K) appears the same number of times in const(y), then the rule $N_i(y) \rightarrow E$ is replaced by the rule $N_i(y) \rightarrow K$.

c) If $K \neq N_i(y)$ and $|K| = 1$ and each constant in const(K) appears the same number of times in const(y), then the non-terminal K is merged with N_i in both H and C.

This process is repeated until $\forall \, r = (A(x) \rightarrow B) \in \Pi, B_{L(x)} \Leftarrow^* A(x)$.

Example: If H contains only the following rules
S(SYD -)→from sydney and X_{48}(SYD -)→sydney
then after normalisation (part c)) these rules will become
S(?fm -)→from X_{48}(?fm -) and X_{48}(SYD -)→sydney.

Completion.
During completion the right hand side of each constituent in C is reduced using a typed leftmost reduction. Specifically for all c=(A(x),B) ∈ C the value D is calculated such that $B_{L(x)} \Leftarrow^* D$.

a) If A ≠ 'S' and a term sequence is encountered while reducing B that begins with A the constituent (A(x),B) is deleted.

b) Otherwise if $D \neq A(x)$ and each constant in const(D) appears the same number of times in const(x) then a rule of the form A(x)→ D is added to H.

c) If $D \neq A(x)$ and $|D| = 1$ and each constant in const(D) appears the same number of times in const(x) then the non-terminal D is merged with A in both H and C.

This process is repeated until no more rules are added to H.

Example: If H contains only the following rule
X_{48}(SYD -)→sydney
and C contains the following constituents
(S(SYD -),from sydney) and (X_{48}(SYD -),sydney)
then after completion the rules of H will be
S(?fm -)→from X_{48}(?fm -) and X_{48}(SYD -)→sydney.

In the substitution phase, normalisation is first performed followed by completion. If the grammar has changed, the process is repeated, beginning with normalization; otherwise, the algorithm continues to the merging phase.

Step 4. (Merging Phase)
During the merging phase, non-terminals are merged by applying the following rules:
- If there exists two rules of the form A(x) → B C(y) and A(q) → E D(z) that can be unified using the mapping σ so that the right hand sides are identical (i.e., $B = E^\sigma$)

with the exception of the last non-terminal on the right hand side of each rule, and the signatures of the last non-terminal can be reordered using the reordering ς so that they unify, i.e., $y \mid\text{-}\mid_\varsigma z^\sigma$ then C and D are merged using ς.

Example: If there are two rules of the form
$X_1(?\text{fm }?\text{to}) \rightarrow$ from City($?\text{fm}$ -) to $X_2(\text{- }?\text{to})$ and
$X_1(?\text{fm }?\text{to}) \rightarrow$ from City($?\text{fm}$ -) to City($?\text{to}$ -),
then the non-terminals X_2 and City are merged.

- If there exists two rules of the form $A(x) \rightarrow B$ and $C(y) \rightarrow E$ where the same right hand side of each rule can be unified using some mapping σ (i.e., $B=E^\sigma$) and the signatures of the left hand sides can be reordered using some reordering ς, i.e., $x \mid\text{-}\mid_\varsigma y^\sigma$ then A and C are merged using ς.

Example: If there are two rules of the form
$X_2(\text{sydney-}) \rightarrow$ sydney and
City(sydney -) $\rightarrow$ sydney,
then the non-terminals X_2 and City are merged.

- If there exists two rules of the form $A(x) \rightarrow \Omega_1\Omega_2 \dots \Omega_n$ and $A(y) \rightarrow \Psi_1\Psi_2\dots\Psi_n$ and $\forall i \text{ root}(\Omega_i)= \text{root}(\Psi_i)$ and there exists a $\sigma1$ such that $A(y)^{\sigma1} = A(x)$, $(\Psi_1\Psi_2\dots \Psi_n)^{\sigma1} = (\Omega_1\Omega_2 \dots \Omega_n)$ but there does not exist a $\sigma2$ such that $A(x)^{\sigma2} = A(y)$, $(\Omega_1\Omega_2 \dots\Omega_n)^{\sigma2} = (\Psi_1\Psi_2\dots\Psi_n)$, then the rule "$A(x) \quad^* \Omega_1\Omega_2\dots\Omega_n$" is deleted.

Example: If a grammar contains two rules of the form
$S(?\text{fm }?\text{to}) \rightarrow$ from City($?\text{fm}$ –) to City(- $?\text{to}$) and
$S(?\text{fm }?\text{fm}) \rightarrow$ from City($?\text{fm}$ –) to City(- $?\text{fm}$),

then the rule "$S(?\text{fm }?\text{fm}) \rightarrow$ from City($?\text{fm}$ –) to City(- $?\text{fm}$)" is deleted. This is because every sentence that can be generated by this rule can be generated from the other rule, although the converse is not true.

The merging phase continues until no more non-terminals can be merged. Once the merging phase has completed, if the number of rules or the number of non-terminals has changed, then the substitution phase is repeated; otherwise, the algorithm may continue to the unchunking phase.

Step 5. (Unchunking Phase)
If there exists a non-terminal A in the grammar where A is not the start symbol such that there is only one rule of the form $A(x) \rightarrow B$, then for all instances of $A(y)$ on the right hand side of any other rule R_1, i.e., $R_1= C(z) \rightarrow D\ A(y)\ E$ a substitution σ is found such that $A(x)^\sigma = A(y)$ and R_1 is transformed to become $C(z) \rightarrow D\ B^\sigma\ E$. The rule $A(x) \rightarrow B$ is then deleted, as well as all constituents of the form $(A(y),F)$.

Example: If there are two rules of the form
$X_{48}(?\text{fm}$ -)$\rightarrow$perth $X_{49}(?\text{fm}$ -) and
$X_{49}(\text{SCT}$ -)$\rightarrow$scotland

and there are no other rules with X_{49} on their left hand side then these rules are replaced by the following rule:

X_{48}(SCT -)→perth scotland.

The unchunking phase is continued until no-more changes can be made. If the grammar has changed during the unchunking phase then the algorithm returns to the substitution phase otherwise it continues to the catch all stage.

Step 6. (Catch All Stage)
In this stage of the algorithm, rules are added to ensure that every sentence in the training set can be generated using the hypothesis grammar. Specifically, an empty set of rewrite rules H_2 is first created. Then if $s_{L(x)} \Leftarrow^* D$ and $D \neq S(x)$, then s is parsed using a chart parser Allen [2]. If $S(x) \stackrel{*}{} s$ then no action is taken otherwise the rule $S(x) \rightarrow D$ is added to H_2. At the end of the catch all stage, all rules in H_2 are added to H.

Step 7. (Final Stage)
In the final stage, rules that are unreachable from the start symbol are deleted. An algorithm for doing this can be found in Aho and Ullman [1].

4   Example

Consider the case where the Boisdale grammar is presented with the following set of training examples:

```
{"from sydney"{ fm=SYD},
"from perth"{fm=PTH},
"to sydney"{to=SYD},
"from perth scotland" {fm=SCT},
"from perth to sydney"{fm=PTH to=SYD}}.
```

At the completion of the alignment phase the hypothesis grammar is as follows:

```
S(SYD -)→from sydney
S(PTH -)→from perth
S(- SYD)→to sydney
S(SCT -)→from perth scotland
S(PTH SYD)→from perth to sydney
X₄₈(SYD -)→sydney
X₄₈(SCT -)→perth scotland
X₄₈(PTH -)→perth
X₄₉(SCT -)→scotland
X₅₀(PTH SYD)→perth to sydney
X₅₁(PTH SYD)→to sydney
```

At the beginning of the substitution phase, the rule "S(SYD -)→from sydney" is examined. The right hand side of this rule is reduced using a typed leftmost reduction as follows from sydney$_{L(\{SYD\})} \Leftarrow^*$ from X_{48}(SYD-). Because the resulting term sequence is not S(SYD-) the rule "S(SYD-)→from X_{48}(SYD-)" is constructed. The right hand side of a rewrite rule cannot contain a constant in a signature therefore the value SYD is replaced by the variable ?fm resulting in the rule "S(?fm-)→from X_{48}(?fm-)". This rule is well-formed therefore it is added to the hypothesis grammar and the rule "S(SYD-) →from sydney" is deleted. The remainder of the rules are similarly examined. At the end of normalisation sub phase all constituents can be parsed using a typed leftmost reduction therefore no rules are added during the completion sub phase. At the completion of the substitution phase, the grammar is as follows:

```
S(?fm -)→from X₄₈(?fm -)
S(?fm ?to)→S(?fm -)S(- ?to)
S(- ?to)→ to X₄₈(?to -)
X₄₈(SYD -)→sydney
X₄₈(PTH -)→perth
X₄₈(?fm -)→perth X₄₉(?fm -)
X₄₉(SCT -)→scotland
X₅₀(?fm ?to)→X₄₈(?fm -)S(- ?to).
```

No non-terminals are merged during the merging phase. During the unchunking phase the non-terminal X_{49} is unchunked. The algorithm then re-enters the substitution phase, because the hypothesis grammar has changed. The algorithm then transitions through the merging, unchunking and catch all stage, without modifying the hypothesis grammar. During the final stage, the non-terminal X_{50} is deleted, and the algorithm returns the grammar shown in Figure 1.

5 Identification in the Limit

A description of a class of unification grammar called Boisdale grammars can be found in Starkie and Fernau [10] along with a proof sketch that the Boisdale algorithm can infer the class of Boisdale grammars in the limit from positive data only. The report Starkie and Fernau [10] also contains a proof that the algorithm can execute in polynomial update time with respect to the size of the training data. A basic ingredient of the identification proof is the following concept.

Definition.
Let C be a set of constituents. A unification grammar G *minimally parses* C if
- the right hand side B of each constituent $c_i = (A(x),B) \in C$ can be reduced to the left hand side A(x) of c using a typed leftmost reduction, i.e.,
  $\forall (A(x),B)\ B_{L(x),G} \Leftarrow^* A(x)$ and
- if any rules are removed from G, then the right hand side of at least one constituent cannot be reduced to the left hand side of that constituent using a typed leftmost reduction.

The report contains the definition of a class of grammar (*typed left-simplex grammar*) such that for each typed left-simplex grammar G, a characteristic set of constituents *characteristic_constituents*(G) can be constructed, such that if any other typed left-simplex grammar H can minimally parse *characteristic_constituents*(G), then G=H. The report also contains a class of unification grammar known as *alignable LL(2) grammars* that have two important properties that enables constituents to be correctly guessed from the a set of sentences by aligning them from the left. The class of *Boisdale grammars* is then defined to be those unification grammars that are both alignable LL(2) grammars and typed left-simplex grammars. It is then shown that for any Boisdale grammar G, a set of characteristic sentences can be constructed such that when these sentences are aligned from the left, the characteristic set of constituents *characteristic_constituents*(G) are recreated. The proof then continues to show that the Boisdale algorithm does not overgeneralise, because all rules that can be incorrectly created during the execution of the algorithm are deleted before the algorithm terminates. Because for all Boisdale grammars there exists a characteristic set of sentences that when presented to the Boisdale algorithm cause the algorithm to reconstruct the original grammar and the fact that the algorithm does not overgeneralise completes the proof that the Boisdale algorithm can identify the class of Boisdale algorithm in the limit from positive data only using the Boisdale algorithm.

The Boisdale algorithm does not enforce the generated grammar to be a Boisdale grammar. This is a deliberate design choice because there exists some training sets for which no Boisdale grammar exists that can generate those sentences (amongst others). Although all Boisdale grammars can be identified in the limit using the Boisdale algorithm and some non-Boisdale grammars can be identified in the limit using the Boisdale grammar, categorising the exact class of grammars that can be identified in the limit using the Boisdale algorithm is an area of future research.

6   Conclusions

This paper introduces the Boisdale algorithm that can identify a class of context-free unification grammars in the limit from positive data only. The Boisdale algorithm infers both the syntax and the semantics of the language. The algorithm executes in polynomial time and can infer a grammar when presented with any set of sentences tagged with any data structure. Determining the exact class of language that can be identified in the limit from positive data using the Boisdale algorithm has not yet been characterised.

The statement that the Boisdale algorithm can infer all Boisdale grammars in the limit from positive data only was empirically tested by creating 400 random grammars, generating characteristic sets of sentences from those grammars, and inferring grammars from the characteristic sets. The inferred grammars were then compared to the target grammars using a tree matching technique. Approximately 150 additional sentences per test where then added to the characteristic set, and the experiment repeated. In all cases, the algorithm inferred the target grammars up to the naming of non-terminals.

References

1. Aho, A. V. and Ullman, J. D., *The theory of parsing, translation, and compiling*, Englewood Cliffs, N.J., Prentice-Hall, 1972.
2. Allen, J., *Natural language understanding*, 2nd ed., Redwood City, Calif., Benjamin/Cummings Pub. Co., 1995.
3. Angluin, D., "Inductive inference of formal grammars from positive data", *Information and Control*, vol. 45, 1980, pp. 117-135.
4. de la Higuera, C. and Oncina, J., "Learning context-free grammars", in Proceedings of ECML Workshop and Tutorial on Learning Context-free Grammars, Cavtat-Dubrovnik Croatia, 2003, pp. 6-19.
5. Gold, E. M., "Grammar identification in the limit", *Information and Control*, vol. 10, no. 5, 1967, pp. 447-474.
6. Otto, F., "On deciding the confluence of a finite string-rewriting system on a given congruence class", *Journal of Computer and System Sciences*, vol. 35, 1987, pp. 285-310.
7. Pereira, F. C. N. and Warren, D. H. D., "Definite clause grammars for language analysis - A survey of the formalism and a comparison with augmented transition networks", *Artificial Intelligence Review*, vol. 13, no. 3, 1980, pp. 231-278.
8. Starkie, B., "Inferring attribute grammars with structured data for natural language processing." in Proceedings of Grammatical Inference: Algorithms and Applications; 6th International Colloquium, ICGI 2002, 2002, pp. 237-248.
9. Starkie, B., "Left aligned grammars - Identifying a class of context-free grammar in the limit from positive data", in Proceedings of ECML Workshop and Tutorial on Learning Context-free Grammars, Cavtat-Dubrovnik Croatia, 2003, pp. 90-101.
10. Starkie, B. and Fernau, H., "The Boisdale algorithm - Identifying a class of unification grammar in the limit from positive data. Addendum A - Proof sketches." University of Newcastle School of Electrical Engineering and Computer Science, Callaghan, NSW Australia 2308 2004.

Learning Stochastic Deterministic Regular Languages

Franck Thollard[1] and Alexander Clark[2]

[1] EURISE,
Jean Monnet University, Saint-Etienne
franck.thollard@univ-st-etienne.fr
[2] ISSCO/TIM, Université de Genève
40 Bvd du Pont d'Arve CH-1211, Genève 4, Switzerland
asc@aclark.demon.co.uk

Abstract. We propose in this article a new practical algorithm for inferring μ-distinguishable stochastic deterministic regular languages. We prove that this algorithm will infer, with high probability, an automaton isomorphic to the target when given a polynomial number of examples. We discuss the links between the error function used to evaluate the inferred model and the learnability of the model class in a PAC like framework.

1 Introduction

Probabilistic automata are compact and efficient devices. They are used in a number of domains including natural language processing [21, 25], speech processing [19, 23, 24] and information retrieval [14, 27].

The increasing amount of data available in different research fields allows the automatic building of these devices. The learnability of Stochastic Deterministic Regular Languages (SDRL) has been studied in the identification in the limit framework. [6] showed that the structure of the target automaton could be identified in the limit with probability one while [9] showed that rational probabilities could be exactly identified. However, the use of these algorithms is still problematic in practice since it is never known if the amount of data available is enough to achieve the identification. For these reasons, we are interested here in a PAC like framework. A subclass of the class of SDRLs has already been studied [22] and the goal here will be the extension of this work to the class of all SDRLs.

Note that some authors have studied machines that define probability distributions over Σ^n or over $\Sigma^{\leq n}$ for a given n [1, 15, 22]. Even if n can be chosen arbitrarily large, these models still define probability distributions over a *finite* set of strings. We study here the inference of probability distributions over $\Sigma^\star$.

The paper is organized as follow. We first present a brief overview of probabilistic grammatical inference and present our new algorithm. We then show that, if enough data is available, the algorithm will infer, with high probability, an automaton isomorphic to the target. We then discuss the link between

G. Paliouras and Y. Sakakibara (Eds.): ICGI 2004, LNAI 3264, pp. 248–259, 2004.
© Springer-Verlag Berlin Heidelberg 2004

the error function used to estimate the quality of the inferred model and the learnability of the model class.

2 Preliminaries

An alphabet Σ is a finite set of symbols. We will denote by $\Sigma^\star$ the free monoid. Symbols from Σ will be denoted by $\sigma_1, \sigma_2, \dots$ and strings from $\Sigma^\star$ by end of alphabet letters (e.g. x, y, z).

A probability distribution over $\Sigma^\star$ (written $\mathcal{D}$) is a function $\Sigma^\star \to [0,1]$ such that $\sum_{x \in \Sigma^\star} \mathrm{Pr}_\mathcal{D}(x) = 1$. A distribution modeled by a machine (e.g. a probabilistic automaton) A, will be written $\mathcal{D}_A$, or A in a non ambiguous context. We will use the L_∞ distance in order to measure the dissimilarity (or similarity) between two distributions: $L_\infty(\mathcal{D}_1, \mathcal{D}_2) = \max_{x \in \Sigma^\star} |\mathrm{Pr}_{\mathcal{D}_1}(x) - \mathrm{Pr}_{\mathcal{D}_2}(x)|$.

The goal here will be the inference of stochastic deterministic regular languages. Even if more general model classes could be inferred (see for example the heuristic techniques of [4] for the learning of Hidden Markov Models or [13] for the learning of residual automata) we prefer the deterministic version for its efficiency at parsing time.

Definition 1. *A* DPFA *is a tuple* $A = \langle Q_A, \Sigma, \delta_A, q_0, F_A, P_A \rangle$, *where:*

- Q_A *is a finite set of* states;
- Σ *is an* alphabet;
- $\delta_A \subseteq Q_A \times \Sigma \times Q_A$ *is a set of* transitions;
- $q_0 \in Q_A$ *is the* initial state;
- $P_A : \delta_A \to (0,1]$ *is the* probability transition function;
- $F_A : Q_A \to [0,1]$ *is the* stopping probability function.

For the automaton to be deterministic, δ_A *must be a function graph, that is*

$$\forall q \in Q_A, \ \forall \ \sigma \ \in \ \Sigma, |\{q' \in Q_A : (q, \sigma, q') \in \delta_A\}| \leq 1 \tag{1}$$

Moreover, the automaton must satisfy the following conditions in order to define a probability distribution: For each state $q \in Q_A$,

$$F_A(q) \ + \sum_{\sigma \in \Sigma, \ q' \in Q_A} P_A(q, \sigma, q') \ = \ 1. \tag{2}$$

Moreover, all accessible states must recognize at least one string of strictly positive probability.

For a given transition $\tau = (q_i, \sigma, q_j)$, state q_i (resp. q_j) will be the origin (resp. the end) of τ. Using deterministic automata, a transition (q_i, σ, q_j) is totally defined by q_i and σ and thus can be equivalently written $(q_i, \sigma, \bullet)$.

A *path* π in a DPFA A is a sequence of transitions $\pi = \tau_1 \tau_2 \dots \tau_n$ with $\tau_i \in \delta_A$. Abusing notation, we will say that the origin (resp. the end) of the path is the origin of its first (resp. its last) transition. We will note $A \overset{x}{\leadsto} q_n$ the path in A that recognizes the string $x = \sigma_1\sigma_2...\sigma_n$ and has q_n as the end of the path; in other words, $A \overset{x}{\leadsto} q_n$ denotes the sequence of transitions $\pi_A(x) = (q_0, \sigma_1, q_1) \ldots (q_{n-1}, \sigma_n, q_n)$ in A.

The probability of a path π will be written $\mathrm{Pr}_A(\pi)$ and computed as follow: $\mathrm{Pr}_A(\pi) = \prod_{\tau_i \in \pi} P_A(\tau_i)$. The probability of a string $x = \sigma_1\sigma_2..\sigma_n$ according to the DPFA A is computed through:

$$\Pr_{\mathcal{D}_A}(x) = \Pr_A(A \overset{x}{\leadsto} q_n) \bullet F_A(q_n) \tag{3}$$

As an example, for $x = ab$, and the DPFA A of figure 1, the path $\pi_A(ab) = (0, a, 1)(1, b, 3)$ has probability $\mathrm{Pr}_A(\pi_A(ab)) = 0.125 \times 0.4$. The probability of the string ab is $\mathrm{Pr}_A(ab) = \mathrm{Pr}_A(\pi_A(ab))F_A(3) = 0.125 \times 0.4 \times 1$.

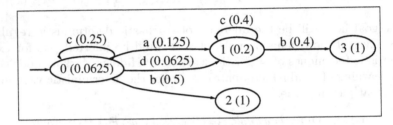

Fig. 1. A DPFA.

As soon as a DPFA A satisfies the conditions (2) it defines a probability distribution over $\Sigma^\star$, that is $\sum_{x \in \Sigma^\star} \mathrm{Pr}_{\mathcal{D}_A}(x) = 1$.

We will note $A_{[q_0 = q_j]}$ the DPFA A in which the initial state has been set to q_j. Note that $A_{[q_0 = q_j]}$ is still a DPFA in that it respects conditions 1 and 2.

Definition 2 (μ-distinguishability). *A* DPFA *A is μ-distinguishable if, for each pair of states q_i, q_j, the distance between distributions $\mathcal{D}_{A_{[q_0=q_i]}}$ and $\mathcal{D}_{A_{[q_0=q_j]}}$ is greater than μ: $\forall\ q_i, q_j \in Q_A$, $L_\infty(\mathcal{D}_{A_{[q_0=q_i]}}, \mathcal{D}_{A_{[q_0=q_j]}}) > \mu$.*

The set of distributions modeled by μ-distinguishable DPFA will be denoted by μ-SDRL. Unless specified, from now, distributions will be a shortcut for μ-SDRL over $\Sigma^\star$.

3   Learning Distributions

While learning a concept, the learner (or the learning algorithm) is given a certain amount of information related to the target concept. In our case, the aim is the approximation of μ-SDRL. Let $\mathcal{D} \in \mu$-SDRL be a distribution and $DRAW_{\mathcal{D}}$ an oracle that, when called, returns an element of $\Sigma^\star$ drawn according to $\mathcal{D}$. $DRAW_{\mathcal{D}}(n)$ will denote the multi-set obtained by n successive calls to $DRAW_{\mathcal{D}}$. Note that $DRAW_{\mathcal{D}}(n)$ produces a multi-set of strings that can be seen as a regular deterministic distribution.

$x^{-1}S$ will be the multi-set obtained from a multi-set S in which the prefix x has been deleted from the strings of S. More formally,

$$x^{-1}S = \{y \in \Sigma^\star : z = xy \wedge z \in S\}_{multi}$$

Having the oracle $DRAW_\mathcal{D}(n)$ is not enough in general to efficiently identify or approximate a target regular distributions $\mathcal{D}$ [1, 15]. More information related to the target concept must be given to the learning process. We now discuss the additional information one wants to provide to the learner.

Σ: Depending on the application, Σ can be given or not. In domain such as continuous speech recognition, an *a priori* vocabulary is given to the learning process. An *ad hoc* technique is used in order to deal with out of vocabulary words. In practice, the size of the vocabulary is a key factor for computational issues. Moreover, [1] showed that the problem of approximating an arbitrary distribution by non-deterministic regular distributions is exponential in the vocabulary size. In parallel, some techniques are used in practice to reduce the vocabulary size [12, 25].

Q_A: The set of states is not given. Nonetheless we give to our algorithm a bound on the size of Q_A. Even if the inference of automata of unbounded number of states has been studied [5, 16, 23, 26], from the practical point of view, a bound on the size is generally known. This bound either comes from domain experts or from computational constraints – large models will not fit in memory or will not be efficient.

δ_A: Describes the structure of the automaton. This function must be inferred from the data. Some authors limit the allowed structures of the model class to allow efficient inference [15, 22]. In the case of learning non deterministic distributions (*e.g.* estimation of Hidden Markov Model) the structure is usually given and the problem reduces to that of estimating the transition probability function.

P_A, F_A: When using maximum likelihood estimate and deterministic machines, these functions are totally defined as soon as δ_A is defined. Nonetheless, while working on real world data, some strings will not be parsed by the model either because they do not belong to the vocabulary[1], or because the model is not general enough. The model must then be smoothed: its probability functions are modified so that a non null probability is provided to each string of $\Sigma^\star$. Although this problem has been studied from its theoretical aspects [18], it has mainly be considered from a practical point of view given its importance for the performance of the final application.

Following [22], we will consider that the target concept will be μ-distinguishable for a given parameter μ. This implies that two states cannot be the same (up to a distance μ) in the model. This constraint can be seen as a constraint on the granularity of the model. Hence we are concerned with the inference of

---

[1] A typical example is encountered in language modeling for speech recognition where proper names often provide out of vocabulary symbols.

probabilistic deterministic μ-distinguishable finite state automata given a bound on the number of states (n), a finite alphabet Σ and an oracle $DRAW$ that provides examples drawn according to the target concept.

4 The Learning Model

The learning model used here is motivated by the ones proposed in [15, 22].

Definition 3 (f-PAC). *Given a class of stochastic languages or distributions C over Σ^*, an algorithm A f-Probably Approximately Correctly (f-PAC)-learns C if there is a polynomial q such that for all c in C, all $\epsilon > 0$ and $\delta > 0$, A is given a sample S_m drawn according to c, and produces a hypothesis H, such that $Pr[f(c, H) > \epsilon] < \delta$ whenever $m > q(1/\epsilon, 1/\delta, |c|)$, where $|c|$ is some measure of the complexity of the class and $f(c, H) \geq 0$ measures a dissimilarity between c and H.*

In our particular case, the complexity of C will be measured by a bound on the number of states of the elements of C and by the distinguishability of the model class. The choice of f will be discussed later in the paper.

5 The ALISA Algorithm

The classic strategy in grammatical inference consists in building a tree shape automaton – called a PPTA for Probabilistic Prefix Tree Acceptor – that is a representation of the maximum likelihood estimate of the data. Then, according to the particular algorithm, two states are chosen. If they are judged equivalent they are merged. The key point consists in deciding whether the states must be merged or not. In [5, 16, 22], the choice is made according to statistical tests applied to the distributions represented by the states (that is the distributions $A_{[q_0=q_j]}$ and $A_{[q_0=q_i]}$ are compared). In [26] a more global criterion is used, based on the analysis of the distribution modeled by the whole model before and after the merge. We follow here [22] and compare the distributions according to the distance L_∞.

The main problems of the above strategy are the following: First it can lead to excessive space requirement. As an example, a PPTA built on the Wall Street Journal database has nearly one million states. As the size of databases naturally increases, and the size of the PPTA grows linearly with the size of the database, problems are inevitable. Secondly, when two states are considered equivalent, they are merged. The resulting state can then be used in other comparisons and other merges. This means that, on the one hand the independence of the statistical tests used is not satisfied and, on the other hand, that a wrong merge will disturb following tests each time the given state will take part in a merge test. For these reasons, we will proceed incrementally: the solution will be built transition by transition[2].

---

[2] Our algorithm can be seen as a modification of the algorithm rlips [6] to guarantee the probable identification of the structure. We nevertheless propose a more algorithmic presentation of the algorithm.

Before the presentation of the algorithm, we provide an extension of the DPFA, the D-DPFA that are DPFA to which a new function that associate a distribution to each state is added.

Definition 4 (D-Dpfa). *A* D-DPFA *is a tuple* $\langle Q_A, \Sigma, \delta_A, q_0, F_A, P_A, S_A \rangle$ *such that* $Q_A, \Sigma, \delta_A, q_0, F_A, P_A$ *define a* DPFA *and* S_A *is a function from* Q_A *to SDRL.*

Algorithm 1 is the pseudo-code of the algorithm ALISA[3] which works in two steps: First the structure is inferred and second the probability functions (transition and final) are estimated.

During the algorithm, the current solution will be a D-DPFA G. At each step of the algorithm (see figure 2 for support of the reading) we aim to create a new transition in G from a state of G (say ν_2 on figure 2). As an example, let us consider the transition $(\nu_2, \sigma, \nu_i) \notin \delta_G$. Let us note x the shorter prefix leading to ν_2 (i.e. $G \overset{x}{\leadsto} \nu_2$). The question now is to identify ν_i. We then consider the DPFA T built from a call to $DRAW_\mathcal{D}(N)$. In T, we find a candidate state cs such that $T \overset{x\sigma}{\leadsto} cs$. On figure 2 the state 2 is the candidate state cs. This state must match the end of the transition we aim to create (here ν_i). In order to find the matching state, we will compare the distribution $T_{[q_0=cs]}$ (represented by $\mathcal{D}_{cs}$ on the figure) with each distribution associated to the states of G, that is the distributions $\mathcal{D}_{\nu_0}, \mathcal{D}_{\nu_1}, \mathcal{D}_{\nu_2}, \mathcal{D}_{\nu_3}$ on the figure[4]. If such a distribution exists, say the distribution associated with ν_3, this means that $\nu_i = \nu_3$. We thus create the transition (ν_2, σ, ν_3). If no state in G matches the candidate state cs, a new state is created in G and the distribution $(x\sigma)^{-1}DRAW_\mathcal{D}(N)$ associated to it.

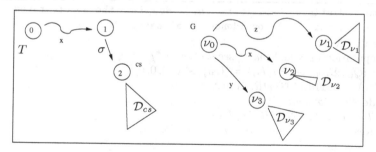

Fig. 2. Adding a new transition in G.

The process is repeated for each relevant[5] state of T. When all the relevant states of T have been considered, there are three possibilities:

1. The user wants a solution: The transition and final probabilities are estimated and G is returned;

---

[3] ALISA stands for Algorithm for Learning Incrementally Stochastic Automata.

[4] Note that another point of view would say that we compare the distributions $\mathcal{D}_{\nu_0}$, $\mathcal{D}_{\nu_1}, \mathcal{D}_{\nu_2}, \mathcal{D}_{\nu_3}$ with the distribution $(x\sigma)^{-1}DRAW_\mathcal{D}(N)$.

[5] The notion of relevance will be made more precise later in this section.

2. The structure of G is a complete graph or G has the required number of states according to the bound on the target number of states: The probabilities are estimated and G is returned;

3. Otherwise, a new sample is drawn and the process is repeated.

We now provide the formal definitions required for the description of the algorithm.

Definition 5 (σ-candidate-state/exit state). *A σ-candidate-state of a DPFA G according to a DPFA T, is a state q_i of T such that: $\exists\ x = \sigma_1...\sigma_n$ and σ such that $T \overset{x\sigma}{\rightsquigarrow} q_i$, $G \overset{x}{\rightsquigarrow} \nu$, and $(\nu, \sigma, \bullet) \notin \delta_G$. The exit state is the target state of the path in G that recognizes x.*

Note that an exit state is totally defined with the σ-candidate state. We will thus consider the exit state associated with a σ-candidate q, written $ES(q)$. On figure 2 state 2 of T is a σ-candidate state and state ν_2 is the exit state associated with the σ-candidate state 2: $ES(2) = \nu_2$.

Definition 6 defines what we mean by *a relevant state*:

Definition 6 (m_0-σ-candidate state). *A σ-candidate state q is a m_0-σ-candidate state if its count is greater than m_0: If $T \overset{x}{\rightsquigarrow} q$, then $|x^{-1}DRAW_{\mathcal{D}}(N)| \geq m_0$.*

Algorithm 1: ALISA.

Data   : distinguishability: μ,   Bound on the nb of states: n, statistical confidence: δ, alphabet: Σ

Result : A DPFA

Computation of N and m_0 /* see section 6 */

$G = \langle Q_G, \Sigma, \delta_G, \nu_0, P_G, F_G \rangle = \langle \{\nu_0\}, \Sigma, \emptyset, 0, 0, 0 \rangle;$

$S_G(\nu_0) \leftarrow \texttt{Build\_PPTA}(DRAW_{\mathcal{D}}(N))$

while *Need to continue* **do**

    $T \leftarrow \texttt{Build\_PPTA}(DRAW_{\mathcal{D}}(N))$

    foreach m_0-σ-candidate state q_{cs} of Q_T **do**

        found $\leftarrow 0$

        foreach state ν of Q_G *and found* $=0$ **do**

            if $L_\infty(T_{[q_0=q_{cs}]}, S_G(\nu)) \leq \mu$ **then**

1

                $\delta_G \leftarrow \delta_G \cup (ES(q_{cs}), \sigma, \nu)$

2

                found $\leftarrow 1$

        if *found* $= 0$ **then**

            /* no node were found similar: creation and link */

            $Q_G \leftarrow Q_G \cup \{\nu'\}$

            $S_G(\nu') \leftarrow T_{[q_0=q_{cs}]}$

            $\delta_G \leftarrow \delta_G \cup (ES(q_{cs}), \sigma, \nu')$

Estimate_Proba (G) /* see section 6.1 */

return G

The comparison of the distributions $T_{[q_0=q_{cs}]}$ and $S(\nu_i)$, $\nu_i \in Q_G$ will be done using the following statistical result:

Lemma 1 ([3], lemma 4) *Let $\mathcal{D}$ be a distribution over Σ^*, and $a > 1$. For sufficiently large values of N, we have*

$$\Pr\left[L_\infty(\mathcal{D}, DRAW_{\mathcal{D}}(N)) \leq \sqrt{6a(\log N)/N}\right] \geq 1 - 4N^{-a}.$$

In order to simplify notation, we will write $I(N) = \sqrt{6a(\log N)/N}$ and $\gamma(N) = 4N^{-a}, a > 1$.

6   Analysis of the Algorithm

Given the distinguishability of the target μ and the confidence parameter δ, we need to define m_0. More precisely, we need to define m_0 such that $I(m_0) \leq \mu/2$ – in order to distinguish μ-distinguishable states – and such that $\gamma(m_0) \leq \delta$ in order to have a sufficiently good confidence in the statistical decisions. The statistical test being applied on independent samples, we need to insure a global confidence δ in order to satisfy the following constraints (with $a > 1$, and m_0 the threshold for a state to be relevant):

$$I(m_0) \leq \mu/2, \qquad (1 - 4m_0^{-a}) \geq \delta \qquad (4)$$

Note that m_0 is polynomial in $\frac{1}{\mu^2}$ since, as $\sqrt{n} \geq \ln(n)$ we have $\frac{\ln(n)}{n} \leq \frac{1}{\sqrt{n}}$ for $n \geq 1$ and thus $m_0 \geq (\frac{24a}{\mu^2})^2$ is enough to satisfy the first constraint.

If m_0 satisfies the above equations, and if N is greater than m_0, then we are sure to produce, with a confidence greater than δ, an automaton isomorphic to the target:

Theorem 1 (G is isomorphic to the target) *If m_0 satisfies equations 4, then, at each time of the algorithm, each state ν of G matches a unique state q of the target C such that*

$$L_\infty(S_G(\nu), C_{[q_0=q]}) \leq \mu/2$$

Let us prove this by induction. At the initial step, the property is true since the unique state of G matches the right state (the initial one) and by lemma 1 the property is true.

Let us suppose now the theorem is true for each state of G and consider q_{cs} a m_0-σ-candidate state of T and q its matching one in the target. Consider now two cases:

1. A state ν in G matches q. Then, by the triangular inequality
    $$L_\infty(T_{[q_0=q_{cs}]}, S_G(\nu)) \leq L_\infty(T_{[q_0=q_{cs}]}, C_{[q_0=q]}) + L_\infty(C_{[q_0=q]}, S_G(\nu)).$$
    Thus, by lemma 1 and the definition of m_0,

    $$L_\infty(T_{[q_0=q_{cs}]}, C_{[q_0=q]}) \leq \mu/2$$

By the inductive hypothesis and because m_0 respects equation 4,
$$L_\infty(C_{[q_0=q]}, S_G(\nu)) \leq \mu/2$$
and thus $L_\infty(T_{[q_0=q_{cs}]}, S_G(\nu)) \leq 2.(\mu/2)$

and the test of line 1 of the algorithm will return true.

2. No state ν of G matches q. Then no state in G will satisfy the line 1 of the algorithm. Indeed, let us consider q' in the target that matches state q_{cs} in T. Then, for each state ν of G, and q its matching state in C, we have:

$$L_\infty(C_{[q_0=q']}, C_{[q_0=q]}) \leq L_\infty(C_{[q_0=q']}, T_{[q_0=q_{cs}]}) +$$
$$L_\infty(T_{[q_0=q_{cs}]}, S_G(\nu)) + L_\infty(S_G(\nu), C_{[q_0=q]})$$

by lemma 1 we have
$$L_\infty(C_{[q_0=q']}, T_{[q_0=q_{cs}]}) \leq \mu/2 \qquad \text{and} \qquad L_\infty(S_G(\nu), C_{[q_0=q]}) \leq \mu/2$$

By the distinguishability of the target, $L_\infty(C_{[q_0=q]}, C_{[q_0=q']}) > \mu/2$
and finally $L_\infty(T_{[q_0=q_{cs}]}, S_G(\nu)) > \mu$
and thus the test of the line 1 will return false for each state ν of G. A new state, say ν_n will be created and the algorithm will associate to it the distribution modeled by $T_{[q_0=q_{cs}]}$ which, by lemma 1 and because m_0 respects equation 4 satisfies $L_\infty(T_{[q_0=q_{cs}]}, C_{[q_0=q]}) \leq \mu/2$.

This shows that at each step of the algorithm the graph G is isomorphic to a subgraph of the target. When the algorithm stops, the automaton produced is isomorphic to the target, either because the target is a complete graph (and the algorithm will stop when the graph is complete) or because it has the required number of states: The automaton cannot have a number of states greater than the number of states of the target since it would require the creation of two states in the automaton matching the same state in the target. □

We have just shown that the algorithm will produce with probability at least δ an automaton isomorphic to the target when given a polynomial number of example. Note here that if N is too small there is the possibility that no m_0-σ-candidate state are available. In order to avoid this problem, we need to sample at least m_0/p with p the probability of having a string that goes through the state: $p = \min_{s \in Q_T} \max_{\pi \in T^x_{\leadsto s}} \Pr_T(\pi)$. Adding p to the measure of the complexity of the model class is reasonable since learning automata with small p should be considered harder that learning ones with great p.

6.1   Estimating the Probabilities

When a new transition (ν, σ, ν_i) is created in G, the probability of this transition can be estimated from the distribution $S_G(\nu)$ which, by construction, holds enough information to provide a good estimate. This probability will be re-estimated later. Indeed, when no state is created, the end of the created transition is an existing state to which a distribution is associated. We can at that point add a new line (after the line numbered 2 in the algorithm) that will perform the merging of the distributions $T_{[q_0=q_{cs}]}$ and $S(\nu)$. The estimate of $S(\nu)$ will then be based on a greater amount of data and thus be more accurate.

6.2   f-PAC Learnability Issues

If we consider learning under the identification in the limit with probability one framework, we can use the technique of [9] which provides the identification in the limit of rational probabilities.

Let us now consider the more interesting f-PAC learning model where the measure of the complexity of the model class (written $|c|$ in the definition of the learning model) is expressed by $\frac{1}{\mu}$ and perhaps also by $\frac{1}{p}$.

When considering the choice of f, a link can be made with the non probabilistic case. Indeed, in the classic PAC framework, some negative results have been bypassed by restricting the class of the distributions from which the samples were drawn. This is true in particular with the regular languages that cannot be learned under the distribution free framework but where positive results exist when restrictions are provided on the distributions [20].

When considering the probabilistic case, the samples are drawn according to the target distribution. We are not yet in a distribution free framework. Nonetheless the difficulty of the learning can be expressed by the measure used to compare the inferred model and the target: When considering the distance L_∞ a simple maximum likelihood estimate is enough to guarantee the quality of the learning: According to Lemma 1, an algorithm that returns $DRAW_D(N)$ will be L_∞-PAC. Worse is the fact that an algorithm that just estimates the strings of probability greater than ε (according to the target) will learn under the L_∞-PAC model. Thus, the L_∞-PAC model is not a good one.

It is much harder to learn when the Kullback-Leibler divergence [8] is used as the quality measure. From the theoretical point of view, such a measure requires that the inferred model is close to the target for all strings, including the low probability ones. Even if this constraint is strong – in that an error on a low probability string can lead to a big value of the divergence – this is the one generally chosen while adapting the PAC framework to the probabilistic case [15, 18, 22]. From the practical point of view, the estimate of low probability strings is a key point in many applications such as speech recognition. The theoretical study of the smoothing is beyond the scope of this article. The interested reader can consider the theoretical works [18, 22], or more practical ones [11, 24, 17].

As a conclusion for this section, when considering n, Σ, μ, δ, and the oracle $DRAW_D$, our algorithm provides an automaton isomorphic to the target with probability δ. When considering a theoretical guarantee of the quality of the final model, the choice of error function must be taken into account. If such a function is the L_∞ distance a simple estimation using the maximum likelihood estimate of the probabilities suffices to guarantee the quality of the model (using Chernoff bounds). If the error is measured using the Kullback-Leibler divergence a deeper analysis is needed in order to take into account the low probability strings. From our opinion, the second framework is more appropriate given the practical importance of smoothing in real world applications. We have elsewhere shown [7] that such learning is possible.

7   Algorithm Complexity

At each state of the algorithm (loop on m_0-σ-candidate states) we consider adding a transition. This step is bounded by $n \times |\Sigma|$. For each of these candidate states, a state of G is considered. There are no more such state than the number of states in the target. The distance L_∞ is thus computed at most $n^2 \times |\Sigma|$. This computation is at most linear in the size of the sets $T_{[q_0=q_{cs}]}$ and $S_G(\nu)$, that is bounded by m_0. The overall complexity of the algorithm is then $n^2 \times |\Sigma| \times m_0$. Note that according to its definition (equation 4) m_0 is polynomial in $1/\mu$ and $1/\delta$. Moreover, n is here the bound on the number of states of the *target* and not the size of the learning sample. The classic algorithms [5, 16, 26] are quadratic in the sample size. Here we are quadratic in the size of the *target* which is supposed to be much smaller.

8   Conclusion and Further Work

We have presented here a grammatical inference algorithm. This algorithm solves some of the classic problems of the most popular algorithms, since the independence of the statistical test is guaranteed and we have a clear sample complexity bound. Moreover, the algorithm is incremental (in that it does not proceed all the data at a time) and can be easily parallelized. From the theoretical point of view, we showed that this algorithm will infer, with high probability, an automaton isomorphic to the target using a polynomial amount of data. This result extends the one of [6] to a PAC like paradigm. The natural further work is the empirical comparison of the algorithm with other algorithms on natural data sets. Preliminary experiments on the Wall Street Journal database show that the ALISA algorithm is much faster in practice than some state merging algorithm [26].

References

1. N. Abe and W. Warmuth. On the computational complexity of approximating distributions by probabilistic automata. In *Wshop on COLT*, pages 52–66, 1998.
2. P. Adriaans, H. Fernau, and M. van Zaannen, editors. *ICGI '02*, volume 2484 of *LNCS*, Berlin, Heidelberg, 2002. Springer-Verlag.
3. D. Angluin. Identifying languages from stochastic examples. Technical Report YALEU/ DCS/RR-614, Yale University, Dept. of Computer Science, 1988.
4. Thorsten Brants. Estimating Markov model structures. In *ICSLP-96*, 1996.
5. R. C. Carrasco and J. Oncina. Learning stochastic regular grammars by means of a state merging method. In *ICGI'94*, pages 139–152, 1994.
6. R. C. Carrasco and J. Oncina. Learning deterministic regular grammars from stochastic samples in polynomial time. *Theoretical Informatics and Applications*, 33(1):1–20, 1999.
7. A. Clark and F. Thollard. PAC-learnability of probabilistic deterministic finite state automata. *Jrl of Machine Learning Research*, 5:473–497, May 2004.
8. Thomas M. Cover and Joy A. Thomas. *Elements of Information Theory*. Wiley Interscience Publication, 1991.

9. C de la Higuera and F. Thollard. Identification in the limit with probability one of stochastic deterministic finite automata. In de Oliveira [10].

10. A. de Oliveira, editor. *ICGI '00*, volume 1891 of *LNCS*, Berlin, Heidelberg, 2000. Springer-Verlag.

11. P. Dupont. Smoothing probabilistic automata: an error-correcting approach. In de Oliveira [10], pages 51–64.

12. P. Dupont and L. Chase. Using symbol clustering to improve probabilistic automaton inference. In *ICGI'98*, pages 232–243, 1998.

13. Y. Esposito, A. Lemay, F. Denis, and P. Dupont. Learning probabilistic residual finite state automata. In Adriaans et al. [2], pages 77–91.

14. D. Freitag. Using grammatical inference to improve precision in information extraction. In *Workshop on Grammatical Inference, Automata Induction, and Language Acquisition*, 1997.

15. M.J. Kearns, Y. Mansour, D. Ron, R. Rubinfeld, R.E. Schapire, and L. Sellie. On the learnability of discrete distributions. In *Proc. of the 25th Annual ACM Symposium on Theory of Computing*, pages 273–282, 1994.

16. C. Kermorvant and P. Dupont. Stochastic grammatical inference with multinomial tests. In Adriaans et al. [2], pages 149–160.

17. D. Llorens, J. M. Vilar, and F. Casacuberta. Finite state language models smoothed using n-grams. *Int. Jrnl of Pattern Recognition and Artificial Intelligence*, 16(3):275–289, 2002.

18. D. McAllester and R. Shapire. On the convergence rate of the good-turing estimators. In *Thirteenth Annual Conf. on COLT*, pages 1–66, 2000.

19. M. Mohri, F. Pereira, and M. Riley. Weighted automata in text and speech processing. In *Workshop on Extended Finite-State Models of Language*, 1996.

20. R. Parekh and H. Honavar. Learning DFA from simple examples. In *International Coloquium on Machine Lerning, ICML97*, 1997.

21. F. Pla, A. Molina, and N. Prieto. An Integrated Statistical Model for Tagging and Chunking Unrestricted Text. In P. Sojka, I. Kopeček, and K. Pala, editors, *Intl. Workshop on Text, Speech and Dialogue*, LNCS/LNAI 1902, pages 15–20, 2000.

22. D. Ron, Y. Singer, and N. Tishby. On the learnability and usage of acyclic probabilistic finite automata. In *COLT 1995*, pages 31–40, USA, 1995. ACM.

23. A. Stolcke. *Bayesian Learning of Probabilistic Language Models*. PhD thesis, Dept. of Electrical Engineering and Computer Science, University of California at Berkeley, 1994.

24. F. Thollard. Improving probabilistic grammatical inference core algorithms with post-processing techniques. In *ICML*, pages 561–568, 2001.

25. F. Thollard and A. Clark. Shallow parsing using probabilistic grammatical inference. In Adriaans et al. [2], pages 269–282.

26. F. Thollard, P. Dupont, and C. de la Higuera. Probabilistic DFA inference using Kullback-Leibler divergence and minimality. In Pat Langley, editor, *ICML*, 2000.

27. M. Young-Lai and F. WM. Tompa. Stochastic grammatical inference of text database structure. *Machine Learning*, 40(2):111–137, 2000.

Polynomial Time Identification of Strict Deterministic Restricted One-Counter Automata in Some Class from Positive Data*

Mitsuo Wakatsuki, Kiyoshi Teraguchi, and Etsuji Tomita

Department of Information and Communication Engineering,
The University of Electro-Communications,
Chofugaoka 1–5–1, Chofu-shi, Tokyo, 182–8585 Japan
{wakatuki,terakiyo,tomita}@ice.uec.ac.jp

Abstract. A deterministic pushdown automaton (dpda) having just one stack symbol is called a *deterministic restricted one-counter automaton* (*droca*). When it accepts by empty stack, it is called *strict*. This paper is concerned with a subclass of real-time strict droca's called *Szilard strict droca*'s. The class of languages accepted by Szilard strict droca's is incomparable to both the class of regular languages and that of simple languages. We show that the class of Szilard strict droca's is polynomial time identifiable in the limit from positive data in the sense of Yokomori. This identifiability is proved by giving an exact *characteristic sample* of polynomial size for a language accepted by a Szilard strict droca. The class of very simple languages is also proved to be polynomial time identifiable in the limit from positive data by Yokomori, but it is still unknown whether there exists a characteristic sample of polynomial size for any very simple language.

1 Introduction

In the study of inductive inference of formal languages, Gold [4] defined the notion of *identification in the limit* and showed that the class of languages containing all finite sets and one infinite set, which is called a *superfinite* class, is not identifiable in the limit from *positive data*. This means that even the class of regular languages is not identifiable in the limit from positive data. Angluin [1] has given several conditions for a class of languages to be identifiable in the limit from positive data, and has presented some examples of identifiable classes. She has also proposed subclasses of regular languages called k-reversible languages for each $k \geq 0$, and has shown that these classes are identifiable in the limit from positive data, requiring a polynomial time for updating conjectures [2].

From the practical point of view, the inductive inference algorithm must have a good *time efficiency* in addition to running with only positive data. One may

* This work has been supported in part by Grant-in-Aid for Scientific Research Nos. 13680435 and 16300001 from the Ministry of Education, Culture, Sports, Science and Technology of Japan.

G. Paliouras and Y. Sakakibara (Eds.): ICGI 2004, LNAI 3264, pp. 260–272, 2004.

define the notion of *polynomial time identification in the limit* in various ways. Pitt [7] has proposed a reasonable definition for polynomial time identifiability in the limit. By making a slight modification of his definition, Yokomori [9] has proposed another definition for polynomial time identifiability in the limit from positive data, and has proved that the class of very simple languages, which is a proper subclass of simple languages, is polynomial time identifiable in the limit from positive data.

This paper deals with a subclass of automata called *Szilard strict deterministic restricted one-counter automata* (*Szilard strict droca's* for short), which are deterministic pushdown automata having just one stack symbol and exactly one transition rule for each input symbol, and discusses the identification problem of the class of Szilard strict droca's. The class of languages accepted by Szilard strict droca's forms a proper subclass of real-time strict deterministic restricted one-counter languages ([5]) and coincides with the class of Szilard languages [6] (or, associated languages) of strict droca's. Furthermore, this class of languages is incomparable to both the class of regular languages and that of simple languages, and is also incomparable to both the class of zero-reversible languages and that of very simple languages. Since a Szilard strict droca has more than one state in general, the class of languages accepted by Szilard strict droca's partially exceeds the ability of not only very simple languages but also simple languages. Note, however, that a Szliard strict droca may have *dead* configurations, and then there may occur some difficulties to identify it.

After providing some properties of languages accepted by Szilard strict droca's, we show that the class of Szilard strict droca's is polynomial time identifiable in the limit from positive data in the sense of Yokomori. The main result in this paper provides another interesting instance of a context-free language class containing nonregular languages which is polynomial time identifiable in the limit. This identifiability is proved by giving an exact *characteristic sample* of polynomial size for a language accepted by a Szilard strict droca, while for the class of very simple languages it is still unknown whether there exist polynomial-sized characteristic samples for these languages.

2 Definitions

We assume that the reader is familiar with the basics of automata and formal language theory. Our definitions and notation are based on [5] and [8].

Definition 1. *A deterministic pushdown automaton (dpda for short) which accepts by empty stack is denoted by* $M = (Q, \Gamma, \Sigma, \delta, q_0, Z_0, \emptyset)$, *where Q is the finite set of states, Γ is the finite set of stack symbols, Σ is the finite set of input symbols, δ is the finite set of transition rules, q_0 is the initial state, Z_0 is the initial stack symbol, and the last empty symbol $\emptyset$ stands for acceptance by empty stack. A dpda which accepts by empty stack is also called a strict dpda. We denote an empty string in Γ^* or Σ^* by ε.*

The set δ of transition rules is a set of rules of the form $(p, A) \xrightarrow{a} (q, \theta)$ with $p, q \in Q$, $A \in \Gamma$, $\theta \in \Gamma^*$, $a \in \Sigma \cup \{\varepsilon\}$, that satisfies the following conditions: (i)

If $(p, A) \xrightarrow{a} (q, \theta)$ with $a \in \Sigma \cup \{\varepsilon\}$ is in δ, then no rule of the form $(p, A) \xrightarrow{a} (r, \gamma)$ is in δ for any $(r, \gamma) \neq (q, \theta)$, (ii) If $(p, A) \xrightarrow{\varepsilon} (q, \theta)$ is in δ, then $\theta = \varepsilon$ and no rule of the form $(p, A) \xrightarrow{a} (r, \gamma)$ is in δ for any $a \in \Sigma$, $r \in Q$, $\gamma \in \Gamma^*$.

For the set δ, define $\mathcal{P} = \mathrm{Max}\{\, \mathrm{Max}\{|\theta| \mid (p, A) \xrightarrow{a} (q, \theta) \in \delta\},\, 1\}$. Here, for a string α, $|\alpha|$ denotes the length of α. Furthermore, for a set S, $|S|$ denotes the cardinality of S.

Such a rule as $(p, A) \xrightarrow{\varepsilon} (q, \varepsilon)$ is called an ε-rule. A dpda is said to be real-time if it has no ε-rules.

Definition 2. A strict dpda M is said to be a deterministic restricted one-counter automaton (droca for short) if $\Gamma = \{Z_0\}$. (Cf. [3, p.201].)

Definition 3. A configuration $c = (p, \alpha)$ of the dpda M is an element of $Q \times \Gamma^*$, where the leftmost symbol of α is the top symbol on the stack. In particular, (q_0, Z_0) is called the initial configuration. The height of $c = (p, \alpha)$ is $|\alpha|$.

Definition 4. The dpda M makes a move $(p, A\omega) \xrightarrow[M]{a} (q, \theta\omega)$ from one configuration to another for any $\omega \in \Gamma^*$, iff δ contains a rule $(p, A) \xrightarrow{a} (q, \theta)$ with $a \in \Sigma \cup \{\varepsilon\}$. A sequence of such moves through successive configurations as $(p_1, \alpha_1) \xrightarrow[M]{a_1} (p_2, \alpha_2)$, $(p_2, \alpha_2) \xrightarrow[M]{a_2} (p_3, \alpha_3)$, ..., $(p_m, \alpha_m) \xrightarrow[M]{a_m} (p_{m+1}, \alpha_{m+1})$ $(\alpha_i \neq \varepsilon$ and $a_i \in \Sigma \cup \{\varepsilon\}$ for $1 \leq i \leq m)$ is called a derivation, and is written as $(p_1, \alpha_1) \xrightarrow[M]{x} (p_{m+1}, \alpha_{m+1})$, where $x = a_1 a_2 \cdots a_m$.

Definition 5. For a configuration (p, α) of the strict dpda M, define $N(p, \alpha) = \{w \in \Sigma^* \mid (p, \alpha) \xrightarrow[M]{w} (q, \varepsilon)$ for some $q \in Q\}$. A configuration (p, α) is said to be live if $N(p, \alpha) \neq \emptyset$. Otherwise, it is said to be dead.

Moreover, the language accepted by M is defined to be $L(M) = N(q_0, Z_0)$, where (q_0, Z_0) is the initial configuration of M.

Definition 6. Let (p, α) be a configuration of the strict dpda M. Then, if $N(p, \alpha) \neq \{\varepsilon\}$, define $\mathrm{FIRST}(p, \alpha) = \{a \in \Sigma \mid (p, \alpha) \xrightarrow[M]{a} (q, \beta)$ for some $(q, \beta) \in Q \times \Gamma^*\}$. Otherwise (i.e., $N(p, \alpha) = \{\varepsilon\}$), define $\mathrm{FIRST}(p, \alpha) = \{\varepsilon\}$.

Moreover, define $\mathrm{EMP}(p, \alpha) = \{q \in Q \mid (p, \alpha) \xrightarrow[M]{w} (q, \varepsilon)$ for some $w \in \Sigma^*\}$.

In this paper, we adopt Yokomori's definition in [9] for the notion of polynomial time identification in the limit from positive data.

For any class of languages to be identified, let $\mathcal{R}$ be a class of representations for the class of languages. Instances of such representations are automata, grammars, and so on. Given an r in $\mathcal{R}$, $L(r)$ denotes the language represented by r. A positive presentation of $L(r)$ is any infinite sequence of data such that every $w \in L(r)$ occurs at least once in the sequence and no other string not in $L(r)$ appears in the sequence. Each element of $L(r)$ is called a positive example (or simply, example) of $L(r)$.

Let r be a representation in $\mathcal{R}$. An algorithm $\mathcal{A}$ is said to identify r in the limit from positive data iff $\mathcal{A}$ takes any positive presentation of $L(r)$ as an input, and outputs an infinite sequence of r_i's in $\mathcal{R}$ such that there exist r' in $\mathcal{R}$ and $j > 0$ so that for all $i \geq j$, the i-th conjecture (representation) r_i is identical to r' and $L(r') = L(r)$. A class $\mathcal{R}$ is *identifiable in the limit from positive data* iff there exists an algorithm $\mathcal{A}$ that, for any r in $\mathcal{R}$, identifies r in the limit from positive data.

Let $\mathcal{A}$ be an algorithm for identifying $\mathcal{R}$ in the limit from positive data. Suppose that after examining i examples, the algorithm $\mathcal{A}$ conjectures some r_i. We say that $\mathcal{A}$ makes an *implicit error of prediction* at step i if r_i is not consistent with the $(i+1)$-st example w_{i+1}, i.e., if $w_{i+1} \notin L(r_i)$.

Definition 7. *A class $\mathcal{R}$ is* polynomial time identifiable in the limit from positive data *iff there exists an algorithm $\mathcal{A}$ for identifying $\mathcal{R}$ in the limit from positive data with the property that there exist polynomials p and q such that for any n, for any r of size n, and for any positive presentation of $L(r)$, the number of implicit errors of prediction made by $\mathcal{A}$ is at most $p(n)$, and the time used by $\mathcal{A}$ between receiving the i-th example w_i and outputting the i-th conjecture r_i is at most $q(n, \sum_{j=1}^{i} |w_j|)$, where the size of r is the length of a description for r.*

3   Szilard Strict DROCA's and Their Languages

For any strict dpda, the next lemma immediately follows from Definition 5.

Lemma 1. *Let $M = (Q, \Gamma, \Sigma, \delta, q_0, Z_0, \emptyset)$ be a strict dpda. (i) [Prefix-free property] For any $x \in \Sigma^*$ and $y \in \Sigma^+$, if $x \in L(M)$, then $xy \notin L(M)$. (ii) If $N(p, \alpha) = \emptyset$ for some $(p, \alpha) \in Q \times \Gamma^+$, then $N(p, \alpha\beta) = \emptyset$ for any $\beta \in \Gamma^*$.*

Now, let $M = (Q, \Gamma, \Sigma, \delta, q_0, Z_0, \emptyset)$, where $\Gamma = \{Z_0\}$, be a strict droca.

Lemma 2. *Let (p, α) be a configuration of some strict droca M. If $N(p, \alpha) \neq \emptyset$ with $|\alpha| \geq |Q|$, then $N(p, \beta) \neq \emptyset$ for any $\beta \in \Gamma^*$.*

Proof. It is clear because $\Gamma = \{Z_0\}$. (See [5, Lemma 3.1] for the details.)   □

From Lemma 1 (ii) and Lemma 2, we can construct a checking procedure whether any configuration $(p, \alpha) \in Q \times \Gamma^*$ of a given strict droca M is *live* or not since it suffices to examine all configurations whose height is at most $|Q| + \mathcal{P}$. Then, the worst-case time complexity of this procedure is polynomial with respect to the size (i.e., the length of its description) of M. This procedure is used for constructing a characteristic derivation tree as shown in Fig. 1.

Definition 8. *A real-time strict droca, that is, a dpda which accepts by empty stack having just one stack symbol Z_0 and having no ε-rules is called a* Szilard *(real-time) strict droca iff for every $a \in \Sigma$, there exists exactly one transition rule of the form $(p, Z_0) \xrightarrow{a} (q, \theta)$ $(p, q \in Q, \theta \in \Gamma^*)$ in δ. Such a rule of the form $(p, Z_0) \xrightarrow{a} (q, \theta)$ for each $a \in \Sigma$ is called an* a-transition rule.

Hereafter, we are concerned with Szilard strict droca's M such that $L(M) \neq \emptyset$.

Example 1. Consider a real-time strict droca $M = (\{q_0, q_1, q_2, q_3\}, \{Z_0\}, \{a_1, a_2, a_3, a_4, a_5\}, \delta, q_0, Z_0, \emptyset)$, where $\delta = \{(q_0, Z_0) \overset{a_1}{\to}(q_1, Z_0), (q_1, Z_0) \overset{a_2}{\to}(q_1, Z_0^2), (q_1, Z_0) \overset{a_3}{\to}(q_2, Z_0), (q_2, Z_0) \overset{a_4}{\to}(q_3, \varepsilon), (q_3, Z_0) \overset{a_5}{\to}(q_3, \varepsilon)\}$. The automaton M is a Szilard strict droca and $L(M) = \{a_1\, a_2^i\, a_3\, a_4\, a_5^i \mid i \geq 0\}$ which is nonregular.

Definition 9. *Let $M' = (Q', \Gamma', \Sigma', \delta', q_0', Z_0', \emptyset)$, where $\Gamma' = \{Z_0'\}$, be a strict droca whose transition rules are uniquely labeled by the symbols of a set C. If a transition rule $(p, Z_0') \overset{a}{\to}(q, \alpha)$ $(p, q \in Q', a \in \Sigma' \cup \{\varepsilon\}, \alpha \in \Gamma'^*)$ is associated with a label $\rho \in C$, we write $\rho : (p, Z_0') \overset{a}{\to}(q, \alpha)$. If a sequence $\sigma = \rho_1 \rho_2 \cdots \rho_n$ $(n \geq 1)$ of labeled transition rules $\rho_i : (p_i, Z_0') \overset{a_i}{\to}(q_i, \alpha_i)$ $(\rho_i \in C, p_i, q_i \in Q', a_i \in \Sigma' \cup \{\varepsilon\}, \alpha_i \in \Gamma'^*)$ for $1 \leq i \leq n$ is applied in a derivation $(r, \beta) \underset{M'}{\overset{x}{\Longrightarrow}}(s, \gamma)$ for some $r, s \in Q', \beta, \gamma \in \Gamma'^*$ with $x = a_1 a_2 \cdots a_n \in \Sigma'^*$, we write $(r, \beta) \underset{M'}{\overset{x}{\Longrightarrow}}{}^{[\sigma]}(s, \gamma)$. The Szilard language [6] (or, associated language) $\text{Sz}(M')$ of M' is defined as $\text{Sz}(M') = \{\sigma \in C^* \mid (q_0', Z_0') \underset{M'}{\overset{w}{\Longrightarrow}}{}^{[\sigma]}(q, \varepsilon) \text{ for some } w \in L(M'), q \in Q'\}$.*

Example 2. Consider a strict droca $M' = (\{p_0, p_1, p_2, p_3\}, \{Z_0'\}, \{a, b\}, \delta', p_0, Z_0', \emptyset)$ associated with a set of labels $\{a_1, a_2, a_3, a_4, a_5\}$, where $\delta' = \{a_1 : (p_0, Z_0') \overset{a}{\to}(p_1, Z_0'), a_2 : (p_1, Z_0') \overset{a}{\to}(p_1, Z_0'^2), a_3 : (p_1, Z_0') \overset{b}{\to}(p_2, Z_0'), a_4 : (p_2, Z_0') \overset{\varepsilon}{\to}(p_3, \varepsilon), a_5 : (p_3, Z_0') \overset{b}{\to}(p_3, \varepsilon)\}$. Then, $L(M') = \{a^i\, b^i \mid i \geq 1\}$ and $\text{Sz}(M') = \{a_1\, a_2^i\, a_3\, a_4\, a_5^i \mid i > 0\}$. It is easily seen that this Szilard language of M' is the same as the language accepted by the Szilard strict droca M in Example 1.

Generalizing the facts in Examples 1 and 2, we can prove the following theorem.

Theorem 1. *The class of Szilard strict droca's forms a proper subclass of real-time strict droca's and the class of languages accepted by Szilard strict droca's coincides with the class of Szilard languages of strict droca's.*

The next lemma immediately follows from the definition of a Szilard strict droca.

Lemma 3. *Let $M = (Q, \Gamma, \Sigma, \delta, q_0, Z_0, \emptyset)$, where $\Gamma = \{Z_0\}$, be a Szilard strict droca and let $w, w_1, w_2 \in L(M)$. Then, for each $a, b, c \in \Sigma$, the followings hold. (1) If $w = ax$ for some $x \in \Sigma^*$, then the a-transition rule is of the form $(q_0, Z_0) \overset{a}{\to}(p, \alpha)$ for some $p \in Q, \alpha \in \Gamma^*$. (2) If $w = xa$ for some $x \in \Sigma^*$, then the a-transition rule is of the form $(p, Z_0) \overset{a}{\to}(q, \varepsilon)$ for some $p, q \in Q$. (3) If $a^n \in N(p, \beta)$ for some $p \in Q, \beta \in \Gamma^+, n > 1$, then $\beta = Z_0^n$ and the a-transition rule is of the form $(p, Z_0) \overset{a}{\to}(p, \varepsilon)$. (4) If $w_1 = xby_1$ and $w_2 = xcy_2$ for some $x, y_1, y_2 \in \Sigma^*$, then there exist $p, q_1, q_2 \in Q$ and $\alpha_1, \alpha_2 \in \Gamma^*$ such that $(p, Z_0) \overset{b}{\to}(q_1, \alpha_1)$ and $(p, Z_0) \overset{c}{\to}(q_2, \alpha_2)$ are in δ.*

For a language L over Σ and $x \in \Sigma^*$, let $x \backslash L = \{y \mid xy \in L\}$. The following lemma comes from the definition of a Szilard strict droca and Lemma 3.

Lemma 4. *Let $M = (Q, \Gamma, \Sigma, \delta, q_0, Z_0, \emptyset)$, where $\Gamma = \{Z_0\}$, be a Szilard strict droca and let $p, p', q, q' \in Q, \alpha, \alpha' \in \Gamma^+, \beta, \beta' \in \Gamma^*, x \in \Sigma^+, u_1, u_2 \in \Sigma^*$. Then, the followings hold. (1) [Forward determinism] If $(q_0, Z_0) \underset{M}{\overset{x}{\Longrightarrow}}(p, \beta)$ and*

$(q_0, Z_0) \xRightarrow[M]{x} (p', \beta')$, then $p = p'$ and $\beta = \beta'$. (2) [Backward determinism] If
$(p, \alpha) \xRightarrow[M]{x} (q, \varepsilon)$ and $(p', \alpha') \xRightarrow[M]{x} (q', \varepsilon)$, then $p = p', q = q'$ and $\alpha = \alpha'$. (3) If
$(p, \alpha) \xRightarrow[M]{x} (q, \beta)$ and $(p', \alpha') \xRightarrow[M]{x} (q', \beta')$, then $p = p', q = q'$ and $|\alpha| - |\beta| =$
$|\alpha'| - |\beta'|$. (4) If $(q_0, Z_0) \xRightarrow[M]{u_1} (p, \alpha) \xRightarrow[M]{x} (q, \varepsilon)$ and $(q_0, Z_0) \xRightarrow[M]{u_2} (p', \alpha') \xRightarrow[M]{x} (q', \varepsilon)$,
then $u_1 \backslash L(M) = u_2 \backslash L(M)$.

For a string $w \in \Sigma^*$, alph(w) denotes the set of symbols appearing in w. For a language L, let alph(L) $= \cup_{w \in L}$alph(w). The following lemma is important for our later discussion.

Lemma 5. *Let* $M_i = (Q_i, \Gamma_i, \Sigma_i, \delta_i, q_{0i}, Z_{0i}, \emptyset)$, *where* $\Gamma_i = \{Z_{0i}\}$, $\Sigma_i = $ alph($L($ M_i)) $(i = 1, 2)$ *and* $\Sigma_1 \subseteq \Sigma_2$, *be two Szilard strict droca's. If* $L(M_1) \subset L(M_2)$, *then for any* $w \in L(M_2) - L(M_1)$, *it is impossible to have* $(q_{01}, Z_{01}) \xRightarrow[M_1]{w} (p, \alpha)$ *for any* $p \in Q_1, \alpha \in \Gamma_1^*$.

Proof. Since $\Sigma_1 = $ alph($L(M_1)$), it follows from Lemma 1 and Lemma 4 (3). $\square$

Finally, we can easily make a characterization on the relationships among the class of languages accepted by Szilard strict droca's and the classes of regular, zero-reversible, simple, and very simple languages. A regular language L is *zero-reversible* iff whenever $u_1 x$ and $u_2 x$ are in L, it holds that $u_1 \backslash L = u_2 \backslash L$ [2]. For a context-free grammar $G = (N, \Sigma, P, S)$ in Greibach normal form, G is said to be *very simple* iff for each $a \in \Sigma$, there exists exactly one production whose right-hand side is of the form $a\alpha$ $(\alpha \in N^*)$ in P [9]. A language L is *very simple* iff there exists a very simple grammar G such that $L = L(G)$.

Let $\mathcal{L}_{SS}$, $\mathcal{L}_{VS}$, and $\mathcal{L}_{ZR}$ be the class of languages accepted by Szilard strict droca's, the class of very simple languages, and the class of zero-reversible languages, respectively. A context-free (nonregular) language $\{a^i b d^i \mid i \geq 0\} \cup \{a^i c e^i \mid i \geq 0\}$ is in $\mathcal{L}_{SS}$ but is not simple. Therefore, this language is neither in $\mathcal{L}_{ZR}$ nor in $\mathcal{L}_{VS}$. On the other hand, a language $\{abcbd\} \in \mathcal{L}_{ZR}$ is in $\mathcal{L}_{VS}$ but is not in $\mathcal{L}_{SS}$. From these results, the next theorem immediately follows.

Theorem 2. *The class of languages accepted by Szilard strict droca's is incomparable to both the class of simple languages and that of regular languages. Furthermore, this class of languages is also incomparable to both the class of very simple languages and that of zero-reversible languages.*

4   Identifying Szilard Strict DROCA's

4.1   An Automaton Schema and Its Interpretation

In a similar way to [9], we introduce a new representation method for Szilard strict droca's called *automaton schemata*. Any Szilard strict droca can be analyzed and decomposed into two constructs: an automaton schema and its interpretation.

Given a finite alphabet Σ, let $V_Q = \{p_a, \bar{p}_a \mid a \in \Sigma\} \cup \{q_0\}$ and let $PAR \, (= \{\theta_a \mid a \in \Sigma\})$ be a finite set of *parameters*, where q_0 is a specific symbol not in $\{p_a, \bar{p}_a \mid a \in \Sigma\} \cup \Sigma \cup PAR$, and the value of each parameter ranges over all elements in $\{Z_0\}^*$. Then, a construct $(p_a, Z_0) \overset{a}{\to} (\bar{p}_a, \theta_a)$, where $p_a, \bar{p}_a \in V_Q, a \in \Sigma$ and $\theta_a \in PAR$, is called a *transition rule form*. We call a 7-tuple $\mathcal{M} = (V_Q, \{Z_0\}, \Sigma, \Delta, q_0, Z_0, \emptyset)$ an *automaton schema* if Δ is a finite set of transition rule forms.

An *interpretation* $I = (f_s, f_p)$ over Σ is an ordered pair of mappings, where f_s is a coding defined on V_Q with $f_s(q_0) = q_0$, and f_p is a homomorphism defined on PAR such that for all $\theta \in PAR$, $f_p(\theta) \in \{Z_0\}^*$. Then, given an automaton schema $\mathcal{M}$, let $I(\mathcal{M})$ be a 7-tuple defined by $(I(V_Q), \{Z_0\}, \Sigma, I(\Delta), q_0, Z_0, \emptyset)$, where $I(V_Q) = \{f_s(p) \mid p \in V_Q\}$ and $I(\Delta) = \{(f_s(p), Z_0) \overset{a}{\to} (f_s(\bar{p}), f_p(\theta)) \mid (p, Z_0) \overset{a}{\to} (\bar{p}, \theta) \in \Delta, p, \bar{p} \in V_Q, a \in \Sigma, \theta \in PAR\}$. Thus, I induces a mapping on the set of all automaton schemata.

Now, we consider the following problem for Szilard strict droca's. Suppose that we are given a finite set of strings $R = \{w_1, w_2, \ldots, w_i\}$ from an unknown language L accepted by a certain Szilard strict droca M_* such that $L = L(M_*)$. Starting with constructing an initial automaton schema $\mathcal{M}_0 = (V_Q, \{Z_0\}, \Sigma, \{(p_a, Z_0) \overset{a}{\to} (\bar{p}_a, \theta_a) \mid a \in \Sigma\}, q_0, Z_0, \emptyset)$, our goal here is to find an interpretation I such that $I(\mathcal{M}_0)$ is consistent with R, i.e., $L(I(\mathcal{M}_0))$ contains R, where $\Sigma = \mathrm{alph}(R)$.

In order to identify such an interpretation $I = (f_s, f_p)$ satisfying the requirements, we have to determine f_s and f_p. Let $\Sigma_s(R) = \{a \in \Sigma \mid ax \in R, x \in \Sigma^*\}$ and $\Sigma_f(R) = \{a \in \Sigma \mid xa \in R, x \in \Sigma^*\}$.

[**Computation of** f_s]   We can define that for all $a \in \Sigma_s(R)$, $f_s(p_a) = q_0$ from Lemma 3 (1). In order to determine $f_s(p)$ for other $p \in V_Q - (\{p_a \mid a \in \Sigma_s(R)\} \cup \{q_0\}) \, (= V_Q')$, we make use of the next fact: for all $w \in R$ with $|w| \geq 2$, for each $a, b \in \Sigma$ such that $w = uabv \, (u, v \in \Sigma^*)$, it holds that $f_s(p_b) = f_s(\bar{p}_a)$. In what follows, we assume that f_s is defined so that for each $p \in V_Q'$, the image $f_s(p)$ is the one with the first index in alphabetical order, among those to be identified.

[**Computation of** f_p]   For all $a \in \Sigma_f(R)$, it is obvious that $f_p(\theta_a) = \varepsilon$ from Lemma 3 (2). Also, for all $a \in \Sigma_s(R) - \Sigma_f(R)$, it is easy to see that $f_p(\theta_a) \neq \varepsilon$. These facts are used for determining f_p. In order to determine $f_p(\theta)$ for $\theta \in PAR - \{\theta_a \mid \theta_a \in \Sigma_f(R)\}$, we make use of almost the same steps shown as [Computation of f_p] in [9, pp.189-191]. We denote a procedure to output $I = (f_s, f_p)$ from a given R by **Consistent**$(R; I)$. The flow of the whole procedure **Consistent**$(R; I)$ is almost the same as **Consistent**(R) in [9, p.192] except the above step of computation of f_s is performed instead of computation of f_n in [9].

Now, we assume that $M_* = (Q_*, \Gamma_*, \Sigma_*, \delta_*, q_0, Z_0, \emptyset)$, where $\Gamma_* = \{Z_0\}$ and $\Sigma_* = \mathrm{alph}(L(M_*))$, is a target Szilard strict droca and that R is a finite subset of $L(M_*)$. Further, let $\mathcal{I}_\Sigma = \{I = (f_s, f_p) \mid I : \text{interpretation over } \Sigma\}$. For any $I = (f_s, f_p), I' = (f_s', f_p') \in \mathcal{I}_\Sigma$, we define a binary relation $\preceq$ as follows: $f_s \preceq f_s'$

iff for every $p, q \in V_Q$ with $p \neq q$, $f_s(p) = f_s(q)$ implies that $f'_s(p) = f'_s(q)$. The symbol $\not\preceq$ denotes the negation of $\preceq$.

We need to show the following series of technical lemmas.

Lemma 6. *Let $I = (f_s, f_p)$ and $I' = (f'_s, f'_p)$ be in $\mathcal{I}_\Sigma$ such that $L(I(\mathcal{M}_0)) \subset L(I'(\mathcal{M}_0))$. Then, it holds that $f'_s \not\preceq f_s$.*

Proof. It follows from the definition of $\preceq$, Lemma 5 and Lemma 1 (i). □

Lemma 7. *Let M_* be a target Szilard strict droca and let $I_* = (f_{s*}, f_{p*})$ be in $\mathcal{I}_{\Sigma_*}$ such that $L(I_*(\mathcal{M}_0)) = L(M_*)$. Further, for a finite subset R of $L(M_*)$ such that $\mathrm{alph}(R) = \Sigma_*$, let $I = (f_s, f_p) \in \mathcal{I}_{\Sigma_*}$ be produced by $\mathbf{Consistent}(R; I)$. Then, it holds that $f_s \preceq f_{s*}$.*

Proof. It is clear from the way to compute f_s and the definition of $\preceq$. □

Lemma 8. *For a finite subset R of $L(M_*)$, where M_* is a target Szilard strict droca, let $I = (f_s, f_p) \in \mathcal{I}_\Sigma$, where $\Sigma = \mathrm{alph}(R) \subseteq \Sigma_*$, be produced by $\mathbf{Consistent}(R; I)$. Further, let $I_* = (f_{s*}, f_{p*}) \in \mathcal{I}_{\Sigma_*}$ such that $L(I_*(\mathcal{M}_0)) = L(M_*)$. Then, it holds that $L(M_*) \not\subset L(I(\mathcal{M}_0))$, i.e., either $L(M_*) = L(I(\mathcal{M}_0))$ or $L(M_*) - L(I(\mathcal{M}_0)) \neq \emptyset$.*

Proof. In the case where $\Sigma \subset \Sigma_*$, it is obvious that $L(M_*) - L(I(\mathcal{M}_0)) \neq \emptyset$. In the case where $\Sigma = \Sigma_*$, it can be proved from Lemmas 6 and 7. □

4.2 A Characteristic Sample

Let $M = (Q, \Gamma, \Sigma, \delta, q_0, Z_0, \emptyset)$, where $\Gamma = \{Z_0\}$, be any Szilard strict droca. A finite subset R of $L(M)$ is called a *characteristic sample* of $L(M)$ if $L(M)$ is the smallest language accepted by a Szilard strict droca containing R, i.e., if for any Szilard strict droca M', $R \subseteq L(M')$ implies $L(M) \subseteq L(M')$.

To obtain a characteristic sample of $L(M)$, at first, we construct a *characteristic derivation tree* T_M of M in a similar way to developing step by step a so-called comparison tree in [5] and [8]. At the initial stage, the characteristic derivation tree T_M contains only a root labeled (q_0, Z_0) which is said to be in *unchecked* status. In each step the procedure considers a node labeled (p, α) such that $(q_0, Z_0) \overset{u}{\underset{M}{\Longrightarrow}} (p, \alpha)$ for some $u \in \Sigma^*$. In case $\alpha = \varepsilon$ or (p, α) is a *dead* configuration or another node (not in *unchecked* status) labeled (p, α) has already appeared elsewhere in the tree, we turn the node to be in *checked* status. Otherwise, we expand it by branching or skipping, which will be described below.

Definition 10. *Let a characteristic derivation tree just having been constructed up to a certain stage be denoted by T_M. If (p, α) and (q, β) are labels of two nodes in T_M which are connected by an edge labeled $x \in \Sigma^+$ such that $(p, \alpha) \overset{x}{\underset{M}{\Longrightarrow}} (q, \beta)$, then we write $\langle (p, \alpha) \rangle \overset{x}{\underset{T_M}{\longrightarrow}} \langle (q, \beta) \rangle$. A sequence of such father-son relations as $\langle (p_i, \alpha_i) \rangle \overset{x_i}{\underset{T_M}{\longrightarrow}} \langle (p_{i+1}, \alpha_{i+1}) \rangle$ for $i = 1, 2, \ldots, m$, is denoted by $\langle (p_1, \alpha_1) \rangle \overset{y}{\underset{T_M}{\Longrightarrow}} \langle (p_{m+1}, \alpha_{m+1}) \rangle$, where $y = x_1 x_2 \cdots x_m$.*

Branching is a basic step of developing a characteristic derivation tree. It is based on moves for configurations by one step.

Definition 11. *Let a characteristic derivation tree which has been constructed so far be denoted by T_M, and let a node labeled (p, α) be in T_M. For each $a_i \in$ FIRST(p, α), let $(p, \alpha) \xrightarrow[M]{a_i} (q_i, \beta_i)$ for some $q_i \in Q$, $\beta_i \in \Gamma^*$. Then, for every $a_i \in$ FIRST(p, α), the tree is expanded as $\langle (p, \alpha) \rangle \xrightarrow[T_M]{a_i} \langle (q_i, \beta_i) \rangle$. The step of developing the tree in this way is named* branching *to the node labeled (p, α).*

In order to prevent a characteristic derivation tree from growing larger and larger infinitely by successive application of branching steps, certain nodes are expanded by another step of *skipping*.

Definition 12. *Let a characteristic derivation tree which has been constructed so far be denoted by T_M. Let a node labeled (p, α) $(\alpha \neq \varepsilon)$ be in T_M, and rewrite the node label as $(p, \alpha' \alpha'')$, where $\alpha = \alpha' \alpha''$ with $\alpha'' \neq \varepsilon$. Furthermore, let T_M contain another node labeled (p, α') to which* branching *has been applied. Then, (i) skipping to the node labeled $(p, \alpha' \alpha'')$ in question with respect to the* branching *node labeled (p, α') is said to be* applicable *in T_M. (ii) A* skipping-end *from the node in question with respect to the* branching *node in T_M is defined to be a node labeled by each configuration in $\{(q, \alpha'') \mid \langle (p, \alpha') \rangle \xrightarrow[T_M]{x} \langle (q, \varepsilon) \rangle, x \in \Sigma^*, q \in$ EMP$(p, \alpha')\}$. (iii) For a skipping-end labeled (q, α'') from the node in question, an* edge label *between them in T_M is defined to be a* shortest *input string (path string) x_0 such that $\langle (p, \alpha') \rangle \xrightarrow[T_M]{x_0} \langle (q, \varepsilon) \rangle$.*

When skipping is applicable to a node in question with respect to some *branching* node in T_M, we expand it by adding all its skipping-ends in *unchecked* status to it as its sons, with the new edges connecting them labeled by edge labels defined above. The step of developing the tree in this way is named *skipping* to the node in question. We introduce here *skipping* status in which a node turns to be when skipping has been applied to it.

Nodes in *skipping* status should be visited over and over again. When a skipping step is applied again to a node in *skipping* status, if additional skipping-ends are found then they are added as new sons. Besides, the edges between the *skipping* node and its sons are relabeled, if necessary, so that the latest labeling should satisfy the condition of Definition 12 (iii). When the tree has been developed enough, if it is confirmed for a *skipping* node to have no more new skipping-ends from it than its present sons, with edge labels between them remaining unchanged, then we let it turn to be in newly defined *s-checked* status.

On the way, the next node to be visited is chosen as the "smallest" of the *unchecked* and *skipping* nodes, where the *size* of a node labeled (p, α) is $|\alpha|$. The exact procedure which constructs a characteristic derivation tree is shown in Fig. 1.

By merging all nodes with the same labels in T_M, we construct a directed finite labeled graph G_M. This graph is called a *characteristic graph* of M.

Input: a Szilard strict droca $M = (Q, \Gamma, \Sigma, \delta, q_0, Z_0, \emptyset)$, where $\Gamma = \{Z_0\}$
Output: a characteristic derivation tree T_M produced by M
Procedure ConstructTree($M; T_M$)
begin
   Let T_M consist of only a root labeled (q_0, Z_0) in *unchecked* status.
  while T_M contains an *unchecked* node or a *skipping* node **do**
    while T_M contains an *unchecked* node **do**
     let P be a smallest such node, and suppose it is labeled (p, α)
     if $\alpha = \varepsilon$ or (p, α) is a *dead* configuration or (p, α) appears as a label of
       another internal node
     then turn P to *checked*
     else if skipping is applicable to P
[Skipping] **then** apply the skipping to P, where all of its newly added sons
       are in *unchecked* status
       if some new nodes are added to T_M by the above skipping
       then turn all *s-checked* nodes to *skipping*   **fi**
       turn P to *skipping*
[Branching] **else** apply the branching to P, where all of its newly added sons
       are in *unchecked* status;
       turn P to *checked* and turn all *s-checked* nodes to *skipping*
     fi **fi** **od**
    if T_M contains a *skipping* node
    then let P be a smallest such node;
[Re-skipping]
      apply again skipping to P, where all of its newly added sons are in
      unchecked status
      if no change has occurred by the above skipping
      then turn P to *s-checked*
      else turn all *s-checked* nodes to *skipping*   **fi** **fi** **od**
   output T_M
end

Fig. 1. A procedure for constructing a characteristic derivation tree.

For each node labeled (p, α) in G_M which is a *live* configuration, define
$\mathrm{pre}(p, \alpha)$ as the *shortest* path string from (q_0, Z_0) to (p, α) in G_M. Moreover,
for (p, α) in G_M and for each $q \in \mathrm{EMP}(p, \alpha)$, define $\mathrm{post}((p, \alpha), q)$ as the *short-est* path string from (p, α) to (q, ε) in G_M. Then, define $R(M) = \{\mathrm{pre}(p, \alpha) \cdot \mathrm{post}((p, \alpha), q) \,|\, (p, \alpha) \text{ in } G_M, q \in \mathrm{EMP}(p, \alpha)\} \cup \{\mathrm{pre}(p, \alpha) \cdot x \cdot \mathrm{post}((q, \beta), r) \,|\, (p, \alpha), (q, \beta) \text{ in } G_M, \langle (p, \alpha) \rangle \xrightarrow[G_M]{x} \langle (q, \beta) \rangle, r \in \mathrm{EMP}(q, \beta)\}$. $R(M)$ is called a *representative sample* of M.

In the above tree T_M, we can show that the size of every node is at most
$\mathcal{S} = \mathcal{P} |Q|$, the number of node labels is at most $\mathcal{K} = (\mathcal{S} + 1) |Q|$, the number
of nodes is at most $\mathcal{K} (|\Sigma| + 1)$, and the length of every edge label is at most
$\mathcal{P} |Q|^3 \mathcal{S}$. Therefore, the worst-case time complexity of the procedure in Fig. 1 is
polynomial with respect to the size of M. Thus, the cardinality of a representative
sample $|R(M)|$ is also polynomial with respect to the size of M.

Example 3. Consider a Szilard strict droca $M = (\{q_0, q_1, q_2, q_3\}, \{Z_0\}, \{a, b, c, d, e, f\}, \delta, q_0, Z_0, \emptyset)$, where $\delta = \{(q_0, Z_0) \xrightarrow{a} (q_0, Z_0^2), (q_0, Z_0) \xrightarrow{b} (q_1, Z_0), (q_1, Z_0) \xrightarrow{c} (q_1, \varepsilon), (q_1, Z_0) \xrightarrow{d} (q_2, \varepsilon), (q_2, Z_0) \xrightarrow{e} (q_2, Z_0), (q_2, Z_0) \xrightarrow{f} (q_3, \varepsilon)\}$. Then, the characteristic derivation tree T_M, and the resulting characteristic graph G_M are shown in Figs. 2 (a), and (b), respectively. Therefore, we obtain that $R(M) = \{bc, bd, abc^2, abcd, abdf, abdef\}$.

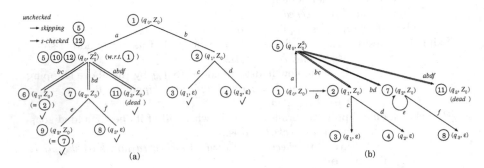

Fig. 2. The characteristic derivation tree (a) and the characteristic graph (b) for Example 3.

The next *key lemma* assures that the representative sample $R(M)$ is a characteristic sample of $L(M)$.

Lemma 9. *The representative sample $R(M)$ of a Szilard strict droca $M = (Q, \Gamma, \Sigma, \delta, q_0, Z_0, \emptyset)$, where $\Gamma = \{Z_0\}$, is a characteristic sample of $L(M)$. That is, it holds that for any language L' accepted by a Szilard strict droca, $R(M) \subseteq L'$ implies that $L(M) \subseteq L'$.*

Proof. Let $M' = (Q', \Gamma', \Sigma, \delta', q_0', Z_0', \emptyset)$, where $\Gamma' = \{Z_0'\}$, be a Szilard strict droca accepting L'. Then it should follow that we have the following claim.

[**Claim**]   Let (p, α) be a label of any node in G_M such that $\alpha \neq \varepsilon$ and (p, α) is a *live* configuration, and let $\langle (q_0, Z_0) \rangle \underset{G_M}{\overset{u}{\Longrightarrow}} \langle (p, \alpha) \rangle$ for some path string $u \in \Sigma^*$. Moreover, let $(q_0', Z_0') \overset{u}{\underset{M'}{\Longrightarrow}} (p', \alpha')$ for some $p' \in Q', \alpha' \in \Gamma'^+$. Then, if $(p, \alpha) \overset{w}{\underset{M}{\Longrightarrow}} (q, \varepsilon)$ with $w \in \Sigma^+$ for some $q \in Q$, then $(p', \alpha') \overset{w}{\underset{M'}{\Longrightarrow}} (q', \varepsilon)$ for some $q' \in Q'$.

[**Proof of Claim**]   This can be proved by induction on $|w| \geq 1$.   □

From Lemmas 8 and 9, the next lemma immediately follows.

Lemma 10. *Let R be a characteristic sample of a language accepted by some Szilard strict droca M and let R' be a finite set such that $R \subseteq R' \subset L(M)$. Then, it holds that for I' (the output of $\mathbf{Consistent}(R'; I'))$, $L(I'(\mathcal{M}_0)) = L(M)$.*

4.3   Identification Algorithm and Its Time Complexity

Let $M_* = (Q_*, \Gamma_*, \Sigma_*, \delta_*, q_0, Z_0, \emptyset)$, where $\Gamma_* = \{Z_0\}$, be a target Szilard strict droca. We now present an identification algorithm IA. This algorithm is given in Fig. 3.

Input: a positive presentation of a target language $L(M_*)$
Output: a sequence of Szilard strict droca's $M_{R_0}, M_{R_1}, \ldots$
Procedure IA
begin
    $R_0 := \emptyset$; $\Sigma_0 := \emptyset$;
    $\mathcal{M}_{0,\Sigma_0} := (\{q_0\}, \{Z_0\}, \Sigma_0, \emptyset, q_0, Z_0, \emptyset)$;   /* automaton schema */
    $M_{R_0} := (\{q_0\}, \{Z_0\}, \Sigma_0, \emptyset, q_0, Z_0, \emptyset)$
    output M_{R_0}
    $i := 1$
    repeat (forever)
        read the next positive example w_i;
        $R_i := R_{i-1} \cup \{w_i\}$; $\Sigma_i := \Sigma_{i-1} \cup \mathrm{alph}(w_i)$;
        $\mathcal{M}_{0,\Sigma_i} := (\{p_a, \bar{p}_a \mid a \in \Sigma_i\} \cup \{q_0\}, \{Z_0\}, \Sigma_i, \{(p_a, Z_0) \xrightarrow{a} (\bar{p}_a, \theta_a) \mid a \in \Sigma_i\},$
            $q_0, Z_0, \emptyset)$
        if $w_i \in L(M_{R_{i-1}})$ **then** $M_{R_i} := M_{R_{i-1}}$
        else call procedure **Consistent**$(R_i; I_i)$;
            $M_{R_i} := I_i(\mathcal{M}_{0,\Sigma_i})$ **fi**
        output M_{R_i}
        $i := i + 1$
end

Fig. 3. The identification algorithm IA.

From Lemmas 9 and 10, the next lemma follows.

Lemma 11. *Let $M_{R_0}, M_{R_1}, \ldots, M_{R_i}, \ldots$ be a sequence of conjectured Szilard strict droca's produced by IA, where $M_{R_i} = I_i(\mathcal{M}_{0,\Sigma_i})$. Then, there exists $r \geq 0$ such that for all $j \geq 0$, $M_{R_r} = M_{R_{r+j}}$ and $L(M_{R_r}) = L(M_*)$.*

Thus, we have the following theorem.

Theorem 3. *The class of Szilard strict droca's is identifiable in the limit from positive data.*

Let $K_i = \sum_{j=1}^{i} |w_j|$ and $\mathrm{size}(M_*) = |Q_*| + |\Sigma_*| + |\delta_*|(\mathcal{P} + 4) + 4$. By analyzing the time complexity of IA in the same way as in [9], we can show that (1) time for updating a conjecture is bounded by $O(\mathrm{Max}\{K_i^{|\Sigma_*|+1}, |\Sigma_*|^3\})$ and (2) the number of implicit errors of prediction IA makes is bounded by $O(\mathrm{size}(M_*))$. Then, we have the following theorem.

Theorem 4. *The algorithm IA runs in $O(m)$-time for updating a conjecture, and the number of implicit errors of prediction is bounded by $O(n)$, where $n = \mathrm{size}(M_*)$, and $m = \mathrm{Max}\{K^{|\Sigma_*|+1}, |\Sigma_*|^3\}$, $K = \sum_{w_j \in R} |w_j|$, and R is the set of positive data provided. Then the time complexity of IA is polynomial when we regard $|\Sigma_*|$ to be a constant as in Yokomori [9].*

5   Conclusions

We have shown that the class of Szilard strict droca's is identifiable in the limit from positive data, and have presented an algorithm which identifies any Szilard strict droca in polynomial time in the sense of Yokomori. This identifiability is proved by giving an exact characteristic sample of polynomial size for a language accepted by a Szilard strict droca. The class of very simple languages is also proved to be polynomial time identifiable in the limit from positive data by Yokomori [9], but it is still unknown whether there exists a characteristic sample of polynomial size for any very simple language.

Acknowledgment

The authors would like to thank Koji Okuo and Takahiro Kikuchi for their contribution in an early stage of this work.

References

1. Angluin, D., *Inductive inference of formal languages from positive data*, Inform. and Control **45** (1980), 117-135.
2. Angluin, D., *Inference of reversible languages*, J. ACM **29** (1982), 741-765.
3. Berstel, J., "Transductions and Context-Free Languages", Teubner Studienbücher, Stuttgart, 1979.
4. Gold, E. M., *Language identification in the limit*, Inform. and Control **10** (1967), 447-474.
5. Higuchi, K., E. Tomita and M. Wakatsuki, *A polynomial-time algorithm for checking the inclusion for strict deterministic restricted one-counter automata*, IEICE Trans. on Information and Systems **E78-D** (1995), 305-313.
6. Mäkinen, E., *The grammatical inference problem for the Szilard languages of linear grammars*, Inform. Process. Lett. **36** (1990), 203-206.
7. Pitt, L., *Inductive inference, DFAs, and computational complexity*, Proc. 2nd Workshop on Analogical and Inductive Inference, Lecture Notes in Artificial Intelligence, Springer, Berlin **397** (1989), 18-44.
8. Tomita, E., *A direct branching algorithm for checking equivalence of some classes of deterministic pushdown automata*, Inform. and Control **52** (1982), 187-238.
9. Yokomori, T., *Polynomial-time identification of very simple grammars from positive data*, Theoret. Comput. Sci. **298** (2003), 179-206.

Learning Syntax from Function Words

David Brooks and Mark Lee

School of Computer Science, University of Birmingham, Birmingham, B29 2TT, UK
{D.J.Brooks,M.G.Lee}@cs.bham.ac.uk

Abstract. This paper presents an approximation of word clustering, using only function words as context. We use this to induce classes of function words. Our algorithm identifies some classes with consistency, and could be useful for guiding greedy grammar learners.

1 Introduction

In this paper we present work-in-progress towards a learning scheme that utilises the strong syntactic role ascribed to function words. We apply standard clustering techniques to learn relations between function words *only*. We believe that such an approach should capture major syntactic regularities very quickly, and thus be more suited to greedy learning frameworks.

Smith and Witten [1] use the relationship between function words and constituent boundaries to learn structure. Their algorithm selects function words on the basis of word frequency, and clusters them into types on the basis of context distribution analysis. The induced function word types are then used as constituent boundaries, dividing the corpus into content word sequences. We extend Smith and Witten's ideas, focusing on learning relations between function words. While it might seem odd to ignore important classes such as nouns and verbs, we believe that this approach will avoid many of the issues of sparse data that follow from using content words.

2 Clustering Function Words

We select the n most frequent words in a corpus as function words. We then cluster, using only *other function words* as contextual information. For each candidate word w, we find its nearest cluster C, using a weighted sum of the similarity of the candidate to each word c in the cluster.

$$sim(w, C) = \sum_{c \in C} \frac{f(c)}{f(C)} \times sim(w, c)$$

Word similarity is measured using context distribution analysis. We define a pair of contexts for each word w_n: $left_n$, the vector of all w_{n-1}; and $right_n$, the vector of w_{n+1}. We use a cosine measure of weighted pointwise mutual information to compare respective vectors:

G. Paliouras and Y. Sakakibara (Eds.): ICGI 2004, LNAI 3264, pp. 273–274, 2004.
© Springer-Verlag Berlin Heidelberg 2004

$$cos(w_i, w_j) = \frac{\sum_{c \in F} wMI(w_i, c) \times wMI(w_j, c)}{\sqrt{\sum_{c \in F} wMI(w_i, c)^2} \times \sqrt{\sum_{c \in F} wMI(w_j, c)^2}}$$

where F is the set of function words, and wMI is a weighted pointwise mutual information function. This yields a similarity score for each vector. We combine these into a single score, using a *directional bias* to weight the significance of left and right components:

$$weight(w_n) = \frac{|left_n| - |right_n|}{|left_n| + |right_n|}$$

This is translated into a pair of scaling factors, which are applied to left and right cosine coefficients respectively, giving a single similarity measure.

3 Experimental Setup

We set up a prototype experiment using a small corpus – document $AA4$ from the British National Corpus – comprising 8283 words of newspaper text. We applied our algorithm to function word clustering for the top 50 words in the BNC. A sample of the resulting classes is shown in Figure 1. The algorithm identifies many classes consistency, notably determiners and verbs. However, some classes are not as easily learned. The principal problem classes are prepositions, where the words often have an alternate sense as particles. Our hard clustering method currently does not allow for multiple senses.

the, a, this, an, his, their	of, and, in, by, from	to, for, with, would, at, will, can
on, as, it, have, all, there	is, was, has, were, had	he, they

Fig. 1. Sample output classes after clustering.

4 Future Work and Conclusions

Our immediate goal is to extend the system to induce rules, and to formally evaluate the resulting grammar. One possible way of doing this would be to use a greedy MDL-based algorithm. Using the techniques outlined here, many of the major classes of function words can be learned consistently. Our preliminary results are encouraging, and we hope that these techniques can be extended to provide a base for full grammar induction.

References

1. Smith, T. C. and Witten, I. H. (1995). Probability-driven lexical classification: A corpus-based approach. In *Proceedings of PACLING-95*, pages 271–283, Brisbane, Australia. University of Queensland.

Running FCRPNI
in Efficient Time for Piecewise
and Right Piecewise Testable Languages*

Antonio Cano, José Ruiz, and Pedro García

Departamento de Sistemas Informáticos y Computación,
Universidad Politécnica de Valencia, Valencia, Spain
{acano,jruiz,pgarcia}@dsic.upv.es

Abstract. The scheme of the inference algorithm known as FCRPNI is applied to the inference of Piecewise Testable Languages and Right Piecewise Testable Languages. We propose efficient algorithms to decide where an automaton contains the forbidden patterns corresponding to those varieties of languages. We also present the results of the experiments done to compare the performance of the FCRPNI and RPNI algorithms for those varieties.

1 FCRPNI Algorithm

FCRPNI Algorithm has been introduced in [1] for any family of languages characterized by the forbidden configurations of their automata, but no specific algorithms for testing forbidden configurations were given.

Proposition 1. *[2] The tranformation semigroup of a given minimal deterministic automaton $\mathcal{A}$ is $\mathcal{R}$-trivial if and only if the configuration*

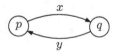

with $p \neq q$ is not present in $\mathcal{A}$.

Theorem 1.1. *[3] The transformation semigroup of a given deterministic automaton $\mathcal{A}$ is $\mathcal{J}$-trivial if and only if the configuration*

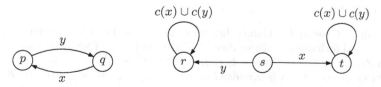

with $p \neq q$ or $r \neq t$ is not present in $\mathcal{A}$.

---

* Work partially supported by Ministerio de Ciencia y Tecnología under project TIC2003-09319-C03-02.

G. Paliouras and Y. Sakakibara (Eds.): ICGI 2004, LNAI 3264, pp. 275–276, 2004.

2   Experimental Results

We have done some experiments in order to compare the behavior of RPNI and
FCRPNI for the cases studied here.

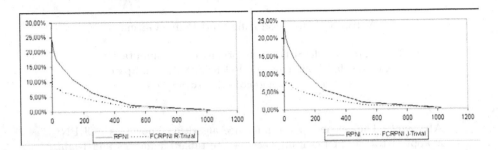

Fig. 1. Error rate for 16 states.

Figures 1 shows the error rate and 2 the running time for Piecewise and Rigth
Piecewise Testable Languages for 16 states and a two letters alphabet. Similar
results are obtained for 8, 32 and 64 states. The error rate for FCRPNI is lower
than for RPNI when the number of examples is smaller. The running time for
FCRPNI is higher than for RPNI but differences are not significant.

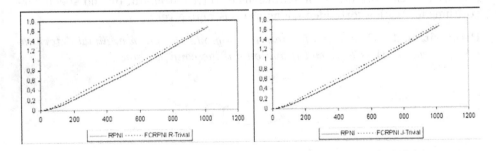

Fig. 2. Running time rate average for 16 states.

References

1. J. Ruiz A. Cano and P. García. Inferring subclasses of regular languages faster using
   RPNI and forbidden configurations. In Henning Fernau Pieter Adriaans and Menno
   van Zaanen, editors, *Grammatical Inference: Algorithms and Applications*, volume
   2484 of *Lecture Notes in Artificial Intelligence*, pages 28–36. Springer, 2002.
2. Joëlle Cohen, Dominique Perrin, and J.-E. Pin. On the expressive power of temporal
   logic. *Jounal of Computer and System Sciences*, pages 271–294, 1993.
3. I. Simon. Piecewise testable events. *2nd GI Conf., Lecture Notes in Computer
   Sciences*, 33:214–222, 1975.

Extracting Minimum Length Document Type Definitions Is NP-Hard
(Abstract)

Henning Fernau[1,2]

[1] School of Electrical Engineering and Computer Science, University of Newcastle
University Drive, NSW 2380 Callaghan, Australia
[2] Wilhelm-Schickard-Institut für Informatik, Universität Tübingen
Sand 13, D-72076 Tübingen, Germany
`fernau@informatik.uni-tuebingen.de`

1 Introduction

XML (eXtensible Markup Language) is becoming more and more popular. Since not all XML documents come with a (proper) accompanying Document Type Descriptors (DTD), it is a challenge to find "good" DTDs automatically. Note that many optimization procedures rely on being given a well-fitting DTD to work properly.

M. Garofalakis *et al.* have developed XTRACT, a system for extracting Document Type Descriptors (DTD) from XML documents. This system may actually integrate many of the other proposals as kind of subroutines, since it finally tries to find the "best" DTD out of those proposals. Due to the connections to regular expression (inference), see [1, 2], any good inference algorithm for regular expressions can hence be incorporated. Observe that the regular expressions which are generated by first using learning algorithms designed for deterministic finite automata and then turning these automata into regular expressions by "textbook algorithms" (as proposed in [2]) tend to produce expressions which are rather "unreadable" from a human perspective. In the envisaged application – the extraction of DTDs – this is particularly bad, since those DTDs are meant to be read and understood by humans. This is one of the reasons why the Grammatical Inference community should get interested in MDL approaches to learning as proposed with the XTRACT project.

XTRACT has two basic steps, which are performed for each element of the DTD which is to be inferred. In a first phase, XTRACT generates DTD proposals matching *some* of the examples in the XML document. In a second phase, a selection of these DTD proposals is generated according to the minimum description length principle (MDL), also known as Occam's razor. In [3], this second phase is implemented using a connection to the facility location problem, which in turn relates to the set cover problem. This way, only an approximation up to a factor of $\log n$, n being the "input size", is possible. Although M. Garofalakis *et al.* claim that these approximations work well in practice, they don't show that this approach is necessary at all. The present paper gives a (partial) justification for their approach, showing that the "selection problem" of the mentioned second phase of their algorithm is NP-hard.

G. Paliouras and Y. Sakakibara (Eds.): ICGI 2004, LNAI 3264, pp. 277–278, 2004.

2   MDL-XTRACT: The Problem

Occam's razor states that the "best" theory is "elegant" and yields the shortest explanation for the given data. The complexity of a set of data can be, according to the MDL principle, therefore measured by:

- the length of the theory in bits, and
- the length of the data in bits, when encoded with the help of the theory.

Since elements in a DTD are basically regular expressions in the classical sense of formal language theory, also see [1], in our case, an application of MDL leads to the following minimization problem we call MDL-XTRACT:

Given:

- a set $R = \{r_1, \ldots, r_m\}$ of regular expressions (over the basic alphabet Σ),
- a set of strings $S = \{s_1, \ldots, s_n\} \subset \Sigma^+$,
- and a positive integer k.

Question: Is it possible to find a subset R' of R with $S \subseteq L(R')$, i.e., each of the given strings can be "explained" by at least one expression from R', such that

$$\sum_{r \in R'} |c(r)| + \sum_{s \in S} |c(s|R')| \leq k \quad ?$$

Here, $c(r)$ is some coding of the regular expression r and $c(s|R')$ is a coding of the string s, given the "theory" R'. We stated above a decision variant of this minimization problem. Details on the chosen coding function can be found in [3].

By a not completely trivial reduction using 3SAT, we were able to show:

Theorem 1. *MDL-XTRACT is NP-complete.*

This somewhat justifies the "heuristic approach" proposed in [3]. Such heuristics can also be used to produce readable regular expressions (REs) from DFA, since each RE can be turned into the normal form $\bigcup R_i$, where each R_i may only contain a union "within" a star. The decision which of the R_i should be finally put into the regular expression could be based on solving MDL-XTRACT. Alternatively, the development of inference algorithms for directly learning REs is welcome.

We gratefully acknowledge discussions with M. Fellows, C. de la Higuera and B. Starkie.

References

1. J. Berstel and L. Boasson. XML grammars. *Acta Informatica* 38:649–671, 2002.
2. H. Fernau. Learning XML grammars. In P. Perner, editor, *Machine Learning and Data Mining in Pattern Recognition MLDM'01*, volume 2123 of *LNCS/LNAI*, pages 73–87. Springer, 2001.
3. M. Garofalakis, A. Gionis, R. Rastogi, S. Seshadri, and K. Shim. XTRACT: learning document type descriptors from XML document collections. *Data Mining and Knowledge Discovery*, 7:23–56, 2003.

Learning Distinguishable Linear Grammars from Positive Data

J.A. Laxminarayana[1], José M. Sempere[2], and G. Nagaraja[1]

[1] CSE Department, I.I.T. Bombay, India
{jalana,gn}@cse.iitb.ac.in
[2] DISC, Universidad Politécnica de Valencia, Spain
jsempere@dsic.upv.es

Abstract. We introduce a new algorithm to infer Terminal Distinguishable Linear Grammars from positive data.

1 Introduction and Preliminaries

Radhakrishnan and Nagaraja have proposed a method[4, 5] to infer a subclass of even linear languages, TDELL, from positive strings. In [6], Sempere and Nagaraja presented a characterizable method to infer a subclass of linear languages, TSDLL, from positive structural information. Recently, Laxminarayana and Nagaraja [1] proposed an incremental tabular method to infer TDEL languages from positive samples.

In this work, a method is proposed to infer a subclass of linear languages from the set of samples which are assumed to be from an even linear language. Sample set may possibly contain erroneous strings. An error model is built to capture the possible errors in the given sample set. The incremental TDELL inference algorithm [1] along with the proposed error model is used to generate a TDEL grammar which can be converted into an equivalent TSDL grammar using a transformation model. The TDEL and TSDL languages are proper subclasses of TDL (Terminal Distinguishable Languages). For further details about these concepts, the reader is referred to [4] and [2]. It is observed that TDELL $\subset$ TSDLL. Hence an equivalent TSDL grammar can be constructed for a given TDEL grammar by using the following transformation model.

Definition 1. *Let G_1 be a given TDEL grammar in normal form. An equivalent TSDL grammar G_2 can be constructed using the following finite steps: 1) For every production rule of the form $A \rightarrow aBb$ in G_1 construct productions $A \rightarrow aA'$ and $A' \rightarrow Bb$ in G_2 where A' is a new non-terminal. 2) Copy all other productions from G_1 to G_2*

2 Using an Error Model

Detection of error, formation of alternatives and selecting a best alternative are the functions involved in the proposed error model. The first function of any error model is to ascertain the existence of an error in the given string. If there is no error or if the error model fails to recognize the error then the input string will be passed to the inference algorithm without any modification. For the sake of simplicity we consider only the detection of single deletion error. Implementation and correctness issues of the error model are discussed in [3].

G. Paliouras and Y. Sakakibara (Eds.): ICGI 2004, LNAI 3264, pp. 279–280, 2004.
© Springer-Verlag Berlin Heidelberg 2004

3   Algorithm to Infer TSDL Grammar

Algorithm 1 TSDL-INFERENCE(S^+)

Require: A nonempty set of positive sample S^+; one sample, say x, at a time.

Ensure: Inferred TSDL grammar

  1: If no more strings are left in the sample set then transform the inferred
     TDEL grammar into an equivalent TSDL and terminate
  2: If $x = \lambda$ then add the production $S \to \lambda$ to the inferred TDEL grammar;
     go to step 1.
  3: If x is not the first string in the S^+ then using the error model obtain
     a preprocessed string of x
  4: Using the incremental TDELL inference algorithm [1], construct a TDEL
     grammar and go to step 1.

Each successive string from S^+ is taken as input to the algorithm. An error model is employed to detect the occurrence of a single deletion error in the input string. If there exists a deletion error then the algorithm will continue with the *processed* string. In all the remaining cases, algorithm proceeds with the given input string. Selection of the appropriate *processed* string for the erroneous string is done using a statistical method.

The inference method proposed for the class of Terminal and Structural Distinguishable Linear Language using error correcting approach infers correctly for many languages. Further, it can be shown that, this method will not over generalize when the samples are from a higher class than linear. In addition, the method can identify any TSDL language in the limit if enough strings are provided.

References

1. J.A.Laxminarayana and G.Nagaraja, Incremental Inference of a subclass of Even Linear Languages, Eleventh International Conference on Advanced Computing and Communications, ADCOM 2003, PSG College of Technology, Coimbatore, India, 2003.
2. J.A.Laxminarayana and G.Nagaraja, Terminal Distinguishable Languages: A survey, A technical report, CSE Dept, IIT Bombay, India.
3. J.A.Laxminarayana and G.Nagaraja, Inference of a subclass of Even Linear Languages: An error correcting approach., A technical report, CSE Dept, IIT Bombay, India.
4. V. Radhakrishnan. Grammatical Inference from Positive Data: An Effective Integrated Approach. PhD thesis, Department of Computer Science and Engineering, Indian Institute of Technology, Bombay (India), 1987.
5. V. Radhakrishnan and G. Nagaraja, Inference of Even Linear grammars and its applications to Picture Description Language. Pattern Recognition, Vol 21, No.1, pp. 55-62, 1988.
6. J. M. Sempere and G. Nagaraja, Learning a subclass of linear languages from positive structural information, Proceedings of the 4th International Colloquium ICGI-98. LNAI Vol. 1433 pp 162-174, Springer-Verlag. 1998.

Extending Incremental Learning
of Context Free Grammars in Synapse

Katsuhiko Nakamura

College of Science and Engineering, Tokyo Denki University,
Hatoyama-machi, Saitama-ken, 350-0394 Japan
nakamura@k.dendai.ac.jp

Abstract. This paper describes recent improvements and extensions of *Synapse* system for learning of context free grammars (CFGs) from sample strings. The system uses rule generation based on bottom-up parsing, incremental learning, and search for rule sets. By the recent improvements, Synapse more rapidly synthesizes several nontrivial CFGs including an unambiguous grammar for the set of strings containing twice as many a's as b's and an ambiguous grammar for strings not of the form of ww. By employing a novel rule generation method called inverse derivation, the form of grammars is extended to definite clause grammars (DCGs) and broader classes of grammars such as graph and hypergraph grammars.

1 Introduction

This paper describes recent improvements and extensions of incremental learning of context free grammars (CFGs) from positive and negative sample strings, that is implemented in *Synapse* system. Main features of our approach are rule generation based on bottom-up parsing, incremental learning, and search for rule sets.

The rule generation in Synapse is based on bottom-up parsing for each positive sample string. The process of goal generation succeeds, if a positive sample is derived from the set of rules in the parsing. If the system fails to parse the string, it generates the minimum production rules and adds them to the set of rules from which the sample string is derived. An important feature of this method is that the system only generates the rules that are applied to in the bottom-up parsing. The goal generation algorithm was called inductive CYK algorithm in our previous papers [2, 3], since it is based on CYK (Cocke, Younger and Kasami) algorithm for the bottom-up parsing.

We are working on extensions of Synapse based on a novel rule generation method called inverse derivation. This method enables Synapse to extend the form of grammars to definite clause grammars (DCGs) [1] and broader classes of grammars such as graph and hypergraph grammars.

2 Rule Generation Based on Inverse Derivation

The inverse derivation can be considered as a refinement of Earley's algorithm by restricting the form to the extended Chomsky Normal Form (CNF) of the

G. Paliouras and Y. Sakakibara (Eds.): ICGI 2004, LNAI 3264, pp. 281–282, 2004.

forms $A \to \beta\gamma$ and $A \to \beta$, where each of β and γ is either a terminal symbol or a nonterminal symbol. The algorithm is to parse a string and generate the test set of pairs (β, γ), which are used in the rule generation section as candidates of right hand sides of rules. In this algorithm, the rules of the form $q_j \Rightarrow p_i$ are generated to represent that when the term $r(j, k)$ occurs, $p(i, k)$ needs to be generated by the rule $p \to qr$, where each term $p(i, j)$ represents that the subsequence $a_i \cdots a_j$ of an input string $a_1 \cdots a_n$ is derived from the nonterminal symbol p.

Definite clause grammars (DCGs) are extended CFGs represented by logic programs [1], in which nonterminal symbols are extended to include symbols with parameters of the form $A(P)$ or $A(P_1, P_2)$, where each of P, P_1, P_2 is a constant or a variable. We can define the derivation of strings by extending the rewriting of nonterminal symbols to the rewriting with substitution of variables. The algorithm can be extended to parse strings in DCG by adding the parameters to the terms $p(i, j)$ as additional arguments.

The inductive inference of DCG rules is closely related to inductive logic programming, especially refinement operators for the Horn clause rules. By using the test set and by extending the methods for CFG in the extended CNF, we can have methods of generating DCG rules.

3   Concluding Remarks

By the recent improvements, Synapse can synthesize CFGs in extended CNF, including an unambiguous grammar for the set of strings containing twice as many a's as b's and an ambiguous grammar for strings not of the form ww, in shorter time.

Since each string is represented by a linear graph in the inverse derivation, the parsing and rule generation method can be further extended to include the rules in graph grammars and hypergraph grammars.

Acknowledgements

The author would like to thank S. Matsumoto, S. Yoshioka and T. Ogasawara for their help in writing and testing Synapse system. This work is partially supported by Research Institute for Technology of Tokyo Denki University.

References

1. F.C.N. Pereira and D.H.D. Warren, Definite Clause Grammars for Language Analysis, *Artificial Intelligence*, **13** pp. 231-278, 1980.
2. K. Nakamura and M. Matsumoto, Incremental Learning of Context Free Grammars, *ICGI 2002, LNAI 2484*, Springer-Verlag, pp. 174 - 184, 2002.
3. K. Nakamura and M. Matsumoto, Incremental Learning of Context Free Grammars Based on Bottom-up Parsing and Search, (to appear in) *Pattern Recognition*, 2004.

Identifying Left-Right Deterministic Linear Languages

Jorge Calera-Rubio* and Jose Oncina**

D. Lenguajes y Sistemas Informaticos, Univ. de Alicante, E-03080 Alicante, Spain
{calera,oncina}@dlsi.ua.es

Abstract. Recently an algorithm to identify in the limit with polynomial time and data Left Deterministic Linear Languages (Left DLL) and, consequently Right DLL, was proposed. In this paper we show that the class of the Left-Right DLL formed by the union of both classes is also identifiable. To do that, we introduce the notion of n-negative characteristic sample, that is a sample that forces an inference algorithm to output an hypothesis of size bigger than n when strings from a non identifiable language are provided.

An important subclass of the linear languages is that of the *Left Deterministic Linear Languages* (Left DLL or LDLL) [1]. They are generated by *Left Deterministic Linear Grammars* such that the next rule to use in the parsing of a string is determined by observing the leftmost terminal in the unparsed part of the string. Regular languages, $\{a^n b^n \mid n \geq 0\}$ and $\{a^m b^n c^n \mid n, m \geq 0\}$ are some examples of languages in the class, while $\{a^n b^n c^m \mid n, m \geq 0\}$ is not.

The class formed by the reversals of the languages in LDLL is called the *Right* DLL (RDLL) and can be defined in a symmetrical way in which LDLL are defined. The regular languages, $\{a^n b^n \mid n \geq 0\}$ and $\{a^n b^n c^m \mid n, m \geq 0\}$ are examples of languages in the class.

Recently [1] it was showed that the class of the LDLL can be identified in the limit from polynomial time and data. Obviously, the class of the RDLL can be identified just by reversing the strings before to introduce them on the LDLL inference algorithm.

In this paper we propose a new class of languages, the Left-Right DLL (LRDLL), formed by the union of LDLL and RDLL. We show that this class can be identified in the limit from polynomial time and data.

In ref. [1] was defined an algorithm LDLGA($\cdot$) that identifies the LDLG. Reminding that RDLL = LDLL^R. Then, it is easy to build an algorithm RDLGA($\cdot$) for RDLG such that RDLGA(S) = (LDLGA(S^R))^R.

Now, for LRDLL let us define an algorithm (LRDLGA) that given a sample S, computes LDLGA(S) and RDLGA(S), and returns the hypothesis grammar with a lower number of non terminals.

* This work was supported by the Spanish CICyT trough project TIC2003-08496-C04.
** This work was supported in part by the IST Programme of the European Community, under the PASCAL Network of Excellence, IST-2002-506778. This publication only reflects the authors' views.

G. Paliouras and Y. Sakakibara (Eds.): ICGI 2004, LNAI 3264, pp. 283–284, 2004.

If the target language is in LDLL − RDLL and the sample is big enough, LDLGA will provide the canonical LDLG for the language, but the RDLGA is going to produce bigger and bigger grammars as the sample grows. Then there has to exist a point when the correct hypothesis will be output.

The case when the language is in RDLL − LDLL is similar. When the target is in both classes, LRDLGA outputs the smaller of both representations.

Now, in order to show the identification in the limit from polynomial time and data, we have to show the existence of a polynomial characteristic set. The idea is to find a sample such that, if the language is not in the class it forces the algorithm to output an hypothesis with size bigger that a given parameter. Let us formalize this idea:

Definition 1 (n-negative characteristic sample). *Let $\phi(\cdot)$ an inference algorithm that identifies in the limit the class of languages $\mathcal{L}$ in terms of the class of grammars $\mathcal{G}$, let a language $L \notin \mathcal{L}$, $C = (C_+, C_-)$ is a n-negative characteristic sample of L (n-NCS) for ϕ if $\forall I = (I_+, I_-) : C_+ \subseteq I_+, C_- \subseteq I_-, \|\phi(I)\| \geq n$.*

In our case, we are going to use the number of non terminals as the size of a grammar. Then, if we can show that for every language in LDLL − RDLL (or RDLL − LDLL) with n non terminals we can find a polynomial size $(n+1)$-NCS for RDLGA (LDLGA), the union of the characteristic sample for LDLGA (RDLGA) of the language with the $(n+1)$-NCS will be a polynomial size characteristic sample for the LRDLGA.

Let us show that this polynomial size n-NCS exists. Following the notation in [1] it is not hard to prove the next proposition and theorem:

Proposition 1. *Let $L \notin LDLL$ and let $n \in \mathbb{N}$. As $L \notin LDLL$ we know that $|\mathrm{Sp}_L|$ is infinite, let Sp_{L_n} be the n smaller $x \in \mathrm{Sp}_L$. Let $S = (S_+, S_-)$ be a sample of L, S is an n-negative characteristic sample (n-NCS) for LRDLGA if:*

1. *$\forall x \in \mathrm{Sp}_{L_n} \, \forall a \in \Sigma : xa \in \mathrm{Pr}(L) \Rightarrow \exists xaw \in S_+$*
2. *$\forall x \in \mathrm{Sp}_{L_n} \, \forall a \in \Sigma : \mathrm{CSF}_L(xa) \neq \emptyset \Rightarrow \mathrm{tail}_{S_+}(xa) = \mathrm{tail}_L(xa)$*
3. *$\forall x, y \in \mathrm{Sp}_{L_n} \, \forall a \in \Sigma : \mathrm{CSF}_L(xa) \neq \emptyset \wedge xa \not\equiv_L y \Rightarrow$*
   $\exists v : xav\,\mathrm{tail}_L(xa) \in S_+ \wedge yv\,\mathrm{tail}_L(y) \in S_- \ \vee$
   $\exists v : yv\,\mathrm{tail}_L(y) \in S_+ \wedge xav\,\mathrm{tail}_L(xa) \in S_-$
4. *$\forall x \in \mathrm{Sp}_{L_n} : x\,\mathrm{tail}_L(x) \in L \Rightarrow x\,\mathrm{tail}_L(x) \in S_+$*

Theorem 1. *For any $L \notin LDLL$ there is an n-negative characteristic sample of polynomial size.*

Acknowledgement. The authors thank Colin de la Higuera for fruitful discussions on the subject.

References

1. de la Higuera, C., Oncina, J.: Learning deterministic linear languages. In: Computational Learning Theory, COLT 02. Number 2375 in Lecture Notes in Artificial Intelligence, Springer Verlag (2002) 185–200

Efficient Learning
of k-Reversible Context-Free Grammars
from Positive Structural Examples

Shinnosuke Seki and Satoshi Kobayashi

Department of Computer Science, University of Electro-Communications,
Chofugaoka 1-5-1, Chofu, Tokyo 182-8585, Japan
shinnosuke@comp.cs.uec.ac.jp, satoshi@cs.uec.ac.jp

Abstract. This paper discusses on the learnability of context free grammars(CFGs) within the framework of *identification in the limit from positive structural examples*. We will introduce a new subclass of CFGs, called a class of *k-reversible context-free grammars* and propose an $O(kdn^3)$ algorithm for learning this new subclass of CFGs, where d is the maximum of the ranks of given skeletal trees, and n is the total size of the given examples.

1 k-Reversible CFG and k-Reversible STA

For any integer $k \geq 0$ and a tree t, by $sp(k, t)$, we denote the subtree of t consisting of all nodes of depth at most k. Let k be a non-negative integer and $G = (N, \Sigma, P, S)$ be a CFG. For $A \in N$, a tree t is said to be a *k-support* of A if there exists a skeleton $s \in K(D_A(G))$ such that $t = sp(k, s)$. A CFG G is *deterministic with look lower k* iff conditions (1) (2) hold: (1) If $S_1, S_2 \in S$ have a common k-support of depth k, then $S_1 = S_2$, and (2) let $A \rightarrow p_1 \ldots p_m \mid q_1 \ldots q_m \in P$ where $p_1, \ldots, p_m, q_1, \ldots, q_m \in N \cup \Sigma$. If for any $i(1 \leqslant i \leqslant m)$, p_i and q_i have a common k-support, then $p_j = q_j$ holds for any j such that p_j and q_j have a common k-support *of depth k*.

A CFG G is said to be *k-reversible* iff G is invertible and deterministic with look lower k. A context free language(CFL) L is said to be *k-reversible* iff there exists a k-reversible CFG G such that $L = L(G)$. The technical terms, k-reversible CFG and k-reversible CFL are written k-rCFG and k-rCFL, respectively.

For a skeletal tree automaton(STA), similar definitions and notations of k-reversibility apply.

Definition 1. *Let $G = (N, \Sigma, P, S)$ be a CFG. We define an STA $A(G) = (Q, Sk \cup \Sigma, \delta, F)$, where $Q = N$, $F = S$, $f \in \delta_k(\sigma, q_1, \ldots, q_k)$ iff $f \rightarrow q_1 \ldots q_k \in P$, and $\delta_0(a) = a$ for $a \in \Sigma$.*

Definition 2. *Let $A = (Q, Sk \cup \Sigma, \delta, F)$ be a deterministic STA. We define a CFG $G(A) = (N, \Sigma, P, S)$, where $N = Q$, $S = F$, and P is the set of all rules of the form $\delta_k(\sigma, q_1, \ldots, q_k) \rightarrow q_1 \ldots q_k$ such that $\sigma \in Sk_k$, $q_1, \ldots, q_k \in Q \cup \Sigma$ and $\delta_k(\sigma, q_1, \ldots, q_k)$ is defined.*

G. Paliouras and Y. Sakakibara (Eds.): ICGI 2004, LNAI 3264, pp. 285–287, 2004.

Proposition 1. *If G is a k-rCFG, then $A(G)$ is a k-rSTA such that $T(A(G)) = K(D(G))$. Conversely if A is a k-rSTA, then $G(A)$ is a k-rCFG such that $T(A) = K(D(G(A)))$.*

Theorem 1. *For any CFL L, there is a k-rCFG G such that $L(G) = L$.*

Our k-reversibility is different from Lopez's k-reversibility[2], Fernau's δ-distinguishability[4] and Oate's k-reversibility[5].

2   Learnability Results

A finite set CS of skeletons is called a *characteristic sample* for a k-reversible set T of skeletons iff T is the smallest k-reversible set of skeletons(k-rSk) containing CS. The existence of characteristic samples is crucially important for the identifiability from positive data.

Theorem 2. *For any k-rSk T, there exists a characteristic sample.*

We can show the existence of the algorithm k-RT satisfying the following theorems.

Theorem 3. *Let Sa be a nonempty positive samples of skeletons, and let A_f be the k-rSTA output by the algorithm k-RT on input Sa. Then $T(A_f)$ is the smallest k-rSk containing Sa.*

We define an effective function RT_∞ from infinite sequences of skeletons $s_1, s_2, s_3, \ldots$ to infinite sequences of guesses $A_1, A_2, A_3, \ldots$ by $A_n = k\text{-RT}(\{s_1, s_2, \ldots, s_n\})$ for all $n \geq 1$.

Theorem 4. *Let A be a k-rSTA, $s_1, s_2, s_3, \ldots$ be a positive presentation of A and $A_1, A_2, A_3, \ldots$ the output of RT_∞ on this input. Then $A_1, A_2, A_3, \ldots$ converges to a correct guess of A.*

Theorem 5. *Let Sa be the set of input skeletons. The algorithm k-RT may be implemented to run in time $O(kdn^3)$, where d is the maximum rank of the symbol σ in Sk, n is the sum of the sizes of the skeletons in Sa.*

Acknowledgements

The authors are heartly grateful to anonymous referees for many constructive suggestions and comments on the draft on this paper, and giving us information as to related references[2],[4].

References

1. Angluin, D., Inference of Reversible Languages. *J. Assoc. Comput. Mach. 29*(1982), 741-765.
2. D. Lopez, Jose M. Sempere, P. Garcia Inference of reversible tree languages *IEEE Transactions on Systems, Man and Cybernetics*, VOL. 34, No. 4, AUGUST 2004
3. Gold, E.M., Language identification in the limit. *Inf. Control 10*(1967), 447-474.
4. H. Fernau. Learning tree languages from text. In J. Kivinen and R.H. Sloan (editors): *Computational Learning Theory COLT*, vol. 2375 of LNCS/LNAI, 2002. pp. 153-168. Berlin: c Springer-Verlag, 2002.
5. T. Oates, D. Desai and V. Bhat, Learning k-Reversible Context-Free Grammars from Positive Structural Examples. In *Proc. of Nineteenth International Conference on Machine Learning*, 2002.
6. Y. Sakakibara, Efficient Learning of Context-Free Grammars from Positive Structural Examples. *Information and Computation 97*(1992), 23-60.

An Analysis of Examples and a Search Space for PAC Learning of Simple Deterministic Languages with Membership Queries

Yasuhiro Tajima, Yoshiyuki Kotani, and Matsuaki Terada

Department of Computer, Information and Communication Sciences,
Tokyo University of Agriculture and Technology
naka-chou 2-24-16, koganei, Tokyo 184-8588, Japan
{ytajima,kotani,m-tera}@cc.tuat.ac.jp

Abstract. We consider a PAC learning problem of simple deterministic languages and show sufficient conditions of it.

1 Introduction

A learning problem for simple deterministic languages (SDLs) has been considered by Ishizaka[3] and it has been shown that SDLs are polynomial time learnable via membership queries and equivalence queries with a hypothesis of a context-free grammar (CFG). Thus, from Angluin[2]'s theorem, SDLs are efficiently PAC learnable with a CFG hypothesis. However, polynomial time learning of SDLs by a simple deterministic grammar (SDG) is not achieved and we cannot reach it by simple extensions of these results. On the other hand, in [4], we have already shown that SDLs are polynomial time learnable via membership queries and a set of representative samples (RS) [1] with an SDG hypothesis. In this paper, we show sufficient conditions and sample complexity to gather a set of RS, and an exponential size search space of hypotheses for these conditions.

2 Gathering a Set of Representative Samples

A CFG is a 4-tuple $G = (N, \Sigma, P, S)$ A CFG G is an SDG iff there exists at most one rule which is of the form $A \to a\beta$ for every pair of $A \in N$ and $a \in \Sigma$. Let ε be the word whose length is 0. We assume that all languages and grammars are ε-free. Let L_t be the target SDL and $G_t = (N_t, \Sigma, P_t, S_t)$ be a SDG such that $L(G_t) = L_t$. Let D be a probability distribution on Σ^* and $Pr(w)$ be the probability for $w \in \Sigma^*$. An example is denoted by $(w, \{+, -\})$ and the word w is called the *example word*. If a hypothesis L_h satisfies $Pr[P(L_h \Delta L_t) \le er] \ge 1 - \delta$ for given $0 < er \le 1$ and $0 < \delta \le 1$ then L_h is PAC. A set Q of RS for L_t is a set of words such that all rules in P_t are used to generate Q. Then, a learning algorithm of SDLs via membership queries and Q is shown in [4]. For every rule $A \to a\beta$ in P_t, let $Z(A \to \beta) = \{w \in \Sigma^* \mid S_t \underset{G_t}{\overset{*}{\Rightarrow}} \alpha_1 A \alpha_2 \underset{G_t}{\Rightarrow} \alpha_1 a \beta \alpha_2 \underset{G_t}{\overset{*}{\Rightarrow}} w\}$

G. Paliouras and Y. Sakakibara (Eds.): ICGI 2004, LNAI 3264, pp. 288–289, 2004.

and, let $Pr(A \rightarrow a\beta) = \sum_{w \in Z(A \rightarrow a\beta)} Pr(w)$. It is to say that $Pr(A \rightarrow a\beta)$ is an appearing probability of $A \rightarrow a\beta$ when an example word is given. Now, let $d = \min\{Pr(A \rightarrow a\beta) \mid A \rightarrow a\beta \ in \ P_t\}$, then a probability that a rule $A \rightarrow a\beta$ does not appear in derivations of m samples is bounded by $(1 - d)^m$. There are $|P_t|$ rules, thus a set of m samples which satisfies $|P_t|(1 - d)^m < \delta$ is a set of RS with a probability at least $1 - \delta$. Let $m > -\frac{1}{d} \log(\frac{\delta}{|P_t|})$, then $|P_t|(1 - d)^m \leq |P_t|e^{-dm} < \delta$. Thus, the following theorem holds.

Theorem 1. SDLs are polynomial time PAC learnable with $er = 0$ via membership queries and m examples, if there exists an SDG G_t such that every rule in G_t has a probability which is greater than or equal to d and the learner knows the size of P_t and d. ☐

When $d = 0$, i.e. there exists a rule which is never used in example words on D then $m = \infty$ and it is impossible to learn in polynomial time. To avoid this restriction, let $m_1 > -\frac{|P_t|}{er} \log(\frac{\delta}{|P_t|})$, and E_1 be the set of m_1 examples. Then, it holds with a probability at least $1 - \delta$ that all rules in P_t which have the appearing probability more than $\frac{er}{|P_t|}$ appear in some derivations of a positive example word in E_1. Since there are at most $|P_t|$ rules to learn, it holds with a probability at least $1 - \delta$ that the total of the appearing probability of rules which are not appear in any derivations of an example word in E_1 is less than er.

Theorem 2. Let E_1 be the set of m_1 examples and $P_1 \subseteq P$ be the set of all rules in P which appear in at least one derivation of an example word in E_1, and $G_1 = (N, \Sigma, P_1, S)$ be an SDG. Then, G_1 satisfies that $Pr[P(L(G_1)\Delta L(G)) \leq er] \geq 1 - \delta$. ☐

3   Conclusions

We can construct a hypotheses space which contains G_1 from E_1 examples and membership queries, but the size of the search space is bounded by an exponential of the size of E_1 and given parameters. Thus, our technique cannot yet achieve efficient learning of SDLs via membership queries with an SDG hypothesis.

References

1. Angluin, D.: A note on the number of queries needed to identify regular languages. Inf. & Cont. **51** (1981) 76–87
2. Angluin, D.: Learning regular languages from queries and counterexamples. Inf. & Comp. **75** (1987) 87–106
3. Ishizaka, H.: Polynomial time learnability of simple deterministic languages. Machine Learning **5** (1990) 151–164
4. Tajima, Y., Tomita, E.: A polynomial time learning algorithm of simple deterministic languages via membership queries and a representative sample. LNAI **1891** (2000) 284–297

Author Index

Lecture Notes in Artificial Intelligence (LNAI)